D. L. MOODY

BY
WILLIAM R. MOODY

NEW YORK
THE MACMILLAN COMPANY
1930

After Bust in Sage Chapel, Northfield, by Hermon MacNeil.

Acknowledgment is gratefully made of help received from a large number of friends, public librarians, and curators of historical societies, too numerous to indicate specifically.

ILLUSTRATIONS

After bust in Sage Chapel, Northfield,
   by Hermon MacNeil   *Frontispiece*

	FACING PAGE
Monument to Early Settlers of Hartford	6
From Records of Mt. Vernon Church	32
Chicago in 1854 and 1857	48
Emma C. Revell	80
Dwight L. Moody	142
Cartoon in "Chicago Tribune" in 1898	274
Round Top	540

BOOK I

D. L. MOODY

CHAPTER I

"A man's life should never be written while he is living. What is important is how a man ends, not how he begins." In these words D. L. Moody replied to a request that he should consent to his biography being prepared during his life. But the end is more readily interpreted against the background of early experiences.

Dwight Lyman Moody was born February 5, 1837. To those who attach great importance to heredity and would trace anything remarkable to the transmitted gifts of distinguished forbears, Moody's genealogy is unproductive. Beyond the communities in which his ancestors lived for seven generations in the Connecticut Valley, their names were unknown.

The Moody family in Massachusetts is descended from John Moody, who, at the age of forty, came to Roxbury in 1633. According to early colonial records, "he was the second son of George Moody of Moulton, County of Suffolk (England), who was famous for his good housekeeping and plain dealing." Governor Winthrop makes the following quaint allusion to him:

> Two men, servants of one Moody, of Roxbury, returning in a boat from the windmill, struck upon the oyster bank. They went out to gather oysters, and not making fast their boat, when the flood came, it floated away, and they were both drowned, although they might have waded out on either side;

but it was an evident judgment of God upon them, for they were wicked persons. One of them, a little before, being reproved for his lewdness, and put in mind of hell, answered, that if hell were ten times hotter, he had rather be there than serve his master.

Lest this uncomplimentary remark might seem prejudicial to the character of the colonist, the Governor added:

The occasion was because the servant had bound himself for divers years, and saw, if he had been at liberty, he might have had greater wages, though otherwise his master used him very well.

In 1635, according to Governor Winthrop, there was a migration from the Bay State Colony to the Connecticut Valley. "About sixty men, women and little children went by land toward Connecticut with their cows, horses, and swine and, after a tedious and a difficult journey, arrived safe." In the Ancient Burying Ground of Hartford a monument to the memory of these original proprietors includes the name of John Moody, and an early plot of the city also indicates his home lot.

The Puritans had sterling qualities. Sacrifices for their views had been great. It was natural, therefore, that they should zealously guard that which they had so dearly bought. Thus it came about that these stalwart men were among those who made vices of their virtues, and strength of convictions was not tempered by breadth of sympathy with opposing beliefs. Soon dissension occurred among the Hartford colonists and these "differences in the churches of Hartford and Wethersfield were the principal cause of the settlement of Hadley." Among the settlers of this new colony of 1660 was Samuel Moody, son of John Moody. Quite possibly the young man was not altogether indifferent to the benefits which the fertile valley offered. These pioneers sometimes found religious convictions coincided with natural advantages.

For years Northfield was the northerly outpost of civilization in New England. The early pioneers, pushing up the Connecticut from Saybrook and Hartford, founded Springfield, Northampton, Hadley and Deerfield. In 1673 a group of daring spirits obtained a grant for the town of Northfield. They were chiefly young men from Northampton, to whom danger gave a zest to life.

> The founding of a new plantation by a small colony, on a frontier so far from help was a bold push [says the historian of Northfield]. Deerfield, the nearest English settlement, planted only two years before, was sixteen miles distant, and intercommunication was difficult. Hadley, to which they must look in case of need, was thirty miles away. In other directions, Brookfield was forty-five miles, Lancaster was sixty and Groton was sixty-five miles. All within this wide circle was wilderness.

The hostility of the Indians made the first efforts for a permanent settlement abortive, and not until 1685 was another attempt made. For the next few years the outcome was uncertain. Indian massacres in neighboring towns and frequent ambushes where a solitary wayfarer was intercepted, made life hazardous for those early settlers. But the meadowlands on the river banks offered rich rewards to the venturesome and gave promise of great returns for their labors. The recent massacres in Hadley and Deerfield made real their peril, but the threatened dangers of Indian cruelty deterred neither the men nor the women.

The early experiences of the Moody family were almost paralleled by the descendants of William Holton, who, at the age of twenty-three, came from England in 1634. Settling in Hartford, he too was probably among the dissidents; for about the same time Samuel Moody moved to Hadley, his neighbor William Holton moved to Northampton, nearly opposite Hadley on the western side of the Connecticut River. Early in the eighteenth century his grandson became one of the settlers in Northfield. For six generations the family has occupied the land acquired by grant.

It was toward the end of the eighteenth century that Isaiah Moody, a direct descendant of Samuel, also moved to Northfield from Hadley. The historian of Northfield tersely records, "He was by trade a brick mason; he came to Northfield about 1796, his whole fortune being the horse he rode and his kit of tools in a bag; died February 20, 1835." It was his son Edwin, born November 1, 1800, who married Betsey Holton. Thus in the sixth generation, the families once neighbors in Hartford are again united. Dwight Lyman Moody was the sixth child by this union.

Isaiah, Noah, Lemuel, Ebenezer and Samuel are typical names chosen for the succeeding generations of Moody's forbears. They testify to the old Puritan traditions inherited by both the Moodys and the Holtons. The marriage of Edwin Moody and Betsey Holton was on January 3, 1828. The groom was twenty-eight and the bride twenty-three. They established their home in a little cottage adjoining the dwelling of the Moody family. Little is known of their early married life but it may be assumed that it did not differ from that of their neighbors. Edwin Moody continued working at his trade as a brick mason which, in those primitive times, not only consisted of building the houses and chimneys but of making the bricks as well.

Edwin Moody was apparently improvident, openhanded and socially inclined. Spending freely, he became seriously involved so that he mortgaged the home and assumed other obligations. At the very time of Dwight's

Monument to Early Settlers of Hartford

birth the straitened circumstances of the family were the subject of anxiety to relatives. A letter from a brother-in-law in Columbus, Georgia, in 1838, in the quaintly formal style of the day counsels thus:

E. MOODY, ESQ.

Dear Sir: Your embarrassing condition is weighing deeply upon your mind and that, however driven may be your pecuniary difficulties, remember that it is easier for a camel to go through the eye of a needle than for a man, thus ashamed, to extract himself while he remains in your section of the country. Taking this view of things I have thought proper to proffer to you my aid and advice as regarding your future movement in life. How far my proffered aid and advice may meet your views subsequent events can only show. I shall make no mention of past transactions. I shall write as I feel. Hope everything will be reciprocal. In the first place you have already a large family. They are the pride of your heart and the apple of your eye and in them are concentrated all your affection. All your future exertions and energies are of course enlisted for their present and future welfare. Yes, and even let you double your diligence and turn where you now are, it will be ever difficult for you to furnish them with the most common necessities of life, and keep even with the world. Now would it not be best for you to save what you can out of the wreck of all your affairs and come south and commence new? Or if you cannot bring your family this fall, come out yourself and spend the winter. You can send money home to support them. The country is as healthy as any portion of the northern states and lands fertile and, in short, no finer country in the world—besides, we can make ourselves in as easy circumstances as one could wish in a reasonable time by economy and industry. It is not worth your while to grieve over misfortunes and past events. Blot them from your memory. Be of good cheer and your pathway may yet be strewn with roses of the brightest hue.

But associations were too strong for the New Englander and the advice was not taken. The strain of the anxiety told upon his constitution, however, for without a moment's warning, at the age of forty-one, he died. His widow was left with the care of seven children and within a month the birth of twins brought an added burden.

At thirty-six years of age, with an impoverished farm heavily mortgaged, and all available chattels seized by creditors, she resolutely applied herself to the task of providing for the little family. Her dower rights secured to her the home itself, otherwise she would have been without a roof over her head.

That she received no help from her family or her husband's family was due in part to their own limited circumstances. But no word of criticism ever came from her. Among the letters which she preserved for more than half a century were two from her husband's sisters. If Edwin Moody did not act upon her husband's counsel to go to Georgia, the first sister would at least express her pity.

> I can assure you, dear sister [she wrote], that you and your little flock around you are constantly in my mind and it would relieve my anxiety in a great measure if I could only know that you are made comfortable and your children had good homes, if obliged to be separated from you. No doubt it will be a great trial for you to part with your little ones; but our wise Providence orders everything for the best and you must bear your afflicted calamities with

Christian fortitude which is the only way to insure happiness in this world and the world to come.

The other sister grieves "to think of your distressed situation—will you be obliged to give up the house and lot? I hope not, but I fear the worst—almost one year has gone since you were called to follow the remains of him who is dearer to you than all earthly things."

CHAPTER II

Less than a century had intervened between the wild unsettled days and the birth of D. L. Moody. It was a primitive community in which he grew up. The railways had not superseded the stagecoach, and childhood memories recalled the annual two-day trip the father made to Boston where he traded the fruits of farm labors and his wife's homely merchandise. There were still those living who could remember the struggles for national independence and even the days of the French and Indian wars.

New England has ever been deemed conservative, and in the first half of the nineteenth century changes were slow. While the dangers of former years no longer threatened, in other respects life continued to be primitive during Moody's youth.

But if there was little contact with the outside world, life had its compensations. Both economically and socially the village was self-sufficing. Necessities were simple and self-provided, and luxuries were few. If social events were infrequent, they were more appreciated on the occasions when they were enjoyed and neighborly intercourse was a pleasing substitute for tedious formalities. If life was no sinecure and "earning a living" the common lot of all, still youth knew how to find fellowship in work, and native genius could find opportunity for expression.

Thus, young Moody's training began in the school of adversity. To be sure, riches and poverty are relative terms. In a community not far removed from pioneer days none were rich. The affluence of the prosperous was potential, measured in land to be cultivated and cattle to be cared for. Though the Moody family were poorer than most of their neighbors, they lived where hardships were the common lot of all. But Moody was endowed with the intangible riches which inhere in the individual—health of body and mind, resourcefulness and self-reliance, habits of industry and thrift, and ideals which resulted from hard discipline. The counsel of a mother who, by example and precept, wisely trained her children and at the same time indicated the nobility of unselfish service for others, was a blessing none can measure. Throughout his life Moody looked on wastefulness and laziness with no leniency.

Early Puritan traditions were strictly observed. The Sabbath was kept from Saturday at sunset to sunset on Sunday. With great regularity Widow Moody's little family, under the guidance of the two older children, trudged a mile and a half to the village church to attend the two regular services and the Sunday school that followed the morning worship. From this requirement there was no appeal, no matter how hard the seats or how long the discourse.

Total abstinence was not commonly practiced in rural New England. Hard cider was a popular drink and in common use. The father had probably followed the congenial custom in his taste for the social glass, and rumor confirms this assumption. But from the time of his death, the widow was an uncompromising enemy of alcohol even in its mildest forms.

Discipline was enforced in the old-fashioned way; there was no sparing of the rod. One so heavily burdened could not adopt the gentler methods in vogue later. Implicit, unquestioning obedience was as necessary in the nature of the case as it was beneficial in the building of character. Truthfulness and punctilious compliance in fulfilling an agreement were emphasized in the training of the young people. On one occasion Moody had agreed to work for a neighbor. The compact included board as well as wages. But a growing boy's appetite was not easily satisfied, and he complained to his mother of the quality and inadequacy of his meals. There was only one question asked and that was, "Did you agree?" He had to acknowledge that he had, and there was no escape until the contract was fulfilled.

But if the mother was a strict disciplinarian and severe in the insistence upon the simple virtues and regulations of the house, she was both wise and tender-hearted, teaching self-denial and sacrifice. Moody often related an instance of this which impressed him for life. A beggar came to the door in search of food, and his request was submitted to the children and determined by vote. Each gave a part of his own evening meal. Often the mother yielded her personal comfort that the children might enjoy themselves after their own fashion. At the end of an arduous day of household duties comprising not only the care of the home but also the weaving of cloth, the making of clothes and the knitting of socks, she let boisterous pranks and hilarious laughter reign unchecked; and, as though her own family were not enough, neighbors' children shared in the mirthful celebrations. Tedious chores were often seen as opportunities for sport, and a novel means of shelling corn was found in hurtling it down the stairs. Her great objective was to strengthen home ties by associating in the minds of her boys and girls the memories of happy fellowship. In this, she believed, would be found a deterrent from evil associations in after life and a bulwark against temptation.

CHAPTER III

Moody's early religious education was meager, and it was largely because of the family misfortunes that he received any at all. At least they were instrumental in bringing about the regular church attendance of the children. Edwin Moody was not strict in his church worship and such associations were not introduced as a tradition into his home. But he died when Dwight was only four years of age. Sorrow and adversity brought to the young widow a sense of need that could be met only by drawing on spiritual resources. In her own youth she had received little training, although she probably followed the common social custom and attended church with some degree of regularity. Betsey Hodges, her mother, is reputed to have been religiously inclined. However that may be, Moody's own mother in those early days seems to have found her creed in the austerities of Puritan *ethics* and a simple belief in God. She apparently had not "experienced religion" in her youth. If challenged to give expression to her faith, she would have probably replied in words to this effect, "Trust in God and do right"; or possibly in the phrase of the prophet Micah, "To do justly, to love mercy, and to walk humbly with thy God." Like the father of Phillips Brooks of Unitarian upbringing, Betsey Holton was "not given to introvertiveness or contemplation, nor seeking the assurance of an inward experience." She was rather an exponent of the gospel of the secular life, faithful in the performance of duty, quick to recognize all obligations. She, too, had "sympathy for all things human."

But whatever may have been the observances of early girlhood, from the time of her marriage church attendance had not been maintained. Parental cares made prior claims, and the inclination could not have been followed even if it had been present.

The death of her husband changed all this, however, and then it was that the faithful young pastor of the church of her fathers, liberal in doctrine but truly imbued with the teaching of Christ, visited the widow and the fatherless not alone with spiritual comfort but with material help which the children could more easily comprehend. To his dying day Moody revered the memory of this true shepherd of God, Reverend Oliver Capen Everett. The baptism of all the Moody children is due to his diligent care. When asked in later life if the ordinance at the hands of the Unitarian satisfied him, Moody replied, "I found I was baptized in the name of the Father, Son and Holy Ghost. I couldn't see that anyone could add to this." Thus it was that the children became regular church attendants. The overburdened mother then probably felt her duty fully met in sending her children to church and Sunday school.

But despite this discipline, young Moody knew nothing of the Bible and had no conception of evangelical Christianity. He related an occasion of great embarrassment to him when at the age of seventeen he went to Boston and became a member of a Bible class. On being asked to read a verse from Daniel, he was at a loss to know whether it was in the Old Testament or the New. That a youth reared within the church and in a nominal Christian home should be so deficient needs some explanation. To do this requires a description of conditions in the Congregational church of New England in the early years of the nineteenth century.

The early settlers in Massachusetts brought with them their prejudices as well as their principles. The spirit of Reformation was still strong among them, and they cherished deep aversion to anything which, in their judgment, savored of Roman Catholic practices. Even the Church of England they regarded with grave misgivings. Doctor Chauncey prayed at a funeral for the first time in Boston in 1766, the practice having been viewed previously as a Roman Catholic custom. For the same reason Christmas and Easter were not generally observed, and the belief continued in rural communities as late as 1870. The memory of the abuses and corruptions in the established Church of England, at the time the early settlers left the homeland, long persisted.

They firmly believed that in a Christian civilization church and state were inseparable, and they attempted to establish a theocracy in their new homes. The Congregational polity was adopted as their state religion; final authority in doctrine and practice they found in a literal interpretation of the Scriptures. Apparently, however, they seemed to have been arrested in the study of God's dealing with mankind in the books of the Old Testament, and great emphasis was laid upon divine austerity. The appeal to fear was most commonly made to bring men to a public profession of faith.

This is clearly evident in the preaching of the latter part of the eighteenth century. The purport of Jonathan Edwards' famous Enfield sermon, when strong men quailed, was the future torment of those without faith. The preacher here portrayed a deity vindictive and vengeful. In upholding his views of divine sovereignty and foreordination, Edwards unwittingly called in question the integrity of God's moral character. If penitent sinners sought forgiveness, "God will not hold himself obliged to show mercy at last," and this in spite of repeated promises of pardon. The joyous note was lacking, for while man was always held up as essentially vile, God was proclaimed as far distant and severe. Such teaching was predominantly depressing and discouraging. In their abhorrence of abuses in the state church in England and of the irreligious life of some of its leaders, these Massachusetts theologians were likewise guilty of distorting sacred truth. Revolting from frivolity, they issued in gloom and sometimes even in hypocrisy.

But extremes engender extremes. Again a revulsion from the somber note occurred. There had been among the early settlers some who had sojourned in Holland where Socinianism, which questioned the Trinitarian doctrine, was beginning to make its impress. There were others who had come under the influence of Emlyn in England; he taught that Christ was not coequal with God but nevertheless was to be worshiped as a divine being. Those who sympathized with the beliefs of the Dutch Socinians and of Emlyn were for a long time numerically weak, but among the more devout New Testament students their views exercised an ever increasing influence. Especially was this true in Boston in the early years of the nineteenth century; and soon William Ellery Channing, Ralph Waldo Emerson, Theodore Parker, James Freeman Clark and Wendell Phillips became protagonists of this new liberalism and opponents of traditions. They fearlessly denounced slavery as a social evil even in face of a conservative element which upheld it on Scriptural grounds. In nobility of character they were outstanding and their brilliant intellectual attainments and oratorical powers drew large numbers.

It is not surprising that, choosing between the older teaching of the nature of God and the New Testament revelation, the younger ministers and theological students should acclaim liberalism. Out of twenty-four "Heralds of a Liberal Faith," designated as prophets by Reverend Samuel A. Elliott, all but three graduated from Harvard. So rapidly had this cause grown that it was said only one minister in Boston adhered to the Calvinistic position, while at Harvard College all the talented young men were Unitarian, and orthodox views were generally ridiculed.

The organization of the Congregational church, with each body of worshipers an independent and self-governing group, made possible the changes of belief without any schism. In most churches a covenant was entered on joining the fellowship, the Westminster confession being assumed but not definitely subscribed to. Naturally when beliefs were altered gradually, the change came about without any alteration in the life of the church in its association with other churches.

Soon the newer views were disseminated throughout the churches in the rural communities. In taking country charges the younger ministers led their hearers to adopt their attitudes, and thus Congregational churches in Massachusetts became Unitarian in doctrine. There were staunch adherents to the traditional teachings of their fathers in some places, and these dissidents broke from the fellowship of the parish and formed Trinitarian churches, but for the most part the older families remained in the place of worship in which their fathers had been reared. Those who seceded paid dearly for their convictions, for, in 1820, the Supreme Court of Massachusetts ordered judgment in favor of the Unitarian churches which involved property and funds to the value of six hundred thousand dollars.

At first the liberals adopted the name of Catholic Christians; and, claiming the utmost latitude in belief, they rejected all historic creeds. It ensued that there was no common expression of faith and widely divergent views were held by those who belonged to the same body.

Among the more conservative, William Ellery Channing was accorded a position of great influence. His loyalty to evangelical faith may be judged from his public utterances. He ascribed to Jesus Christ a unique position, subordinate to God the Father but more than man; He existed before the world; He literally came from heaven to save our race; He sustains other offices than those of a teacher and witness to the Truth; He still acts for our benefit and is our intercessor with the Father. He affirmed:

> The truth of Christianity is a growing evidence. When we begin our enquiries into the truth of Christianity, we are impressed with the miraculous works of Christ, those exertions of divine power which prove that the Father was in him, that he was commissioned from heaven. In proportion as we attend to the subject, a new source of evidence springs up and brings new conviction to our minds. In the moral character of Jesus we see a miracle more striking than the most stupendous work of a physical nature. We see in a brighter and clearer light, the impressions and evidence of a sincere, upright, devout and most benevolent heart. We see a character most original and yet most consistent; such as the evangelists could never have feigned, such as imposters would never have imagined, but which is exactly suited to the wants and miseries of man, and to our highest conceptions of the Divinity.

Thus the movement which had its inception in an attempt to vindicate the character of God and to protest against early Puritan theology made a metaphysical distinction between the deity and divinity of Christ.

But soon the liberals came to a parting of the ways. The more radical leaders were not satisfied with the evangelical position of Channing; and Ralph Waldo Emerson and Theodore Parker, who became known as Transcendentalists, avowed a disbelief in the views held heretofore and a schism grew up among themselves. "The

Transcendentalists substituted ethical culture for revealed religion, and for a time the momentum of early Christian training carried the adherents of this new cult: Puritan earnestness had not died out; the sense of responsibility was as lively as ever—to earn one's living by honest labor; to be pure, upright, charitable; to be a good son, father, citizen—these things were essential to the well-being of society, and to that of the individual as part of it; but they awakened no enthusiasm, gave no scope for self-devotion, since the end in view, however desirable, came short of the ultimate and total welfare of the individual."

It was in the transitional period from the conservatism of Channing to the radical school of his successors that Moody passed his youth. The Moody and Holton families had maintained their associations with the church of their fathers which had accepted the Unitarian position. The controversial questions absorbing the ministry made no appeal to young Moody. Aggressive propaganda for liberalism and apologetics for the newer attitudes apparently failed to stir his interest. In his religious background, therefore, there was no doctrinal teaching in the Christian faith.

Educational opportunities were similarly limited. Each community had the church and school which were the first provisions made by the early settlers in Massachusetts. As homes were established, "little red schoolhouses" were to be found scattered throughout rural districts. There in one room, under the instruction of an untrained teacher, children of every age and degree of ability learned the rudiments. School desks and seats were made for two occupants and succeeding generations left roughly carved emblems and initials. In cold weather a large wood stove, often red-hot, baked those close by, while others in remote parts of the room felt the chill of the atmosphere through the shrunken window frames.

Furthermore, the terms were not uniform. If the annual town meeting failed to make adequate provision for three full terms, the school sessions were accordingly shortened. Older students often failed to receive consecutive teaching by being forced to leave before the close of the term to work on farms.

One of Moody's earliest ventures was to drive a neighbor's cows to pasture in the morning and to bring them home after school. He received one cent a week.

In the face of such hardships young Moody received his early and his only systematic schooling. All in all it probably lasted for eight years—from the time he was five until he was thirteen. The reputation of his lively sense of humor and of his combined energy and resourcefulness long lingered. It accorded him a leadership among the boys of his own age. His was the conceiving and directing spirit of many an inventive escapade which in after years he would recount with genuine relish. The fun of his pranks were well worth the double thrashing which surely followed from teacher and parent.

Moody was a normal boy. His love of mischief was at this time his most distinguishing characteristic. The monotony of village life at times seemed to pall upon him and he had recourse to many inventions to relieve the tedium of daily routine. Once he posted a sign upon the schoolhouse door announcing a lecture to be delivered at early candlelight. Such an event drew many neighbors all ready to contribute a tallow dip to provide the necessary illumination. When no lecturer appeared no one was so indignant as the young culprit who was not suspected of the hoax. On another occasion when he was to declaim at the closing exercises of the school term he chose Mark Antony's oration over the dead Cæsar. To add a dramatic touch to the scene he had placed before him a long box supposed to be the bier of the assassinated Roman. In the height of eloquence

Moody fiercely struck the box and, to the surprise and consternation of the audience, a large cat sprang out. Again he led a group of boys into a farmer's shed where a large number of young cattle were kept. Quietly creeping to the loft above, the boys let out a wild war whoop, raising such a racket as to stampede the yearlings so that they fled in terror, leaping over fences, and were brought back to their enclosure only with greatest difficulty. In after years the scenes which the relating of these escapades brought to mind were an unfailing delight not only to his children but to the narrator as well.

But one teacher who came to the little school impressed Moody. First, she opened the exercises with prayer and later she announced that she proposed to rule the school without the old-fashioned whippings. It was not long before Dwight had broken a rule, and with the summons to remain after school, he expected the customary punishment and immediately assumed the air of injured innocence. To his surprise, when they were alone, the teacher began to talk kindly to him and to tell him how sorry she was to have him disobey. This treatment was worse than the birch rod, and Dwight did not like it. After telling him how it grieved her to find that he could not be trusted, the teacher said, "I have made up my mind that if I cannot rule the school by love, I will give it up. I will have no punishment. If you love me, try to help me." This was too much for Dwight. "If anyone troubles you, I'll whack him!" he said. And the new champion for reform had soon to be restrained from his vigorous methods so chivalrously exerted in supporting the system of the teacher.

The attempt to secure better educational advantages when he was ten years old met with indifferent success. A brother one year his senior who was working for his board and attending the public school in Greenfield, the county seat fourteen miles away, found a similar place for Dwight. They left home on a cheerless November day and the distance seemed formidable. From an elevation across the river the boys looked back for their last view of the village. A sense of awful loneliness swept over the younger one; and, recalling the experience later, he would attribute to the memory of this incident the feeling of dreariness that November always brought. But the incident had its beautiful aspect which may best be related in Moody's own words:

> When at last we arrived in the town I had hard work to keep back my tears, and my brother had to do his best to cheer me. Suddenly he pointed to someone and said, "There is a man that'll give you a cent; he gives one to every new boy that comes to town." He was a feeble, white-haired man, and I was so afraid that he would pass me by that I planted myself directly in his path. As he came up to us my brother spoke to him, and he stopped and looked at me. "Why, I have never seen you before. You must be a new boy," he said. He asked me about my home, and then, laying his trembling hand upon my head, he told me that, although I had no earthly father, my Heavenly Father loved me, and then gave me a bright new cent. I do not remember what became of that cent, but that old man's blessing has followed me for over fifty years; and to my dying day I shall feel the kindly pressure of that hand upon my head.

An old catalogue of a private school in the village known as the Northfield Institute includes the name of Dwight L. Moody with that of a brother and cousin for the year ending 1853. In later life he never referred to this school but often said his school days ended when he was thirteen so that if he actually attended the institute, it was for a very brief period. This is further confirmed by the fact that he worked on neighboring farms during the last year at home, and he left Northfield to find employment in Boston in April, 1854, four years after his schooling definitely terminated.

During those years no ambition roused the boy to supplement his inadequate education by any serious reading, and he seemed destined to follow the uneventful course of his forbears. This is less surprising when the circumstances are considered. His only time for reading was at night by the dim light of a tallow candle, and books were scarce in rural communities. Then, too, he was physically exhausted after a long day of arduous toil; his spirit and energy proved him equal to a man's task and the day's toll of strength was great. Intellectual awakening was to come later.

By the nature of his labors he often worked alone. What thoughts came to him and what youthful visions he may have had is not known. In after years he could not himself recall what experiences led to the decision to try his fortune in some place where greater scope would be given to his energies. In any case, increasing restiveness developed during his last two years at home and the growing consciousness of initiative and awakening ambition impelled him. Finally he sought an opportunity to demonstrate his powers, and it mattered little where he found it.

CHAPTER IV

For some time his project of going to Boston to seek employment was the subject of home discussion. He encountered opposition from the two whose judgment he valued most, his mother and his brother George. Though there was less than four years difference in their ages, George Moody, as an elder brother, had been accorded a deference beyond that which his seniority would imply. But Dwight had now arrived at an age where he believed he should and must decide for his own future. Only seventeen, he was immature, inexperienced and crude, yet he believed himself capable of determining how and where those powers with which he felt himself endowed could best be employed.

All arguments proved unavailing, and he received from his mother a reluctant consent to his plan. He had no means wherewith to make the journey, for his wages had gone into the family purse. But go he would if he had to walk.

In after years he related with no little feeling how George, who disapproved of his leaving home, met him on the road and gave him five dollars. With this as his only capital, Moody began his own life.

An old daguerreotype from this period pictures an ingenuous youth. His eyes are wide apart, clear and frank; the jaw firm and not large; the lips full. The ears are small and close set; the head rests upon broad, sloping shoulders and is surmounted with heavy locks of hair. The face is pleasing and handsome; the expression genial and alert. It is the likeness of a youth who has lived cleanly and challenges life unafraid.

There is the temptation of crediting to a youth those qualities which his subsequent career reveals. But the most diligent study of young Moody would not have shown any indications of a future different from that of thousands of his contemporaries. Nothing of outstanding character in intellectual gifts was evident. His first letters indicate his immaturity and are inconsistent with the resolute determination which he showed in making the venture. But against his handicaps, and of inestimable value, he presented rugged health of body, mind and spirit.

Thus as the career began, with his temperament and disposition, his gifts of leadership, his energy, resourcefulness and sense of humor, Moody was potentially a power for good. His alertness of mind found its counterpart in a physical nimbleness. He was willful and quick-tempered but these qualities were moderated by a susceptible heart.

In going to Boston, the youth had the ambition of amassing wealth and considered it a worthy object. European traditions which award public service with honors, have never prevailed to the same extent in America. To acquire affluence has appealed to young America as a shorter method for obtaining the means wherewith to wield power. Wealth is in every generation a relative term, and according to the standards of the day the possession of one hundred thousand dollars constituted a fortune. To procure such a sum was the dream of the young man.

Success was not Moody's initial experience. It was not easy for a lad whose knowledge was limited to farm work, to find employment. Possibly the reputation for capacity and industry which he had in his native town gave him an exaggerated opinion of his own gifts and resulted in an appearance of self-confidence that made an unfavorable impression. His first efforts left him chagrined, homesick and discouraged.

Finally, when his pride gave way under the dreadful sense of being adrift in a world that seemed to care nothing for him, he turned to his mother's brothers who conducted a small retail boot and shoe business. Why he did not first seek a position with them is not clear.

The uncles seized the opportunity to offer frank criticism.

> Dwight, I am afraid if you come in here you will want to run the store yourself [said Mr. Holton]. Now, my men want to do their work as I want it done. If you are willing to come and do the best you can, and do it right, and if you'll ask whenever you don't know, and if you promise to go to church and Sunday school, and if you will not go anywhere that you wouldn't want your mother to know about, we'll see how we can get along. You may have till Monday to think it over.

Moody accepted the offer. The experience had greatly humbled him and the memory of his previous bitter disappointment and utter loneliness was never effaced. During his entire life the vain efforts of a youth seeking work or discouraged in his first employment wakened Moody's warmest sympathy. More than forty years after, when preaching in Boston, he made reference to those days:

> I remember how I walked up and down the streets trying to find a situation, and I recollect how, when they answered me roughly, their treatment would chill my soul. But when someone would say, "I feel for you; I would like to help you, but I can't, but

you will be all right soon, I went away happy and light-hearted. That man's sympathy did me good.

It seemed as if there was room for everyone else in the world, but none for me. For about two days I had the feeling that no one wanted me. I never have had it since and I never want it again.

Sixty-seven years later a member of Mr. Moody's family, while crossing the ocean, was introduced to a gentleman who told with deep emotion his own experience with the evangelist. At the beginning of his business career in the early eighties, he was sent to Chicago to represent a large European mercantile house. His first efforts had been totally disheartening and futile. One Sunday night he attended a meeting Moody was conducting.

I was utterly downcast and lonely, in a foreign land, in a large city, and among strangers [he said]. I do not know why I was impelled to wait to speak to your father. It must have been a sense that somehow he would understand. I shall never forget his talk. He laid his hand on my shoulder and told me he knew all about it. He had been through my experience and he said he believed I would make good, and I have. But I shall always feel I owe much to that great-souled man for the cheer and help he gave a lonely, discouraged boy.

It was characteristic of Moody that every joy and every sorrow; all successes and all reverses, enlarged his capacity for understanding others; he entered into the closest fellowship with those that wept as well as those that rejoiced. This faculty, to a large extent, expressed the genius for friendship which he carried through life.

CHAPTER V

BOSTON was the scene of stormy events in 1854 at the time Moody came to the city. The anti-slavery agitation was at its height. He worked on Court Street, a short distance from Faneuil Hall, where the leading abolitionist speakers were to be heard on frequent occasions. It was natural that he should seize every opportunity to hear the fiery eloquence of men whose names were upon every one's lips, and it is not difficult to imagine the effect of all this on an impressionable youth from the country.

A memorable event occurred soon after his arrival. This was the rendition of the fugitive slave Anthony Burns. The old Court House where the negro was held was opposite the shop in which Moody worked, and he was an interested observer. He was in the mob which threatened to free the prisoner forcibly and which was only dispersed when shots were fired over the heads of the people. If the attempted liberation failed, the memory remained. Fires of abolitionist zeal, which burned with increasing intensity during the trying days of the succeeding decade, were kindled. The pitiable sight of Burns carried through the streets in chains to be returned to bondage affected Moody much as Lincoln was affected in witnessing ten or a dozen slaves shackled together on a river steamer, like so many animals, which was for him "a continual torment."

In all these distracting weeks Moody was learning to be a salesman and he rapidly became proficient. Conventional but unfruitful methods he discarded, and adopted others more aggressive. When the window display failed to attract customers, he did not hesitate to embrace the medieval practice of accosting passers-by with an invitation to enter the store and examine the goods. Soon he induced his employer to permit him to forego holidays and share the profits gained by keeping the shop open when other places of business were closed. On such occasions there was always a large number of country visitors only too glad to find they could combine necessary trading with a pleasure trip to the city.

It is not surprising that the country lad should find the new conditions irksome at times. The love of mischief would again assert itself. On one occasion the cobbler was the victim of the youthful clerk. Moody carefully made a little slit with a sharp knife in the leather seat of the bench. He placed beneath this a pan of water so that when the occupant placed his weight on it, the small aperture opened and the water beneath came through. The mystified cobbler only discovered the secret of his annoyance by the ill-concealed amusement of the young clerk.

After a long day's work in the little store Moody would often take exercise by running around Boston Common. Once he walked up to a stranger and, without accosting him, silently accompanied him. Accommodating his gait to that of the stranger, he continued to walk until the Boston citizen, thoroughly convinced that the youth was demented, fled precipitately.

From a day book with entries from July 1, 1854, to June 4, 1856, there are items against the name of D. L. Moody indicating that his salary was small. He had already been in his uncles' employ for over a year before any credit entries appeared, apparently indicating that during this period his wages were sent directly to his mother. From June, 1856, to September his total payments were but $57.28.

On April 9, 1854, he writes his brothers:

I sleep on Court Street. I have a room up in the third story. I went to Sunday school in the morning and then I went to one this noon but I don't belong to only one. I am going to join the Christian Association tomorrow night. Then I shall have a place to go to when I want to go anywhere. And I can have all the books I want to read free from expense. Only have to pay one dollar a year. They have a large room and the smart men of Boston lecture to them for nothing and they get up and ask questions. The place where I board, there are about twenty-five clerks and some girls. We have a jolly time. I wanted to go over to Chelsea and so I went over there and it was about four o'clock when we see a ship yonder and we soon passed it. You know a steamboat goes faster than a ship. And we got on the wharf first and waited to see that ship come in. It was a ship from Liverpool loaded with immigrants. All the Greeks in town were there—the sailors sang a song when they came in sight. Such meetings as there were!

Goodbye from a true friend,

DWIGHT.

As the Boston Young Men's Christian Association had been established in 1851, Moody was among its earliest members, and the interest recounted in this letter was to continue throughout life.

There seems to have been some uncertainty of the duration of stay in Boston for shortly after the above letter he writes his youngest brother, "I don't have anything to do but trade. I took as much as anyone last Saturday. Tell William Alexander I shan't be back there to work for him till June. I wish when you get a good chance, Samuel, you would send me a Greenleaf's arithmetic too, for I get some time to study and the spring is very backward." To a sister he sends, "You wanted me to write and tell you how the pickpockets get fat picking my pockets." Other letters are full of inquiries about farm life in Northfield, "Have you got your planting done?" he asked. "Isn't the spring backward?" He thinks he can advantageously provide his brothers with shoes and "will endeavour to help you more."

Immature and crude as these letters are, they reveal a love for home and thoughtfulness of those dear to him. Home is the great reality, and city experiences only a passing phase.

CHAPTER VI

The two years spent in Boston not only awakened qualities which gave promise of business success but widened his horizon. Here at the age of seventeen he was converted and this event determined his whole career. In a sermon preached in the same city many years later he thus referred to the experience: "Some day you will read in the papers that D. L. Moody of East Northfield is dead. Don't believe a word of it. At that moment I shall be more alive than I am now. I shall have gone higher, that is all; gone out of this old tenement of clay into a house that is immortal; a body that death cannot touch, that sin cannot taint, a body like unto His own glorious body. I was born of the flesh in 1837. I was born of the spirit in 1854. That which is born of the flesh may die. That which is born of the spirit will live forever."

In complying with the conditions imposed by his uncle, Moody attended the Mount Vernon Church of which Doctor Edwin N. Kirk was pastor and became enrolled in a Bible class conducted by Mr. Edward Kimball. At first Dwight was embarrassed by his conscious lack of knowledge of the Bible. When he had the temerity to remark naïvely upon the subject under discussion, he was made to realize his ignorance by the expressions of surprise and, at times, by the ill-concealed mirth of his fellow scholars, some of whom were students at Harvard. In illustrating the Bible class narrative in after years he would relate how he caused great amusement by commenting, "That Moses must have been *smart*." He suffered in consequence, and soon assumed an attitude of taciturn observation.

Mr. Kimball was one who did not feel that his duties were fully discharged when the hour of Bible instruction was over. There was that in the awkward country boy which engaged his teacher. Kimball determined to seek an opportunity for a personal interview, realizing the ineffectiveness of a general appeal and Moody's embarrassment in being addressed before others. With great tact and wisdom he went to the boy's place of employment where he found Moody engaged in wrapping up shoes. What was said could not be definitely recalled, but the decision was made by the youth to yield to the claims of Christ. Apparently there was no deep conviction of sin or wrestling of spirit. His allegiance was a reasonable service joyously rendered. The few words wisely spoken achieved what sermons and class work had failed to bring about. That one conversation was the turning point in Moody's life. There was a new incentive, ultimately revolutionizing all his early objectives.

No longer was he to view religion as a set of inhibitions, but as a power applicable to daily life and an unfailing source of joy. Sunday henceforth became a day of spiritual privilege.

Though the choice was decisive, there was great immaturity. Moody did not become miraculously informed in doctrine and knowledge of the Scriptures. Such was his ignorance that there were those who entertained grave misgivings of his fitness for church fellowship. When he appeared before the committee for examination and was asked, "What has Christ done for you and for us all, that especially entitles Him to our love and obedience?" his reply was, "I think He has done a great deal for us all, but I don't know of anything He has done in particular."

It is not surprising then, in those days when membership in evangelical churches was based upon strict acceptance of doctrine, that young Moody's admission was deferred until after a season of probation. Under the guidance of three church officers he was remanded for counsel and instruction.

His progress is noted in the church records:

> No. 1079. Dwight L. Moody. Boards, 43 Court Street. Has been baptized. First awakened on the 16th of May. Became anxious about himself. Saw himself a sinner, and sin now seems hateful and holiness desirable. Thinks he has repented; has purposed to give up sin; feels dependent upon Christ for forgiveness. Loves the Scriptures. Prays. Desires to be useful. Religiously educated. Been in the city a year. From Northfield, this state. Is not ashamed to be known as Christian. Eighteen years old.
>
> No. 1131. March 12, 1856. Mr. Moody thinks he has made some progress since he was here before—at least in knowledge. Has maintained his habits of prayer and reading the Bible. Believes God will hear his prayers, and reads the Bible. Is fully determined to adhere to the cause of Christ always. Feels that it would be very bad if he should join the church and then turn. Must repent and ask forgiveness, for Christ's sake. Will never give up his hope, or love Christ less, whether admitted to the church or not. His prevailing intention is to give up his will to God.

Nothing is so misleading as to conceive of the youth abandoning all his previous ambitions at this time, but the direction of his life had become fixed. He was a beginner in the school of Christian experience—experience which, day by day, was to bring fuller knowledge.

At all times and in any way thereafter, he was eager to serve his new found Master.

It would be interesting to learn how he related to his mother the story of his conversion, but no letter is to be found in which he imparts the news of his great decision. Possibly the mother felt that the nature of his confidence was too sacredly intimate ever to come under the eye of an unsympathetic reader. Or, perhaps, the zeal of the young convert may have made such appeals in behalf of others in the family that they seemed to reflect upon the faithfulness of home instruction. In any event, after the first few weeks in Boston no letters to his mother are to be found; and natural curiosity respecting his own descriptions of his experiences is not satisfied.

Many years later, however, when preaching in Boston, he speaks of those early days. "I thought the old sun shone brighter than it ever had before. I thought it was just smiling upon me. As I walked upon Boston Common and heard the birds singing in the trees, I thought they were all singing a song to me. Do you know how I fell in love with the birds? I had never cared for them before. It seemed to me that I was in love with all creation—I had not a bitter feeling against any man, and I was ready to take all men to my heart. If a man has not the love of God shed abroad in his heart, he has never been regenerated. If you hear a person get up in prayer meeting and he begins to find fault with everybody, you may doubt whether his is a genuine conversion; it may be a counterfeit. It has not the right ring, because the impulse of a converted soul is to love, and not to be getting up and complaining of everyone else and finding fault."

CHAPTER VII

AFTER two years in Boston Moody went to Chicago. He found the position with his uncles to be "not very pleasant." It may well be that he chafed under business methods which he thought irksome and antiquated, or that his services were not sufficiently recognized. Whatever caused the unpleasantness is not known, for in later years he never alluded to it, and what seemed so serious at the time may have been exaggerated in his boyish mind.

Having once determined on making the move, he consulted no one, doubtless fearing dissuasion. A letter to his mother, from Chicago, dated September 20, 1856, is thoroughly characteristic of his immediateness.

> Uncle Sam objected to my going and as he had been so kind to me when I left home and went to Boston as to give me employment and keep me out of bad company I could not help feeling I had to go against his will, so I thought the quicker I went and got out of his way the better—for you must know I had no money too, with only enough to get here. When I got to Keene (N. H.) Monday night I thought I was near you. God knows there was no one under the sun that would have liked to see you more than I should. But I thought of the meeting, then the parting, then I thought I would drive right through and reach my western home as quick as I can. I have found some nice people and have not been sorry I came, although I love Boston.

Two weeks later he again writes his mother:

> It made me feel bad to read that you could not think of me without crying. You think I am a good way off, but I don't feel as if I was so far from home as I did in Boston and I think I shall go East as often as once a year. Although I don't like living here as well as I did in Boston I like it better than I expected to before I came out here.
>
> I was fairly drove out of Boston—But never mind! I can make more money enough faster than I can in Boston and go home once a year. At that you will see me as often as you would if I had stayed in Boston, and I think oftener.
>
> I have one of the best situations in the city. This city covers over a good deal of ground, three times as much as Boston, but it is not so thickly settled. There are some of the nicest buildings in this city that I ever saw. They claim they have the best spot in the country. It is surely the best I ever saw. It is a very lively city, much more so than Boston.

From the first he met with success. The growing city offered greater opportunities. Three months after arriving in Chicago he "is doing well—first rate. I came very near going East last week as a man offered to pay my way if I would go on with him to buy some goods. But Mr. W. (his employer) was so drove up for help he could not spare me." Again to his mother he confides, "I have made thirty dollars a week ever since I came out here." This was a large salary, according to the times, for a lad of nineteen.

The change to the West was not without waves of homesickness. He went to the post office "one thousand times" before he received the longed-for letters and "never knew what it was to want to get a letter before." When one came he read it "over and over." Again:

You must know how lonely it feels to be off in a city like this, for it is so wicked. The stores are all open on the Sabbath—a great many of them. I think of home and of Boston often but don't wish to go back to live there, although I have some warm friends in Boston. But I won't say anything for I may do injustice to someone that I would not do for anything.

For some time the unpleasantness he had experienced annoyed him, and in his loneliness seemed to rankle. He wrote a brother who was in Boston:

I did not think when I left you at Tremont Temple that Sunday that I should see the far west before seeing you again—But as it happens I am writing you Sunday, something I have not done for more than two years. But as my friend is going to Boston tomorrow morning before I get up, I write you a few lines to let you know I have not forgotten you and hope you have not me. I think of your situation often and then of mine and I hope you will never have anyone cross your path as they have mine and blast your hopes, although I think it has turned out for the best: but I could not think so when I left Boston. God has been with me since I left Boston. I have met with the very best of success. I got me a good place. I am in the largest retail store in the city; get good pay and a good man to work for.

National affairs continued to hold his interest and he thought Chicago "good for Fremont fifteen thousand" and wants the local county paper to be forwarded that will tell "how old Northfield is going" in the coming election of 1856.

Opportunities to make money appeared on every side, and the spirit of enterprise and speculation made their appeal. Nothing depicts young Moody's double interests at this time more than his letters home. Thus to his elder brother George he writes:

If I get a hundred dollars, I lay it right into land and at the rate it has increased I can make twenty-five per cent on my money. I bought some woodland out in Desplaines and I have the wood almost off and I shall double my money on it. I was offered fifty dollars for my bargain before I paid one cent down, but if nothing happens I shall make a good deal more. I can lend money here for two per cent a month and get good security. I lent one hundred dollars the other day for seventeen per cent a day! I tell you here is the place to make money. I can make more here in one week than I could in Boston in a month. And that is not all, I can enjoy myself here. I have enjoyed more religion here than ever in my life. I wish sometimes you were out here. Although we did not just get along very well, I think we could love well enough now.

Do you enjoy as much religion as you have? I hope you will hold on to the promises in the Bible. I find the better I live the more enjoyment I have and the more I think of God and His love the less I think of this world's troubles. George, don't let anything keep you from the full enjoyment of God's love. I think we have some things come upon us some times to try our faith and God likes to see us cling on. As the Psalmist says in one place God likes to chastise them whom he loves. So let us pray for each other, for I think it becomes Christians to pray for each other. I have brought you before God in my prayers and I hope you have done the same. Yours in Christ,

D. L. Moody.

This letter, so full of shrewd money-making plans, closes with phrases that sound foreign and unfamiliar and were probably acquired through attendance at testimony or prayer meetings.

Thus are conflicting influences at work in young Moody. He is equally fervent over business affairs and religious interests. His ethical perception lacks balance, recognizing nothing inconsistent in lending money at usurious rates of interest and at the same time appealing to his brother to "hold on to the promises in the Bible." Is there danger of his living in compartments, never permitting his religious professions to invade his business dealings? Misgivings on this score are immediately dispelled in the realization that this confusion of motives is due to the immaturity and crudity of early youth. Later events demonstrate that he held *no* sacrifices too great on behalf of Christian principles.

CHAPTER VIII

CHICAGO was the scene of a spiritual revival in the winter of 1856. It immediately enlisted Moody's interest. He felt the genuineness of the spirit in the meetings he attended and responded to the glow of fellowship which characterized them. Yet he, who was soon to influence thousands by his presentation of the gospel, was at this time unable to give expression to his own deepest feelings. Consequently he borrowed stereotyped phrases, foreign to his own thought and ill-adapted to his youth, and from which his conversation in later years was peculiarly free.

During this revival special services were held in many churches. Testimony to the power of God to break the hold of sin and the joy of a life yielded to His will, were familiar themes. He wrote home:

> I go every night to meeting—O, how I do enjoy it! It seems as if God was here Himself. Pray that this work may go on until every knee is bowed. I wish there could be a revival in Northfield, that many might be brought into the fold of Christ. Oh, Mother, keep the family away from Spiritualist meetings, for I am afraid they may be led astray.

To this letter there is an amusing postscript:

> Mother, you said in your letter that you were glad to hear I was getting good pay. I think you did not understand me, for I did not say I got that amount, but that I could make it soon. If I should build a house out here that would cost me one hundred

dollars, I could rent it for seventy-five dollars a year. That is making money. That is if I was able to do it, you know.

His industry and his absorption in business prevented the long-anticipated trip home. In August, 1857, he wrote:

> I received a letter from you yesterday saying you were much disappointed in my not coming home. I should like much to come, but my employer is East most of the time—so you see it is not because I don't want to come, for I have been looking forward to it and expect a good time, but that will come soon.

Soon after coming to Chicago, he was transferred from the retail department and became a traveling salesman; he also did the work of a credit man. In his journeys through Illinois he was impressed with the rich farm lands in the central and southern sections of the state. A letter to a brother reported:

> I like the land better this way than I do in the northern part but the people are more like heathens. They all smoke, chew, swear, drink and steal. They are shiftless, ignorant, miserable people. A Yankee can do well here, I think. I have no doubt told you, but you would like to know what I am up to traveling all the time. Well, I will tell you. I am collecting for a house in Chicago. I like it better than anything I have ever done. It is nothing but excitement all the time. I don't have to go back into the country. Most of our customers are on the railroad, so I seldom have to cross the prairies with a horse and if I do I have a good one. I drove a horse into a slew the other day so that nothing but his head stuck out. I didn't expect to see him out again but I made to get him out. My hair stood right on end.

I will send you a lock so you can see for yourself. Are times hard in Massachusetts? They are hard here. I don't collect hardly anything. I started the first of this month with ten thousand dollars worth of notes and have not collected one thousand yet. There is no money. I met a lot of the Chicago and Cincinnati collectors, and they do not collect enough to pay for their expenses. The reason we travel at this time for these merchants is to secure a good many of the bills. The merchants are failing or making assignments, or selling out and running away. I had a case the other day of a man who went to New York and bought six thousand dollars worth and then came back to Chicago and bought six thousand more, and he had three thousand dollars. That made fifteen thousand dollars before he got all of his goods into his store. He made an assignment. His preferred creditors were his father and brother. They take all and we have got to stand back. That is the way they do it out here this year. We have to take horses, cattle, wheat, corn, oats, barley, reapers and mortgages on lands, houses, and stores—everything you can think of.

The death of a friend impressed him with the brevity of life, and he expressed solicitude for the spiritual welfare of his brothers.

Another time he explained how a draft might be collected for the benefit of his mother to whom he made regular remittances.

Early in 1858 he accepted a position with a large wholesale boot and shoe firm and traveled "most of the time." The spirit of the West was reflected in his correspondence. His travels took him "down in Missouri and also in Iowa, Wisconsin and Indiana." The country was wild and unsettled and "as you cross the prairie you can see the prairie wolf, and deer and prairie chickens are as thick as grasshoppers in August." For some time he "has not had time to turn around. The folks I am now with do a very heavy business, the largest this side of New York. In the busy season we have to jump all hands of us as tight as we can jump."

He yearned for a sight of loved ones in the old home but a visit was contingent upon the pressure of business. "You see I have a good position and I want to work my cards to make it better. I have been very successful so far and if nothing happens I will do well."

There had been criticism at home for leaving his former employers but he assured his mother:

> I have got me a position that is worth five of that and if I have any health and my God is with me I shall succeed here in Chicago better than I ever thought I should. I hope you will never forget to pray for your son here in the west surrounded by temptation. I never worked in a place before, since my conversion, that there are so many wild young men as there is here. I hope you will plead with God that I may live a consistent Christian life before them, that they will not lead me. I am in hopes to live before them that I may be successful in winning their souls to Christ. Pray for me dear Mother.

Moody possessed, however, a spirit of humility and a recognition of the subtlety of temptation. In the face of physical danger he was brave, but of unseen temptation he lived in fear and never ceased to pray "Lead us not into temptation but keep us from evil." Referring, in conversation with a friend, to the moral collapse of a man of prominence Moody exclaimed, "You know I'm not afraid to die but there are times when I am almost afraid of living." Those who heard him preach the sermon "Sowing and Reaping" will recall his emphasis on the possibility of a man destroying a reputation of years of upright living by one lapse from rectitude. With a note of genuine fear he would make personal application saying, "In one brief moment I can undo what I have taken a lifetime to build up."

Early in his career he must have impressed his associates with his sincerity and unusual ability. On January 12, 1859, he wrote his mother:

> On my return from the country last week I found my hopes all vanished. The one I looked to for advice and counsel, who had proven to be more than a friend was dead and his remains taken East before I got the news. That man was my employer, Mr. Henderson.

Less than a month later Moody reported that the widow had asked him to serve the family as administrator. He recognized his own limitations and concluded:

> I am not old enough (he was but twenty-two) to take such an estate on my shoulders but they insisted that I should have the settling up of the business. So I have set to work and have had all the property divided and the son and daughter, also the widow, take their share. The heirs put the business all in my hands to collect something like one hundred and fifty thousand dollars worth of property. It will take three years to close it up at least. I think I will have all I want to do for the next few months to straighten out things. I feel highly honored for they had a great many friends here, two nephews who are good business men. But they would not have them and said I must take it. I never have been put in so responsible a situation in my life and my prayer is that I may do myself credit and I am in hopes you will not forget to pray for me.

CHAPTER IX

SPEAKING was not Moody's gift; of this he had been assured by his elders in Boston. His zeal therefore must find some other channel for expression. On arriving in Chicago, he placed his letter from Mount Vernon Church with the Plymouth Church and immediately sought some form of service for which he would be adapted. Originality may lie as much in perception of opportunity as in invention! Hiring a pew, he proceeded to fill it by recruiting attendants from street corners and boarding houses. Although he could not speak himself, he brought listeners for those who could. To such a degree was this effort a success that ultimately he was engaging four pews which he kept full.

But some other outlet was needed for his energies, and he proffered his services to a mission Sunday school on North Wells Street. Probably his appearance was not convincing, for he was told that no class was available, and that if he would teach he must provide himself with a class. Thereupon he collected a group of nondescript children and brought them to the school.

His labors were more successful in behalf of the Sunday school than in behalf of the church. Some members had not taken kindly to those who accepted the hospitality of his pews; but, on the other hand, his efforts among children were so encouraging that thenceforth he gave increasingly of his time and thought to work with young people. As he visited different sections of the city, he perceived the need of a Sunday school for slum children and determined to start one.

In a letter to his home he gives his impressions.

I suppose you would like to know what kind of a looking place Chicago is. Well you will see on the map that Lake Michigan is almost as high as Chicago itself. I believe the land is about three feet the highest. As there are but two or three months in the year that water stands in the streets, we have plank sidewalks. The streets are very dirty, but nevertheless it is healthy. Here I don't believe you would know me if you were to see me tonight. When I came out here I only weighed about one hundred and thirty-five, now I weigh one hundred and fifty-five. The streets are all laid out straight and broad. You can look as far as the eye can reach and try to walk out of the city, but it is almost impossible for you to get out of the limits of the city. The population of the city is more than one hundred thousand, but it is so scattered, it covers four times the ground that Boston does. It has the most dwelling houses I ever saw. There are Michigan Avenue and Wabash Avenue. These avenues run along close to the lake. The business districts are Water Street for wholesaling and for retailing Lake Street. There are a good many more, but these are the leading streets. The men that came out here and settled ten years ago are worth from ten to fifty thousand dollars. We seldom ever see a poor person here, there is very little stealing going on. Goodnight.

Old Chicago newspapers of the time when Moody came to the city give further idea of its life. Large space is allotted to railroad schedules and shipping notices. Advertisements of toilet articles in the Chicago Weekly Press sound strangely familiar, assuring "a beautiful complexion and a roseate hue." Political and social conditions are reflected in editorials which discuss "the Mormon abomination" and an attack of "border ruffians." Jenny Lind's concerts in London and the provinces are asserted to have been a great success, gross receipts amounting to a hundred thousand pounds. Marvelous incomes of lawyers are reported; twenty thousand and even fifty thousand dollars a year "have been alleged." The failure of the national figure, P. T. Barnum, is announced, with letters from him protesting his innocence. Henry Ward Beecher writes a letter which is widely published, in answer to an inquiry of his belief in spiritualism. He declares himself among the unbelievers in the cult, but is convinced that it should have a scientific investigation. An editorial in the Democratic Press advocates a projected railroad to be built to Council Bluffs, making Kansas more accessible and thwarting the machinations of Douglas to make it a slave state; the writer affirms, "Build the railroads and Kansas shall be free."

The growth of the city had been too rapid to permit of careful planning. Strangers were impressed with the way it sprawled out from the lakeside into the prairie. In twenty years, from 1856 to 1876, the population increased nearly fivefold as follows: 1856—84,113; 1867—169,353; 1876—407,661. To a large extent the buildings were of wood, although in the business section offices and stores were of brick or stone. As many had been built without thought of future street grading, sidewalks later had to be accommodated to the varying elevations of adjacent fronts, necessitating frequent steps up and down in a single block. The growing business area invaded that part of the city where homes were formerly located, and the result was a commingling, in a strange confusion of levels, of warehouses, residences, factories and slums.

In this district Moody found his opportunity. In 1858 he began a Sunday school without the support of any church or society. He rented a hall over one of the large city markets known as North Market Hall and enlisted the coöperation of a group of friends, notably Mr. John

Lake Street, Chicago, in 1854

Clark Street, Chicago, in 1857

V. Farwell. This was the inception of a work which was destined to issue in a wider service than Moody ever imagined.

A letter home from LaCrosse, Wisconsin, where he was traveling for his firm, indicates the varied character of his activities.

> Dear Brother, I meant to write you last week but did not for the very reason that it slipped my mind. How I wished you were with me last week. My business was so that I had to be on the Mississippi River and I never was on it when it looked as well as it does now. Everything looked so nice. The western country has not looked so well for years, great billows of grain as far as the eye can reach. I tell you if wheat brings a good price this fall things will look differently in this western country. I wish you would write me how you are getting on with your Sunday school and who is superintendent of it now and how large a school you have. Tell me all about it. If I was in your place I would not have it stop every winter but keep it agoing. I shall expect to have a good time when I get home, for I have been away some time. Now the children are so glad to see me when I return. I think I have got the best school there is in the west. Anyway it is the largest there is this side of New York. I wish you could see it. It is one I started the next month after Luther went home. I hold it in North Market Hall, one of the largest halls in the city. If you know of anyone coming to Chicago tell them to call on me and they can give you a better idea what I am doing than I can tell you. Yours,
>
> D. L. Moody.

An early associate described the Sunday school:

> It was a large, dingy, dilapidated-looking brick

building on the outside, while the inside was a great grimy hall with blackened walls and ceiling, as bare and uninviting as can be imagined. But it was soon crowded to the doors with classes of boys and girls of a type entirely new to me; largely the "gamins" of the streets—bold, restless, inquisitive youngsters, whose wardrobe was often limited to trousers, shirt and suspenders, and even these in a very advanced stage of decay. The scholars were bubbling over with mischief and exuberance of vitality and sorely tried the patience of the teachers; but the singing was a vent for their spirits, and such singing I had never heard before. The boys who sold papers in the street had an indescribable lung power, and the rest seemed not far behind. There must have been five or six hundred scholars, and it was no easy task to govern such a boisterous crowd, but the teachers seemed to interest their classes, and the exercises passed off with great enthusiasm.

At the close of the school Mr. Moody took his place at the door and seemed to know personally every boy and girl; he shook hands and had a smile and cheery word for each. They crowded about him tumultuously, and his arm must have ached many a time after those meetings. It was easy to see the hold he had on those young lives, and why they were drawn to that place week after week. The institution was a veritable hive of activity—meetings almost every evening, with occasional picnics and sociables, and services on the sabbath that occupied most of the day.

Apparently no attempt was made at first to organize the school into classes. Order was maintained by singing, which was followed by a brief talk. This, it was felt, was all that *could* be accomplished.

Moody devoted himself more and more to distinctly evangelistic work, sometimes speaking himself, but oftener securing other speakers. He continuously re-enforced the membership of his Sunday school, and to keep the interest from flagging he had recourse to innumerable devices for sustaining its popularity. He made much of picnics, entering into the spirit of them with as keen zest as the youngest child. He was not only an unusually strong man, but also a very fast runner. At one of these outings he picked up a barrel nearly filled with apples. Holding it so the apples would spill out, he ran ahead followed by the boys who gathered up the fruit as it dropped.

One summer fourteen boys were promised a new suit each at Christmas if they would attend regularly until that time. Their descriptive names indicated their social status: Red Eye, Smikes, Madden the Butcher, Jackey Candles, Snidericks, Billy Bluecannon, Billy Bucktooth, Darby the Cobler, Butcher Kilroy, Greenhorn, Indian, Black Stove Pipe, Old Man and Rag-breeches Cadet. All but one fulfilled the conditions, and Moody had them photographed before and after donning the suits. The pictures were entitled, "Will It Pay?" "And It Does Pay!" and this uniformed group became known as "Moody's bodyguard."

Thirteen years later one of Moody's friends called at a railway ticket office. The agent, after looking at him curiously for a moment, asked him to step inside, and said, "You do not seem to know me." "No, I have not that pleasure." "You remember Mr. Moody's bodyguard?" "Yes, I have a picture of them at home." "Well," said the agent, "when you go home take a square look at the ugliest of the lot and you will see your humble servant, now a church member and heir to Mr. Moody in his work."

Prayer meetings and cottage meetings were held in the

homes of the members of the Sunday school. "Some of the happiest nights I ever had were in these children's prayer meetings," Mr. Moody used to say. "Many people don't believe that early conversions hold out. They think that fathers and mothers should take care of religion. Well, that is not my experience. Some of the most active men that I had to help me in Chicago were little barefooted boys picked up in the lanes and by-ways whom I had in my children's meetings."

Nearly seventy years after these days an old man wrote to Moody's family:

> I am one of five brothers that attended the Sunday school in the North Market Hall, and the first Sunday school in the saloon or store, it must have been, near the old Market Hall. I can remember we sat on long benches. Your father often called on us. We lived near the corner of Wells and Madison Streets. I am the only one of the five boys now living. . . . I remember the little pony your father bought. We called it the little piebald pony and we had many a good ride on our hand sleds with your father holding all of our ropes. He always invited us to come to school next Sunday. I attended the school till the latter part of 1864 when I enlisted.

The plan by which the incompetent teachers were weeded out was as novel as it was effective. Membership could be transferred from one class to another simply by notifying the superintendent of the desired change. Only the fittest of the teachers survived this process of elimination. By degrees the school increased to fifteen hundred, and order and system were established. It was before the day of International Lessons and there was but one textbook, the Bible, for scholars and teachers; denominational differences were not recognized.

Moody's methods for financing the school were eminently successful. He issued stock certificates on the "North Market Sabbath School Association; Capital, $10,000; 40,000 shares at twenty-five cents each. For dividends apply at the school each Sabbath at three P.M." The purchase of these shares enabled the erection of a new building.

Remembering his own youthful experiences, Moody dealt sternly with mischief makers in a few instances. On one occasion a certain young bully, the ringleader of the worst "gang" in the city, persistently and maliciously caused great annoyance. In response to repeated warnings, he assumed a more threatening attitude and mocked at every effort to induce him to behave. It was against the rules to turn out a scholar. Grace having failed, Moody said to Mr. Farwell, "If that boy disturbs his class to-day and you see me go for him and take him to the anteroom, ask the school to rise and sing a very loud hymn until I return." The boy continued to disturb. Moody thereupon seized him, hurried him to the anteroom before he realized what was happening, and locked the door. While the school sang lustily, Moody gave the boy such a whipping as he himself had received in early life. The boy was converted soon afterwards, and years later acknowledged to a friend that he was still enjoying the benefits of that gospel exercise!

Moody was subjected to a great deal of annoyance from those who attended the open-air services and noon prayer meetings for the express purpose of making a disturbance. At the close of a prayer meeting one day he was standing at the door shaking hands with the people as they went out. As an added trial to his patience, one of the most persistent and irrepressible disturbers advanced extending his hand. For an instant Moody hesitated; then, accepting the proffered hand, he said, "I suppose if Jesus Christ could eat the Last Supper with a Judas Iscariot I ought to shake hands with you."

His spirit of genuine humility and the ready wit made him a difficult man to criticize. At another time he was one of several speakers at a convention. A minister who spoke after Moody took occasion to censure him, saying that his address was made up of newspaper clippings. When the critic sat down Moody stepped to the front again and said that he agreed; that he recognized his want of learning and inability to make a fine address; he thanked the minister for pointing out his shortcomings, and asked the man to pray that God would help him to do better.

There were times when his old quick temper broke out again, but it would seem that the momentary weakness was turned to good, so sincerely did he repent. One evening after an unusually earnest appeal Moody was standing near the door of the inquiry room, urging the people to come in. The entrance to the room was by the lower landing of the stairs and Moody was just at the head of a short flight. While he stood there a man approached him and deliberately and grossly insulted him. Moody never repeated the insult, but it must have been a very bitter one. Instantly he thrust the man from him, and sent him reeling down the remaining steps to the vestibule. The man escaped injury, but having given way to a sudden temptation, Moody was keenly rebuked by his conscience for what might have caused a serious accident. A friend who was present and witnessed the scene described what ensued:

> When I saw Mr. Moody give way to his temper, although I could not but believe the provocation was extraordinary, I said to myself, "This meeting is killed. The large number who have seen the whole thing will hardly be in a condition to be influenced by anything more Moody may say to-night." But before Moody began the second meeting that night

he arose, and with trembling voice, made a humble apology.

"Friends," he said, "before beginning to-night, I want to confess that I yielded just now to my temper, out in the hall, and I have done wrong. Just as I was coming in here to-night I lost my temper with a man, and I want to confess my wrong before you all, and if that man is present here whom I thrust away from me in anger, I want to ask his forgiveness and God's. Let us pray." There was not a word of excuse or vindication for resenting the insult. The impression made by his words was wonderful, and instead of the meeting being killed by the scene it was greatly blessed by such a consistent and straightforward confession.

Moody never lost an opportunity for reaching those whom others could not reach. Once he was invited, as a joke, to the opening of a great billiard hall and saloon. He saw the owners, and asked permission to bring a friend. They consented, but asked who the friend was. Moody replied that it wasn't necessary to tell, but that he never went without Him. They understood his meaning and then protested:

"Come, we don't want any praying!"
"You've given me an invitation and I'm going to come."
"But if you come you needn't pray."
"Well, I'll tell you what we'll do," was the answer, "we'll compromise the matter and if you don't want me to come and pray for you when you open, let me pray for you both now."

To this they agreed. Moody made them kneel down and then prayed that their business might go to pieces but that God would save them!

As the work for children developed, adults were included in Moody's interests. "I learned," he would say, "that it was not enough to get the child. At first I thought it was. But you can get the child but one hour one day in the week. You work against great odds unless you can get someone in the home to help the child."

Beginning with children because he felt himself unqualified to work among their elders, Moody was soon led into a ministry for older people. It was a natural development rather than a sudden change. Calls upon his children in cases of absences often revealed the domestic tragedies of many homes. While offering sympathy in sorrow or in adversity, he made contacts which brought him face to face with opportunities for service.

It was natural for him to seek to meet the needs of men with what he felt to be the only panacea for human ill, the gospel of Christ. Thus he began evening meetings of an evangelistic character, and for the purpose rented an old saloon. At first Moody invited city ministers to preach, while he himself acted as usher. But those to whom he had been friend and counselor felt that his message would be of greater help, and before long he yielded to their importunities. If, as he had been informed, he could not speak to the privileged classes, he discovered that the common people heard him gladly.

The demands upon Moody's physical resources were exacting. How great they were is best told in his own words:

> Sunday was a busy day for me then. During the week I would be out of town as a commercial traveler selling boots and shoes, but I would always manage to be back by Saturday night. Often it was late when I got to my room, but I would have to be up by six o'clock to get the hall ready for Sunday school.

Every Saturday night a German society held a dance there, and I had to roll out beer kegs, sweep up sawdust, clean up generally, and arrange the chairs. I did not think it right to hire anyone to do this on a Sunday, so sometimes with the assistance of a scholar, and often without any, I would do it myself.

This usually took most of the morning, and when it was done I would have to drum up the scholars and new boys and girls. By the time three o'clock came we would have the hall full, and then I had to keep order while the speaker for the day led the exercises. We had to keep things going to keep up the children's interest. When school was over I visited absent scholars and found out why they were not at Sunday school, called on the sick, and invited the parents to attend the evening gospel service. By the time I had made my rounds the hour had come for the evening meeting in a near-by building, formerly occupied by a saloon, where I presided, and following that, we had an after-meeting. By the time I was through the day, I was tired out. I didn't know much at that time, for after going from early morning till late at night with only a few crackers and some cheese, I was faint and fatigued. Sometimes after such a day's work I thought I sinned in going asleep over my prayers, when really I was a fool for neglecting the dictates of common sense. God is not a hard taskmaster, and in later years I have learned that to do your best work you cannot afford to neglect the common laws of health.

It was not Moody's plan to act as superintendent of the school. He wisely associated with himself such men as John V. Farwell, at that time the largest dry goods merchant in the city, and Isaac H. Burch, president of one of the banks. These gentlemen assisted Moody and superintended the school in turn, contributing largely to its success.

At no time in his life was Moody willing to submit to tradition if it did not appear to him to be as effective as an original course. He was fond of quoting an old Scotch saying, "They say! What do they say? Let them say!" This spirit manifested itself in the North Market School, where the order of exercises was never determined by a prearranged program. Moody or some other helper would read a passage of Scripture, announce a hymn, tell an anecdote—anything to maintain interest.

The experiences of these years provided the training for subsequent service. Confronted with varying conditions where classes from the ends of the world merged into young America, the resourcefulness of the New Englander developed.

While the Christian ministry was encroaching more and more upon Moody's time and thought, he did not disregard the interests of his employers. But soon he began to feel the pull in two directions; full devotion to his voluntary Christian service on the one hand and increasing demands attendant upon his marked success in business on the other. After the death of his former employer, he had accepted a position with another large wholesale house. His ambition was still keen. His associates were for the most part young men like himself, sharing the same ambitions, destined in some instances to achieve eminence in the financial and industrial life of the nation.

In his business trips Moody seized every opportunity of "witnessing for Christ." The free and easy customs of those early days in small communities readily lent themselves to out-door preaching. Moody's compelling sense of earnestness attracted and held the attention of the casual crowd; his talks were characterized by timely and pertinent illustrations which always appealed to the audience. Often he had to meet coarse witticisms and to foil the scoffer's jibe in a way to win and not repulse. He became a discerning judge of human nature. Even in a rebuff he recognized interest. "I don't mind if a man is angry," he would say. "It may mean that he is waking up. A child wakes up cross."

His discernment is illustrated by an incident he used to relate. While preaching on a street corner in a Michigan town, his attention was attracted to a man who drove up to the outskirts of the group and listened with every evidence of disdain. Apparently he was a man of means; he drove a pair of good horses and wore a silk hat, insignia of prosperity in those days. The second night he again appeared, quite casually, but Moody was convinced that the man's interest was aroused despite his affected contempt. Moody inquired concerning him and was told that he had derided all that had been said. This reaffirmed Moody's conviction and he intimated that he was going to call. His friends tried to dissuade him. The man was notoriously profane and he had the reputation of exerting a bad influence upon young men. He was one of the most prosperous men of the town; he had an attractive home, a charming wife, and children.

True to his purpose Moody went to this home. As he approached the man came out on his way to business. Moody stopped him and asked if he was Mr. ——. He replied that he was. "I hear," said Moody, "that you have been prosperous beyond most men here, that you have a beautiful home, an attractive wife, and lovely children. But with all these blessings God has bestowed on you, all you give Him in return are curses and blasphemies. I want to ask you why you treat my Master so?" "I did not know but he would knock me down," Moody commented in relating the story, "but I thought I would give it to him straight."

Possibly it was the daring of the assault, or the weakening of defenses from awakened conscience which accounted for the result, but the man replied gruffly, "Come in." Moody followed him into the house, and was led into the library. When they were seated, to Moody's surprise, the man said, "All you say is true. I have been prosperous. I have a beautiful wife, and children. But profanity has so become a habit that I don't know when I swear. Only the other evening when we had company for dinner my wife was so mortified at my swearing that she wanted to sink through the floor; and I did not know that I had sworn." The young traveling salesman told of the One who breaks the power of sinful habit. The men knelt together in prayer, and he who had been an addict to profanity gave his allegiance to Christ. Thirty years later at the close of a service in California, a man came forward and asked if Moody recognized him. Time had effaced the name, but Moody remembered the derisive blasphemer. Moody immediately questioned, "Have you ever sworn since that day of your conversion?" The answer was an emphatic "Never!"

Many stories are told of his aggressiveness in dealing with those whom he sought to win. He is reputed to have addressed a stranger with the inquiry, "Are you a Christian?" To the obvious reply that it was none of his business Moody said, "Yes, it is!" which elicited the rejoinder, "Then you are D. L. Moody." The story is probably apocryphal, but at any rate it illustrates his reputation for zeal in doing personal work.

Moody had come to Chicago, a crude, raw youth of nineteen. His limitations were noticeable; in ordinary social intercourse he was ill at ease. Stories that would be humorous but for the conscious suffering they imply, are told of awkward situations, unkindly criticism, and gross injustice to which he was subjected. It was this lack of social education, as it might be termed, which led him in his zeal to offend many. The accounts of his impulsive approach to men under any and all conditions are doubtless untrue or greatly exaggerated. Even if they are substantially true, a wrong impression is frequently given by quoting only a part of the interview, without fully recording the attendant circumstances. Too often the ardent youth is pictured as utterly lacking in all sense of the fitness of an occasion or the sensibilities of another. This is to misrepresent Moody entirely, for if he might not be conversant with the outward social usages he was, even at this time, ever thoughtful of the feelings of people. He was always essentially a gentleman.

BOOK II

CHAPTER X

"IF you would gain mankind the best way is to appear to love, and the best way of appearing to love is to love." This is the observation of an eighteenth century philosopher and jurist, and, if true in the field of social science and statecraft, it is more clearly evident in Christian service. To account for Moody's extraordinary influence one must look beyond all other gifts to his natural capacity for the love of mankind. From the day of his great decision in Boston his horizon was changing continuously. While at first his early ambitions were not abandoned, they were given less and less consideration; increasingly his efforts in behalf of the needy engrossed his thought.

The choice between his divided interests came about two years after his arrival in Chicago. One incident became the determining factor in his giving up business and devoting himself entirely to Christian service. In his Sunday school one class of girls presented a baffling problem. Frivolous and careless, they attended school apparently with the sole object of enjoying the discomfiture which they caused their teacher. Successive attempts to find some one who could hold their interest had failed. Moody himself was discouraged. Finally he found a man who was able to control the class, and in this Moody rejoiced. One Sunday this teacher was absent, and then a second Sunday passed. Moody did not have an opportunity of calling on his associate but early one Monday morning he came to Moody's office. There was evidence of recent illness and he explained that he had had a severe hemorrhage and that the doctors had advised him to return to his home in the East. He had come to say good-by and said that he probably had not long to live. That which concerned him most was the belief that he had made a complete failure of his class. Moody emphatically disagreed. Still the teacher insisted, offering as proof of his point that he had not led one of his girls to Christ. This was an amazing aspect to Moody. His aim for these heedless girls had not reached beyond interesting them sufficiently to insure healthy occupation of idle hours and imparting such Bible instruction as was possible.

Then Moody in his characteristically impulsive way, exclaimed, "Let's go and tell your girls how you feel. I will go with you." Together they started on this round of visits; "the best journey I ever made," Moody termed it. Explaining his reason for leaving Chicago and confessing his sense of failure, the teacher would state the purpose of the call and urge the surrender of the young life to the Master. He would pray for the girl, then Moody would pray. In describing the experience Moody said, "I had never done such a thing in my life as to pray God to convert a young girl then and there, but we prayed God and he answered our prayers."

During the ensuing week the two young men continued their task until every scholar was interviewed, although occasionally business prevented Moody from accompanying the teacher. Moody thus relates the story of their labors: "He came to my store one day with his face literally shining. 'The last of my class has yielded herself up to Christ,' he exclaimed. That night he had to leave for his home and I called the class together for a prayer meeting and God kindled a fire in my soul that has never been quenched. The height of my ambition had been to be a successful merchant and if I had known that that meeting was going to take that ambition out of me I might not have gone. But how many times I have thanked God since for that meeting. The teacher sat in the midst of his class and talked with them and then read the fourteenth chapter of John. We tried to sing, 'Blest Be the Tie That Binds,' after which we knelt in prayer. I was just rising from my knees when one of the class began to pray, then another and another till every one had prayed. As I went out from the meeting I said to myself, 'Oh God, let me die rather than lose the blessing I have received to-night.' When the train left for the East one by one the group gathered without prearrangement to bid farewell to the one whose life in its sunset glow had brought light to those careless souls." Sixty years later the daughter of one of this class, herself an earnest Christian worker, met a member of the Moody family and testified the abiding influence of that teacher.

"The hardest struggle I ever had in my life was when I gave up business," Moody commented in later years. He enjoyed commercial life. The thrill in matching himself against his competitors, in persuading new customers to place a good order, in advising retailers in methods of salesmanship, made work pleasantly exciting to him.

By special commissions in addition to his regular salary, Moody had an income at this time of more than five thousand dollars, a splendid beginning for a youth of only twenty-four. Already he had acquired by savings and shrewd investments, seven thousand dollars, providing the nucleus of the prospective fortune which had been his goal.

Furthermore, he had recently become engaged to Emma C. Revell. Privations he could endure himself; but to renounce an assured income and to risk the imposition of hardships on the one he loved was a severe challenge to Moody's faith.

The national crisis was another consideration which weighed against his devoting himself wholly to Christian service. Since his days in Boston Moody's convictions respecting the evils of slavery had strengthened and he was among the throng which welcomed with enthusiasm the nomination of Abraham Lincoln in the Wigwam erected in Chicago for the Republican convention. Conflict and secession threatened, and if there was to be war, Moody would wish to give himself to the cause of abolition.

Without ecclesiastical training and with meager educational advantages, he would not be eligible for appointment under any board. Then, too, his Sunday school, which was an undenominational enterprise, would demand his time and energies. But this had no organized support and all the workers were volunteers. He would, therefore, be entirely dependent upon his savings.

The struggle ended as anyone who knew Moody could have foreseen. If once convinced of duty to God, there was no compromise. He resigned from business to become a nondescript, independent city missionary in connection with his Sunday school in the old North Market Hall. It was a venture, for as he later expressed it, "I said to myself, 'I'll live on what I've saved. When that is gone and there is no means of support I will take it as a call to return to business where I know I can earn my living.'"

CHAPTER XI

To effect economies was now Moody's aim. Leaving the comforts of his boarding place with its congenial associates, he slept in the prayer meeting room of the Y. M. C. A. and boarded in cheap restaurants. His régime would have killed a man of less sturdy physique. In later years he realized that his had been a poor economy and would say, "I was an older man before thirty than I have ever been since. A man's health is too precious to be carelessly neglected as mine was."

Moody persisted in his usual but effective methods of rendering Christian service. He would often hail children on the street and ask for an introduction to their parents in order that he might secure consent for the enrollment of the children in his school. Once he made such a request of a little girl whom he met casually. The child had reasons for not wanting him to see her home and asked him to wait on the corner until she had discharged her immediate errand. Patiently he waited, wondering why she was so long delayed. Finally he realized it was but a ruse of the youngster to get rid of him. Some time later he again met the little girl and recognition was mutual. She fled, pursued by the determined missionary. Up and down the sidewalks the chase continued, only ending when the child darted into a saloon, through the bar, and upstairs. There she was found hiding under a bed. Moody persuaded her to come out and he was introduced to the mother to whom he explained the purpose of his call. Subsequently the child's reluctance to have Moody visit her home was revealed. The father had been a carpenter who had come to Chicago seeking employment. Unsuccessful in this attempt, he had finally opened a saloon. Soon after he had died, leaving the saloon as the only means of support for his widow and children, but they had never become reconciled to this source of livelihood. The children became members of Moody's school, and not long after, the saloon was closed. Years later in a distant city, Moody met the little girl who had led him such a chase, now the wife of an earnest church worker and herself devoted to Christian service.

The early references to Moody in the Chicago press reflect the varied character of his activities. A lad has been arrested for "forging orders to obtain letters from the post office." It is not indicated that he is a member of the North Market Sunday school but he is released from imprisonment on two hundred dollars bail, "D. L. Moody becoming surety for his appearance." Later a news item shows Moody in a very different rôle. According to the *Tribune* of January 2, 1862, two men are arrested on a complaint of Moody who has discovered that they have been fraudulently delivering coal which had been secured for poor relief. "It appears that Mr. Moody, having a donation of several hundred tons of coal, hired the Fishers to transport the same from the Rock Island freight depot to the society's [City Relief Society] yard." Moody apparently acted as his own detective and made the complaint himself.

One who knew Moody at this time wrote many years later:

> D. L. Moody was a picturesque figure in the city. I taught in the Sunday school in which he was interested. He actually washed and dressed the children and personally conducted them to school. Many of the stories told of him are apocryphal but he really

did put his hand on the arm of a stranger going into a basement saloon and said, "My friend, you are going straight to hell." "Just my luck," the man answered.

He did get up in service and announce he had just become engaged to Miss Emma Revell and could not be depended upon to see the girls home from meetings any more. However, he developed as the city did, and it was not many years before that city was building a great temporary auditorium to hold the people who wished to hear him speak.

Always direct in dealing with a situation, Moody was unawed by dignitaries. His Sunday school sessions were frequently disturbed by rowdies. Appeals to the priest of the parish to which they belonged were ineffective, so Moody sought help from Bishop Duggan. The bishop was busy and an immediate audience was denied. "Never mind," said Moody, quietly taking a seat in the hall, "I will remain till he can see me." The servant was not at all sure that the bishop would care to receive the persistent caller but found it impossible to dissuade him. Moody had come to see the bishop and would wait, if necessary, for the remainder of the day—or until he could be seen. When at length the bishop consented to the interview, the young missionary briefly stated that he was engaged in work for children in a section neglected by every one else and that he regretted his inability to carry it on unmolested. He asked that the bishop give orders prohibiting further interference. The bishop at first refused to believe that any of his people were among the offenders but Moody replied that the rowdies had declared themselves Roman Catholic. The bishop then recalled that there was in his district a group over which he had little or no control and for that reason he could not assure Moody of help in the present difficulty.

"Your zeal and devotion are most commendable, however," he added, "and all you need to make you a great power for good is to come within the fold of the only true church."

"But whatever advantage that would give me among Catholics would be offset by the fact that I could no longer work among Protestants," Moody answered.

"Certainly you could," replied the bishop.

"But," exclaimed Moody, "surely you would not let me pray with a Protestant."

"Yes," said the bishop, "you could pray with Protestants as much as ever."

"Well, I did not know that. Would you pray with a Protestant, Bishop?"

"Yes, I would."

"Well then," was the immediate response, "I wish you would pray for me now that I may be led aright in this matter." And forthwith kneeling, the bishop and the Protestant missionary prayed for guidance. The result was the eventual cessation of all further annoyance in Moody's school and a lifelong friendship with Bishop Duggan.

Moody was increasingly in demand in places outside Chicago as a speaker. As the reports of his success spread, interest in his methods grew. Home letters were full of Sunday school work.

> I was away all last week at a Sunday school convention [he wrote his mother]. I have to go this week again and have got to go all of next week so you see I am driven more now than ever in my life. I have crowds wherever I go. Last week where I was the house was full and the sidewalk outside so they had to open another church, and I had to speak in two houses. The Lord blessed me very much and

work commenced in good earnest so they have sent for me again.

[Then he added, apparently in the effort to reconcile his mother to his new calling]: If you could be out here you never would be sorry I gave up business for if I had not I should have lost everything I was worth for all but one or two merchants in the boot and shoe business have failed. No business is good for anything now, Mother. Do not think for a moment but I love you as much now as ever for I do.

There may have been a feeling that his new interests had eclipsed home responsibility, for in another letter he wrote that he attended meeting every night but two, for eight months. "If I could see you and tell you how the Lord is blessing me in my labors, I think you would say, 'God bless you. Go forward.'"

Again, during the winter of 1861, he described how absorbing was his work among the children: "It takes all my time."

Alluding to the business depression he said, "There are ten young men to one place. I have never seen things in so poor a condition as they are at present. I do not know what is to become of us out here if the strife goes on South, but I suppose it will come out all right." Like tens of thousands, Moody was solaced by a false optimism even when the nation was on the very brink of civil war.

An interesting picture of Moody at this time is given by his friend D. W. McWilliams.

> It was at the house of a friend in Peoria, Ill., in 1861, that I first met Mr. Moody. Our host had invited several ministers and two laymen to meet him at dinner. When they arrived Mr. Moody was not with the others, but enquiry led to the informa-

tion that he had come early and was upstairs in a room at prayer with an unconverted friend of the host, who had been induced to call upon Mr. Moody for this special purpose.

On being introduced to those present Mr. Moody soon turned to one of the ministers and said, "How do you explain this verse in the Bible?" giving the verse in full. Soon after he turned to another minister, quoted a verse, and asked, "What does it mean?" The entire conversation that day was exposition of the Scripture in reply to Mr. Moody's rapid questions, and a stirring of hearts in the direction of personal work for the salvation of others. The impression made upon the guests that day was of Mr. Moody's love for the souls of others, and his intense desire for Bible knowledge.

Soon afterward I called upon Mr. Moody in Chicago, and was conducted through his parish. We went to what would now be called the slums. Soon a crowd of street gamins, boys and girls of all ages, were following us with loud shouts of "Oh, here's Moody! Come, here's Moody!" Evidently they all knew him as their best friend. He had candy in both side pockets, and gave it freely. We visited house after house of the poor, sick, and unfortunate. He was everywhere greeted with affection, and carried real sunshine into these abodes of squalor. He enquired for the absent ones by name.

In one letter, found among the few his mother preserved and dated November 19, 1861, Moody confided his early successes in preaching. "I wish you were out here this fall. I think you would like to attend our prayer meetings. Some nights there are fifteen or twenty who rise for prayers."

The Rev. James S. Chadwick became city missionary at the Methodist Episcopal church in Chicago in 1861. His office was in the building in which the Young Men's Christian Association had rooms before the erection of Farwell Hall. With reference to Mr. Moody's work, Mr. Chadwick said:

> I have known him to start from the Y. M. C. A. with baskets of provisions for poor families, many of whom would have been neglected or overlooked but for his timely interest. He always urged those to whom he thus relieved to attend church and become Christians. In many instances whole families were thus brought to know and serve the Lord Jesus Christ. In the noonday prayer meetings men have risen and told how Mr. Moody visited their homes with substantial relief for hungry children, and then joined in prayer for all the family.
>
> Mr. Moody would regularly station himself at the entrance to the Y. M. C. A. rooms, just before the hour of noon, and distribute to passers-by invitations to go upstairs to the prayer meeting. Christians and persons who were not Christians were frequently prevailed upon to spend a few minutes in the helpful and inspiring service. Many conversions resulted from these invitations.

The phenomenal growth of the North Market Sunday school had attracted attention throughout the country. It became one of the sights of Chicago. President Lincoln, shortly after his election to the presidency, came to Chicago to meet Vice President-Elect Hamlin and other political advisers. On Sunday, November 25, 1860, Mr. Lincoln attended service in Bishop Cheney's church in the morning and in the afternoon visited Moody's Sunday school.

One of the scholars who was present that day relates the event. "Mr. Lincoln had been assured that he would not be called upon to make an address, but as he was leaving and was already halfway down the hall Mr. Moody said, 'We promised not to ask Mr. Lincoln to speak, but this does not prevent his saying a word to us if he wishes.' Stopping where he was in the aisle on the way out, in the midst of the boys and girls, he briefly expressed his pleasure in being with them and admonished them to govern their lives according to the precepts they learned from their study of the Bible."

When the war broke out a few months later, over fifty young men from the North Market Sunday school answered the President's call for troops.

The memory of these years in Chicago was never effaced. Often his mind would recur to those children in the slums who were deprived of the enjoyments of country life. Once at Northfield he enlisted the help of young people in the town to pick apples, and by special arrangement with the railroads he was able to send hundreds of bushels to Boston for distribution through the city missionary to children.

But Moody was not forgetful of home and he coveted for loved ones in Northfield the privileges of Christian service which he himself enjoyed. On July 3, 1862, he wrote to his mother:

> The good folks of Boston have raised money to send a man of God to Northfield. He will be there to-morrow. I am anxious to have a good house for he is one of the greatest preachers of the state. I want George and Edwin [his brothers] to stir up the folks and get them out. If you could get word to John Fisher and the folks up in that district I would like it. Oh, work now for I do not know as you could or would ever be able to get such a man in

the town again for years. Often I have thought of Northfield since I left there and have been praying God to raise up some one to preach to them. I think He has heard my prayer for I am confident you will like this man.

CHAPTER XII

THERE was no one to whom Moody owed so much as to his wife, Emma C. Revell. She was the second of the three daughters of Fleming H. Revell who had been a shipbuilder in London. Meeting with severe reverses, he had brought his family to America, and, in 1849, went to Chicago seeking to retrieve his impaired fortune. Here he resumed his former trade and built boats for Lake Michigan traffic.

The family was composed of the parents, three daughters and one son, Fleming H. Revell, Jr., who has since achieved distinction as a publisher. They lived on Washington Street close to the courthouse and maintained a gracious hospitality, making the home a natural meeting place for young people.

Under what circumstances Moody and Emma Revell met is not now known. It is probable that some common friend brought Moody into the Revell home soon after he came to Chicago, for in a letter to his mother, dated June, 1861, he thus alludes to his fiancée:

> I shall also send the daguerreotype of myself and Miss Emma Revell whom I shall bring down East with me the next time I come—when that will be I do not know. Miss Revell I have known ever since I came west or at least I got acquainted with her in May, I came here in September. You know she was then only twelve years old. I think, dear Mother, you would love her if you could get acquainted with her. I do not know of anyone that

knows her but that does. She is a good Christian girl.

Their early experiences, to a certain degree, had been similar. Like her fiancé, Emma Revell had known financial anxiety for it had not been easy for the father, broken in health and in spirit, to adjust himself to new business conditions and methods. The Revell children had attended the public schools and Emma, acknowledged to be the scholar of the family, continued through the high school and then became a teacher in grammar school. By experience and by training, therefore, she was equipped to be in the truest sense a helpmeet to the one with whom she threw her lot in life.

It was while a school-teacher, but seventeen years of age, that she became engaged to Moody. He had just relinquished his business prospects and had no assured income; but the unconventional, uneducated youth so zealous and so seemingly unmindful of common prudence had won her heart. She staked all on that.

The "good Christian girl" was a loyal, sympathetic companion and an efficient and unobtrusive fellow worker. In her wise counsel, which he esteemed above that of all others, Moody found an unfailing source of help. Though modest and retiring, she possessed reserve forces which were veiled by a gracious personality. Moody was by nature impulsive and was sometimes tempted to act rashly, but in his wife he found what he termed his "balance wheel." With advice, sympathy and faith this girl labored with him; and by her judgment, tact and sacrifice she contributed to his every effort. It is significant that through thirty-seven years of married life she alone of all his associates never sought to dissuade Moody from any undertaking. Hers was a "heart at leisure, from itself set free."

One who saw her shortly after her marriage related

how impressed he was with her youthful appearance. While visiting the North Market Sunday school his attention was arrested by a class of fully forty middle-aged men being taught by a young girl. Turning to Moody who was showing him about, the guest expressed surprise that one so immature should be given such a responsibility. Moody replied casually that she seemed competent. Later, however, the visitor reverted to the subject and with evident signs of disapproval said, "Mr. Moody, I cannot but feel that that lady must be altogether too young to instruct such a large company of men. Will you, sir, please to inform me who she is?" "Certainly," answered Moody, "she's my wife."

Her tact and wisdom are illustrated in a letter she wrote to her fiancé's mother. The announcement of Dwight's engagement to a girl of English parentage had not been received with any enthusiasm by the Widow Moody for there still lingered within her smoldering embers of the "ancient grudge." She recalled the stories of the domineering Britishers of Revolutionary days and within her own memory neighbors' sons had been recruited for the War of 1812. Moody had been ill and was staying in the Revell home. He asked Emma to read to him a letter just received from his mother, in which she had pointed out the differences in the religious training of the two young people. To this objection the girl replied:

> Dear Mrs. Moody: Your last letter was received by Mr. Moody about three weeks ago, and as he was then sick and at our house he requested me to read it to him, which I am glad I did as by it I learned the false impression you had in regard to me because of our different views on religion.
>
> I thought by what you wrote that you had the idea that because I was a Baptist and you were of

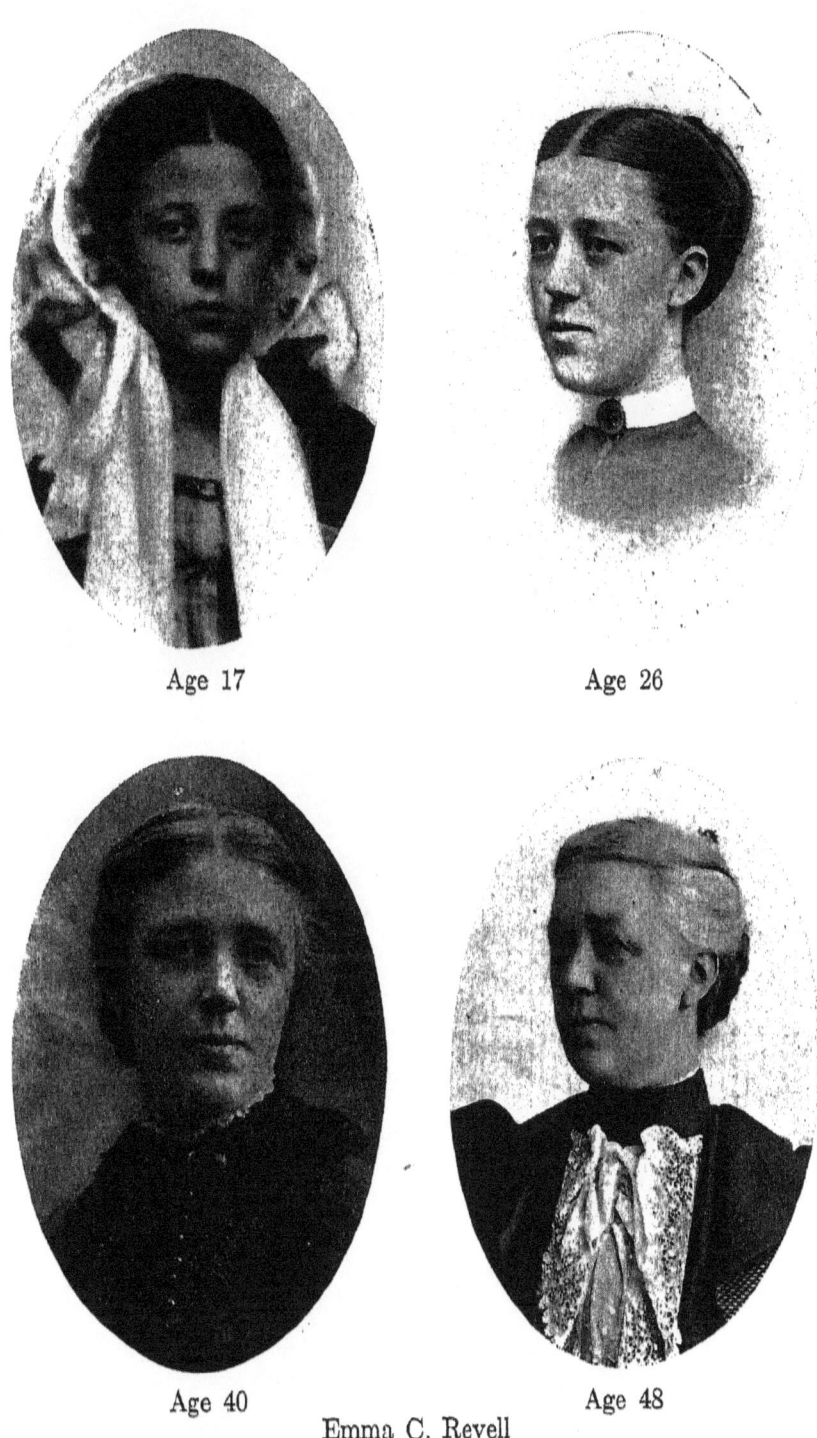

Emma C. Revell

a different sect, that I would not esteem you, but please do not think so a moment longer for I assure you it makes no difference in regard to my feelings. I think it makes very little difference to what sect we belong as long as our hearts are right in the sight of God.

I thought also that you might have thought that because Mr. Moody was of a different denomination to what I had been trained in youth that his love and respect for his mother had abated, but I know such is not the case. Besides some of Mr. Moody's warmest friends are Unitarian.

It seems strange to me when I first thought of writing to one I had never seen as it is something I have never done before, but I have heard Mr. Moody speak of you so often that it seemed as though I too knew you and felt that I loved you.

When your letter was received Mr. Moody was quite unwell, but don't be alarmed about him now, as he has entirely recovered and is now enjoying good health. While he was sick he was at our house and, though I did what I could for him, I know it was very little compared to a mother's tender care. I think he must have missed you very much as he spoke of you often then.

Believe me to be truly yours in much esteem and love,

EMMA C. REVELL.

Her whole heart was with her husband from the first and those who met her during her early married life sensed the latent forces which were to find expression in her husband's labors. Thus three months after her marriage she wrote to Moody's mother again:

My dear husband arrived safely home last Tuesday. It was the first time we have been separated since our marriage and I was very glad to see him home again. We are hoping and praying for a revival in our city this winter. There seems to be much interest in the mission schools. I feel that God will answer our prayers for we do so much need our Saviour's blessings.

I have often thought of you and though I have never seen you I feel quite well acquainted. I hope we will become still better acquainted. Pray for us.

The help his wife gave Moody was as varied in its scope as were his duties. She made the home a sanctuary of restful fellowship and for years she had entire charge of Moody's ever-increasing correspondence; she even aided in the preparation of his addresses. There was no bank account in Moody's name, but his wife achieved masterly results in financing. To all this was added the care of three children who ultimately made up the family circle and, besides, there were the social demands on Mrs. Moody's time because of the public nature of her husband's work.

The greater social and educational advantages his wife had enjoyed enabled her to render Moody a peculiarly delicate service that none other could have proffered. From the time of his marriage Moody became a scholar in the social amenities, under the tutelage of his wife.

Yet Mrs. Moody was not robust. During her girlhood she was a sufferer from asthma and had an organic heart difficulty. But these weaknesses were never allowed to limit her activities.

Years later in Edinburgh, a friend fully confirmed the selfless quality of the assistance Emma Revell gave her husband.

> We had just begun to know Mrs. Moody [wrote Mrs. MacKinnon] but one day was enough to show what a source of strength and comfort she was to her

husband. The more I saw of her afterwards, the more convinced I was that a great deal of his usefulness was owing to her, not only in the work she did for him, relieving him of all correspondence, but also from her character. Her independence of thought, not a mere unthinking echo of a master mind and will; her calmness, meeting so quietly his impulsiveness; her humility, her great nobility of character, and her sincerity, her crystal-like purity and transparency, could not but make her an unspeakable help to him in his arduous and trying work.

CHAPTER XIII

THE years 1861-1865 were eventful to Moody not only because they marked the beginning of his missionary service and the establishment of his own home, but also because they were epochal in American history. For more than a generation the mutterings of impending strife had persisted. In the firm where Moody had worked the clerks had formed a "lyceum" where, with young men from neighboring houses, heated debates were held over such issues as States' rights, abolition, and the several compromises on the slavery question. Lines of political allegiance were closely drawn. Soon after going west, Moody had allied himself with the Republican party and remained one of its staunch supporters.

On April 12, 1861, the Confederate forces fired on Fort Sumter. Three days later the president's proclamation called "seventy-five thousand militia for three months' service," and the last possible hope of averting war was dispelled. Events followed swiftly on one another in the ensuing weeks. "The chivalrous South rose in blind passion for a cause at the bottom of which lay the narrowest of pecuniary interests," says an unprejudiced student of these events, "while the oversharp Yankee, guided by a sort of comic backwoodsman, fought, whether wisely or not, for a cause as untainted as ever animated a nation in arms."

Many were urging Moody to join a company being organized from among the members of the Chicago Y. M. C. A. Former business associates and even boys from the North Market Sunday school were enlisting. From the first Moody had zealously championed the cause of the Union and vigorously expressed his allegiance to Abraham Lincoln. To prove the genuineness of his professions did not duty demand that he enroll as a soldier in defense of his principles? On the other hand, having dedicated himself to Christian service, could he morally take up arms? Moody made his decision in the light of what he believed his immediate duty and continued in the service of peace instead of war.

But if he was not to serve the cause as a soldier, he would serve the soldiers themselves. He organized an Army and Navy Committee of the Y. M. C. A. which later merged with the National Christian Commission, and he threw himself into the work of this agency with enthusiasm.

Some idea of the character of Moody's activities may be gained from a brief newspaper announcement. The nineteenth Illinois regiment known as the Zouaves were encamped in Elizabethtown, Kentucky. Here they published the *Zouave Gazette* and under date of October 30, 1861, appears an article entitled "A Welcome Visit" and reads:

> D. L. Moody, the active missionary of the Y. M. C. A. having been invited by the chaplain of the Nineteenth to visit our regiment, arrived at Lebanon Junction Wednesday evening last; since which time he has labored unceasingly, both day and night, in distributing books, papers, tracts, hymn books, etc. . . . The secret of Mr. Moody, both here among the soldiers and at home, is that he makes a personal application of the gospel truths to those whom he meets and living a life devoted to his Master, his advice and example convinces and converts.

The diversified nature of the Christian Commission, combining what, two generations later, are the activities of the Red Cross and the Y. M. C. A., was a work of demands as multifarious as the wants of suffering humanity. At times Moody would be found among the stretcher bearers, and again giving assistance to the hospitals. He held meetings under all conditions in camps, recruiting stations, and military prisons. There were letters to be written bearing sad intelligence to relatives, a cup of water to be given to a dying boy, accompanied by some word of comfort or spiritual solace.

Moody's letters home are even more brief than usual. In March, 1862, he wrote his mother:

> I am at Cairo (Ill.) with things to relieve the wants of the sick and wounded soldiers. I was up at Fort Donaldson, Tenn., last week and as soon as I got home they sent me back with seven or eight hundred dollars worth of things for the wounded. One hospital has fourteen hundred, another eight hundred. I tell you Mother as I was going through the hospitals to-day I remarked to the lady that was with me "if I was going to be sick I would want to be home" for there is nothing like home. Who could take such care of me as you could? The sympathy goes a great way too, I tell you. You do not know how roughly the poor fellows are treated in the army. . . . I was on the battlefield before they had buried the dead. It was awful to see the dead lying round without there being anyone to bury them. . . . Mother, I am getting homesick. I suppose you think I do not think of home. If I did I would write you, but that is not so. I think of home so often daily, but I am so busy I do not get the time to write as often as I would like to.

On September 13, 1862, he briefly announced, "I was married on the twenty-eighth of last month" and from that time apparently delegated to his wife the duty of keeping the home circle informed of his plans and activities. Occasionally he wrote a few brief sentences to say he was "holding meetings at the camp every night with the soldiers. A good many are turning from the evil of their ways. God seems to be waiting to have this nation call upon Him." His younger brother Samuel, who visited Moody in his new home wrote to Northfield, "Dwight is on a run from morning till night. He barely gets time to eat. Camp Douglass is situated here and he holds meetings down there most every night. It is a treat to go down there and hear the soldiers sing."

A friend has described one of the journeys Moody took to the battlefields:

> During the winter and spring of 1861 and 1862 I was a medical student in the city of Chicago, and saw Mr. Moody almost every day as he went hurrying about busily engaged in his good work. That was in the early days of the Young Men's Christian Association and he was looked upon as one of the most active promoters of the institution. The great battle of Pittsburg Landing was fought . . . and a call came for physicians and nurses for the wounded, for the supply of both was entirely inadequate for the work to be done. Accordingly the Young Men's Christian Association was called upon to send as many nurses as possible, and I, being a medical student, was invited to be one of the company.
>
> Our train was a heavy one, carrying about sixty or seventy-five physicians and about three hundred nurses, besides many supplies. I had a seat in the centre of the car, which was comfortably full.
>
> When we were two or three hours out of Chicago and everyone was getting settled down in his seat for the night (we had no sleepers then) I was aroused

by a gentle tap on the shoulder and asked if I would
not attend Mr. Moody's prayer meeting, which was
then to be held in the front end of the car. I wasn't
a Christian then and I didn't go, but nevertheless
my conscience gave me a stinging rebuke and I was
set to thinking. In the forward end of that car was
Mr. Moody, engaged in conducting a prayer meeting; in the rear end was a company of men playing
a game of cards. I couldn't help realizing the wonderful zeal of the man in his great work, and how
earnest and how careful he was that no duty be neglected, no opportunity lost. We reached Cairo on
Thursday, April 10, were transferred from our train
to the steamer, and were soon on our way up the
Ohio and Tennessee Rivers.

When evening came the passengers were sitting
about in groups in the large cabin. Mr. Moody,
with his Young Men's Christian Association assistants, passed through the crowd of the large room.
There again he conducted a service. I don't remember seeing anything more of the card players. As
on the first evening, so the next, I didn't attend
prayers, but I remember that among those who didn't
there was no effort made to disturb the meeting.
Nor was any evidence of disrespect shown, as far
as I could see.

On Friday afternoon about three o'clock we
reached Pittsburg Landing, and were at once sent
to the different steamers that were standing there,
loaded with hundreds of wounded soldiers waiting
for our arrival, and so were scattered in all directions. I saw no more of Mr. Moody during that trip,
but have thought of this circumstance many, many
times, and of the intense Christian zeal by which
he was always impelled.

Moody never kept a diary, wrote but brief letters, and destroyed those he received. Consequently the record of those years is fragmentary. From incidental references in conversation but chiefly from illustrations which he used, drawn from personal experience, a general impression is given of his rapidly changing sphere of service during the war. Nine times he is at the front, the visits lasting for weeks and even months. War has revealed the genuine devotion of the man. His sacrifices to the welfare of the soldiers have won the confidence and esteem of many who in former times looked upon his labors with suspicion and even ridiculed him.

The daily press follows Moody's activities with increasing interest. A news item reports his attendance as a delegate to a Sunday school convention in April, 1862. A month later a paragraph announces that "at or near Pittsburg Landing at the request of the Chicago Sanitary Commission D. L. Moody who has just returned from the camps and hospitals, will address a meeting." The writer adds "no one who has gone to our army on a similar errand can give such thrilling incidents as Mr. Moody." Such notices appear with greater frequency in subsequent months, always referring to new scenes of labor.

To add to his cares at this time his newly established home was burned. The incident was worth only a passing allusion in a letter to the effect that "we have got settled again after the fire." That to which Moody attached importance was the fact, "The meetings are full of interest." He appended almost casually that he thinks of taking his young bride into the midst of suffering. "I think," he wrote, "of going to Tennessee, Kentucky, and Alabama in a few days. If I go I shall take Emma and she will write to you while we are gone."

Moody did not neglect the spiritual interests of the

Chicago Y. M. C. A. despite his active service for the soldiers at the battlefront. In the sixth annual report (1864) it is recorded that "D. L. Moody addressed the meeting on 'The Power of Earnest Prayer.' . . . The meetings are rapidly increasing in interest. Many ministers are in attendance and larger congregations than for many years."

It was at this time that Moody experienced his first real sorrow. He had been too young to sense the loss of his father, and though he had known the pinch of poverty, he had never suffered any great personal grief. He was now called upon to suffer keenly in the affliction of another, his youngest brother Samuel, who held a peculiar place in Moody's affections. He had long anticipated welcoming Samuel as a guest in his home. The brother gave promise of being a good business man, and Moody hoped to help in the fulfillment of his ambition to make his start in Chicago. But shortly after his arrival Moody learned that Samuel had epilepsy, a tragic secret that the mother had never betrayed. It was a severe shock to Moody to have all his fond hopes for his brother shattered. Moody wrote him later:

> I love you dearly. There is nothing I can do for you but I will do it if it is in my power. May God bless and keep you faithful. The good Lord will hear your prayers and answer them if you will only keep near the cross. I hope you will do all you can personally for the Saviour. Talk to Him; pray to Him; labor for Him; and the good Lord will never leave you. Read often the fourteenth chapter of John and the Lord may hear your prayer and remove your disease. I will pray for you my dear Brother.

Moody's sorrow was mitigated to a degree at this time by the birth of his first child. His references to his wife and baby are ingenuous. "The baby is cunning," he wrote his mother. "I love it dearly. I used to think a wife and child would make us love others less; but they don't. I love them more."

The war years brought Moody face to face with such sin and suffering as he had never known before. At times a dying youth yearned to be told the "old, old story" and in the simplest and briefest terms to learn the way to God. Such experiences aroused Moody to the immediacy of the need for the gospel, for simplicity in its statement and for definite decision. Frequently a meeting would be held on the eve of a battle, and the knowledge that some listening to his message were attending their last service challenged him to his utmost efforts to bring the men to an acceptance of Christ.

Those who heard Moody in later years recall the wealth of illustration which he acquired from this ministry and realize what an ineffaceable impression it made upon the man and his message.

Moody found friendships which broadened his outlook during these rushing days. Through the Christian Commission he was brought into contact with prominent Christian laymen from different sections of the country as well as with those engaged directly in the service. Among them were General O. O. Howard and Major D. W. Whittle with whom he maintained a lifelong intimacy.

CHAPTER XIV

WITH the close of the war, Moody not only continued the work in his mission, now grown to an independent church and Sunday school, but also devoted himself to service with the Young Men's Christian Association. Its interdenominational character appealed to him. He saw in the movement a common ground for all Christians to achieve more by concerted action than they could through sectarian agencies.

The Chicago association, founded in 1855, was one of the earliest established in America. It was launched with great enthusiasm but its impetus had waned during the distractions of subsequent years. Although the officers of the association realized the need of an adequate building, no results had issued from several conferences on the subject. At length one of the officers said, "The only way for us to obtain a new building is to elect Mr. Moody president of the association." Moody was elected to that office in the spring of 1866.

Apparently he had served as secretary prior to this. Under his leadership the noonday prayer meeting had grown until it had become a center of Christian fellowship. It was widely known and prominent Christian leaders passing through Chicago were drafted by the enterprising secretary to speak of religious activities in other sections of the country. This meeting had come to fill a unique place in the religious life of the city and even of the entire surrounding region.

On assuming the presidency of the association Moody first of all defined its scope. To allay any misgivings among ministers that the organization might infringe upon the sphere of service of the church, Moody invited the pastors and leading laymen to a meeting. Here he outlined the work he felt the association should accomplish and tactfully asked advice as to how he might best achieve this end. The press report of the meeting states that on this occasion Moody announced that the new building was "in a fair way for completion and when finished the rental of certain portions of the structure will be a source of income." The report added that the success of the work of the Chicago association had attracted nation wide interest, and that Philadelphia and New York were inquiring concerning the methods of operation employed in the western city.

Moody's scheme for carrying out the erection of the new building was unusual. First he obtained a state charter exempting the property from taxation. Subscription to stock was then invited whereby donors both large and small might have a share in the project. Mr. John V. Farwell gave the site, Mr. Cyrus McCormick made the first cash contribution of ten thousand dollars and his example was soon emulated by others who swelled the total to a sum which insured "the first hall ever erected in America for Christian Association work."

When the building was completed many felt that to name it for Moody would be an appropriate recognition of his labors. Learning of the plan, he anticipated the action of his friends by moving that inasmuch as Mr. Farwell had given the valuable land for the building it should be known as Farwell Hall. The motion was carried.

Farwell Hall met a real municipal need quite apart from the association. The large auditorium was used for lectures, concerts and various public meetings. By location and appointment it was the most commodious and convenient place of assembly in the city. When it was destroyed by fire on January 7, 1868, the *Chicago Tribune* on the following day stressed the loss which the city had sustained. This paper said:

> A great calamity befell this city yesterday. The magnificent building known as Farwell Hall, which on Monday evening was filled with the beauty and fashion of the city, which gave back echoes to the strains of sweet music, lies this night a heap of broken bricks and mortar. . . . Farwell Hall was not old enough to have any memories clustering about it, save in the eyes of the members of the Y. M. C. A., to whom each pillar, each window, each stone, almost, was fraught with associations. Yet since it was thrown open to the public use, many audiences have assembled there, many good, brave words have been spoken there; it has heard discussions on manufacture and on the rights of naturalized citizens. It has served as a place where working men could state their wrongs and preachers have gone to "vindicate the ways of God to man." . . . So this, the largest hall in the city, was not entirely destitute of a history. Not only hymns and psalms of praise have been chorused there, but the sweetest violinist (Ole Bull) has chosen it as the spot on which to exercise his gift of pleasing and it was only the night before last that hundreds sat delighted where now there is but a mass of smoking ruins.

While the building was still in flames, numerous handbills were distributed on the streets announcing that the noon prayer meeting that day would be held in the Methodist Church block. The late Dr. David J. Burrell was among those who were called upon to assist in circulating these notices. He frequently related the incident in after years as evidence of Moody's energetic methods.

Moody immediately called a meeting of the trustees to plan for the erection of a new building. It was completed and dedicated in the following year. This second Farwell Hall suffered the fate of its predecessor in the great Chicago fire of 1871.

The third Farwell Hall was erected while Moody was in England in 1872-1875. Yet for this one also he shared the responsibility of raising money. After the close of his mission in Chicago in 1877 he secured the balance of the money necessary to clear the building from debt.

Moody's interest in the Y. M. C. A. was lifelong. He continuously sought to forward its cause.

> In every city in which he worked, on both sides of the ocean, his work and words summoned to the association a group of consecrated laymen, and with them financial resources which everywhere promoted the extension and usefulness of our work for young men [writes the late Richard C. Morse, veteran general secretary of the International Committee of the Y. M. C. A.]. In almost every city his efforts were always not only to promote the spiritual life of the association but also to procure for it better accommodation and appliances, and in many instances, a building. . . . No lists of amounts raised in the various cities can show a total amount which represents to any degree the financial help that came to the association through this agency.

Direct evangelistic preaching, often in the streets, was a prominent feature of these early years in association work; Moody could frequently be seen on summer nights speaking from the courthouse steps assisted by a group of young people as his choir. Supplementing these outdoor services were meetings held in the common jail, talking, reading and praying with the prisoners.

Experience acquired in this work—the necessity for

the seasonal word; readiness in meeting opposition; strength in standing unflinchingly for conviction and duty—provided a better equipment for a wider range of service.

In 1867 Mr. Richard C. Morse, then a recent graduate of the theological seminary, recounted his impressions in attending a Y. M. C. A. convention in Cincinnati. Particularly was he struck with the evangelistic enthusiasm of the delegates combined with the sanity of their pointed and terse language. "Moody especially made this impression."

"The reward of service is more service," a favorite proverb of Moody's, found full expression in his life. From 1865 to 1871 state conventions of Sunday schools and meetings of Y. M. C. A. leaders made constant demands on his time. Even ministerial gatherings asked him to explain his effective methods and sought to benefit by his inspirational addresses.

The increased power of his message drew a greater response from the public. In 1867 a newspaper paragraph reported that "an interesting revival" was in progress in Moody's mission. "The average attendance is from one hundred seventy-five to two hundred and from fifteen to twenty are converted every evening."

Dr. Charles R. Erdman, a warm friend of the Y. M. C. A., says:

> In subsequent years the Association has lost much of its evangelical conviction and of its evangelical fervour. With its superb equipment and its efficient organization, it is still accomplishing a great work, but educational and social and athletic features obscure its religious aim. Its best friends would rejoice if the movement could be reanimated by the spirit which impelled Mr. Moody, and which would make the Association more as it was in his day, a

recruiting station for Christian volunteers, a training ground for Christian leaders, a rallying center for united spiritual campaigns.

As a relatively new movement, the association gave full scope, in the sixties, to all forms of Christian activities. Moody's conception of the purpose of the organization was that it should serve as an agency for enlisting young men in Christian effort. It was not in his nature to exert himself solely for entertainment or instruction. He believed that temptation could best be met by bringing young men into a personal relationship with Christ and setting them to work in behalf of others. While pool and gymnasium had their rightful province, Moody did not believe they should hold as important a rôle as the spiritual activities of the association.

CHAPTER XV

It has been shown that Moody's efforts to reach the parents of his scholars led to a Sunday evening service distinctly evangelistic in character. Later these services were protracted to week days with gratifying results and growing interest. From this it was not far to the establishment of a union or interdenominational church. Naturally those who had found spiritual blessing in the North Market Hall desired a bond which would hold them together.

For some time Moody demurred. He wanted them to join the neighboring churches but the new recruits earnestly wished to conserve the fellowship with those whom they knew and with whom they had labored. Nevertheless Moody's inexperience and lack of special training made him hesitant. Finally his objections were overruled and a union church was formed, its members bound by a common loyalty to Christ.

A difficulty was at once experienced in the formulation of a creed as the basis of the union. These people, drawn from such varied and motley backgrounds, had widely divergent views. There were national sympathies to be considered as well as temperamental inclinations. From the Scotch, trained in Presbyterian doctrine, there was insistence upon Calvinistic statements of faith; those of early Methodist training were no less staunch for Arminian tenets; the Baptists placed the emphasis upon believer's baptism and the form of its administration. But there was one bond of unity, though there were many beliefs.

After repeated sessions of the group assigned to the task of drawing up a creed, a happy solution was found in so framing the confession of faith as to confine it to the words of Scripture itself. Any dissident would then be taking issue not with any sectarian opinions but with the Bible; at the same time there would be a degree of freedom through individual interpretation. Thus was conserved the evangelical character of the union with the spirit of personal liberty.

There was a mutual concession in unessentials. If some parents wished to have their infants christened this was permissible; but if there were others who were convinced that they must receive the believer's baptism and that by immersion, this too was provided for by a special baptistry built beneath the pulpit. In the fellowship of the Illinois Street Church, at its inception, was illustrated the spirit of the old Latin motto: "In essentials loyalty; in unessentials liberty; in all things charity."

Moody has been termed an "unordained pastor." He was without theological training but, though he had not undergone a systematic preparation, he may be truthfully described as a "foreordained minister." His duties at the mission demanded the services of the ordained pastor, yet Moody performed all rites with the one exception of the marriage ceremony.

During Moody's sojourn abroad the church was without a regular pastor. When the parishioners learned that Moody would probably be unable to resume the personal direction of the church for some time, they felt that a pastor should be called "whose support Mr. Moody himself guaranteed." There were no denominational qualifications stipulated but he was to be selected as one who "should teach the essential truth of the Bible in unquestioned orthodoxy and be a competent interpreter of the Scriptures." Such a one was found in Rev. William J. Erdman, whose thorough college and seminary training, scholarly attainments, and unquestioned loyalty to the Scriptures made him a wise choice.

Successive pastorates were held by Revs. Charles Morton, George C. Needham, Charles F. Goss, Thomas B. Hyde and R. A. Torrey.

Twenty-five years after Moody had passed from his labors, the church, having grown out of its humble beginning as a mission school, erected "the Moody Memorial Church," an imposing edifice with a seating capacity for over four thousand and with splendid Sunday school facilities capable of accommodating twenty-five hundred scholars. Under an earnest pastor, Rev. W. P. Philpott, and after seventy years, the work which began in the dingy quarters of the old North Market Hall is still carried on.

CHAPTER XVI

In his zeal to miss no spiritual privileges, Moody eagerly sought instruction from all sources. His wife had been reared in an Anglican home but in her early girlhood she had been immersed and had joined the Baptist church. The reasons which influenced her naturally had considerable weight with her husband, and it was with the question of immersion still undetermined in his mind that Moody entered upon his war experiences. In these years of service on the battlefield and in the hospitals, it not infrequently happened that a wounded soldier asked to be baptized. If a chaplain was available he was asked to administer the ordinance but often Moody himself did it. To refuse a dying man the privilege of entering the fellowship on the ground that circumstances did not permit the correct performance of the rite was repugnant to Moody's conception of Christian teaching. And if exceptions were permissible in case of sickness, Moody could not see that the method was essential. He became convinced that Christ had not ordained a ceremony of baptism which could not be administered under any and all conditions.

For a time Moody came under the influence of the Plymouth Brethren. Their familiarity with the Scriptures, their assiduous study of the Bible, and their spiritual insight into its truths made a strong appeal to him. C. H. MacIntosh and J. N. Darby were prominent leaders among the body, and Moody became a diligent student of their works. With a spiritual perception they combined a thorough scholarship. Though their views were not in accord with the recognized religious teachers of the day, they were men capable of clearly and logically defining their position.

The Plymouth Brethren withdrew from the Anglican church in 1830 as a protest against its formalism and worldliness and they established their own simple organization. Sundays they met to partake of the communion and to listen to expositions of Scripture. Like the Quakers they had no salaried clergy, and the services were characterized by the greatest simplicity. In Scripture interpretation they were literalists; prophecy made a strong appeal to them and the decipherment of the symbolism of the apocalyptical books led to elaborate systems of eschatology.

Moody would invite to his home any visitor to Chicago belonging to the Brethren in order to learn from him any new truth or exposition. An amusing incident is connected with such a visit from a distinguished Plymouth Brother. At the end of a very busy day of visiting, preaching and ministering through long hours, Moody returned home late at night, and at his request evening prayers were led by the guest. Apparently the Brother "enjoyed great liberty" in expounding the Word for at some length he explained the involved symbolism of a portion of Scripture. In prayer he was no less fulsome, and when at last the worship ended, Moody remained upon his knees. Mrs. Moody was at first impressed by his devout spirit, but as he continued, her first sense of admiration gave way to alarm lest Moody, like his father, had suddenly suffered a stroke. At last she tried to arouse him and was immediately successful, his sheepish expression betraying the fact that he had been sound asleep.

Moody described his deep chagrin when the visitor remarked, "The spirit is willing but the flesh is weak." "It was nothing of the kind," Moody would say in relating the incident. "He was to blame for going on so long after a hard day's work. At the time I thought it was because I wasn't spiritual. It was because I was a fool. The Lord isn't a hard taskmaster and I was nearly killing myself by foolishly working day and night and going without meals. I have learned since then if I am to do my best for God I must use sense. Since then I've had prayers only in the morning when I'm wide awake."

But even if some Brethren were prolix, Moody knew they had the Bible knowledge he needed. It was this eager yearning to equip himself more fully for service that led him to go to Europe for a brief trip in 1867. Reports of conventions having for their object increased spiritual power had reached Moody from time to time and he longed to go to some of these gatherings that he might hear many of whom he had read and have fellowship with men of wide and rich spiritual experience. In a characteristically abrupt manner he announced before his mission that the next week he was sailing for England.

He was anxious to meet Mr. George Williams, the founder of the Y. M. C. A. and others engaged in similar service. As leader of the Chicago association, which naturally was a center for the exchange of methods and ideas, Moody wished to be fully informed and to be able to make available the best results of the broad experience of these men.

Every line of Christian activity in church, Sunday school and mission hall challenged his eager and sympathetic inquiry. He planned to go to Bristol to see the work of George Müller, and such places as Exeter Hall and Spurgeon's Tabernacle were objects of his pilgrimage. The "May Meetings," the annual assemblies of the leading missionary organizations and other religious bodies, were another attraction. This spring season would afford an exceptional privilege of hearing the prominent ministers and missionaries from the British Isles and from foreign fields.

There was an additional reason for the prospective trip. Mrs. Moody, as already stated, had been since childhood a sufferer from valvular heart trouble and asthma. A physician had expressed the opinion that an ocean voyage might prove beneficial. The benefit was not immediately apparent for, writing to a brother, Moody reported, "Emma's cough is not any better. I am sorry her journey has not been of any help to her." The physician's judgment was confirmed later, however, for asthma never affected her again after that trip.

Moody, who had often taken trips on the Great Lakes with no discomfort, looked forward to the crossing with keen anticipation. But he proved to be a very poor sailor and, far from being able to help his wife, he was the important subject of care. He crossed to Europe five times in subsequent years yet he always faced the voyage with a sense of dread.

Under date of March 16, 1867, Mrs. Moody wrote to Samuel from Liverpool, "Mr. Moody was sick more or less from the time we started till the time we landed in Liverpool, which was two weeks."

Of her first Sunday's experiences she does not draw a very attractive picture. They disembarked too late to attend morning service but they began observations in the afternoon. To the American couple, so watchful for all that might be effective at home, the Sunday school they visited seemed "rather a dull formal one and the room was very gloomy and dark." In the evening Moody went alone to a service conducted by "Mr. Lockhard who is a Liverpool merchant and preaches Sunday evenings in the large circus."

First impressions were evidently not happy, and he who was to become so ardent a lover of Old England wrote:

> I know you will be glad to hear from us. We are well and having a good time. We had a long voyage but very rough. I was seasick most of the way. I do not expect to visit this country again. One trip across the water is enough for me. I do not like the old country as well as our own. I cannot tell you how glad I am I was born and brought up in America. I shall be glad when I get back. I am not sorry I came for I very much value the information I am gaining here. But it is a horrible place to live in.

But English hospitality was soon extended to them. Mrs. Moody sent from London on May 3 an account of their engrossing interests:

> We have invitations nearly two weeks ahead to take tea, dinner, etc. . . . The anniversaries are taking up our time now. All the anniversaries are in April, May and June, most of them in May. They are held now every day and five or six meetings the same day in different places. We are anxious to attend for we have an opportunity of hearing the first men of Great Britain. . . . I think I'll like the English better than when I first came. I do not think them as reserved as I expected to find them, but do not think them as free and open as Americans.

Several weeks later Mrs. Moody wrote again, this time with almost girlish enthusiasm:

> You see I am in Scotland and in the quaint city of Edinburgh. Everything seems a little strange. The houses are all built of stone and many of the oldest buildings are such queer specimens of architecture. Then the city is covered with houses, hill and vale, and you may go upstairs, quite a long flight, apparently leading you up to the upper stories

of houses. But instead of that you are landed in
another street, and so you may go down a long flight
of stairs and think you are going into a cellar or
some other subterranean place, and you likewise find
yourself in another street. But with all I think
Edinburgh is a beautiful city.

In another letter she described their sight-seeing:

> I have just been out for a walk with Mr. Moody
> and I went into one of the churches John Knox
> used to preach in and also went through the house
> where he used to live, nearly three hundred years
> ago. It is a very old-fashioned-looking house. The
> only thing left in the house at present, that used to
> belong to him, is an old chair in which Mr. M. and I
> both rested for a few minutes. . . . We have had
> a very pleasant time in London and met many valuable acquaintances. I think Mr. M. will regret to
> leave it. I suppose Sam has received the papers
> Mr. M. sent so I will not need to tell you more of
> the many prayer meetings now formed. We have
> had some delightful times. With very much love
> for you.

There appeared in a religious weekly on April 18, 1867,
what was probably the first notice of Moody in Great
Britain. The notice read, "Mr. D. L. Moody of Chicago,
who is now in London, gives a most gratifying account of
the Lord's work in different parts of America." In the
next issue was an extract from the *New York Independent*
of an unusual interest that had been awakened by a visit
to Providence of

> D. L. Moody of Chicago to commence an organized
> system of missionary labor among the saloons.
> Appointing prayer meeting on Saturday evenings,
> at their (Y. M. C. A.) hall they went in groups of

three and four into all the saloons, and all places of idle resort, courteously but earnestly inviting those present to attend the meeting.

The efforts evidently met with success—so great success, in fact, as to arouse strong opposition.

In May at the annual breakfast of the Aldersgate Y. M. C. A. Moody seems to have been the principal speaker. He related his experiences in the Chicago Y. M. C. A. and described the various activities of the organization and laid great stress upon the inspiration derived from the daily noon prayer meeting. The suggestion of similar meetings in London met with a cordial reception, for a week later *The Revival* contained the following article:

> More than once have we heard our dear brother, Mr. Moody of Chicago, say that he would rather be used of God to establish in the city of London a lively, well-conducted, and well-attended daily prayer meeting, than leave any other result of his visit to England, inasmuch as he believes nothing can be so important and so likely to lead to great and blessed consequences, not only to London, but to our country at large, and possibly to the world; and to Mr. Moody we owe that such a prayer meeting has been set on foot.
>
> Hitherto we have been greatly encouraged; the attendance during the first week has ranged from sixty to eighty, and—best of all—much of the Lord's presence and blessing has been realized, hearts have been warmed and stirred, and there has been much more of that simplicity and freedom which characterize the daily prayer meeting in America than is usual with us. We certainly have a lesson to learn in this matter from our American brethren.

The simple rules for conducting the meeting probably originated with Moody as they reflect his sound, practical judgment and his aversion to long prayers.

> *Regulations.* Begin and close punctually.
> No prayer or remarks to exceed three minutes.
> Not more than two prayers or addresses consecutively.
> No tracts or papers to be distributed in the room.
> No announcement of meetings to be made, directly or indirectly, except by the chairman, at his discretion.
> No solicitation for money allowed.

The unconventional ways of this young American must have been surprising if not an actual shock. In accordance with English custom a vote of thanks to the chairman, a well-known nobleman, was assigned to Moody at some meeting. The chair was yielded to the vice chairman in order that the motion could be offered. The vice chairman announced that they were glad to welcome their "American cousin, the Rev. Mr. Moody of Chicago," who would now "move a vote of thanks to the noble Earl." With refreshing frankness and an utter disregard of conventionalities, Moody burst upon the audience with the bold announcement:

> The chairman has made two mistakes. To begin with I'm not the "Reverend Mr. Moody" at all. I'm plain Dwight L. Moody, a Sabbath school worker. And then I'm not your "American cousin." By the grace of God I'm your brother, who is interested, with you, in our Father's work for His children.
>
> And now about this vote of thanks to the "noble Earl" for being our chairman this evening. I don't

see why we should thank him, any more than he should thank us. When at one time they offered to thank our Mr. Lincoln for presiding over a meeting in Illinois, he stopped it. He said he'd tried to do his duty and they tried to do theirs. He thought it was an even thing all around.

This fairly took the breath away from Moody's hearers. Such talk could not be gauged by any standard. Its novelty was delightful, and he carried his English audiences from that time on.

It was not alone in London that Moody left the impress of his zeal, for in a certain journal, under date of July 4, 1867, there is a report that daily prayer meetings have spread to Paris and are held at the *Salle Evangelique*. In the same publication is a description of Moody as a prominent Christian speaker there.

The trip abroad was remarkable in effecting mutual introductions between Moody and many evangelistic workers. On numerous occasions he had described his manifold activities in Chicago and had thereby aroused great interest in his efforts. Annual reports of the Chicago Y. M. C. A. were thought sufficiently important to be recorded in a religious paper having circulation among all denominations.

On July first a farewell dinner was tendered Moody. In reporting the event *The Revival* said:

> Few men who have visited a foreign shore have endeared themselves to so many hearts in so short a time, or, with an unknown name and without letters of commendation, won their way so deeply into the affections of a multitude of Christian brethren who had never heard of him before, but who, having talked with him or heard him speak of Jesus asked for no other warrant to yield him a large measure of their love.

At this dinner there was present a Mr. Palmer of Boston who had known Moody when he lived in that city. Being called upon to speak Mr. Palmer said:

> I knew this brother when quite a lad in the Sunday school. He came in, scarcely knowing what a Sunday school or a prayer meeting was; but he devoted himself to the study of the Word of God, and very gradually was brought to the knowledge of the Truth. When I came over to this country I went to the May meetings at Exeter Hall, and at one of them, to my astonishment, heard my brother Moody announced among the speakers, and I have not seen him since until to-night.

Perhaps the most impressive tribute to Moody was by Dr. Newman Hall whose distinguished ministry had given his name international recognition.

> I do thank God that He has put it into the heart of our brother to interest himself as he has done in the work of the Lord in this land. He might have come to look at our places of interest, but he has rather come to do us good. I have been to the daily prayer meeting, and have been struck with the absence of red tape and starch, pleased with the honesty I found there.

At this time Moody himself wrote home:

> I have sent you an account of the daily union prayer meetings I have at last got started here. It is a great success and they are starting them in different parts of the city. I am in hopes great good will come of it. They are also starting them in different parts of the kingdom. I was out to Bristol the other day. They are talking about one there. I am in hopes to get a good many started before I go back

to America. Bristol is where the great orphan schools of George Müller are. He has eleven hundred and fifty children in his home, but he never asks a man for a cent of money to support them. He calls on God and God sends the money. It is wonderful to see what God can do with a man of prayer.

Moody used his brief visit in England to advantage. In addition to starting the Aldersgate noon meeting, still continued after sixty years, he was instrumental in establishing several others. He attended the Exposition in Paris and remained about ten days, returned to London, made a hurried trip to Scotland to be present at a missionary meeting where he was disappointed in not hearing the famous Scotch missionary, Alexander Duff, and, early in July, Moody returned to America after an absence of nearly four months.

CHAPTER XVII

As the success of Moody's evangelistic efforts began to be noticed, he received letters from all parts of the country soliciting his aid in behalf of wild or dissipated young men who had wandered to Chicago. A friend, describing this personal feature of Moody's work, said:

> At one of these Sabbath evening services I saw one of the most distinguished lawyers of Illinois, from the heart of the state, sitting by the side of his son, who had been snatched as a brand from the burning by the earnest appeals and prayers of Moody. The lawyer had written to Moody to save his son if he could. Words cannot tell of the work accomplished in those days, nor describe the intense earnestness of the audiences nor the enthusiastic singing of the old evangelical hymns and the Sabbath school tunes. If ever the Lord was praised from full hearts, it was at these meetings.

Moody was always too engrossed in his work to be a good letter writer. There is, nevertheless, a letter written to a friend in England which indicates the character of his work at this time. It is dated August 30, 1867, and reads:

> There have been about forty county conventions held in Illinois since I returned. I have been to many of them, and God has blessed them wonderfully. In one county over a thousand people came together from all parts. Some two hundred and fifty were anxious about their souls on the two days of the conference. God is working in our land and we

are praying for you, that England and America may be blessed together. Over eight hundred have united with our association since I returned, and they are coming from all denominations and meeting with us. We are going out in companies of from twenty to one hundred in a group, and holding open-air meetings in different parts of the city. We afterwards adjourn to the church, and some of the most wealthy and conservative churches have thrown their doors open to the crowds that come thronging in from the outdoor meetings, and the enquiry is heard on every side, "What must we do to be saved?" I hope you will pray for us that God may keep us humble and near to Himself. I cannot tell you how very much I enjoyed my trip in your dear land. My mind is often wandering off over the Atlantic to your home and my heart goes out to my dear Saviour in gratitude and love for ever permitting me to visit Old England, and there to become acquainted with so many whom I expect to meet in the better country, and there to talk of the great Redeemer who came into this dark world to save us.

I sometimes look forward with joy to the day when I am to lay my armour by and sit down with my Lord and Master; but at other times, when I see how much there is to do, and so few to do it, my hope is that my days may be continued, and that God may give me strength, heart, and wisdom to do the work He has for me to do. Give my love to all friends, I pray daily for your noon meeting, and shall look for fruits of you in heaven. Your brother in Christ.

D. L. Moody.

It was natural that a man so practical as he should have a strong desire to see definite results and at times he became depressed if he failed to bring about immediate conversions. In a characteristic story he described how he learned to put away doubt and discouragement:

"One Sunday I had preached and there did not seem to be any result. On the Monday I was very much cast down. I was sitting in my study, brooding over my want of success, when a young man who conducted a Bible class of one hundred adults in my Sabbath school called upon me. As he came in I could see he was away up on the mountain top, while I was down in the valley. Said he, 'What kind of a day did you have yesterday?'

"'Very poor. I had no success, and I feel quite cast down. How did you get on?'

"'Oh, grandly! I never had a better day!'

"'What was your subject?'

"'I had the life and character of Noah. Did you ever preach Noah? Did you ever study up his life?'

"'Well, no, I don't know that I ever made it a special study. I thought I knew pretty well all there was in the Bible about him. You know it is all contained in a few verses.'

"'If you never studied it before you had better do it now,' replied he. 'It will do you good. Noah was a wonderful character.' When the young man went away I got out my Bible and some other books and read all I could find about Noah. I had not been reading long before the thought came stealing over me, 'Here is a man who toiled on for a hundred and twenty years and never had a single convert outside his own family. Yet he did not get discouraged.'

"I closed my Bible; the cloud had gone; I started out to a noon prayer meeting. I had not been there long when a man got up and said he had come from a little town in Illinois. On the day before he had admitted a hundred young converts to church membership. As he was speaking I said to myself, 'I wonder what Noah would have given if he could have heard that! He never had any such results from his labors.'

"Then in a little while a man who sat right behind me stood up and said, 'I wish you would pray for me; I would like to become a Christian.' Thought I to myself, 'I wonder what Noah would have given if he had heard that! He never heard a single soul asking God for mercy yet he did not get discouraged.'

"I have never hung my harp on the willows since that day. Let us ask God to take away the clouds and unbelief; let us get out of Doubting Castle; let us move forward courageously in the name of our God, and expect to see results."

A friend recalls these times when first he observed Moody and his work.

> The Moody of later years, in his great evangelistic triumphs, was simply the Moody of that early time expanded, enlarged, manifolded by the thousand and one auxiliaries and coadjutors which, by his matchless magnetism, he ever continued to gather about him. He had the greatest power to set others to work, and thus multiply himself, of any man I ever knew.

Dr. Rufus Clark records an illustrative experience of Moody's early mission work.

> He had been twice invited to come and hold meetings in a certain county in the State; but a pressure of duties compelled him to decline. Having in the summer a leisure week, he sent word to one of the pastors that he was coming, and took the next train.
> On his arrival he called upon the pastor, who said to him, "I'm sorry that you have come. When we wrote you all seemed fair for a revival; now all

promise is gone." He went immediately to see another pastor, who told him, "You might better have staid at home; winter is the time; in summer people here are too busy." Mr. Moody was left to his meditations; but it did not take "the Lightning Evangelist" long to decide what he would do. He persuaded a few persons to go with him to the corner of a public square. Discovering a dry goods box on the opposite side of the street, he tumbled it over, and mounting upon it, began to speak. At first a few stopped to listen; others came, until a crowd of eager listeners had gathered around him. Many seemed deeply moved, while some wept. At the close, he invited all to attend another meeting to be held in a church near-by. Such a multitude flocked to the church that it would not hold them. Other meetings followed, increasing in interest. God poured out his Spirit, and a blessed revival followed. The first pastor called upon said, "I made a mistake; the Lord knew where to send you." The second pastor said, "I see that summer is just the time for a revival."

The year 1867 was of further significance in Moody's life for it was during his visit to England that he met Mr. Harry Moorehouse from Birmingham. All the circumstances were extraordinary and did not predispose Moody in Moorehouse's favor. In the first place he was known as the "Boy Preacher" and Moody hated such sensational cognomens. Furthermore, Moorehouse introduced himself and said he wanted to come to Chicago; this advance, Moody felt, was not in good taste and increased his prejudice. Moreover, the youth's appearance was not prepossessing; he looked like a beardless boy of seventeen.

Apparently Moorehouse followed Moody to America,

for an account of services he conducted in New Jersey appears in a London journal under date of September 30, 1867. "Harry Moorehouse came to Millville September 30, after preaching about a fortnight in Presbyterian and Baptist churches, and in Spring Garden Hall, Philadelphia."

Moody himself described the experience which had so great an influence on his future service. "I hadn't been in Chicago a great many weeks before I got a letter saying that he had arrived in America, and that he would come to Chicago and preach for me if I wanted him. Well, I sat down and wrote a very cold letter—'If you come West, call on me.' I thought that would be the last I should hear of him. I soon got another letter saying he was still in the country, and would come to Chicago and preach for me if I wanted him. I wrote again, 'If you happen to come West, drop in on me.' In the course of a few days I got a letter stating that on a certain Thursday he would be in Chicago and would preach for me. Then what to do with him I didn't know. I had made up my mind that he couldn't preach. I was going to be out of town Thursday and Friday, and I told some of the officers of the church, 'There is an Englishman coming here Thursday who wants to preach. I don't know whether he can or not.'

"They said there was a great deal of interest in the church, and they did not think he had better preach then; he was a stranger and he might do more harm than good. 'Well,' I said, 'you might try him. I will announce him to speak Thursday night. Your regular weekly meeting is on Friday. After hearing him you can either announce that he will speak again the next night or you can have your usual prayer meeting. If he speaks well both nights you will know whether to announce him or me for the Sunday meeting. I will be back Saturday.'

"When I got back Saturday morning I was anxious to

know how he got on. The first thing I said to my wife, when I got into the house, was, 'How is the young Englishman coming along? How do the people like him?'

" 'They like him very much.'

" 'Did you hear him?'

" 'Yes.'

" 'Well, did you like him?'

" 'Yes, I liked him very much. He has preached two sermons from that verse of John 3:16, "For God so loved the world, that He gave His only begotten Son, that whosoever believeth on Him should not perish, but have everlasting life," and I think you will like him, although he preaches a little differently from you.'

" 'How is that?'

" 'Well, he tells the worst sinners that God loves them.'

" 'Then,' said I, 'he is wrong.'

" 'I think you will agree with him when you hear him,' said she, 'because he backs up everything he says with the Bible.'

"Sunday came, and as I went to the church I noticed that everyone brought a Bible. The morning address was to Christians. I had never heard anything quite like it. He gave chapter and verse to prove every statement he made. When night came the church was packed. 'Now, beloved friends,' said the preacher, 'if you will turn to the third chapter of John and the sixteenth verse, you will find my text.' He preached the most extraordinary sermon from that verse. He did not divide the text into 'secondly' and 'thirdly' and 'fourthly'; he just took the whole verse, and then went through the Bible from Genesis to Revelation to prove that in all ages God loved the world. God had sent prophets and patriarchs and holy men to warn us, and then He sent his Son, and after they killed Him, He sent the Holy Ghost. I never knew up to that time that God loved us so much. This heart of mine began to thaw out; I could not keep back the tears. It was like news from a far country; I just drank it in. So did the crowded congregation. I tell you there is one thing that draws above everything else in this world, and that is love. A man that has no one to love him, no mother, no wife, no children, no brother, no sister, belongs to the class that commits suicide.

"It's pretty hard to get a crowd out in Chicago on a Monday night, but the people came. They brought their Bibles, and Moorehouse began, 'Beloved friends, if you will turn to the third chapter of John and the sixteenth verse, you will find my text,' and again he showed on another line, from Genesis to Revelation, that God loved us. He could turn to almost any part of the Bible and prove it. Well, I thought that was better than the other one; he struck a higher note than ever, and it was sweet to my soul to hear it. He just beat that truth down into my heart, and I have never doubted it since. I used to preach that God was behind the sinner with a double-edged sword ready to hew him down. I have got done with that. I preach now that God is behind him with love, and he is running away from the God of Love.

"Tuesday night came, and we thought he had surely exhausted that text and that he would take another, but he said, 'If you will turn to the third chapter of John and the sixteenth verse, you will find my text,' and he preached again from that wonderful text, and this night he seemed to strike a higher chord still. 'God so loved the world that He gave His only begotten Son, that whosoever believeth on Him should not perish, but have'— not going to have when you die but have it right here now—'everlasting life.' By that time we began to believe it, and we have never doubted it since. For six nights he had preached on this one text. The seventh night came, and he went into the pulpit. Every eye was upon him. He said, 'Beloved friends, I have been hunting all day for a new text, but I cannot find anything so good as the old one; so we will go back to the third chapter of John and the sixteenth verse,' and he preached the seventh sermon from those wonderful words, 'God so loved the world.' I remember the end of that sermon: 'My friends,' he said, 'for a whole week I have been trying to tell you how much God loves you, but I cannot do it with this poor stammering tongue. If I could borrow Jacob's ladder and climb up into heaven and ask Gabriel, who stands in the presence of the Almighty, to tell me how much love the Father has for the world, all he could say would be: "God so loved the world, that He gave His only begotten Son, that whosoever believeth on Him should not perish, but have everlasting life." ' "

This experience supplied the "wooing note" which had been largely missing from Moody's sermons up to this time.

Moorehouse revisited America in August, 1868, and labored with Moody for two months, preaching in his church and in Farwell Hall. During this time, accompanied by Moody, he went to various other cities, holding some seventy-two meetings. In the winter of 1878 he assisted Moody's evangelistic work in a New England mission.

Quickened in his desire to familiarize himself further with methods of work and of religious instruction, Moody returned to England in 1870, this time for a briefer trip and unaccompanied by his wife. He attended a conference in Dublin and enlarged his circle of friends. It was during this visit that he was impressed with the remark, "The world had yet to see what God can do with a man wholly surrendered to His will." It is not known who made this statement but it was the kind of statement that was always arresting to Moody. It thereupon became the purpose of his life to be wholly surrendered.

Mr. Charles Inglis, who was present at the Dublin conference, describes his impression of Moody.

I recall first meeting Mr. Moody at the Dublin Convention in 1870 when he was an entirely unknown man in Great Britain, and I remember to this day that he was dressed in a suit of Scotch tweed with pockets on the hips. The convener of the meeting, who was a Quaker, said in his quiet way, "Well, Mr. Moody, I hope you are taking back with you to America some happy reminiscences!" "Well," he said, "my pockets are full of papers with Bible readings and notes."

When we were going into the convention one night Moody was sitting under a tree in those beautiful grounds of Mr. Bewley's. He summoned me and said, "You men need not go in there. You have been feeding all day long. Come and sit under this tree and give me some new illustrations."

It was Moody's intention on this visit to assume the rôle of a learner and not do any speaking. But in spite of his resolution he was drawn into active work. A pastor in a London church asked him to occupy his pulpit, and Moody accepted the appointment. At the morning service there was no indication of any special interest; at the evening service, however, there was prevalent a deep spiritual sense. When the service was ended Moody asked all who wished to signify their desire to become Christians to rise. In response so many people rose all over the church that Moody thought to himself, "These people do not understand me. They do not know what I mean when I ask them to rise." He therefore repeated the invitation by asking all who really wanted to become Christians to withdraw to the vestry. The attendance was so large that it was necessary to bring in extra chairs. The pastor of the church was no less surprised than Moody. Neither had expected such results. Then Moody asked all in the room who in sincerity of spirit desired to enter the Christian life to meet the pastor in the church the next evening. On Monday Moody went to Dublin; a telegram followed him, urging his immediate return and saying that the work was going on and a larger number had attended the after-service on Monday night than on Sunday. Moody returned and conducted meetings for ten days; and four hundred were taken into church fellowship.

Moody often related an incident in connection with these meetings which deepened his sense of the efficacy of prayer. There were two sisters belonging to the church, one of whom was a confirmed invalid. The sufferer, no longer able to attend worship, began praying for a spiritual awakening. One day she read of the work which Moody had been conducting in Chicago and prayed definitely that he might be sent to their community. On the Sunday morning when Moody had preached, the sister who was in attendance returned from the morning service and asked the invalid, "Who do you think preached this morning?" Not knowing of Moody's being in the country she named several whom she thought might have been invited to occupy the pulpit. When at last her sister said it was "Mr. Moody from America," the invalid replied, "I know what that means. God has heard my prayers."

CHAPTER XVIII

To those of Moody's generation who lived in Chicago, the Great Fire, which occurred on the night of October 8, 1871, was a historic event. All incidents in life were related to it as "before the fire" and "after the fire." Everything conspired to further its rapid spread over a large area. There had been a season of protracted drought followed by high wind. Only a few of the buildings were of fireproof construction but even these could not resist the intense heat. No barrier could withstand the advancing flames in either the business or residential section. The irregular basement line necessitated differences in the elevation of the sidewalk in a single block. These varying levels created currents of air, converting the sidewalks into roaring chimneys. Glowing embers falling into the cracks between the boards found dry and combustible material so that in an incredibly short time the very avenues of escape became fiery furnaces.

Awful in its devastation, cruel in its wantonness, remorseless in its onslaught upon thousands of homes, the catastrophe was appalling. According to authorities, "The glow was seen for hundreds of miles over the prairie and the lake. The river seemed to boil and mingle its steam with the smoke." Estimates of the direct monetary losses in the destruction of buildings were variously estimated from one hundred and ninety to two hundred million dollars, while the indirect injury to business interests was probably another hundred million dollars. Nearly a hundred thousand people were homeless and it is estimated that two hundred and fifty lost their lives.

When, after two days, the fire had spent itself the total destruction had to be measured not by buildings burned, but by the area covered, and twenty-one hundred acres of the business and home sections of the city were smoldering ruins.

During the previous summer Moody had visited California with a party of friends. In resuming his work, he found that summer attractions had seriously reduced attendance at his church. To reawaken and maintain interest in the Sunday evening service, he determined to give a course of addresses on Bible characters, which would readily lend themselves to a closing gospel message. The subjects met with a popular reception, and the audiences steadily increased. Moody purposed devoting the last six nights to the consideration of the character and mission of Christ beginning with the nativity and ending with the passion. The fifth Sunday, the fateful night of the fire, there was the largest audience he had ever addressed in Chicago. His text was "What then shall I do with Jesus who is called Christ?" In concluding he urged his audience to give careful thought to this important question and to return the following Sunday when, in the presence of Calvary and the Cross, he would call upon all to make their decision. As the audience was dismissed, the fire bells were ringing.

During the World's Fair in 1893, on the anniversary of the fire, Moody referred to that Sunday evening.

> I have never seen that congregation since [he said]. I have looked over this audience, and not a single one is here that I preached to that night. I have a great many old friends and am pretty well-known in Chicago, but twenty-two years have passed away, and I have not seen that congregation since, and I never will meet those people again until I

meet them in another world. But I want to tell you of one lesson I learned that night, which I have never forgotten, and that is, when I preach, to press Christ upon the people then and there, and try to bring them to a decision on the spot. I would rather have that right hand cut off than give an audience now a week to decide what to do with Jesus. I have often been criticised; people have said, "Moody, you seem to be trying to get people to decide all at once; why do you not give them time to consider?" I have asked God many times to forgive me for telling people that night to take a week to think it over, and if He spares my life, I will never do it again. This audience will break up in a few minutes—we may never meet after to-day. There is something terribly solemn about a congregation like this.

You will notice that Pilate was just in the condition of my audience that night—just the condition that you are in to-day—he had to decide then and there what to do with Jesus. The thing was sprung upon him suddenly, although I do not think that Jesus Christ could have been a stranger to Pilate. I do not believe that He had preached in Judea for months, and also in Jerusalem, without Pilate having heard of His teachings. He must have heard of the sermons He had preached; he must have heard of the doctrine He had taught; he must have heard of the wonderful miracles He had performed; he must have heard how Herod had taken the life of His forerunner by having him beheaded, and of the cruel way Herod had treated him. Jesus of Nazareth was no stranger to Pilate.

Ever since the night of the great fire I have determined as long as God spares my life to make more of

Christ than in the past. I thank God that He is a thousand times more to me to-day than He was twenty-two years ago.

The Great Fire swept out of existence tangible evidence of Moody's work. As he went home that Sunday night he saw the glare of the flames. About one o'clock Farwell Hall was burned; and soon his church went down. At midnight the fierceness of the flames seemed to be waning, and it was thought that the fire department could gain the upper hand. The family retired, but within an hour all the residents of the street were warned to flee. The fire had crossed the river and was advancing rapidly.

A friend took Moody's two little children with his own family to a place of safety in a carriage. Any effort to save household goods was futile. No conveyances could be obtained, the roads were crowded, and all that could be rescued was a few cherished tokens valued chiefly for their sentiment. The Moodys filled a baby carriage with such clothing and articles as there was room for, and started away. Suddenly Mrs. Moody remembered an oil portrait of Moody by the artist Healey which she prized both for its own sake and on account of the giver. The artist had presented it to her after her return from Europe in 1867. It hung upon the wall in the little parlor of the home that had been presented to Moody. completely furnished, and Mrs. Moody valued that painting above anything the home contained.

A stranger who had entered the room assisted in taking it from the wall. Calling her husband, Mrs. Moody urged him to take it for her. The ludicrous side of the situation at once appealed to him. "Take my own picture!" he said. "Well, that would be a joke. Suppose I meet some friends in the same trouble as ourselves, and they say, 'Hullo, Moody, glad you have escaped; what's that you have saved and cling to so affectionately?'

Wouldn't it sound well to reply, 'Oh, I've got my own portrait!'"

No entreaty could prevail on Moody. The canvas was hastily knocked out of its heavy frame, and carried off by Mrs. Moody herself. It is now the cherished possession of a son.

CHAPTER XIX

THE winter following the Chicago fire offered new opportunities. Naturally destitution and suffering were widespread. Organized welfare bodies did not exist and human need was great. Voluntary help was provided both willingly and generously from all parts of the nation, largely through separate and independent channels. Churches, fraternal orders and societies aided those of similar faith or associations. There was no lack of warm sympathy and readiness to extend help, but there was wanting one thoroughly organized medium through which this good assistance could be applied.

Moody, like many other Christian ministers and philanthropic workers, entered upon a campaign in the East to raise funds and to organize forces for emergency relief in Chicago. George H. Stuart, who had been head of the Christian Commission, John Wanamaker, and R. K. Remington were among those who lent Moody their whole-hearted coöperation. When taking leave of Mr. Remington, Moody expressed the hope that he might some time return the kindness which he had received. "Don't wait for me," was the reply. "Do it to the first man that comes along."

On this hurried trip Moody raised three thousand dollars which enabled him to erect a small temporary building known as the North Side Tabernacle. One story high and with a seating capacity for fifteen hundred people, it served as a center for Moody's relief work. It was dedicated Christmas eve, just two and a half months after the fire.

Though Mrs. Moody and the children stayed with relatives during the winter months, Moody slept in the tabernacle with a corps of fellow workers. The winds from Lake Michigan searched through the cracks and crevices and made it difficult to keep warm. Moody often told with amusement how, on retiring, shoes were carefully placed over the knot holes to protect the sleepers from the chilling draughts that penetrated the floor.

But there were gratifying incidents as well as trials that year, making it one of the happiest and most eventful of Moody's life. At the close of a service two women whom he had frequently noticed in attendance, came forward and said they were praying for him, as they felt he needed the "power of the Spirit." "I need power! Why," said he in telling of the interview, "I thought I had power! I had the largest congregations in Chicago, and there were many conversions. I was, in a sense, satisfied. But right along those two godly women kept praying for me, and their earnest talk about 'anointing for special service' set me thinking. I asked them to come and talk with me, and they poured out their hearts in prayer that I might receive the filling of the Holy Spirit. There came a great hunger into my soul. I did not know what it was. I began to cry out as I never did before. I really felt that I did not want to live if I could not have this power for service."

Moody was passing through this spiritual unrest at the time of the fire. If new spiritual resources were available, he wanted them; and his prayers were answered while he was soliciting relief funds in the East. He seldom alluded to what happened, as the reality of the experience made it too sacred to be discussed. Then too, he realized that many would attribute it to causes other than that from which he was convinced it came. In recording the incident he said:

My heart was not in the work of begging. I could not appeal. I was crying all the time that God would fill me with His Spirit. Well, one day, in the city of New York—oh, what a day!—I cannot describe it. I seldom refer to it; it is almost too sacred an experience to name. Paul had an experience of which he never spoke for fourteen years. I can only say that God revealed Himself to me, and I had such an experience of His love that I had to ask Him to stay His hand. I went to preaching again. The sermons were not different; I did not present any new truths; and yet hundreds were converted. I would not now be placed back where I was before that blessed experience if you should give me all the world—it would be as small dust of the balance.

In passing it may be observed that this state of ecstasy came upon him not in the seclusion of some retreat, nor in the act of wrestling in prayer, but in the midst of a busy day in a thronged city on the world's famous thoroughfare, Broadway. To attempt to explain such great moments is impertinent. Moody was convinced it was God's appointment for service, and who may have the temerity, in light of later events, to question it?

The genuineness of Moody's "anointment for service" was in no way so fully demonstrated as by his willingness to *serve*, no matter how mean the task. During the long winter of 1871-1872 he labored for the physical welfare of those in whose behalf he had so earnestly labored for spiritual blessings.

With this spirit of loving service the new tabernacle was continuously blessed and within a year steps were taken to build a new church. The lot on which the old Chicago Avenue Church had stood for more than fifty years was secured and contributions came in from all quarters, thousands of Sunday school children giving five cents each to provide one brick for the new edifice. A brief acknowledgment to a donation of three dollars and sixty-five cents, in Moody's own handwriting, is preserved. It reads, in part, "We will put in seventy-three bricks for the dear children." For two years the basement of the building was roofed over temporarily and used for meetings.

BOOK III

CHAPTER XX

DURING his brief visits to England in 1867 and 1870 Moody had made the acquaintance of a group of Christian leaders prominent in evangelistic circles. From several he had received invitations to return and conduct missions. The time seemed opportune; his church was provided with a place of worship and the Y. M. C. A. was again established in a new Farwell Hall. After serving as president of the organization four years Moody had now resigned that the work might benefit by a change in leadership.

A six months' absence, at the most, was all that Moody contemplated. He supposed that his life was firmly rooted in Chicago and he looked to an early resumption of his labors there. Accepting the invitation to Great Britain, he made his plans with the precipitation that was so characteristic. Moody always worked at a given task with such complete absorption as to preclude any thought of the future. When one goal had been realized it was time to consider the next move. So, considering his immediate duties in Chicago now fulfilled, he decided to seize the opportunity for a change of activity.

In his church work Moody had been compelled to prepare addresses simple and concise in their statement and accompanied by apt illustrations. A union church was not a place to discuss controversial views; to denominationalism, as such, he was almost indifferent. Early in his experience he had discovered that the supremacy of Christ is the essential. Again, the varied character of his church work and mission activities had taught him the necessity of combining tact and fearlessness in dealing with opposition born of bigotry. The years in Chicago were therefore in reality an apprenticeship for the work to which his life was to be given. The Chicago experiences were to afford repeatedly the understanding and means of grasping and meeting situations in his evangelistic work both in Great Britain and America.

In contrast to the America which Moody knew, England was a land of ancient tradition. Great Britain itself, however, was feeling new impulses and was awakening to fresh social and intellectual influences. The ten years preceding Moody's visit saw man, in all his relationships, receiving a new evaluation. The Reform Bill of 1867 extended the franchise to the laboring man, a recognition he had not had before. The conscience of the nation immediately became vocal, legislating against the wrongs which had long been recognized but neglected.

Mr. J. A. Spender thus describes the changes taking place in the decade following 1869:

> The ministers, great and powerful, knew secrets which would not bear whispering; they could set armies in motion, make powerful sovereigns tremble at their nod. We get the atmosphere of it best in Disraeli's novels. His world is peopled with resplendent ambassadors, talking secrets of State to high-born ministers, with half-confidences permitted to great ladies and Princes of the Church. Days spent in Chancelleries are wound up in gilded salons where the great game goes on to an accompaniment of enchanting music in a dazzling throng of superbly dressed women. This, one divines, is what in Disraeli's thought made the public life worth living, gave it romance and dignity and atoned for the vexation and vulgarity which had to be endured in the business of vote-collecting. . . .

From 1869 onwards the public man was in the open, and a faithful Press followed him to the platform whence he now made appeals which were at least equal in importance to those which he had made from his place in Parliament. The whole modern business of organization and propaganda was soon on foot. With the localities stirred up to a political life of their own, it became more and more difficult for wealthy and well-born individuals to obtain safe seats in the House of Commons by arrangement with the whips and the political clubs. Political programmes became a necessity for both parties, and both endeavoured to broaden their appeals so as to make them acceptable to the largest numbers. The extension of the franchise in town and country went on concurrently with this extension of the appeal and promise. Discrimination between people, all of whom were now assumed to be educated, no longer seemed logical or just. If the old idea of leaving most things to settle themselves was abandoned, the masses whose interests were bound up in the new legislation had a right to be consulted. The Liberal was no longer, in Bagehot's phrase, "shocked to hear himself called anything else; and most Tories were at pains to prove that they were in reality just as democratic as their opponents."

The times are described by a modern writer in terms of perhaps unwarranted severity, but nevertheless deserving in part. Mr. J. A. Stewart describes what he is pleased to term "Victorian Religiosity."

> The unctuous smugness of the mid-Victorian era has often been remarked. Carlyle in apocalyptic style might cry "woe, woe," might denounce shams and simulacra, invoke the Eternal Verities and point

menacingly to Avernus; he was but a voice crying in the wilderness. Matthew Arnold's stall-fed, self-righteous Philistine possessed the field and pocketed the revenues, with a grand air of patronising High Providence. Church and State were vastly at ease in a Zion of roast beef and port wine, lapsing, though they did not know it, into the lethargy of fatty degeneration.

Carlyle from his home in Chelsea was viewing the world with a sense of disillusionment.

> The only progress to which Carlyle would allow the name was moral progress [writes his biographer], the only prosperity, the growth of better and nobler men and women.... The hope, if there is a hope, lay in a change of heart in the English people, and the reawakening of the nobler element in them; and this meant a recovered sense of religion.

But "he himself had for many years attended no place of worship," failing to find what appealed to him as the truth.

Darwin was challenging scientists with his evolutionary theory, his *Origin of Species* having appeared in 1859 and his *Descent of Man* in 1871. Any theory of creation other than the literal record in Genesis was a sacrilege to many and any other than an anthropomorphological view of God and His ways rudely offended their sensibilities. Some regarded science as the direct enemy of faith.

The religious world was unsettled. The Tractarian Movement at Oxford had influenced a large number of young men, and any effort under the leadership of laymen was looked upon with suspicion. Dissenters were strongly distinguished from the Established Church. On one occasion when Moody asked Spurgeon to preach for him, even on his second mission in the eighties, the invitation was resented by some devout people. That Moody was an American layman they could overlook, but they could not believe any spiritual blessing could come from a dissenting preacher.

Disturbing among traditionalists was the growing influence of those who no longer accepted literal views respecting the Bible. Higher criticism was the denial of supernaturalism in God's Word. It was not enough to acknowledge a divine architect; each draughtsman must be duly accredited. The very names of certain scholars were anathema. The letter was exalted at the expense of the spirit.

Evangelism was largely associated in the minds of the public with emotionalism and hysteria. Revivals had been characterized by it in the past. Crying out and even falling into a state of catalepsis were common occurrences. These extravagances had prejudiced many sober-minded people.

But Moody's work was free from this. In fact, Moody himself looked with suspicion upon any such displays. He believed that the gospel message was to be received in reverence and that the success of a mission was not to be measured by any numerical results, but rather by the accessions to churches, individual activity in Christian service, and higher ethical standards of living. Profession of faith was to be confirmed by the evidence of works. Salvation was for service and not for ecstasies nor personal happiness, although the latter would probably follow in the degree to which the individual worked for others.

The Anglicans were divided among themselves into broad, evangelical, and high. Various groups of Methodists were known as Wesleyans, Primitives and other less familiar terms. Congregationalists and Baptists also were divided on theological grounds. Attempts to unify only too often led to emphasizing the differences and what was needed was one great common cause, apart from doctrinal dispute.

Such were the conditions under which Moody began his mission in England in the seventies. To this situation is unquestionably due the character of the reception accorded him. The fervor of those who threw themselves whole-heartedly into the work, and the democratic and catholic spirit in which the mission was conducted were features of the movement. Where the spirit of God is there can be no distinctions either social or denominational. In Moody's mission, common loyalty to Christ led many of different denominations to become broader in their sympathies and to adopt a more truly Christian view of the nature of God and of their attitude to one another.

CHAPTER XXI

In an old diary which Mrs. Moody kept during a period of two years there are two brief entries, "June 7th, 1873, sailed from New York on S.S. *City of Paris* for Liverpool. June 17th, reached Liverpool and were met by Mr. Moorehouse." "Sailed from Liverpool for New York, August 4, 1875, reached New York August 14, reached Northfield August 16."

Within this period Moody entered a work of wider service. Suddenly he emerges into the bright glare of public notice. One familiar with his early disadvantages and the obscurity of his origin, might have questioned the result on him. Praise and criticism, attention and obloquy, were each in turn to test him.

Expenses of this trip for Moody and his family had been assured by three gentlemen: Mr. Henry Bewley at whose place in Dublin Moody had attended a conference, Rev. William Pennefather and Mr. Cuthbert Bainbridge of Newcastle-on-Tyne. They also guaranteed the salary and expenses of any helper Moody might bring.

Feeling the need of an assistant for music Moody had turned first to Philip Philips and then to P. P. Bliss but neither was available. A short time before Moody had engaged a young man, Ira D. Sankey, to be chorister in his church and Sunday school. He was the next one whom Moody asked to be his helper. Sankey had a special gift of singing the simple gospel hymns; according to George C. Stebbins, Sankey had no knowledge "of the art of singing and the use of his voice was intuitive rather than through cultivation, showing that he possessed gifts of an extraordinary character to have accomplished what he did."

But Moody's faith was to have a severe trial. The funds which had been promised to meet expenses did not come. To pay the steamship passage to Liverpool he was compelled to draw upon his savings, and when he arrived in England he learned that all three friends had died within a brief period. Moody found himself three thousand miles from home, with no arrangements made for his visit, no committee to plan for his time, and with the personal responsibility for a singer whose salary was one hundred dollars a month.

Just before leaving America he had received a letter from a Y. M. C. A. secretary in York expressing the hope that if Moody ever came to England, he would visit the York association and speak. Moody now seized this possibility of an opening and wrote that he was ready to begin meetings in York at once. In reply he received word that it would require a month to make necessary preparations and was asked to fix a date for consultation regarding plans. Meanwhile Moody and his family had proceeded to London whence he replied, by telegram, "I will be in York to-night."

The situation was not encouraging. Moody, after looking it over carefully, declared that "every man must make his own way," and that "he was ready to go in at once," and the meetings opened immediately. The next morning application was made to several ministers of the town for the use of their pulpits on the coming Sabbath, and a Baptist, a Congregational and two Wesleyan churches were placed at his disposal.

The following modest introductory notice appeared in one corner of *The Christian*, entitled, "Mr. D. L. Moody in England":

Mr. Moody has just arrived in England with his family, and is accompanied by a Christian brother, who leads the singing at his meetings, after the manner of our well-known and much-loved, Philip Philips. Mrs. Moody and her children remain with her sister in the neighbourhood of London while her husband is holding meetings in the provinces. Last Lord's Day he preached in Independent and Wesleyan chapels in York, and we believe that he intends to continue awhile in the North of England and then go to Scotland. He prefers preaching in chapels, and so strengthening existing causes, to commencing a new work in public halls, etc. Any friends who desire his help, especially in the North, should write to him at once, Young Men's Christian Association, York. We will notify change of address from week to week, as we receive it from him.

In contrast with this short notice, the later issues of religious papers gave extensive reports during the two years that covered Moody's campaign in Great Britain. the *London Christian* published double numbers, the extra pages being devoted entirely to articles concerning the great meetings.

At first the clergy were strongly inclined to look upon the newcomers with suspicious and disfavor, and the attendance at the services was small; but gradually the meetings grew in interest, the clergy coöperated, and both the preaching and the singing became the subject of public conversation throughout the community.

Moody wrote from York on June 30 to Mr. Farwell of Chicago,

> You will see by the heading of this note that I am in York. I began here one week ago yesterday, and have had splendid success so far. Yesterday we had

four meetings. They were large, and I think very profitable. God was with us. I preached in the morning on "They that be wise shall shine"; in the afternoon on "No difference"; and in the evening from the text, "The spirit of the Lord is upon me, because He hath anointed me to preach the gospel." Sankey sang the hymns finely; all seemed to be much pleased with him. I think he is going to do much good here. All the chapels are open to us, and invitations are coming from all over the country; I think we shall have all we can do here. I think of you all, and get fearfully homesick at times.

Keep me posted in regard to the Young Men's Christian Association building, and all about the stock. I should like to see a good building go up there. I do not see any better opportunity to work for Christ than in that field. I do not know what is to become of the Young Men's Christian Association in England and America if something of the kind is not done. I send you some flower seeds, I think the one marked 1-6 is beautiful, and never have seen anything in America like it. I hope you will have success with them. Remember me to Wells and all your own family. Yours thro' the Grace of God.

Rev. F. B. Meyer who met Moody for the first time in York recalls the small beginnings of the mission:

I can see him now, standing up to lead the first noon prayer meeting in a small, ill-lit room in Coney Street, York, little realising that it was the seed-germ of a mighty harvest, and that a movement was beginning that would culminate in a few months in Free Assembly Hall, Edinburgh, and ultimately in the Agricultural Hall and the Royal Opera House, London. It was the birth-time of a new conception of ministry, new methods of work, new inspiration and hopes.

What an inspiration when this great, noble soul first broke into my life! I was a young pastor then, in the old city of York, and bound rather rigidly by the chains of conventionalism. Such had been my training, and such might have been my career. But here was a revelation of a new ideal. The first characteristic of Mr. Moody's that struck me was that he was so absolutely unconventional and natural. That a piece of work had generally been done after a certain method would probably be the reason why he would set about it in some fresh and unexpected way. That the new method startled people, was the greater reason for continuing with it, if only it drew them to the Gospel. But there was never the slightest approach to irreverence, fanaticism, or extravagance; everything was in perfect accord, with a rare common sense, a directness of method, a simplicity and transparency of aim, which were as attractive as they were fruitful in result.

The first ten days of his meetings were only moderately successful, and he gladly accepted my invitation to come to the chapel where I ministered, and there we had a fortnight of most blessed and memorable meetings. The little vestry there—how vividly I remember it—was the scene of our long and earnest prayers as we knelt around the leather-covered table in the middle of the room. Two Presbyterian students, from Dr. Mackay's church in Hull, brothers, often used to pray with us, and I remember that Mr. Moody, at the great Free Trade Hall, Manchester, referred to that little room as the fountain from which the river of blessing for the whole country had sprung.

Many recollections of those days come back as I

write; how in the midst of tea at home Mr. Moody suddenly felt that he should preach his afterward famous sermon on Heaven, and started off on a three miles' walk to fetch his notes; how Mr. Sankey went over to see Mr. Rees, of Sunderland, the sailor-preacher, of whom I had spoken to them, and proved his singing powers in the little back parlour of W. D. Longstaff, to the entire satisfaction of both minister and elder; how we had our all-day meeting, the first of its kind in England; and how the fire of God burnt hot in all our hearts.

CHAPTER XXII

FROM York Moody went to Sunderland, Bishop Auckland, Carlisle and Newcastle, the interest and attendance increasing in each succeeding place. Mrs. Moody wrote to her family in Chicago of chapels overcrowded, overflow meetings, and Moody preaching four times daily and "every time to crowded audiences." She added, regarding the stay in Darlington, "I heard it was thought that two hundred were converted the last twenty-four hours." A meeting of mothers whose home duties did not permit attendance at the regular services was arranged by a group of ladies in Newcastle. According to Mrs. Moody:

> The ladies themselves went to the poorest, meanest streets and told the women to come and bring their babies with them. Such a squealing! First a bass voice, then a shrill tenor, then a go-between. I could not help thinking of the Pied Piper of Hamlin town when he charmed the rats from the houses. Their squeals were in fifty different sharps and flats and I thought it was a good deal so with the babies. But the poor women listened while the tears ran down their faces and Mr. Sankey and Mr. Moody were both able to continue their talks remarkably well.

Here in the north of England Moody has entered upon a new experience. Heretofore his labors for the most part were among those who knew him. Now, however, all is strange and he is solely dependent upon the message he has to deliver and his own resources. It is the initial effort of its kind; he is unknown and confronted with strong prejudices; his colloquialisms, American accent and unusual methods do not commend him to many. Songs are used that are popular in character, and solo singing is a novelty in a mission. The "inquiry meeting" following the preaching in which those who are interested have an opportunity to meet with experienced Christian workers, has to establish itself, by its results, in the favor of the people who have never seen anything of the kind before. In fact everything is strangely unfamiliar to Moody's hearers; it is the introduction of a new type of evangelism.

Undaunted by circumstances or criticisms Moody labored on and in each city the attendance at the services grew. Many came out of curiosity, but it mattered not to him what the impelling motive of his hearers might be, provided it afforded him the opportunity of delivering his message. These months in the autumn of 1873 were his introduction not only to Great Britain, but, through the attention attracted to the scope and results of his work, to his own country.

Moody had power which overcame prejudices and won him friends in every place he visited. Even among those who never accepted his methods, he won friendship by the force of his personality. One writer reporting the services says:

> He is genuine to the backbone. He is not eloquent but very fluent, not poetical or rhetorical but he never talks twaddle and seldom utters a sentence that is not well worth hearing—he is American to the core, in speech, intonation and vigor. His anecdotes are, for the most part, the acquisition of his own experience; they are apt, often most pathetic, and sometimes appalling. His earnestness is intense,

his energy untiring, his courage leonine, his tact uncommon, and his love for souls most tender.

But in spite of these qualities Moody was often misunderstood. In Sunderland a delegation from the Y. M. C. A. waited on Moody to invite him to address a meeting under their auspices. The interview made an unfavorable impression because of Moody's abrupt manner and apparent brusqueness. His appearance was neither ecclesiastical nor dignified. In reply to the invitation to speak for them Moody said:

"Oh, yes. I'll preach for you."

"We don't want you to preach for us; we want you to preach for Christ," the leader of the delegation answered.

"Oh, yes, yes! All right. I'll preach for you," was Moody's response. The delegation then explained that the association had not given evidences of their sympathy earlier because Moody had come to the city on the invitation of a Baptist minister, and they had feared that the organization would lose friends if they coöperated in what might be a sectarian movement. To this Moody replied, "I go where I can do the most good; that is what I am after. It is souls I want; it is souls I want." But even with this assurance there was distrust for one of the group thought there were mercenary motives behind the work.

Methodists felt that Moody was a Calvinist and they held aloof until Rev. William Moreley Punshun, who had known Moody in America, came from London to attend the services, thereby allaying the misgivings of his fellow ministers. Some objected to Moody's "throwing about the gospel promiscuously into the crowds." Others took exception to solo singing which, it was contended, did not constitute worship. That men and women could "decide for Christ" in an "enquiry room" meeting and immediately become Christians was also an offense to many;

they maintained that sudden conversion was not a permanent experience. But in spite of opposition from many sources both among those in the Established Church and Dissenters, confidence grew increasingly as the results and the genuine character of Moody's selfless service were recognized.

Moody made various impressions, of course. In the *Newcastle Chronicle* the editor, a member of Parliament, wrote an article upon "the wonderful religious phenomenon," and as the paper wielded a wide influence and the writer was sympathetic, many were induced to follow the movement.

That which impressed some was the dissimilarity of Moody's preaching to that of missioners to which they were accustomed. "Mr. Moody preaches," says one writer, "but conventional use of the word 'preaching' does not convey any notion of Mr. Moody's talk. He is a business man, and he means business; every word he speaks is meant to lead to a definite result; if it doesn't do that, he regards it as thrown away."

In Newcastle, for the first time, the interest of the privileged classes was awakened. Moody protracted his stay in this city with the purpose of living down such prejudices as arose from misunderstanding, and of proving the value of the methods he employed. Popular songs to convey a religious truth, solo singing, the "enquiry room" and other innovations in conducting a mission, he wished to commend to the community by a practical demonstration of their value.

One feature of the services was an all-day meeting or conference at the close of each mission. This was an important factor in bringing together the Christian forces; its effect was to break down sectarian prejudices.

> Denominational lines have been, in a great measure, obliterated [writes an observer]. Ministers of

various sects have assembled in crowds under the banner of one God, one faith, one baptism and one sublime destiny. Efforts for ecclesiastical unity that had extended over years have been crowned with success in a day. . . . Beyond the limits of the meetings held, an unwonted seriousness has spread over vast communities, solemnizing the thoughtless, checking the vicious, silencing the scoffers, and leading multitudes, not yet brought to Christ, to think of death, the judgment and eternity.

CHAPTER XXIII

DURING the mission in Newcastle the Rev. John Kelman of Leith, a suburb of Edinburgh, came to study the character of the work, the reports of which had awakened a good deal of curiosity on the part of the ministry throughout Scotland. So fully was he in sympathy with the spirit which prevailed in the mission, and so greatly was he impressed by what he saw that he warmly espoused the cause and urged his fellow ministers to invite Moody to Edinburgh. Another eminent minister, Rev. J. H. Wilson of the Barclay Church, interested by reports from friends in Sunderland, warmly seconded the suggestion. Through the instrumentality of these men a committee extended the invitation to Moody.

He was familiar with the general knowledge that the north was reputed for its theological scholarship and as the home of metaphysics. Scottish theology he contemplated with awe; he was fearful of the pitfalls into which, with his lack of training, he might inadvertently fall. But in the very consciousness of his inadequacy was strength. It is doubtful if he ever exercised greater courage or felt a greater sense of dependence upon God than when he went to Scotland for the first time. He had previously known few Scots, but their reputation for unresponsiveness had created in his mind the picture of a people cold and unemotional to whom the gospel story as he presented it would be ineffective. It was with grave misgivings and only after careful consideration that Moody accepted. His decision, however, resulted in one of the greatest labors of his career.

But in reality, conditions in Scotland were most auspicious for Moody's mission. Of these conditions he was unaware, yet they bear a direct relation to the success of his work there.

"It were to miss the aim of biography to lose sight of the story of a life in the events of an epoch," according to a distinguished scholar and biographer. But to understand a man's life he must be placed in his day and generation. Particularly is this true in recounting Moody's life and influence in Scotland for he came at an opportune time in its religious life and history.

The response to Moody's message was instantaneous for it met a need which the church was inwardly voicing; a long-drawn-out and bitter controversy had been succeeded by a religion of convention. This was the issue of the Disruption which had antedated Moody's visit by thirty years.

The Established Church of Scotland had always been Presbyterian and administration was rigidly applied throughout the country. Under its rules a minister received his charge through the nomination of a patron although the appointment was slightly safeguarded by being subjected to the approval of the presbytery. But the system had led to many abuses and had long been a subject of contention within the church; "Riding Committees," sometimes under military escort, had ordained a patron's nominee in spite of local opposition; irreligious ministers were forced on protesting congregations. The practice continued in the face of vain objections until the situation became intolerable.

One case was put to the test. The presbytery refused to proceed in confirming the appointment of a minister duly nominated by a nobleman with the concurrence of only two members of the congregation. Thereupon the patron and nominee appealed to the civil court which ruled the presbytery had acted illegally and that it was bound and astricted to admit the minister to the charge. A long and bitter struggle followed which ultimately went to the House of Lords. There the ruling of the lower court was sustained; judgment went against the presbytery and upheld the plea of the patron.

It is not surprising that such a decision, subordinating the spiritual interests of the church to the temporal powers should have shaken Scotland. Such names as Chalmers, Rainy and Hugh Miller will ever be cherished for their leadership in the struggle into which the church entered.

But all efforts to bring about any possible settlement proved futile and in May, 1843, there occurred the "Disruption," the greatest event in Scottish religious life since the Reformation. Every community was affected by its far-reaching influence. Four hundred and seventy-four ministers, constituting nearly half of the entire number in the church, withdrew from the fellowship in which they had been reared. Among this number were many of the oldest and most spiritual leaders of Scotland; the sacrifice they made for conscience sake was real and vital. They relinquished their salaries, vacated their manses and went forth in faith to begin their Christian service anew by establishing the Free Church.

The days following Disruption were filled with unrest. It was a time of instability both in church policy and in statement of belief. The rapid advancement of science challenged old established convictions; even the Westminster Confession of Faith was no longer regarded by some as infallible. "All over Scotland many ministers were afraid of being renounced as being unsound if they did not affect and echo a certain theological jargon. Some avoided their natural voice, and cultivated precious tones of unctuous religiosity." Having cast off state control, the church gave greater liberty to individual belief and interpretation which issued in numerous cross currents of religious thought.

But in the course of time the spiritual quickening of the Disruption waned; "a time of ebb succeeded the mighty surge." Reverence for a great tradition was succeeded by the idolatry of so great and noble an event; formalism settled upon many of the churches, and outward observance stifled genuine life.

> North of the Tweed, where character shares the austerities of nature, an obstinate Calvinism still pervaded the land like an atmosphere. Sunday was a day of high penance, as if the sins of six days were to be expiated in a batch by intensified self-torment on the seventh. A child who absent-mindedly hummed a profane tune on the Sabbath sent a genuine thrill of horror through the nursery and even the occasional singing of the national anthem in church produced an uncomfortable feeling.

Sir William Robertson Nicoll, the brilliant literary critic, and editor of the *British Weekly*, thus characterizes the generation which followed the Disruption, and the one in which Moody began his work:

> The time was critical. The Free Church had been founded in a time of intense Evangelical faith and passion. . . . The obvious danger was that the Free Church should become the home of bigotry and obscurantism. This danger was not so great at first. There was a lull in critical and theological discussion, and the men were sure of their ground. The large and generous spirit of Chalmers impressed itself on the Church of which he was the main founder, and the desire to assert the influence of religion in science and literature in all the fields of

knowledge was shown from the beginning. . . .'. The Free Church was apparently refusing to shape the dogmas of traditional Christianity in such a way as to meet the subtle intellectual and moral demands of an essentially scientific age. There was an apparent unanimity in the Free Church, but it was much more apparent than real. For one thing, the teaching of some of the professors had been producing its influence. Dr. A. B. Davidson, the recognised master of Old Testament learning, a man who joins to his knowledge imagination, subtlety, fervour, and a rare power of style, had been quietly teaching the best men amongst his students that the old view of revelation would have to be seriously altered. He did not do this so much directly as indirectly, and I think there was a period when any Free Church minister who asserted the existence of errors in the Bible would have been summarily deposed. The abler students had been taking sessions at Germany, and had thus escaped from the narrowness of the provincial coterie. They were interested, some of them in literature, some in science, some in philosophy. At the New College they discussed in their theological society with daring and freedom the problems of the time. A crisis was sure to come and it might very well have been a crisis which would have broken the Church in pieces. That it did not was due largely to the influence of one man—the American Evangelist, Mr. Moody.

Now a real voice, peculiar to many in its accent but throbbing with deep emotion in preaching the love of God; a messenger apparently so engrossed in individuals and their relation to Christ as to be unmindful of their struggle with the state; one who ever seemed to know nothing of the Disruption and only "Christ and Him crucified" challenged the attention. And when the message itself they discovered was the very word they had all unconsciously been yearning to hear the people came to listen and many found a new life of privilege in Christian service. As one expressed it, "It seemed as though someone set to music the tune which had been haunting thousands of ears."

CHAPTER XXIV

EDINBURGH was the first large city in which Moody conducted a mission. The city prided itself as a great center of learning. That methods had proved successful in the smaller cities of the north of England was no assurance that the same would be true in Edinburgh. But from the first the meetings were largely attended, and wide interest was awakened, not only in Edinburgh but throughout Scotland.

Members of all the Protestant denominations professed themselves quickened. The prejudices of those who for years had resisted every attempt to introduce instrumental music into public worship were overcome, and they lustily sang with Mr. Sankey and his organ. The most respected leaders of religion spoke from the evangelist's platforms, helped in the enquiry rooms and instructed the young converts. . . . On all sides the fire spread. Hundreds of converts were gathered from the careless and formal members of the Church, as well as from among people who never went to Church. In contrast to most congregations, the number of men at the meetings equalled, and sometimes exceeded that of women. It was possible to fill one church after another with young men, and to see in each a hundred rise to confess that they had been converted by God's Word.

The secret of all this lay open. The evangelists themselves were obviously men of sincerity and power. They made mistakes. Mr. Moody said some rash things, as a foreigner could not help doing, and many crude ones, as an uneducated man must. While some of his addresses were powerful, others were very poor. But these faults soon sank from sight in the deep impression of a true zeal to win men for a better life, and to pour fresh power into the routine of Christian work.

Moody laid no claim to theological training, but with singleness of purpose he labored to bring men to a knowledge of the gospel. Men felt themselves in the presence of a power influencing them persuasively with no outward demonstration of hysteria or excitement. Methods were sane and practical, and as such, commended them to experienced pastors and Christian workers. "Mr. Moody suffered no fools, and every symptom of the hysteria which often breaks out in such movements was promptly suppressed." The preaching won Scotsmen's hearts by its loyalty to the Bible and its expository character. Moody's American accent gave "an edge of the real and even the occasional glint of humor swept the address clean of every appearance of unreality."

With a view to making the movement more widely known and familiarizing the Christian public with the salient features of the mission, Moody suggested that a fund of two thousand pounds be raised to send reports of the meetings as published in the *London Christian* to all ministers in the United Kingdom. By the end of 1874 a brief notice in that paper announced the success of the appeal whereby "thirty thousand copies of the periodical have gone to ministers for the past quarter."

Special meetings were reported for young men, for university students, for Sunday school teachers; and in the Corn Exchange a service brought three thousand from the slums to hear the gospel. Apparently the largest churches were available and fully taxed to their capacity for special services as well as the Free Assembly Hall, the Established Assembly Hall and the Music Hall.

On one Sunday evening he preached to students of the university and theological seminary on "There Is No Difference." An observer writes:

> This was one of the most magnificent sights I have ever witnessed. On the platform with him were numbers of professors of both colleges. The hall was densely crowded, and I question whether he ever addressed a more intelligent audience, or one that gave him more profound and riveted attention. Had they not had confidence in him and felt his power, and, we trust, the higher power of God's Spirit and truth, they would not have sat for more than two hours with such quietness. He commanded that immense meeting of about two thousand men, as no man on that platform, save Dr. Duff could have done.

One incident occurred, however, during these early meetings in Edinburgh which threatened to jeopardize the work. A man in Chicago apparently cherished some grudge against Moody and wrote to an Edinburgh minister charging Moody with having inspired an article in the *Edinburgh Daily Review* which contained statements "that are misleading and some that are positively untrue." The letter also charged that Moody had on one occasion, while still in business, been guilty of a gross breach of confidence and disloyalty to his employer.

Moody was troubled. It was not his custom to respond publicly to any criticism, and the bitterly vituperative character of the letter would almost seem to have been a sufficient answer to itself. Nevertheless, he earnestly requested the committee upon whose invitation he had come to Edinburgh to investigate the charges. Accordingly a letter was addressed to Mr. John V. Farwell whose standing as a prominent merchant and well-known Christian layman was readily confirmed.

The reply was an enthusiastic testimonial to Moody's work. It was signed by thirty-five prominent ministers and Christian workers and supplemented by a letter from the head of the firm in which Moody was employed at the time of the alleged disloyalty. What threatened to undermine confidence in Moody's work ultimately resulted in the strongest kind of endorsement. The outcome gave Moody a firmer hold upon Great Britain.

During these early days in Scotland Mrs. Moody several times makes note of the fact that Moody suffered from hoarseness. At the opening of the Edinburgh mission she writes, "November 22, 1873. Arrived in Edinburgh and came to Rev. Dr. W. G. Blaikie. D. L. very hoarse. Professor Simpson sent for. 23rd. Disappointment to many. D. L. not able on account of his throat to go out." Entries elsewhere give light upon the cause of this hoarseness and at the same time of the extraordinary physical endurance which apparently was being taxed to the utmost. "D. L. preached outdoors at Arthur's Seat to an audience of ten thousand." "D. L. preached at 9 A.M., again at 11 A.M., again at 6 P.M. and 8 P.M. in the open air. At 9:30 P.M. had a prayer meeting for thirty minutes and then talked with anxious ones till eleven o'clock." It must be remembered that Sunday was not the only strenuous day; that he was also preaching daily two or three times with prayer meetings and inquiry meetings in addition.

Evidently Moody soon won the Scotch heart, for twenty-six years later Mrs. W. G. Blaikie who was his hostess writes:

> After Mr. Moody came to stay with us in Edinburgh in 1873 and when his successful work became known, several friends sent invitations to our house

to beg that he would go and visit them. These notes were shown to Mr. Moody but with the assurance that we did not wish him to leave us, his answer was, "The Master says 'Whatsoever house ye enter into, there abide, and thence depart,' so I shall remain here!" We rejoiced in his decision and always remember the winter of 1873-74 as one of the happiest times we ever enjoyed!

In a letter to her mother dated January 8, 1874, Mrs. Moody wrote:

> I think the people here would do anything for Mr. Moody. One of the newspapers has just published his biography and has sold, as a consequence, thirteen thousand copies already, but the great trouble to Mr. Moody is that the person who wrote the article mentions money in it. I think on that account if they give him a present here he will have it sent to the church. It will show them that he is not after their money and do the church good these hard times. God is very good to us and does not let us want for anything.

On the first Sunday in 1874, at seven different times, Moody preached to audiences aggregating fifteen thousand.

> He is the most powerful speaker—the most eloquent preacher—who most fully carries an audience with him and produces the greatest results [writes one who attended the meetings]. If Mr. Moody is judged by such a rule, he is one of the most eloquent of living men, for none of us here who are ministers feel the least desire to speak if he is present, for with all our university training we acknowledge his superior power as a heaven-commissioned evangelist. . . . What masses of young people from the schools crowded the meetings during the holi-

days! And so great has been the attraction of the singing of the one and the eloquence of the other, that hundreds of young persons, especially of the higher classes, who were formerly accustomed to go to the theatre, opera, and pantomime, gave them up deliberately and from choice and the force of conviction attended the gospel and prayer meetings.

Among the warm-hearted and sympathetic fellow workers on this first visit to Edinburgh were a Mr. and Mrs. Peter MacKinnon of Campbeltown, Scotland, and Mrs. MacKinnon recorded the impressions of the various missions in which she took part. The first impression she had of Moody was that "of an ordinary, very decided, businesslike person, not polished in manner or style." Regarding the meetings she writes,

> At every point, at every turn, in those days one met something touching in connection with the work. People were thoroughly roused to opposition, or to sympathy. It was the subject of conversation everywhere, and everyone had a position to take up—for, or against. It was an easy thing to show one's colours; in fact it was impossible not to do so. . . .
> And yet I have scarcely spoken of the man around whom all this interest circled. This fact is fitting; for while thousands listened with intense interest to his words, he himself seemed to be forgotten—the subject, which was the Gospel always, quite covered up the speaker. And I am glad to find that, on recalling these days, it is the work itself that comes uppermost, the worker is almost forgotten. I marvel at it, for his personal influence was wonderful.

A familiar dictum of Moody's was, "I would rather set ten men to work than do the work of ten men." As a matter of fact he did both. Among the number of men who gathered about Moody at this time was Henry Drummond who had entered upon theological studies, less from personal inclination than from a desire to gratify the wishes of his parents. Natural sciences appealed to him strongly, and geology had a special fascination for him. But he pursued his studies in theology conscientiously, and his earnestness and discernment had already attracted attention by a paper which he had read before the Theological Society on "Spiritual Diagnosis." In this essay he had contrasted the clinic of the medical profession with an analogous service in ministerial life showing that the most effective work is to be accomplished in personal dealing with individuals; that the sermon from the pulpit needed a supplementary work in which experienced Christians could come in direct contact with the individual. The innovation of the "enquiry room" in Moody's meetings was directly in line with this form of ministry for which he had made appeal.

Both in early training and in manner of thought no men could have been more unlike than Drummond and Moody. Thoroughly educated, widely read, extensively traveled, Drummond enjoyed the advantages of culture; Moody, with no academic training, limited in his reading, and largely self-taught, had had few of the privileges which his friend had received. But their loyalty to Christ, their love for their fellow men and their genuine joy in service formed a common bond, and each recognized in the other qualities that awakened a mutual love. Writing of Moody twenty years later Drummond describes him as "the greatest human" he ever knew.

The influence of the mission in Edinburgh left its impress upon Drummond. Sir George Adam Smith refers thus to it:

> The religious movement in Great Britain, from 1873 to 1875, stands supreme, and deserves most

thorough treatment. The history of this has never been written. The present generation do not know how large it was and with what results upon the life of our nation. As for Drummond, it made him the man he was in his prime; in his expertness in dealing with men, in his power as a speaker, nay, even in some principles of his faith, he is inexplicable without it.

Rev. John Watson (Ian Maclaren) in an introduction to Drummond's posthumous work *The Ideal Life* says: "As soon as Moody came to Edinburgh, Drummond allied himself with the most capable, honest, and unselfish evangelist of our day, and saw strange chapters in religious life through the United Kingdom. This was the infirmary in which he learned spiritual diagnosis."

Among other influential leaders in Scottish religious life whose coöperation did much for the success of the Edinburgh meetings were Drs. Horatius Bonar, Alexander Whyte and Archibald Charteris. Rev. Arthur Gordon, in the biography of Dr. Charteris refers to his sympathetic attitude:

> Spiritual stagnation was to him the great enemy which all were bound to attack. When, therefore, Mr. Moody and Mr. Sankey were asked by a representative committee (of which Dr. Charteris and the Rev. George Wilson were members) to visit Edinburgh in 1873, he had first satisfied himself of the spiritual genuineness of their work, and then threw himself into it with characteristic eagerness and hope. He attended an early meeting in Queen Street Hall, and thereafter addressed a letter to the Rev. John M'Murtrie: "Do try to attend Moody and Sankey's meeting to-morrow in Free Assembly Hall at twelve. Queen Street Hall too small. I had to

stand to-day. There is no Plymouthism; but many members of your own and other Church of Scotland congregations. I heard nothing and saw nothing you would not approve of." Dr. Charteris also brought Dr. Maxwell Nicholson to the noon meeting. The fourth week of special meetings began in St. Stephen's parish church on Tuesday evening, December 16, 1873, where for three nights the church was crowded by two thousand people. Many ministers of all denominations throughout the country attended. Dr. Nicholson himself presided, and a deep and abiding impression was made. Coöperation among ministers of different communions was then sadly unusual, but in presence of that fear of the Lord which was upon them all, denominational differences were forgotten. Brotherhood in Christ was remembered. The Free Assembly Hall and the Tolbooth were the centre of the movement. The present writer remembers first hearing Mr. Moody, when passages were crowded as never on the most popular Assembly day. Professor Charteris was on his right, Professor Blaikie of the Free Church on his left; and as it began, so it continued. Dr. Charteris and Mr. Moody were greatly drawn to one another, not only by oneness of faith in things fundamental, but by a common aim in practical evangelization. Moody thoroughly believed in an educated ministry, and quaintly observed that he had never had a college education himself; but, as he did not get it, he was doing the best he could without it. He fully recognized that steady ministerial work in Scotland was what made his mission so successful. Twelve years later Dr. Charteris in a Guild sermon used the illustration:—"Of all ministers who preach, there is not one in our day to whom so many souls owe their new life as to Mr. Moody; and did you ever hear of one whose power was so guided by a purpose, strong as a passion, to win souls to his Saviour?" . . .

And now what shall we say when we look back upon the whole movement in Edinburgh? Although there are some minor details in which I could have wished to see some change, yet, in *all that is essential and really characteristic,* it seems to me to be such that the words which naturally occur are, "It is the Lord's doing, and marvellous in our eyes." In so far as we can judge, a real revival of religion has been granted to us. Men old and grey have sought and found Christ; young men have flung off the thraldom of former sins.

As minister of Free St. George's Dr. Alexander Whyte occupied a position of great influence in Presbyterianism and the fact that he manifested his sympathy in the movement contributed not a little to giving confidence to the public. "Whyte gladly bore his share in the work which went on in Edinburgh during the winter of 1873-1874," writes his biographer.

Toward the end of the Edinburgh meetings Dr. Horatius Bonar sent a letter which, although not intended for publication, had been so frequently requested that it was printed. An extract reads,

> These American brethren bring to us no new gospel, nor do they pretend to novelty of any kind in their plans, save perhaps that of giving greater prominence to the singing of hymns, conveying the good news to their hearers through this instrumentality. We may trust them. They fully deserve our confidence; the more we know of them in private the more do we appreciate them and the more do we feel inclined to cast in our lot with them. We ask for soundness in faith, and we do well. These men are sound. We ask for a consistent humble life, and

we do well. These men are self-denying, hard-working men, who are spending and being spent in a service which they believe to be not human but divine. We ask for definite aims, an ultimatum in which self shall have no place, and we do well. These men have the most definite of all definite aims—winning souls to everlasting joy, and they look for no fame and no reward save the Master's approval—the recompense in reserve for those who turn many to righteousness. They have in view no sinister nor sordid motives, as their past history shows, as every one who associated with them must feel. Besides all this, it is vain to try to stop them. They will work and they will speak whoever shall say nay. Let us work along with them. Rowland Hill was once asked the question, "When do you intend to stop?" "Not until we have carried all before us," was his answer. So say our brethren from Chicago. We say "Amen." This needy world says "Amen." The work is great and the time is short, but strength is not of man but of God.

In *Brother Scots* by Donald Carswell out of six Scotsmen whom he selects as representative men of their time, the author records how four felt the influence of Moody's personality and work: Henry Drummond, the professor in science; Keir Hardy, the Labor leader, who "when he was seventeen succumbed to the general influence (of Moody's mission) and became converted"; Lord Overtoun, the rich capitalist, who under "the guidance of that great American evangelist was brought out as a leader in evangelical Christianity in Scotland"; and Sir William Robertson Nicoll, the journalist who felt "the quickening which no preacher who knew his business would think of ignoring."

It was the same message which arrested the eager

attention of all. Nothing so testified to the genuineness of the character of the meetings as the obliteration of artificial barriers, not only ecclesiastical and social but even the natural distinctions of age and education.

The question is always asked how permanent the results of a mission are. It is significant then to note that forty years after this visit to Scotland an editorial appears in an Edinburgh evening paper referring to the lasting influence of the mission. The writer says:

> Moody set a torch to Scotland. Not only was Christian life revived, but all kinds of religious enterprise benefited by his work. Philanthropy took a new lease on life. The spirit of Chalmers reasserted itself. . . . Moody showed a new line of evangelism by pointing the way to a new Christianity in works as well as faith.

At the close of the Edinburgh mission there is a simple entry in Mrs. Moody's diary, "February 5, 1874. D. L. just thirty-seven years old."

CHAPTER XXV

THE evangelism of which Moody was an exponent worked from within outwards. He maintained that a man who comes into right relations with God will soon find that "old things pass away and all things become new." Profligacy and drunkenness give place to thrift and sobriety; cleanliness is a natural sequence to godliness.

Although Moody labored in behalf of the individual, he was also interested in society. His conception of the gospel was comprehensive and he was not indifferent to man's intellectual and physical needs. He placed first emphasis upon the spiritual values because he insisted that the most efficacious means of social reformation was through the individual. A distinguished scholar and teacher of divinity has expressed dissent with present tendencies in the statement, "In modern discussions on religion the tendency is to lose the individual in the sociological aspects of religion." Moody was ever actively sympathetic with every and any sane effort to mitigate squalor and vice. But he recognized that social evils had their origin in man himself. If the individual was rightly oriented, temptation itself became impotent and many so-called social evils disappeared. He often said, "Whitewashing the pump won't make the water pure. A heart that is right with God and man seldom constitutes a social problem and by seeking first the kingdom of God and His righteousness nine-tenths of social betterment is effected by the convert himself and the other tenth by Christian sympathy."

In a report which Moody made in 1867 he enunciated this principle even more emphatically:

> Opportunities have been afforded for reaching a large number of people with the gospel of peace, otherwise almost unapproachable, simply because its forerunners were bread, coal and clothing. The heart as naturally opens to such kindness as flowers to the sunshine; and when Christianity thus opens human hearts, its power with God and men is recognized and felt. To give is not the gospel. To work is not the gospel. To pray is not the gospel. To believe is not the gospel. But put these all together into an active life, and we have the gospel personified, and then there are added to the church daily such as are saved in this life, and in the life to come.
>
> It is a wonderful fact that men and women saved by the blood of Jesus rarely remain subjects of charity, but rise at once to comfort and respectability.

These principles found practical application from the very beginning of Moody's work, and they were maintained throughout life. Wherever he held missions he assisted local charities which aimed to alleviate misery and suffering.

In organizing relief work in Chicago his methods were sane and practicable. He maintained a wood yard and the genuineness of an applicant for work was soon tested for opportunity was immediately given to earn sufficient for urgent necessities. Often Moody would relate his experiences: "I kept a few cords of wood and some saws and saw-horses in the yard behind my office. When a man came with a pitiful tale of want I would offer him work. It was extraordinary what ingenuity was displayed in dodging my woodpile. Sometimes he wanted to go and tell his friends of his good fortune in finding employment, but I would never see him again. It took a long time before I had a cord of wood sawed."

A perusal of the files of Chicago newspapers fully confirms the statement that his interest was in behalf of all classes and every agency for social betterment. A proposal for the establishment of a State Reform School for Girls in Illinois is reported in the Chicago Tribune in 1864 which states that among those who support the movement is D. L. Moody who has evidently made a study of the subject and claims that the project "has the hearty coöperation of the chief cities in the state and of our representatives at Springfield."

Hardly a week passed in those early Chicago days but some brief notice appeared in the press of Moody's active service in behalf of some class of society. Now it is for those in jail; again it is for the lonely pioneer in the undeveloped Northwest; he has charge of furnishing and arranging a library in the new Y. M. C. A. building; he is elected a director of the Washingtonian Home.

It was estimated that twenty thousand men worked on the docks at Liverpool. They had to be in readiness though it could not be indicated exactly when they would be needed. This meant that there were often many hours of waiting in the piercingly cold mornings. No shelter was provided for them, and the only places to which they could go for warmth were the neighboring public houses and saloons. Some public-spirited men had realized that the situation demanded an effort on the part of Christians to provide resorts where shelter, warmth and good cheer might be found. At the close of a mission there Rev. Charles Garrett was invited to speak on the best method of dealing with the situation. His appeal was in behalf of the formation of a company to open a shelter for the workmen. Moody immediately supported the idea and asked for subscriptions, "If anyone wished to give a thousand pounds let him come up. Mr. Balfour, come forward and you must preface your remarks by giving a thousand pounds." Just then some one announced his readiness to give ten pounds but Mr. Moody was obdurate in not wishing to accept small donations until later. Then Mr. Lockhart contributed five hundred pounds, until in this manner the stock was entirely subscribed.

It was not enough to preach temperance, but it was incumbent upon the community so far as was in them really to remove temptation from the path of their fellow men. The success of that one movement is remarkable. In one week in November some years later, over one hundred seventy-five thousand customers were served and many of these, but for the coffee-houses, would have patronized the saloons. The capital stock was ten thousand pounds and the first branch was opened in August, 1875. Twenty-two years later the report of the Liverpool British Workmen's Public House Co., Ltd., stated that the capital was approximately fifty-five thousand pounds and that there were sixty-seven branches at work.

It was Moody's sympathy with those who suffered from social ills, from squalor and poverty, that accounted for his strong convictions in regard to the sale of liquor. He had witnessed misery, shame and suffering which drunkenness entails in every walk in life and he hated and feared alcohol from what he knew of its treachery and merciless tyranny. Thus it came about that he was the relentless foe of the manufacture and sale of all stimulants and from his earliest days in Christian work in Chicago to the end of his career he was ever ready to assist in every movement having as its objective the furthering of the temperance cause.

If Moody was an enemy of the saloon and the public house, and he most emphatically was, he was the friend of its victims. At the close of his Glasgow service he wrote to the *North British Daily* from Dublin on October

22, 1874, appealing to the Christian public in behalf of the city waifs of Glasgow:

> Rags are the emblem of the drunkard's child. . . . It is for these worse than orphaned children I venture now to plead. Were they really orphans they would be taken in and clothed, educated and fed. Meantime there are hundreds of budding lives anchored down to vice. . . . What is wanted is a home for these children of the streets. If it is to be done let it be done at once before the cold winds of the coming winter have pierced the thin little rags. . . . Let it be gone about in faith and I know there are many open purses as well as willing hands in Glasgow to respond. May God put it into some kind gracious heart to take up this mission in the Master's name.

Two days later a Mr. William Quarrier wrote to the same paper, referring to Moody's letter. He stated that he had already made his beginning but needed at once substantial help to enable him to render adequate service.

> We have been carrying on work on a limited scale during the past two years [he writes] and in that time we have been the means of helping some hundreds of poor girls and boys. . . . My estimate is that it will take three thousand pounds to build a place to carry on the work indicated above and if any kind friends see their way to send that sum I can promise that with God's help in a year hundreds of the class named in Mr. Moody's letter will be helped and blessed.

He continued to outline his plan advocating that

> the city authorities should be empowered to have stricter supervision of the children in the streets and prohibit them from selling, singing or begging. Any

hardships to the child or its dependent mother which might arise by the magistrates in this would be relieved, I am sure, by the Christian public. Why should not our magistrates have this power? It is a thing essential for the child's sake if not for the sake of the people who have to pay for the crimes which spring upon them from the wrong deeds of the child.

Again in two days another letter appears from the same Mr. Quarrier stating that he has received the needed three thousand pounds to start the work and that there is further need of twenty thousand pounds to erect, in a suitable rural community, cottage homes for the children.

After half a century it is impressive to note the magnitude to which this work has grown. Over two thousand needy children are given a home, and special departments are assigned to the care of consumptive and epileptic patients. The plant involves in buildings and equipment three hundred and fifty thousand pounds and the work is maintained at a daily cost of one hundred pounds.

Independent philanthropies also followed. Notable among these was a home for children of drunken and dissolute parents at Saltcoats. "In these Homes the children got a good plain education" under influence of a healthful atmosphere, the girls having elementary instruction in "home making" and the boys in lines that would fit them for useful occupations. "In this way hundreds of the poorest of the city's waifs got a good start in life, and while a majority of them went forward to lives of Christian respectability and usefulness in this country (Scotland) and Canada, some of them rose to positions of high honour and influence."

In a report of the Carruber's Close Mission in Edinburgh for the year 1898-99 it is stated that mainly through Moody's exertions the sum of eleven thousand pounds was raised, with which an excellent site facing High Street was acquired, and the present commodious building was erected upon it, and opened for use by Mr. Moody himself on March 4, 1884.

The Sunday Free Breakfasts in Edinburgh and Glasgow were another result of Moody's Scotch mission. For years a heterogeneous crowd has gathered in large buildings in these cities and has been served hot tea and rolls. After the breakfast there are gospel hymns and a brief talk. Through this agency alone many men have been reached by the gospel and helped to lives of industry and self-respect.

Perhaps one of the greatest achievements in Edinburgh was the Gaiety Club. During the mission a group of young men who had worked in the inquiry room or conducted meetings among their fellow students were drawn into a close intimacy. Leadership in this group was naturally accorded to Henry Drummond, upon whose initiative the Gaiety Music Hall was engaged for Sunday nights in the season of 1875-76. The audiences were largely of university students and young business men. Participants in the work were some who were to become well known in later years, notably Professor James Stalker, Provost Swan, Rev. John Watson (Ian Maclaren) and Sir George Adam Smith.

Many other instances could be cited of varied forms of philanthropy which had their origins in missions which Moody conducted in Great Britain and America or which derived their impetus from the influence of his work. Numerous mission halls in Great Britain, which bring to drab and colorless lives the one opportunity for sane and healthful social life with their women's clubs and sewing circles and occasional socials, date from the London mission of 1884. Numerous Y. M. C. A. buildings and institutions for practical training in Christian service are living monuments to Moody's labors.

Surely this is an answer to the criticism that the evangelism of the previous generation did not take cognizance of the implications of the so-called Social Gospel. The charge is made that the future welfare of the soul eclipsed the present needs; that want and suffering were viewed with indifference; that efforts for social betterment and for eradication of the causes of vice were overlooked. The critics would imply that solicitude for soul salvation obscured, in the minds of these older evangelists, the sense of social responsibility for health of mind and body; that tracts and testaments made a poor substitute for food and clothing for cold and starving humanity.

What Morley says of Gladstone is equally true of Moody, "All his activities were in his own mind one. . . . It was religious motives, through a thousand avenues and channels, steered him and guided him in his whole conception of active social duty."

CHAPTER XXVI

In January, 1874, Moody accepted an invitation to visit the city of Glasgow. Two weeks intervened between the close of the Edinburgh mission and the inauguration of work in Glasgow. He might have seized this opportunity for a brief respite from his work but instead, characteristically, he accepted three other invitations, visiting Berwick-on-Tweed, Melrose and Dundee. In each place his work was intensive; he spoke frequently—five times in one day at Berwick-on-Tweed; in Dundee he started a work which he would not complete until his return five months later.

On reaching Glasgow on February 7 to begin the mission on the following day Moody found that thorough preparation had been made. Meetings had been conducted uninterruptedly since he had accepted the invitation. At nine o'clock Sunday morning a stirring meeting of Sabbath school teachers was held in the City Hall, attended by about three thousand. The evangelistic service was held at half-past six, but more than an hour before that time the City Hall was crowded, and the great multitude outside were drafted off to the three nearest churches, which were soon filled. The next day a prayer meeting began in the morning in the United Presbyterian Church.

At the very beginning the work seemed in interest and evident results but a continuation of the mission in Edinburgh. Here, as elsewhere, he had the sympathetic coöperation of the clergy. This Moody recognized, for in his opening address to the Sunday school teachers he intimated that he had met with them first "because he knew that no class would welcome him more heartily, with the single exception of the ministers, and that it would be presumption in him to lecture them."

For three months meetings were held with apparently undiminished interest. Reference to contemporary reports gives an impression of the general awakening throughout the city and surrounding towns as well. From such centers as Greenock and Paisley and towns on the Clyde visitors attended the services in large numbers.

A notable part of the Glasgow mission was the interest awakened among young men. One particular meeting was memorable and became known as the "One Hundred and One Night" from the fact that one hundred and one young men professed their allegiance to Christ for the first time on that occasion.

> It took place in Ewing Place Congregational Church which was filled with young men [says Sir George Adam Smith]. Mr. Moody had sent to Edinburgh for a deputation of students and Stewart, Miller, Gordon, Brown, Henry (Drummond) and I went. Mr. Moody did not speak at all himself; but Dr. Cairns of Berwick, delivered a powerful address on Immortality; then the students spoke one after another; and Dr. J. H. Wilson wound up. As the meeting proceeded, the spiritual power was such as I have never experienced on any other occasion; and when Mr. Moody, at the close, ordered the front seats to be cleared, and invited those who wished to be prayed for to occupy the vacant pews, a hundred and one came forward. As the evangelist pleaded and that solemn stream began to gather from every corner of the church, the sense of Divine power became overwhelming, and I remember quite well turning round on the platform and hiding my face in my hands, unable to look on the scene any more.

Yet all was perfectly quiet, and the hundred and one were men of intelligence and character, who were not carried away with excitement, but moved by the force of conviction. I did not remember anything remarkable in Henry's speaking that night; the address which told most was, I think, that of Frank Gordon, whose speaking was characterized by a wonderful pathos and passion. When we six went back to the hotel, we sat very late discussing the remarkable scene we had just witnessed. Some one started the question whether it is usual to remember the date and incidents of one's own conversion. At such a moment it is easy to be confidential, and it turned out that we were equally divided, three remembering the circumstances in which their spiritual life began, and three not. Henry was, I think, among the latter. Each of us possesses an interleaved Testament, beautifully bound in morocco, as a memorial of that night; and each book contains the signature and mottoes of all six. These Testaments were Henry's idea, and he presented them to the rest. His own copy went with him through his subsequent evangelistic wanderings, and was worn to rags.

Writing more than fifty years later Mr. William M. Oats, also in attendance on this service, records his vivid impressions. The after results he reports, in part, from his personal observations:

> That night was known in Glasgow as the "one hundred and one night." Did these young fellows stand? Did the decision mean reality? The writer was present that evening, and has since kept trace as far as that is possible. The first to come to the front pews was Henry Downie; he served God in the city for fifty years, passing away only a year ago, and bore a fine testimony.

Twenty-five years ago, the writer was walking along a street in Adelaide, South Australia, when he was accosted by an architect in that city, who said, "I was one of the one hundred and one in Glasgow."

Crossing to Tasmania, a leading Christian worker introduced himself as "one of the one hundred and one." In one of the busy centres of London, there is today a missionary at work, who was brought to the Lord at that time.

From that notable night, right on for three months, a young men's meeting went on, and thousands were led to trust the Saviour.

Shortly after Moody left Glasgow, these young men were formed into the Young Men's Christian Union, which later was united to the Y. M. C. A. When summer came a large tent was pitched upon Glasgow Green, a central public park, and this band of young men conducted meetings nightly. Many of the slum dwellers were reached, and the workers bethought themselves of a "breakfast" on Sunday mornings for those who had been sleeping out. The first Sunday when the young fellows went out with their invitation, they were received with suspicion. Some smiled, some cursed, but some accepted and came. When it became known that there were actually sandwiches to be had, and hot tea, the numbers increased until there was a company of two thousand. A report of the work reads:

> That "Free Breakfast" has continued for fifty-one years, and is to-day as great a blessing as when it was first begun. A great work has developed, a large hall now accommodates the crowds and hundreds of the very worst characters in the city have been changed into new creatures in Christ Jesus.

In every form of aggressive work in the city, the young men were prominent. The stamp of Mr.

Moody seemed upon them, and much of his ingenuity and forcefulness. And as young men go into all parts of the world, for trade and commerce, as well as for Missionary service, every land has benefited by that wonderful evangelistic mission in Glasgow in 1874.

According to the historian Buckle, the Scotch have always been great "sermon tasters." He speaks of services when one man would preach for five or even six hours. "On great occasions," he states, "several clergymen were present in the same church in order that when one was fatigued, he might leave the pulpit and be succeeded by another, who in his turn was followed by a third; the patience of the hearers being apparently inexhaustible." This referred to the seventeenth century, but there still lingered in the Scotch great powers of endurance on the part of both minister and the audience. Scotland, therefore, took readily to the idea of an all-day conference with a succession of meetings. It was an innovation and yet found a certain precedence in the time of the Covenanters.

Moody himself used to relate an amusing experience he had during a visit to the Highlands. One Sunday morning he made an address of the usual length, thirty-five to forty minutes. On resuming his seat the minister, greatly agitated, whispered, "You're not through, are you?" to which Moody replied that he had concluded his address. Scandalized at anyone preaching so short a sermon in his pulpit the old pastor exclaimed, "Tut, tut, man! What apology shall I make to the audience?"

It is not surprising, therefore, that the mission in Glasgow was concluded with nine convocations held during six days in the Crystal Palace. Admission was by ticket.

It was a novel general assembly, with representatives of almost every class of society and every

Protestant church in the land [says one observer]. It may be safely said that no other cause of interest whatever has so often drawn together so many thousands in Glasgow. Three months daily use had not worn off the edge of freshness or spiritual attraction.

Dr. John Cairns was credited with saying that it was "unparalleled in the history of Scottish, perhaps of British Christianity."

CHAPTER XXVII

THERE is almost a sense of weariness in following Moody during his first year in Great Britain. From the time of landing in Liverpool he had no cessation from arduous and continuous work and his physical endurance became an object of wonder. Even his companions from time to time had to find respite, but Moody renewed his strength daily. This was due to the fact that he did not worry. With implicit and childlike faith throughout life, having done all he could, he cast his burden upon the Lord. A second resource was to be found in his ability to sleep soundly. It was undoubtedly a real gift which enabled him, in the midst of labors, to snatch a brief nap from which he would wake thoroughly refreshed. Often only a short time before addressing a large throng he would throw himself down on a couch or settle back in a chair and, glancing at his watch, ask a friend to awaken him in ten minutes, the very time that it would be necessary to start for a service. In railway journeys, even in carriages, he could find reinvigoration.

But it is not so much the physical resources which impress one in following these indefatigable labors as it is the spirit in which he works under such widely differing conditions. As the days passed he became increasingly conscious of what he could do as well as what he could not do. His judgment had so often been vindicated that he felt justified in following it even in the face of the advice of others. A friend records:

> Every few minutes he meets a new set of people to work with, and at their head, men who them-

selves are accustomed to lead, and therefore the less suited to follow; and yet he succeeds in overcoming all these difficulties, and reigning by consent of all. Of course he had troubles and difficulties, but he seemed never to meet an insuperable one. Somehow it could be got over. At one place, the committee were not willing to give in to his ways, and there was a talk of their retiring when he said, "Gentlemen, let us understand one another. It is not a question of your retiring or not; you asked me to come here, but if we cannot get on, I am the one to retire, not you." This soon settled the matter.

Entries in Mrs. Moody's diary are infrequent and chiefly valuable for determining the dates of certain missions. The following items leave much to be desired but they indicate Moody's activity.

> May 21st D. L. preached out doors at Arthur's Seat to an audience of ten thousand. May 22nd D. L. went to Kilmarneck. . . . D. L. is to go within a week to Ayr, Stirling, etc. May 30 D. L. went to Perth. June 1st went to Perth and met D. L. June 9 went to Dundee to our friend Mrs. Mackies. D. L. preached out doors. June 13 came to Aberdeen. July 5 D. L. preached in Blairgowrie, *good* meetings, July 17 came to Inverness, D. L. preached in the evening.

As the summer wore on Moody's energies were unremitting and he visited Elgin, Nairn, Grantown, Keth, Banff, Craig Castle, Wick and Thurso. Once Mrs. Moody records, "D. L. rather tired." On Sunday "August 2nd D. L. preached at 9 A.M. at 11 A.M., enquiry meeting at 3 P.M. and at 7 P.M. out doors. Large crowds of people in Banff from the country to attend the meetings."

These entries record only the dates, but from religious

journals of the time and the witness of observers the story is related which to the reader would be a repetitious monotony of crowded churches, outdoor services and filled inquiry rooms. Though speaking with such frequency Moody's labors were not perfunctory, for the power of his message was in large part due to his sincerity and earnestness.

During these days of strenuous labors Moody had little time to devote to a steadily increasing correspondence. Letters of all descriptions poured in upon him from every direction, many pitifully revealing tragedies of domestic life, confessions of past guilt, or such problems as are met with in every pastorate. These called for counsel, compassion, possibly tactful admonition, and could be entrusted to only wise and sympathetic co-laborers. These Moody found first in Mrs. Moody and later in Henry Drummond. No less remarkable than Moody's endurance was Mrs. Moody's capacity to supplement his work by assuming the heavy responsibility of his correspondence.

In his missions at this time he was accompanied by a group of friends who had assisted local workers in inquiry rooms or conducted overflow meetings and special services. From Craig Castle to Aberdeen the party included "Mr. Drummond of Stirling." Further entries in Mrs. Moody's diary indicated the itinerary during the remainder of the summer of 1874 which included Goldspie, Strathpeffer, Oban, Campbeltown, Dingwall, Blairgowrie and Rothsay.

CHAPTER XXVIII

In September Moody left Scotland for Ireland where he was received cordially. In Belfast an attendance of "from ten to twenty thousand" is reported at the out-door meetings and a unique inquiry meeting lasted from two to ten P.M. Rev. E. J. Goodspeed writes, "It is worthy of remark, the great contrast in outward manifestation between the present work and that of 1859. I have not heard of or noticed any physical excitement—not even an outcry, much less what were known as 'prostrations.'"

In fact, once while Moody was preaching some one in the audience was deeply impressed and cried out and fell down apparently in a cataleptic condition. There were exclamations from every side and a tenseness in the very atmosphere. Some earnest souls rejoiced that "the days of '59 have returned." But Moody ceased speaking, pronounced the benediction, and dismissed the audience. To some who looked for a "sign" this was slighting the Holy Spirit, and it was felt that his work could no longer be owned of God. But in the light of subsequent experience it was this very intolerance of anything that verged upon hysteria or excessive display of feelings that commended Moody and his work to thoughtful men and women.

Fifty years later under date of September 6, 1924, the *Northern Whig* and *Belfast Post* remind their readers of Moody's mission.

> It is interesting to recall that Messrs. Moody and Sankey began their first evangelistic campaign in Belfast on the first Sunday in September, 1874. The

older generation will recall that the first prayer meeting was held in Donegall Square Church, and the forenoon service in Fisherwick Place Church. Meetings went on in other centres throughout the entire day. The sacred edifices were all crowded, and many hundreds were unable to obtain admission to any of the services.

Dublin was no less cordial to Moody than Ulster. Priests and many of the Roman Catholic faith, whom he never attacked, attended his mission. In a news item in the *British Weekly*, written twenty-four years later, the Dublin mission is thus referred to:

> In Ireland he enjoyed quite as phenomenal a success as anywhere else. Indeed, his audiences in Dublin in 1874 were, I think, the largest he addressed in the three kingdoms, for the Exhibition Building, where the meetings were held, accommodated about twenty thousand people; and a sight of the vast audience from the angle of the two immense transepts, whence Mr. Moody spoke, reminded one of nothing so much as the day of Pentecost. It was this which made Moody mighty. His plain, blunt speech, his intensity, his fervour, his homely wit, his melting pathos, his shrewdness which amounted to genius, his superb and kingly leadership, had won universal admiration, but it was the subtle, sacred thing which they called "unction" that gave saving power to his ministry. They might not possess the towering gifts of this massive and majestic man, but they might all possess the gift of the Holy Ghost.

To such an extent had Moody won the heart of Dublin that in the theaters an effort to burlesque the meetings was promptly met with marked disfavor. During a pantomime at one of the Dublin theaters a clown entered and said, "I feel rather Moody." His companion rejoined, "I feel rather Sankeymonious." Upon this the gallery hissed them, and then, not content with a negative form of expressing respect, some one started "Hold the Fort, for I Am Coming," and, according to an English journal, the whole assembly in the higher story joined in the chorus, and the curtain fell until the hymn was concluded.

Roman Catholic journals were sympathetic in attitude. The *Nation* of ultramontane principles published an editorial significant for its tolerance. It is entitled "Fair Play" and reads:

> The deadly danger of the age comes upon us from the direction of Huxley, and Darwin, and Tyndall, rather than from Moody and Sankey. Irish Catholics desire to see Protestants deeply imbued with religious feeling, rather than tinged with rationalism and infidelity; and as long as the religious services of our Protestant neighbors are honestly directed to quickening religious thought in their own body, without offering aggressive or intentional insult to us, it is our duty to pay the homage of our respect to their conscientious convictions; in a word, to *do as we would be done by*. It would surely be a bright and blessed day for our country, if this spirit of mutual respect and toleration were everywhere honestly acted out amongst us. Mr. Moody never makes controversial reference to others. His success in attracting the favorable attention of our brethren of a different faith has been unexampled in the history of our city.

The *London Times* correspondent writes of the Dublin meetings:

> The most remarkable ever witnessed in Ireland. . . . This new mission has been of a character essen-

tially different and seemed to possess elements of vitality which were wanting in others. There was nothing sensational though much was novel and attractive, in the nature of the services and the mode of conducting them. . . . How, then, is his marvelous success to be explained? His great earnestness is perhaps the secret of it. His heart as well as his head seems to be full of his subject and he has no difficulty in giving effective expression to his thought.

A special correspondent in the *Daily News* reports:

> Like Bunyan, he has the great gift of being able to realize things unseen, and to describe his vision in familiar language to those whom he addresses. . . . He filled the lay figures with life, clothed them with garments, and then made them talk to each other in the English language as it is today accented in some of the American states. . . . When he was picturing the scene of Daniel translating the king's dream he rapidly repeated Daniel's account of the dream and Nebuchadnezzar's quick and delighted ejaculation, "That's so! That's it!" as he recognized the incidents. I fancy it was not without difficulty some of the people, bending forward and listening with glistening eye and heightened color, refrained from clapping their hands with glee that the youthful Daniel, the unyielding servant of God, had triumphed over tribulation, and walked out of prison to take his place on the right hand of the king.

Mr. George A. Sanford relates an incident illustrating the warmth of esteem in which Moody's memory was held in Ireland many years after:

> I happened to be traveling that summer and, as is my custom, reported at the local Y. M. C. A. to find out a desirable place to put up during my stay in Dublin. As is always the case every courtesy was

extended to me and I was informed of a nice home in the immediate vicinity where lodgers were sometimes received. Willing Y. M. C. A. members insisted on carrying my baggage and on piloting me to the house. The wife of the gentleman said they were no longer taking lodgers but on ascertaining that I was an American they received me. After a stay of about a week I asked for my bill and was surprised to be informed that there was no bill. Thinking that perhaps I was not understood I said that I meant my bill for lodging and food. Then I was informed that there was just one way in which those items could be paid, namely, by staying another week. At once I saw the drift which matters were taking and insisted to the utmost on settling my account. In reply the lady said, "A few years ago our home was the home of a drunkard and you know what that means. Through the influence of one of your Americans, Mr. D. L. Moody, my husband was converted and my home is now a Christian home. It is very little that we can do to show our appreciation; but hospitality is one of the few things we can do and we hope you will not take that pleasure away from us." Of course on my arrival in New York I sent back a token of my appreciation and a few weeks later while at Northfield had the pleasure of running across Mr. Moody as he was driving down the street on which the East Northfield Post Office is located and near to his own corner got his attention for a few minutes. I can see him now as he was sitting in his buckboard wagon. I told him the story of Mrs. K. and the home in Dublin where I had been so welcomed and that the reason was himself. That was in 1899, the last year he attended the conference. I can never forget how pleased he was by the little incident.

CHAPTER XXIX

AMERICA is essentially sectional. There is no central nerve ganglion such as European countries find in their capitals whence impulses reach all parts of the land. London is England, and Paris is France in a peculiar sense; but an event which is of unusual local interest in Philadelphia or Boston may not be deemed worthy of record in the daily press in other cities of the United States. In the United Kingdom, however, stimuli in any center immediately is registered in London and at once becomes of national interest.

The Edinburgh meetings projected Moody's figure prominently before the public. The notices accorded the work by the local press attracted attention not only in Scotland but throughout the kingdom. The confidence Moody enjoyed in the esteem of Scotchmen of national reputation, not only among clergymen but also among professional and business men, assured him a wide sympathy and coöperation.

After Dublin, missions in Manchester, Sheffield, Birmingham and Liverpool occupied the months of December, January and February. In each new place the interest already awakened elsewhere had prepared the way for a favorable beginning; for sixteen months the public had been hearing of the throngs attending the services in the north of England, in Scotland, and in Ireland.

Manchester was peculiarly a new field because it was a great industrial center. The mission began, as had already become the custom with Moody, at an eight o'clock service on Sunday morning, primarily for Christian workers. It was his purpose always to seek to prepare the Christians themselves in any mission, realizing that success was dependent not upon the visitors, but upon the real coöperation of all Christians.

In Manchester Moody evinced his interest in the Y. M. C. A. and in one of the last meetings held there its cause was presented and the need of providing a suitable building. Moody made an urgent appeal for funds and with the help of friends ultimately secured thirty thousand pounds, the full amount needed for the building and equipment.

Fifty years after these meetings the *Manchester Guardian,* under date of July 20, 1923, prints an appreciation of the permanent value of the mission and quotes the words of Dr. Philip Shaff, the well-known ecclesiastical historian:

> As the Methodist Revival more than a hundred years ago stopped the progress of deism, so these plain men from America turned the tide of modern atheism. . . . He was not what is called an educated man; yet as we have said, he captured the churches with the best educated ministry in the world. And he did it, because he never indulged in those cheap sneers against a college bred ministry in which evangelists have so often been guilty, because he never posed as an authority on debatable subjects about which he knew nothing. If he had talked as though no man was serving the church of Christ who was not serving it in his way, he would have blocked his own path at the outset; Scotland would have turned a deaf ear to him.

In Sheffield, another industrial center, Moody's experiences were similar to those recorded elsewhere.

> The merits and demerits of the American evangelists are keenly discussed by excited groups at the

corners of streets [writes the *Daily Review*], and the opponents of the movement attribute its success to vulgar curiosity, sensational advertising, and press exaggeration. Meanwhile the meetings in connection with the movement are on the increase. The city has the reputation of being hard to arouse, its citizens being sturdy, independent, unimpressionable; like the metal in which we work in these parts, true but hard as steel.

But Moody crowded the churches and assembly halls and left a lasting impression on the city.

In Birmingham Moody enjoyed the coöperation of one of the most influential personalities in England, Dr. R. W. Dale. He recorded his first opinions of Moody's power.

At the first meeting, Mr. Moody's address was simple, direct, kindly, and hopeful; it had a touch of humour and a touch of pathos; it was lit up with a story or two that filled most eyes with tears; but there seemed nothing in it very remarkable. Yet it *told*. A prayer meeting with an address, at eight o'clock on a damp cold January morning, was hardly the kind of thing—let me say it frankly—that I should generally regard as attractive; but I enjoyed it heartily; it seemed one of the happiest meetings I had ever attended; there was warmth and there was sunlight in it. At the evening meeting the same day, at Bingley Hall, I was still unable to make it out how it was that he had done so much in other parts of the kingdom. I listened with interest; everybody listened with interest; and I was conscious again of a certain warmth and brightness which made the service very pleasant, but I could not see that there was much to impress those that were careless about religious duty. The next morning at the prayer meeting the address was more incisive and striking, and at the evening service I began to see that the stranger had a faculty for making the elementary truths of the Gospel intensely clear and vivid. But it still seemed most remarkable that he should have done so much and on Tuesday I told Mr. Moody that the work was most plainly of God, for I could see no real relation between him and what he had done. He laughed cheerily and said he should be very sorry if it were otherwise.

I had seen occasional instances before of instant transition from religious anxiety to the clear and triumphant consciousness of restoration to God; but what struck me in the gallery of Bingley Hall was the fact that this instant transition took place with nearly every person with whom I had talked. They had come up into the gallery anxious, restless, feeling after God in the darkness, and when, after a conversation of a quarter of an hour or twenty minutes, they went away, their faces were filled with light, and they left me not only at peace with God but filled with joy. I have seen the sunrise from the top of Helvellyn and the top of the Righi, and there is something very glorious in it; but to see the light of heaven suddenly strike on man after man in the course of one evening is very much more thrilling. These people carried their new joy with them to their homes and their workshops. It could not be hid.

Dale's biographer continued:

Dale flung himself into the work, and his open admiration of Mr. Moody amazed many of those who thought they knew him well. It was an offence to some, a problem to others. During the mission Mr.

Bright came down to address his constituents, and Mr. Moody, with characteristic common sense, insisted that Bingley Hall—the only building that could hold the crowds who wished to hear their great representative—should be placed for the evening at Mr. Bright's disposal, and that he should not be prevented from discharging a public duty. Some who listened to Dale that night as he enforced Mr. Bright's plea for church disestablishment, and who heard him in the same week helping Mr. Moody on the same platform, or saw him at work in the enquirer's gallery, found it hard to understand how he could thus blend political and religious enthusiasm. That political interest should be supreme at one time, and religious interest at another would have been intelligible; but how both could coexist, each inflaming and intensifying the other—this was an insoluble enigma. The paradox of his life, one might say, in this instance was focussed at a point.

At Liverpool a temporary structure was erected with a seating capacity of ten thousand and to a larger extent than heretofore, Moody enlisted the coöperation of ministers of the Anglican church.

An incident occurred here which left a deep impression on him. It seemed a supernatural intervention and for that reason he never referred to it in public; only on few occasions did he ever relate the experience and then only to his most intimate friends. During the Civil War in America, sympathy with the cause of the South had been predominant in Liverpool, due largely to the close association through the cotton interests. Because of this the press in Liverpool had been outspoken in its criticism of the mission. At this time Moody was alone, his family being with friends in the country. Naturally a fearless man, he could not account for a peculiar sense of dread which came upon him suddenly. If anyone approached him rapidly from behind he would draw aside to let him pass or would cross the road. On returning to his hotel after service, he locked his door, looked under his bed and examined his closet. This continued for several days until his anxiety about himself was greatly aroused. He questioned if the strain of continuous work for more than a year might possibly have affected his mind. He told no one of the cloud under which he was working.

At the close of a service one day he was detained by his committee, who formed a circle about him. They engaged in conversation which to Moody seemed trifling and unusual. Surely they knew that he was tired and anxious to get rest. After a little while an officer of the police force came up and, touching his cap, reported that they "had the man." It was then explained to Moody that for a week the police had been trying to locate a maniac who had escaped from a local asylum. He had divulged to somebody that he felt himself commissioned by the Almighty to assassinate the Yankee preacher and he had been seeking an opportunity to achieve his end. Unwittingly Moody had protected himself.

CHAPTER XXX

Moody gave prominence to singing in his missions because he believed that it prepared his hearers for the sermon by creating a receptive frame of mind. Furthermore, he regarded the use of hymns as an invaluable medium by which the gospel message might be conveyed to those on whom the spoken word had no effect. He was always insistent that every one take part in the song service. This was remarked on by many especially as it became known that Moody himself was not musical and was even tone deaf so that he could hardly recognize an air.

In Sunderland there had been a demand for the songs which had been popular. But the hymns had been gathered from many sources and since some had never been published, there was no book to be recommended. *Hallowed Hymns,* a book previously introduced by an American visitor, had lost its demand when the visitor had departed, and a large number were unsold in the hands of the English publishers. At first this book was used in the meetings, but there were a few solos not included.

As the demand for the popular solos increased Moody was anxious to have a small supplement added to this book. He laid the plan before the publishers but they were loath to incur any further expense, fearing they would simply add to the loss already sustained. The man with whom Moody conferred stated that the firm already had all it wanted of "those damn Yankee songs."

Shocked at this rebuff, Moody turned to Messrs. Morgan and Scott and asked them if they would undertake the publication of a book to be known as *Sacred Songs and Solos*. They too were unwilling to risk a possible loss. Then Moody asked Mr. Sankey to share with him a guarantee against any loss to the publishers. But Sankey too was not convinced that such a venture would be safe and declined to assume any responsibility.

Moody returned to Messrs. Morgan and Scott and guaranteed personally to a sum not to exceed sixteen hundred dollars any loss incurred. This guarantee was the total amount of Moody's sayings; he offered it with the knowledge and concurrence of Mrs. Moody who had faith in her husband's judgment.

The first advertisement of *Sacred Songs and Solos* appeared in the *London Christian* on September 18, 1873, only three months after Moody began his mission in Great Britain. The venture met with immediate success; two more editions were published in the next two months.

At the close of the English mission the sale of these books had been so large that the royalties alone exceeded five thousand pounds. To the surprise of the publishers, however, Moody positively declined to accept any part of this. He seemed to fear the possession of material things. His decisions were made in relation to what would help or hinder "the work" by which term he always alluded to his mission in life. The absolute rights or wrongs of a thing in itself was not enough for him. It had to be considered in its relation as an influence upon his calling. It was represented to him that, inasmuch as he had made a guarantee personally against loss, the royalties were due him; but he could not be dissuaded from his decision. He suggested, however, that the sum be made over to the London committee in charge of the meetings. It had incurred great expense by hiring halls and advertising. But the committee had already met its expenses and was not willing to accept any such financial aid from Moody.

Mr. Farwell of Chicago was in London and heard of the embarrassment encountered in disposing of the sum. He suggested it be used to rebuild the Chicago church which Moody had established at Chicago Avenue and La Salle Street and had been destroyed by the "Great Fire" three years before. Farwell's suggestion was accepted, and the Chicago Avenue Church was rebuilt by funds accruing from royalties upon the English edition of *Sacred Songs and Solos* used in missions conducted by Moody in Great Britain from 1873-75.

The existence of copyrights owned by different authors and publishers prevented Moody from using *Sacred Songs and Solos* when he returned to America in 1875. He therefore, in collaboration with friends and publishers, issued a new book called *Gospel Hymns*. This book at once became popular, and large numbers were sold during the missions held in Philadelphia, Chicago and Boston. Mr. Bliss, Mr. Sankey, Mr. McGranahan, Mr. Stebbins and others continued writing new hymns as Moody's work went on and "Gospel Hymn" No. 1 was followed by Nos. 2, 3, 4, 5, and 6.

Again the question of royalties arose. As in England, Moody insisted that none should come to Mr. Sankey or himself. He would never permit anyone to say that he or his associate derived any pecuniary advantage from the sale of books used in the meetings. The cause to which he had devoted his life was the one thought uppermost in his mind.

It was arranged, therefore, that all royalties from the sale of the American books were to become a trust fund to be used in Christian service, and three prominent Christian business men consented to act as trustees and almoners of the money, Messrs. William E. Dodge of

New York, George Stuart of Philadelphia and John V. Farwell of Chicago.

Mr. Dodge, who acted as chairman of the trustees, has made the following statement:

> Mr. Moody was greatly pained when in Great Britain, to find that those who were opposed to the new religious life had circulated reports that large sums of money were made from royalties on the hymn book, and that the meetings were really carried on for the purpose of selling it, thus increasing the income of those conducting them. On his return to America, and before visiting the great cities of the country, he felt the need of a book of hymns and tunes adapted to his use here, and determined to arrange its publication so as to avoid all possible criticism.
>
> He invited me to visit Northfield to confer with him on the subject, which he felt to be of great importance. I met there Mr. Sankey and Mr. Bliss, and found a most delightful and unusual spirit of Christian self-sacrifice on their part. They were willing to contribute their own hymns and tunes, and the copyrights which they held. They joined with Mr. Moody in giving up all possible claim to any benefits which might arise from their publication.
>
> Mr. Moody urged me to act as trustee, to arrange with the publishers for a royalty and to receive any money which might come from this source and distribute it at my discretion for religious and benevolent purposes. I declined to act alone, but promised Mr. Moody that if two other gentlemen were selected I would gladly serve with them, and suggested the names of George H. Stuart of Philadelphia, and John V. Farwell of Chicago; a board of trustees was thus formed.

The sale of the first editions of the books greatly exceeded our expectations, and, although the royalty was, on a single copy, small, as trustees we received up to September, 1885, the large sum of $357,388.64. All of this was carefully distributed among various religious and educational institutions. It was finally determined to be wise and right that as the schools at Northfield had become so firmly established, and were doing such great good, the entire royalties of these books should be turned over to the trustees of these schools, and this was accordingly done under careful legal advice.

During all these years neither Mr. Moody nor Mr. Sankey had any fixed income. Mr. Sankey especially had given up copyrights that would have brought him in a large sum yearly, and opportunities to hold musical institutes and conventions which would have added largely to his income. Neither of them during the whole continuance of the trust received one dollar of personal advantage, and as they had no definite means of support the self-sacrifice and the unselfishness of this course, in order to prevent the slightest breath of scandal and not weaken the influence of their personal work, were very remarkable and very beautiful. I have never known anything like it.

In closing the trust, which was a peculiar one, after getting full legal advice, I submitted the opinions to a lawyer of very high national reputation—the leader of the bar in New York in all matters of consultation. He was greatly interested in the form of the trust, though he had but little sympathy with the religious work. He gave a large amount of time and thought to the matter, and after giving his opinion I asked him to be kind enough to send me a memorandum, so that I could personally send him a cheque, which I supposed would necessarily be a large one. He told me that under no possible circumstances would he accept a cent; that the unselfishness and splendid quality of men who could make such a sacrifice was a revelation of human nature that made him feel better disposed toward mankind.

I have ventured to go into this matter somewhat at length, because while Mr. Moody and Mr. Sankey have not received a cent of personal benefit from the royalties on the hymn books, unkind and ignorant assertions have been made to the contrary in some quarters.

Years later Mr. Edmund Coffin, a New York lawyer, wrote to add his testimony to that of Mr. Dodge:

> I have glanced at the pages about the hymn books and am glad to find the words of Mr. Dodge which in many things revive my memory, especially as to the advice given by eminent counsel to the trustees. That counsel was Mr. Southmayde, partner of Senator Evarts and the late Mr. Joseph Choate. I remember very well that he was selected for advice, not only because of his legal prominence, but also because of his known antipathy to all evangelistic matters. I was directed to consult him and when I called and mentioned the names of your father and Mr. Sankey he called them all sorts of bad names and stated that they were making large money out of their meetings. When I explained the facts and that I wanted to consult him as to that very matter, he would hardly believe me; but I persuaded him to look over the papers. He sent for me later, and said he would withdraw the charge that they were rascals, but would say, instead, that they were d—d fools to let such money slip through their hands. I

am glad to know from Mr. Dodge's report that Mr. Southmayde may have used more complimentary language to him. I remember that he told me he would be ashamed to ask any fee for his advice in the consultation I had with him in such a matter.

The collection of simple airs made a phenomenal appeal to the Christian public throughout the English speaking world. They possessed sufficient variety to appeal to all classes. In 1926 T. R. Glover of Cambridge University, England, a classical scholar, but one probably even more popularly known as a student of the Bible, writes his impression of that old collection of hymns in the London *Daily News,* after half a century:

> Most of us grow more conscious that we need guidance, and many of us that we need forgiveness. Here it is that my old hymn book comes in, with more hope and assurance than some collections can give me. In homely language that one cannot mistake, it speaks of sin, of man's need of forgiveness and salvation, and of God's provision in Christ for all man's need. Must you tell me that Moody and Sankey and the Salvation Army teach a great deal that I do not believe? Perhaps so; but I offer an obvious suggestion as to that. If my doctor will cure my rheumatism, I will forgive him saying "The Taming of the Shrew" is as good as "As You Like It." Deplorable as that judgment seems to me, there are moments in the life of the rheumatic when he thinks of something else. If a man can show me the path of deliverance from sin, his decision that the Chronicles and the Gospels are equally inspired, is to me a thing of secondary interest. There is such a thing as proportion in ideas, and I think Moody and Sankey put the main emphasis on the main ideas, and some good friends of mine do not.

It is strange that one who was in no sense musical could compile a popular hymn book. Yet even as far back as 1868 Moody had demonstrated his ability to judge what the people would sing, for in that year, in Chicago, he published a collection of popular sacred songs "adapted to church, Sunday school and revival services" known as the *North-Western Hymn Book*.

Therefore in the book compiled in England in 1873 Moody was not without experience. Many of the songs were of little permanent value. They served their day and "fell in sleep." Many Moody himself outgrew. "We have been singing 'Hold the Fort' too long," he would say. "It is not a question of keeping a stronghold, but of aggressive warfare." This song had been written shortly after the close of the Civil War; Major D. W. Whittle thus relates the occasion from which it took its origin:

> During October, 1864, just before Sherman began his famous march to the sea, while his army lay camped in the neighborhood of Atlanta, the army of Hood in a carefully prepared movement passed the right flank of Sherman's army and gained his rear, commenced the destruction of the railroad leading north, burning blockhouses and capturing the small garrisons along the line. Sherman's army was put in rapid motion, following Hood, to save the supplies and larger posts, the principal of which was located at Altoona Pass, a defile in the Altoona range of mountains, through which ran the railroad. General Corse of Illinois was stationed here with a brigade of troops, composed of Minnesota and Illinois regiments, in all about sixteen hundred men, Colonel Tourtelotte being second in command. A million and a half of rations were stored here, and it was highly important that the earthworks commanding

the supplies should be held. Six thousand men, under command of General French, were detailed by Hood to take the position. The works were completely surrounded and summoned to surrender. Corse refused, and sharp fighting commenced. The defenders were slowly driven into a small fort upon the crest of the hill. Many had fallen, and the result seemed to render a prolongation of the fight hopeless. At this moment, an officer caught sight of a white signal flag, far away across the valley, twenty miles distant, upon the top of Kenesaw Mountain. The signal was answered by the commander of the Federal troops and soon the message was waved across from mountain to mountain: "Hold the Fort; I Am Coming."

Other songs were associated with some passing phase of social life. At an Industrial Exposition held in Chicago, a common rendezvous, was a large central fountain and "Meet Me at the Fountain" was frequently heard. This phrase suggested to Rev. R. Lowrie a song which began "Will you meet me at the fountain, when we reach the glory land?" "Let the Lower Lights Be Burning" by P. P. Bliss was suggested by the help afforded a skipper in making Cleveland harbor one stormy night when the regular harbor lights were not discernible and only the lower lights could be picked up.

Some compositions were nothing less than sentimental and even mawkish; Moody himself soon discarded them. To many they were valued from association, and sometimes were used as solos elsewhere than in his meetings. The very titles are sufficient to denote their character, "If Papa Were Only Ready," "My Mother's Prayer," "Little Mary," which related some simple and touching death scene. Though in early years he used these songs they were soon rejected; for he learned that emotionalism was to be distrusted and might be a real menace to genuine and permanent spiritual results.

It would almost seem as though Moody's own religious experience were revealed in the hymns and found favor with him at different times. Early in the sixties Moody wrote to a friend, "Hawley, were you ever homesick for heaven?" and shows the following passage from Rutherford which he has marked,

> His absence is like a mountain upon my heavy heart; oh, when shall we meet? Oh, how long it is to the dawning of the marriage day. O, sweet Lord Jesus, take long steps. Oh, my beloved, flee like a roe or a young hart upon the mountains of separation. Oh, that He would fold the Heaven together like an old cloak, and shovel time and days away, and make ready the Lamb's Wife for her Husband. Since He looked upon me, my heart is not my own; He hath run away to Heaven with it. How sweet the wind that bloweth out of the quarter where Christ is!

Thus it is explicable that in early years there appeared so many songs of yearning for heavenly joys. Such were "Waiting and Watching for Me," "Shall We Meet beyond the River," "One Sweetly Solemn Thought," "By the Gate They'll Meet Us," "I Long to Be There," "What Must It Be to Be There."

But when he broke down in Kansas City and was within a few weeks of laying down his life-work he wrote to an intimate friend in Scotland:

> I cannot tell you how much I miss dear Drummond. It does not seem possible I shall not see him again on earth. What a good time we shall all have when we get to heaven! Only think what a lot have gone on since 1873, when we first met. I get home-

sick for them sometimes, and yet I would not be off until the work that the Lord has given me to do is finished. The work is sweeter now than ever, and I think I have some streams started that will flow on forever. What a joy to be in the harvest field and have a hand in God's work!

This letter expresses devotion to his work and longing for fellowship with loved friends rather than the selfish luxury of ecstasy. It corresponds with Moody's later standard that the permanent value of a hymn depended on the truth it taught. He said, "For a hymn to live it must be based upon some great doctrine of the Christian faith. Music alone will never make it live." And then he would name the great hymns of the Christian church, such as "Rock of Ages," "Ten Thousand Times Ten Thousand," "Jesus Lover of My Soul," showing how those that have endured through the generations have been founded upon some great evangelical truth.

In a study of Moody an able and discerning writer says:

> Moody was as untrained as Shakespeare and Whitman were. And, like them, he loved to do great things with words. But words were never toys to him. They were clubs, they were slings, they were arrows, with which to go out and do battle against the clinging overmastering evil of the world.

Music to Moody was as feathers to an arrow, bringing words to the thought and to the heart. Music for music's sake made no appeal to him; to music as a means to evangelistic endeavor he ascribed great value.

On Moody's subsequent evangelistic campaigns in Great Britain the royalties of *Sacred Songs and Solos* were turned over to the trustees of the Northfield schools, and at the close of the mission in 1882-84 the amount was sufficient to erect two much-needed recitation halls, one at Northfield Seminary, and the other at Mount Hermon School.

The extent to which Moody's judgment had been confirmed in the sale of these books was no less surprising to him than to others. The popularity of the collection is unique in the history of publishing. After fifty-five years *Sacred Songs and Solos* continue to sell in large numbers. Nearly a quarter of a million copies were sold in the year ending December 31, 1927; seventy million copies have been sold since the first edition appeared.

CHAPTER XXXI

THROUGHOUT January and February, 1875, extensive preparations were made for the proposed mission in London. The need for evangelistic services in London at that time may be gathered from statistics which were published shortly before Moody went there. The promoters of Special Services in Theaters and Halls made the following statement concerning the city's need, in the report of their fifteenth series of services:

> 117,000 habitual criminals are on its police register, increasing at an average of 30,000 per annum.
>
> More than one-third of all the crime in the country is committed in London.
>
> 23,000 persons live in its common lodging houses.
>
> Its many beer shops and gin palaces would, if placed side by side, stretch from Charing Cross to Portsmouth, a distance of 73 miles.
>
> 38,000 drunkards appear annually before its magistrates.
>
> It has as many paupers as would occupy every house in Brighton.
>
> It has upward of a million habitual neglecters of public worship.
>
> It has sixty miles of shops open every Lord's day.
>
> It has need of nine hundred new churches and chapels, and two hundred additional city missionaries.

On Friday, February 5, 1875, Freemasons' Hall in London was crowded with ministers and other Christian workers from all parts of London and its suburbs, to confer with Moody in reference to the services soon to begin. It was estimated that over two thousand persons were present, and that it was the largest and most varied meeting of a ministerial order ever held for any purpose in England.

The chair was occupied by a leading London merchant. Moody made a brief statement. He said that there were many obstacles to the proposed work in London which could be put out of the way if they could only meet together and come to an understanding. He found some of the very best men kept out of the work because they had heard this and that. Perhaps some things they heard were true and some not; and if they only had a fair and square understanding, he thought it would be helpful. He spoke frankly to his new friends, telling them that the great difficulty with which they had to contend was prejudice, and he urged the ministers to come into sympathy with the work at the beginning, and invited questions from everyone. He continued:

> A great deal has been said about our making a fine thing financially out of this movement from the sale of the hymn books, organs, etc. Now I desire to say that up to the first of January we received a royalty from the publishers of our hymn books, but from that date when the solo-book was enlarged, we determined not to receive anything from the sale and have requested the publishers to hand over the royalty upon all our hymn books to one of your leading citizens, Mr. H. Matheson, who will devote the same to such charitable objects as may be decided upon.
>
> In regard to the organ question, I want to say, once for all, that we are not selling organs—that is not our mission, nor are we agents for the sale of organs; nor do we receive a commission or compen-

sation in any way whatever from any person or persons for the organ that Mr. Sankey uses at our meetings.

I hope that no one here will think I have made these statements to create financial sympathy on our behalf. We do not want your money; we want your confidence, and we want your sympathy and prayers, and as our one object in coming here is to preach Christ, we believe we shall have them, and that with God's blessing we shall see many brought into His fold. If we make mistakes, come and tell us. Then I shall not fear for the result.

Many questions were asked Moody and many misstatements corrected. One clergyman wished to know whether the work had the effect of estranging people from the communion. If so, he could not uphold the mission without being false to his ordination vows and the Holy Ghost. Moody replied that his one object was to preach the gospel, a statement which was greeted with cheers.

The next questioner wanted to know if it were true that a Roman Catholic took the chair at one of Moody's meetings in Ireland. Moody said that he was not responsible for the chairman, and added amid laughter that his meetings were attended by "Jew, Greek and barbarian."

One interrogator was anxious to have Moody make a statement of faith to which he replied, "It is already in print." Immediately notebooks were forthcoming and the inquiry was made as to where it could be procured. "In the fifty-third chapter of Isaiah," was the reply.

Four centers were selected for preaching: Agricultural Hall at Islington in north London, capable of seating over fifteen thousand persons, with standing room for four or five thousand more; Bow Road Hall in the extreme east, with ten thousand seats; the Royal Opera House in the west; and the Victoria Theater in the south, and later

Camberwell Green Hall. In this way it was hoped to reach all sections and the largest building in each instance was secured.

Moody's work is to attract attention far and wide, for what impresses London makes impulses reach to the uttermost parts of the world. Rich and poor, learned and illiterate, noble and pauper, are to feel the influence of his message. Even if not in sympathy they are at least to take cognizance of his work. Disraeli in opposing Plimsoll in his humane efforts in behalf of British seamen, charges him with being a "Moody and Sankey in politics." Queen Victoria has heard of their work although she is suspicious apparently of anything outside her own Anglican church. From Windsor Castle she writes to the Countess of Gainsborough under date of April 27, 1875:

> DEAR FANNY,
> I received your letter yesterday on the subject of Moody and Sankey, "the American evangelists." It would never do for *me* to go to a public place to hear them, or anything of that sort, nor, as you know, do I go to *any large public places now*.
> But independently of that, though I am sure they are very good and sincere people, it is not the *sort* of religious performance which I like. This sensational style of excitement like the Revivals is not the religion which *can last*, and is not, I think, wholesome for the mind or heart, though there may be instances where it does good.
> Eloquent, simple preaching, with plain practical teaching, seem to me far more likely to do *real* and *permanent* good, and this can surely be heard in all Protestant churches, whether in the Established Church or amongst Dissenters, *if* the ministers are thoroughly earnest. . . .
> V. R.

CHAPTER XXXII

THE London mission began in Agricultural Hall, an enormous structure which had two principal uses; one for the Smithfield cattle show at Christmas, and the other for the great horse fair in June. At the outset Moody addressed himself to Christians, saying that he "would rather wake up a slumbering church than a slumbering world," and that "the man who does the most good in the world is not the man who works himself, but the man who sets others to work." He was able to help people more in a few minutes in the inquiry room than he could in a whole sermon. "You have had enough of pulpit preaching," he said, "and very good preaching too; what we want now is hand-to-hand work, personal effort, individuals going to people and pressing on them the claims of Christ."

An eyewitness thus describes the scene outside Agricultural Hall at the opening of the meeting:

> Many policemen to keep the way; multitudes of young men full of fun and joking; multitudes also of evil women and girls, gaily dressed, joining in the ribaldry; the two together forming a mass of well-dressed but disreputable blackguardism, proving to demonstration that the American evangelists had come at last exactly where they were sorely needed. Omnibus men, cabmen, tram-car men, board men, and loafers of every description took part in the universal carnival. Oaths, jests, slang, and mockery were all let loose together; but not one serious face, not one thoughtful countenance, not an idea of God's

judgment or of eternity in all the vast changing multitude outside.

After the service inside had ended, and partly during its continuance, detachments of choirs belonging to the neighboring missions had stationed themselves near the hall and occupied themselves in singing the "Songs and Solos" and delivering addresses of the briefest character. But all seemed in vain; the very spirit of mockery seemed to possess the great majority. There was nothing like spiteful opposition, much less of interference; the singers and speakers were merely regarded as amiable enthusiasts, who had rashly delivered themselves to the merciless mockery of a London mob.

The mob was not the only form of opposition. The *Saturday Review* expressed surprise that "so many persons go to hear the Americans. As for Moody, he is simply a ranter of the most vulgar type. His mission appears to be to degrade religion to the level of the 'penny gaff.'"

Even the *New York Times,* at that period, was nearly as strong in its opposition to the evangelists. In its issue of June 22, 1875, in the editorial column, the statement occurs that "we are credibly informed that Messrs. Moody and Sankey were sent to England by Mr. Barnum as a matter of speculation."

Society papers devoted a great deal of attention to Moody on this visit. Caricatures of him and Mr. Sankey appeared in *Vanity Fair.* The tone of the articles and paragraphs describing the meetings was at first contemptuous; but, as eminent leaders of society began to attend, it became more respectful in tone. There was a wide difference of opinion regarding the work at its inception. Some notices were guardedly sympathetic; others treated the movement with contemptuous ridicule and others were frankly noncommittal. Under date of April 3, 1875, *Vanity Fair* refers to Moody's labors:

> The "Revival" of religious enthusiasm which has lately been attempted in England is one of the many remarkable proofs that lie ready to hand for those who will see them, that there is in mankind a strong desire and yearning for something more than mere material existence. That Mr. Moody should have caught at that desire is not remarkable, for many have done so before; but what is remarkable is the success with which he has vulgarized his entirely new treatment of it. . . .
>
> He has held meetings all over the country, and, to the despair of ordinary practitioners, has assembled greater multitudes than have been brought together for a like purpose in this generation. For he has discovered that "Christianity is dying with respectability," and he has not hesitated to dissociate it from so fatal a disease. . . .
>
> It is a sufficient comment on the Anglican hierarchy that there is not a Bishop or other dignitary of the Church whose presence could command a tenth part of the audiences which Mr. Moody brings together daily, and as large meetings for conversion mean large subscriptions for "the work" represented by Mr. Moody, he has every cause to be satisfied with the amenability of the English to American methods.

In striking contrast with the flippant attitude of some papers was a leading article in the *Times* which referred pleasantly to Mr. Sankey's singing, and then added:

> But the people would not come together for weeks merely to hear expressive singing, nor to yield to the impulse of association. They come to hear Mr.

Moody, and the main question is: What had he to say? Is any Christian church in this metropolis in a position to say that it can afford to dispense with any vigorous effort to rouse the mass of people to a more Christian life? The congregations which are to be seen in our churches and chapels are but a fraction of the hundreds and thousands around them, of whom multitudes are living but little better than a mere animal existence. If any considerable proportion of them can be aroused to the mere desire for something higher, an immense step is gained; if the churches are really a higher influence still, Mr. Moody will at least have prepared them better material to work on.

The *Christian World* reflected religious sympathy:

We may not be able to say, with a respected contemporary, that Mr. Moody is a modern Wycliffe— a name we should rather assign, if we used it at all, to a great English preacher who has been proclaiming the Gospel to multitudes in London every week for more than twenty-one years. Neither are we prepared to coincide with the magnanimous assertion of a Wesleyan Methodist journal, that this movement puts the revival which was wrought by Whitfield and Wesley into the shade, in respect, at least, to the numbers brought under the sound of the Gospel. These are statements, as it seems to us, which would require to be greatly qualified before they could be accepted by thoughtful men. Yet, without going the length of our too exuberant friends, we can testify that the success of the gatherings over which Mr. Moody presides has been simply marvelous, and in its way quite unexampled, either within the memory of living men, or in all that has been recorded by the pen of the English historian of the Christian church. Whatever may be the view he takes of the work, as to its true spiritual significance and value, every candid onlooker must acknowledge that the present is a phenomenon which cannot be too carefully scanned, or too fully described by the contemporary journalist. It will unquestionably claim for itself a chapter of no inconsiderable magnitude in the book that deals with the religious history of England in the last quarter of the nineteenth century. Some little service to the future, as well as to the present day reader, may, therefore, be rendered by an attempt to gather up the salient points in the story of the first month spent by Messrs. Moody and Sankey in London.

Week after week interest in the noon prayer meeting was sustained. Soon it outgrew Exeter Hall and plans were made to hold it in the Opera House, Haymarket. It would seem that Moody himself was put to almost every trial that a man can experience. Ridicule and adulation; contempt and popularity; denunciation and praise, alike seemed ineffective. One paper affirmed that "judged by the low standard of an American ranter, Mr. Moody is a third-rate star." His reading of Scripture was severely censured. "Mr. Moody with a jocular familiarity which painfully jarred on our sense of the reverent, translated pages of the Bible into the American vernacular. The grand simple stories of holy writ were thus parodied and burlesqued." But in spite of all aspersions Moody steadily went on. The epithets "Pernicious humbugs," "crack-brained Yankee evangelist," "pestilential vermin," "abbots of unreason," at last gave way in the face of continued popularity and references to the work and the workers became respectful.

One writer in an English journal gave him the following sympathetic criticism:

Whatever size the audience may be, he is at home with them at once, and he makes them feel that they are at home with him. . . . In addition to all this, he has a deeply pathetic vein, which enables him to plead very earnestly at the very citadel of the heart. . . . The vein of pathos comes out tenderly and beautifully. But, most important of all, he seems to rely for effect absolutely on divine power. Of course every true preacher does, but in very different degrees of conscious trust and expectation. Mr. Moody goes to his meetings, fully expecting the Divine Presence because he has asked it. He speaks with the fearlessness, the boldness, and the directness of one delivering a message from the King of kings and Lord of lords; and he takes pains to have his own heart in the spirit of the message. He tries to go to his audience loving them, and actively and fervently longing for their salvation. He says that if he does not try to stir up this spirit of love beforehand, he cannot get hold of an audience; if he does, he never fails. He seems to try, like Baxter, never to speak of weighty soul concerns without his whole soul being drenched therein.

With all this, there is in Mr. Moody a remarkable naturalness, a want of all approach to affectation or sanctimoniousness, and even a play of humor which spurts out sometimes in his most serious addresses. Doubtless he gets the tone of his system restored by letting the humor out of him after a long day's hard and earnest work. For children he has obviously a great affection, and they draw to him freely and pleasantly. We should fancy him a famous man to lead a Sunday school excursion party to the country, and set them agoing with all manner of joyous and laughing games. We are sure he would be the happiest of the party, enjoying the fun himself, as well as pleased at their enjoyment of it. The repression of human nature or the running of it into artificial moulds is no part of his policy. His instincts of sagacity make him recoil from all one-sidedness, and desire that men and women under God's grace should hide no true accomplishment and lose no real charm.

One of the annoyances to which Moody was subjected was a sale of photographs on the streets alleged to be copyrighted. He was powerless to prevent this, but he felt that the pictures themselves afforded the best refutation to the charge, for no one who saw them could believe they resembled him. The rumor, however, was finally scotched when a photographer in one of the largest provincial towns wrote a letter to the *Times* to the effect that he had offered one thousand pounds for permission to photograph and copyright Moody and Sankey but that the offer had been refused. Another petty annoyance was the sale of a penny biography.

The ingenuity of the critics was severely taxed, and every effort was made on their part to discredit Moody. It was alleged that the firm of Samuel Bagster and Sons gave Moody a commission for using and recommending their edition of the Bible. To this criticism Moody would make no reply, but at the time of Moody's decease Mr. Robert Bagster, the head of the firm, wrote the family:

> Mr. D. L. Moody was a great influence on the sale of Bibles—especially the Bagster Bibles—thousands of which were sold during his visit, owing to the fact that he used one himself.
>
> It has been said that Mr. D. L. Moody received benefits or commissions from the books he recommended. I have for many years had the pleasure of acquaintance with him and long continued business connections, and never on any occasion has a suggestion or thought of commission arisen. He liked

our Bibles—thought them good—and in his usual direct way said so.

The Bow Road Hall was in the east end of London, adjacent to some of its worst slums. An American spending a few weeks in London at the time sent this description to a home paper:

> The Bow Road Hall is a capacious frame building, sheathed with corrugated iron, which was erected for these meetings in the East End of London; it is in easy reach of a vice-infected, poverty-stricken district, which Mr. Moody thinks "comes nearer to hell than any other place on earth." A thick carpeting of sawdust, laid upon the ground, forms the floor. It is seated with cane-bottomed chairs, of which, I am told, it holds over nine thousand. Scripture texts in white letters two feet high, on a background of red flannel, stretch along several walls. A choir of one hundred young men and women occupies a part of the platform.

Many came from other parts of London and Moody was disappointed in finding that the class in attendance was more respectable than he had anticipated. He yearned to proclaim liberty to the poor and oppressed.

A striking incident connected with this campaign was the publication of a letter written by the Archbishop of Canterbury (Dr. Tait) to a friend:

> Many of our parochial clergy, as you are aware, have been present at the meetings in question, and those who have stood aloof have not done so from any want of interest, but because they have felt that, greatly as they rejoiced that simple gospel truths were urged on their people's consciences, there were circumstances attending the movement to which they could not consistently give their approval. If there

is a difficulty in the clergy's giving their official sanction to the work, you will at once see that in the case of the bishops there are greater difficulties in the way of any direct sanction, which, coming from them, could not but be regarded as official and authoritative; and I confess that the objections I originally felt still remain in full force, now that we have had time to examine and to learn from various quarters the exact nature of the movement.

But looking to the vast field that lies before us, and the overwhelming difficulties of contending with the mass of positive sin and careless indifference which exists on all sides against the progress of the gospel, I, for my part, rejoice that, whether regularly or irregularly, whether according to the Divine Scriptural and perfect way, or imperfectly with certain admixtures of human error, Christ is preached, and sleeping consciences are aroused.

CHAPTER XXXIII

THE London mission is described by one who had known Moody in Chicago:

The preaching begins at eight o'clock. At half-past seven every chair in the hall is filled. Late comers, who cannot be packed upon the platform, or find standing room out of range of those who are seated, are turned away by the policemen at the entrances. The choir fills the time with hymns familiar to American Sunday schools and prayer meetings: "Sweet Hour of Prayer," "When He Cometh," "Come to the Saviour," but mostly unknown here until Mr. Sankey sang them into notice and favour.

A Christian cannot look into the faces of this serious, hushed, expectant audience of eight or ten thousand people without being deeply moved by the thought of the issues that may hang on this hour. Most of them seem to belong to a class of shopkeepers and thrifty working people. But here and there a diamond flashes its light from richer toilettes, while some of the faces evidently belong to the very lowest classes. Hundreds, if not thousands, of them have come from other quarters of the city, from five to ten miles away. They sit so closely packed that the men wear their hats. Ushers, carrying their tall rods of office, are thickly scattered along the entrances and aisles. In a great tent at the rear a prayer meeting is going on for the blessing of God on the evening's service.

Promptly at eight Mr. Moody steps out and plants both hands on the rail that runs along the front of the platform and forms his pulpit. He has grown stout since leaving America, and wears a flowing beard, but there is no mistaking the man as soon as he opens his mouth. He sees too many people, he says, whose faces are getting familiar at these meetings. "It's time for Christians to stop coming here and crowding into the best seats. It's time for 'em to go out among these sailors and drunkards and bring them in and give them the best seats."

In the very midst of one discourse, and the height of its interest, two or three quickly succeeding shrieks came from the centre of the audience. Mr. Moody stopped as if at a signal, and, with Sheridan-like promptness, said: "We'll stand up and sing 'Rock of Ages, Cleft for Me' and the ushers will please help that friend out of the hall. She's hysterical." There were no more "hysterical" demonstrations during the evening, and the congregation scarcely realised that there had been any interruption in the service.

At the close of the address, which was something less than an hour long, those who wished to become Christians were invited to stand up, and several hundred arose. While they remained standing all Christions present were asked to rise. Apparently not a tenth of the audience kept their seats under both invitations. The congregation was then dismissed, but with an urgent request to stay to the second meeting, for conversation and prayer with inquirers. Many remained, perhaps twelve or fifteen hundred, but much the larger part were Christians. As there were opportunity and occasion, they scattered about the hall, talking and praying with those who had asked for prayer. The interest in this second meeting did not, somehow, seem to match that of the preaching service. . . .

Nothing is clearer than that London has been remarkably stirred by the labors of these two evangelists. The windows of every bookseller are hung with their pictures. Penny editions of Mr. Sankey's songs are hawked about the streets. The stages and the railway stations are placarded to catch the travelers for their meetings. The papers report their services with a fulness never dreamed of before in reporting religious meetings. Yet it is doubtful whether, with services held almost every day since about the first of March, five per cent of the people of this great city have ever heard them, or fifteen per per cent ever heard of them.

While Moody was reaching the slum population in the crowded East End, he was also holding services in the fashionable West End at the Royal Opera House. In addition to the noon prayer meeting and a Bible lecture in the afternoon, he preached twice every evening except Saturday, being driven rapidly from the Opera House to Bow Road Hall. One Sunday he preached four times and, being ignorant of the distance, walked sixteen miles to deliver the sermon as he would not use a public conveyance on Sunday.

"I walked it," he announced later when preaching on the Fourth Commandment, "and I slept that night with a clear conscience. I have made it a rule never to use the cars, and if I have a private carriage I insist that horse and man shall rest on Monday. I want no hackman to rise up in judgment against me."

In a later visit to Scotland a committeeman went to a livery stable keeper, without Moody's knowledge, to secure a carriage to take him to a distant meeting on the following Sunday. "It will hurt him less to walk," said the owner of a thousand horses, "than to drive a horse and carriage four miles through the decalogue." Moody was greatly pleased with the reply when it was related to him and often repeated the incident, remarking that he wished more employers were as careful of the interests of their men and dumb animals.

Moody preached the same message in the West End, in the heart of the wealth and aristocracy of the British capital.

> With him, a sinner riding in a carriage emblazoned with a coat of arms, was just as much in need of a Saviour as a poor dog-fighter [writes an observer]. It was his calling to preach the gospel here, as he had preached it elsewhere; and his simple, manly earnestness, and utter forgetfulness of himself, soon won for him not only the respect, but the admiration of those cultivated noblemen and ladies, than whom no people in the world are more ready to honour genuine excellence, or acknowledge the influence of real genius or piety. To them Mr. Moody was a rare Christian. The fact that he was not a scholar was forgotten. He evidently knew Christ and His gospel. . . .

It was said that Dean Stanley, hearing there was difficulty in finding a suitable place for Moody's mission in the west of London, declared he should preach in Westminster if no other place could be secured.

During the meetings in Haymarket an incident occurred which was to have far-reaching influences. At a luncheon one day a group of gentlemen who were keen sportsmen began discussing the general topic of the day— Moody and his work. Much adverse criticism was expressed. One of the members, Mr. Edward Studd, a retired East India merchant who had amassed a fortune and returned to England, was an enthusiastic racing man, being an original organizer of the Liverpool Steeple Chase. He had a large stud in Wiltshire and had been successful on the turf. In every sense a sportsman, he felt that no man should be censured unheard and announced his intention of going to hear this Yankee in order to inform himself before judging the American. The declaration aroused a good deal of amusement among Studd's friends but he asserted that as a gentleman and sportsman he was determined to give Moody a fair chance. From the luncheon table he went to the Haymarket Theater where he was converted. Such a thorough experience was it that his whole manner of life was changed, and the same enthusiasm which he had manifested in racing was now diverted to Christian service. He sold his stud and devoted himself to personal work, seeking to bring his former associates into the knowledge he had himself acquired.

One of Mr. Studd's six sons was at Eton. The father sent for the boy to come to London to attend the meetings at the Haymarket where he too was converted.

During the meetings in the Haymarket Opera House an amusing incident occurred which revealed the sensitiveness and the excitable nature of English society in those days, at the slightest suggestion of an invasion of their prerogatives and exclusiveness. Moody had been asked by some youthful admirers to come to Eton to address the students. Whether the invitation came from students then enrolled or from former Etonians is not known. Little suspecting any untoward results Moody accepted the invitation. Immediately a storm was aroused and the authorities became alarmed. It was said that a clerical dignitary at Windsor feared for the castle and asked for a reinforcement of troops as a protection against the dire consequences of the Americans preaching of Republicanism. To such an extent was antagonism aroused that a question was asked on the subject in the

House of Lords. The excitement subsided as quickly as it grew and the meeting in Eton took place in private grounds and Windsor Castle remains to this day unmolested.

Moody used to say: "Some audiences you count but others can only be weighed." To the latter group he assigned these meetings in Haymarket. At the services were men and women whose educational privileges and social positions accorded them great influence. But Moody was strangely indifferent to this personal advantage and coveted them for the service they were capable of rendering among those whom he felt they could reach.

Among those who attended the London meetings was Mr. Gladstone, who entered heartily into the service. At the close, Moody was presented to him. The conversation was characteristic in its abruptness, and in reply to an inquiry as to its nature, Moody said: "Oh, he said he wished he had my shoulders, and I said I wished I had his head on them . . ."

CHAPTER XXXIV

A newspaper report graphically describes the scenes which characterized the Camberwell services, in the south of London:

The cry is "Still they come." From all points; by bus, tram car, carriage, cab, or on foot; young and old, rich and poor, clerics and laity, soldiers in uniform, come scurrying to the Camberwell shrine, pilgrims by thousands, to share in this our Pentecost of the period. Camberwell scarce knows itself. The old park keeper, with the seedy coat (by which strangers from afar, as they pass through and admire the beauty of our park, must be also struck with the economy of our Vestry), the old man stands amazed at the streams flowing steadily toward Mr. Moody's hall, and doubtless thinks how different it was when a boy. The trams and busses, bearing the words "Near Messrs. Moody and Sankey's Hall," discharge cargoes either at the Father Redcap or the top of Brunswick Road, according to their journey, and no person with eyes in his head need use his tongue as to "the way to walk in," for on the top of a house on the green is a monster announcement directing you aright, another in a garden opposite the Vicarage wall, another opposite the east end of Waterloo Street, whilst posters in scarlet and black show the immediate locality of our new minister.

The London mission which closed with the Camberwell meetings on July 11, 1875, had lasted four months. The extent of the work may be appreciated by the number of services held and the estimated attendance during this time which are reported by one authority as follows:

> In Camberwell, sixty meetings attended by 480,000 people; in Victoria, forty-five meetings, attended by 400,000; in the Opera House, sixty meetings attended by 330,000; in Bow, sixty meetings, attended by 600,000; and in Agricultural Hall, sixty meetings, attended by 720,000. The amount of money expended for buildings, printing, stewards, etc., is $140,000. Messrs. Moody and Sankey have declined to receive any compensation from the committee. It is stated that a prominent business man has bought the Victoria Theatre, and intends to fit it up for religious work.

To a large extent the success of the London mission was due to the staff of volunteer workers who loyally supported the work and assisted in various ways. Among the number were scores of prominent laymen and distinguished ministers such as Dean Stanley, Dr. Newman Hall, Rev. Charles Haddon Spurgeon and Dr. Marcus Rainsford, while the Earl of Shaftesbury and many others of the nobility were frequently in attendance.

Mr. Quintin Hogg and the Hon. Arthur Kinnaird, later to become Lord Kinnaird, also gave fully of their time and energy. The former had entertained Moody in his home in 1872, and an intimate friendship grew up between the two men. In the biography written by his daughter the circumstances of their meeting in London is related:

> That summer they [the family] had arranged to go to Urrard together, but ten days before they were to start, Edwards, their butler, came and told of a wonderful American preaching at Frank White's

Chapel. His name? Mr. D. L. Moody. Mr. Hogg had met him in America, and when he heard that the evangelist had no friends in London, and was going to a hotel, he immediately sent and invited him to make Richmond Terrace his home during his stay in London. That evening he took some of his boys to hear the visitor. They were so greatly impressed that the next night a contingent of about fifty boys turned up. Mr. Moody had the same magnetic power over masses of people that Quintin Hogg possessed over individuals, and the influence he exerted on these poor boys was so marked that their leader felt it was an opportunity he dared not let slip. The boys were some of them quite broken down by the service, and were more open to religious influence than they had ever been. It was a terrible disappointment, but Mrs. Hogg swallowed all personal feeling as usual, and agreed at once that it was a crisis in which the influence of one they knew and trusted must not be removed. She went north with her baby, leaving her husband to cultivate the good seed that had been sown so plenteously.

Hon. Arthur Kinnaird, a keen athlete, diligent in business and thoroughly democratic in spirit, found in the mission the same religious service in which he heartily believed and to which he could devote himself. During the mission it was from young men that Moody received most valuable help, for Drummond, Hogg and Kinnaird were all under thirty at this time.

Surely the value of a work is to be measured by the lasting impression it makes upon lives. It is for this reason that special significance may be given to the testimony of one who sat under Moody's preaching in 1875, and fifty-three years later can recall not only the general impressions which he felt but illustrations which he used.

In a letter to the *British Weekly* dated February 2, 1928, a correspondent writes:

> Two impressions remain clear and fixed. A service held at Agricultural Hall at seven in the morning. For the whole remainder of that day I felt as one under a spell that altogether refused to be relaxed. Nor could I cease to recall the following very significant incident. At this early meeting I had sat immediately behind a hard-headed man of letters whom I happened to recognize and who was about the last person I should have expected to be there, or to show himself otherwise than contemptuously critical; yet by some slight movement of his person it was made plain to me that the speaker I was listening to had succeeded in opening the fountain of tears.
>
> But very soon this novel and daring evangelistic attack, which had been begun in the humbler parts of London, was repeated in even bolder form at the very centre. The Grand Opera House, in the most fashionable quarter of the great English metropolis was taken by these two rough and uncultured visitors from across the Atlantic, and not only thrown open for revival meetings at different hours of the day, but were hugely attended, and this, let it be remarked, not by middle-class audiences alone or chiefly, but by crowds of the very highest rank, by aristocrats of the bluest blood, and it can be shown, even by ladies from the Royal circle at Windsor who were so favourably impressed that, as I have recently seen recorded, they actually suggested to Queen Victoria that a visit to the Opera House was well worthy of Her Majesty's consideration.

From Henry Drummond's letters at this time further impressions of the work are gleaned. To his father he writes:

I suppose I am fairly engaged now to follow Moody all winter and take his young men's meetings. I cannot help thinking more and more every day that this is the work God has planned for me. I do not believe there has ever been such an opportunity for work in the history of the church. Why I should have such a tremendous privilege is the only mystery to me. Moody says if the young men's meetings can be kept up in every town, he believes there will be ten thousand young men converted before the winter is over. What a tremendous thought!

We have never less than a thousand each night, and that is full six weeks without a break. There is not a man in the world that would not envy such a congregation. One can do a year's work in a month in times like these. I have no doubt but that we shall turn out a number of missionaries from among the young men here.

I got a treat last night. Moody sat up alone with me till near one o'clock telling me the story of his life. He told me the whole thing. A reporter might have made his fortune out of it.

Moody is not at all the worse for this great work here; speaking to fifteen thousand people every night. These figures are not exaggerated. He is very careful, and he says so himself.

Everything is bright outside and inside, and I only wish you were here to share in the enjoyment. How would you like to see *an acre of people?* That is exactly the size of the audience to which Mr. Moody preaches every night in the East of London. Here is Moody's programme: Drive three miles to noon meeting; lunch; Bible reading at 3:30 followed by enquiry meeting till at least five; then preaching in the Opera House at 6:30; then very short enquiry meeting; then drive five miles to East End to preach to twelve thousand at 8:30; then enquiry meeting; then drive five or six miles home. This is *every day* this week and next, a terrible strain, which, however, he never seems to feel for a moment.

On August 26, 1875, appeared an audited account of all expenses and receipts of donation signed by the chairman, secretary and treasurer of the committee, totaling approximately thirty thousand pounds of rents, alterations, janitors, lighting, printing, postage, etc. There is nothing for the remuneration of Moody and Sankey. On October 7, 1875, there appeared a letter in the *London Christian* from the chairman of the London Committee that makes a statement respecting the finances of the mission as follows:

Dear Sir:

I ask to make a statement on the subject of Messrs. Moody and Sankey's expenses and especially regarding the disposition which I have made of the amount produced by the royalty on the hymn books sold from January first last, to the close of the mission.

When Mr. Moody was invited to come to England to engage in the evangelistic work which has been so signally blessed, his expenses and those of Mr. Sankey were guaranteed. But, in the providence of God, the honored friends who had addressed to him the invitation had been removed by death before his arrival, and Mr. Moody unexpectedly found himself without resources. As, however, it soon became necessary to print a volume of the solos and other hymns sung at the meetings, an arrangement was made with the publishers to allow him a royalty on the proceeds, as a fund to provide for the expenses of the evangelists and their families.

This arrangement continued all through the mission in Scotland and Ireland, but when Mr. Moody came to London last January, and met the ministers of all denominations at Freemason's Hall, to prepare the way for the mission here, he voluntarily announced in public that he did not mean to take another shilling of this royalty, as sufficient for the expenses of the whole visit had already been received. He added that the amount of royalty from the first of January would be paid over by the publishers to me, to be disposed of afterwards for any object of Christian work that I might determine. This was just at the time when the sales were about to enormously increase, and while this renunciation undoubtedly removed out of the way the only possible ground upon which any could have alleged that Mr. Moody had a pecuniary interest in the success of the work, I feel assured there can only be one opinion—that it was on his part an act of noble disinterestedness.

The royalty between the first of January and the thirtieth of June, the virtual close of the London work, had amounted, with a small sum of bank interest, to five thousand six hundred sixty-seven pounds, seventeen shillings, six pence.

After reference to the Chicago church and its needs the writer continued: "I have just remitted to a well-known and greatly esteemed friend, Mr. George A. Stuart, of Philadelphia, a bill on demand for twenty-seven thousand ninety-two dollars; being the exact equivalent of the sterling exchange of the day, requesting him to appropriate it to the object I have indicated."

This mission concluded Moody's first campaign in Great Britain. In August he left London for Liverpool, the city in which he had arrived unknown two years previously. Now religious leaders there paid tribute to the effectiveness of his labors in a farewell meeting. He was returning to America.

BOOK IV

CHAPTER XXXV

ONLY ten years had elapsed since the close of the Civil War. During this period America was characterized by

the reconstruction of industries, an adjustment of new sources of supply to new processes of manufacture, a coördination of means of transportation with the demands of population, an adaptation of national vision to the new order of things and a realization that neither secession, civil war, nor reconstruction had circumscribed the future of the republic.

Historians are in agreement in recording the marvelous development in industry. The acquisition of wealth became nothing less than an obsession with many and the day of large fortunes dawned upon the land. Stock gambling was widespread. Small firms became merged into large combinations with unprecedented aggregations of capital. Those upon whom fortune smiled indulged in all kinds of luxuries; the simplicity of former days gave place to ostentation and unimagined conveniences. Formal and lengthy letters which had constituted a literature of themselves were superseded by the insistent message of telegraph and telephone. The slow moving horse car was displaced by the clanging trolley. The first bathtub in this country was installed with considerable criticism and ridicule in Cincinnati in 1846 and not until 1851 was one placed in the White House. In twenty years what had been viewed as a luxury had become commonplace in almost every city. "To so many persons the accumulation of wealth had become the one absorbing and all-important object in life that the methods by which the end was gained, no matter how abominable, shocked nobody."

The genius of the American people and the discovery and development of natural resources increased manufacturing and added to the national wealth. The year 1876 marked the permanent shifting of balance of trade in the United States from the import to the export column.

With this unprecedented national expansion there was a corresponding development in population. The vast wealth and the industrial growth offered attractions to the overcrowded areas of Europe and the phenomenal tide of immigration had begun.

The sudden wealth brought opportunities for education and travel. There was a growing appreciation of culture and new times brought new manners; America, emerging into a consciousness of unity and power, realized the need of better educational privileges. Colleges and universities were established and older institutions broadened their scope. Libraries multiplied; foreign travel began to attract large numbers and each year thousands made pilgrimages to the shrines of culture in the Old World.

In short, the social and political conditions were strikingly like those of our day. The news of half a century ago reads like that of yesterday. In the early seventies the newspapers report that Dr. Döllinger of Bonne is calling a convention in his native city with the purpose of effecting church unity upon some basis of common belief; he is inviting representatives of all religious bodies throughout Christendom. Crime waves came with the spirit of unrest that followed the Civil War. There is the "Tweed Ring" of New York, the "Whiskey Ring" of Chicago, and the "Molly Maguires" in Pennsylvania. News seekers who thrived on sensationalism found ample subjects in the kidnapping of Charlie Ross and the mad rush to the gold fields of the Black Hills. The New York press commented editorially on the high cost of living, the street car rates, and the purity of the milk supply.

In describing the religious conditions Hadley says: "It was a time when as in ancient Rome the world needed a moral, spiritual and religious regeneration and a dedication to high ideals of service."

German theology, with scientific methods of historical research, was being applied to the Bible, and traditional views respecting the authorship of the different books composing the Scriptures were being vigorously assailed. It was not enough simply to build upon the customs of the fathers, for in a transitional age every tenet is challenged.

Atheism in its bolder, blatant vogue of the previous century had given place to a politer agnosticism. It was not good form to acknowledge skeptical views, with the result that within the church there were those who would have been outside had they openly avowed their views. Doubtless among these were some who were superficial but still there were many others who, convinced of the soundness of recent scientific discoveries, found difficulty in accepting traditional religious teaching but were not prepared to disavow their faith.

Professor Royce of Harvard, writing of Professor William James' life and work, thus describes the period:

> William James began his work as a philosopher, during the '70s of the last century, in years which were, for our present purposes, characterized by two notable movements of world-wide significance. These two movements were at once scientific in the more special sense of that term, and philosophical in the broad meaning of that word. . . . He belongs to the age in which our nation, rapidly transformed by the occupation of new territory, by economic growth, by immigration, and by education, has been attempting

to find itself anew, to redefine its ideals, to retain its moral integrity, and yet to become a world power. . . . The problems involved in such a civilization we none of us well understand. . . .

Our nation since the Civil War has largely lost touch with the older forms of its own religious life. . . .

Since the war our transformed and restless people have been seeking not only for religious, but for moral guidance. What are the principles that can show us the course to follow in the often pathless wilderness of the new democracy? . . .

Royce answers that maxims are needed—maxims that "combine attractive vagueness with an equally winning pungency." They must seem obviously practicable; but must not appear excessively vigorous. They must arouse a large enthusiasm for action, without baffling us with the sense of restraint, or of wearisome self-control. The wayfaring man, though a fool, must be sure that he at least will not err in applying our moral law. Efficiency is the watchword needed.

Charles Eliot Norton voiced the feeling of many thoughtful men when he wrote a friend, "The world has never been a pleasant place for a rational man to live in. I doubt if it is a worse place for him now than it has been in past times . . . " And again he writes:

> Inveterate and persistent optimism, though it may show only its pleasant side in such a character as Emerson's, is dangerous doctrine for a people. It degenerates into fatalistic indifference to moral considerations, and to personal responsibilities; it is at the root of much of the irrational sentimentalism in our American politics, of much of our national disregard of honour in our public men, of much of our unwillingness to accept hard truths, and of much of

the common tendency to disregard the distinctions between right and wrong, and to excuse the guilt on the plea of good intentions or good nature.

Dr. Lyman Abbott referring to the religious setting of Moody's work says:

> When Mr. Moody began his evangelistic ministry, as when John Wesley began his, over a century earlier, the preaching in the regular pulpits and by the duly appointed ecclesiastical teachers too often lacked the simplicity of Christ's spirit. Sometimes it had become the repetition of a theological system; sometimes a course of instruction in ethical culture; sometimes a proclamation of law, a Thou Shalt and Thou Shalt Not; sometimes a species of emotionalism more or less successfully attempting to be dramatic, sometimes it could hardly be distinguished from literary essays or political stump speeches.

Theological seminaries were apparently unconscious of the needs of the times and failed to adapt their preparation of the ministry to the needs of the coming day. According to Bishop Lawrence:

> Professors in their theological interests and traditions were to me as the monks of old. When I entered college in 1867, the great mass of intelligent Christian people believed, or thought that they believed, that this world was created in six days of twenty-four hours, and that that event happened in 4004 B.C. for was it not so written in the margin of the first page of the King James Bible?

In such a period, very briefly, Moody's message came with refreshing power. To him Christian faith was not dependent upon inflexible doctrinal formulas but on a relationship with a Person. Science dealt only with the realm of sense; but there was a realm of the soul no less real. Each was to be known by compliance with simple rules and proved by experience.

It was at the very time when it would have appeared most difficult to turn men's thoughts from the material to the spiritual.

Moody's success abroad had been so signal that his return to America aroused much curiosity. On landing in New York, he was interviewed in typical American fashion, and articles and editorials sought to explain him. These are for the most part kindly and sympathetic, if not understanding.

The *New York Herald* on August 15 thus describes Moody: "He is about five feet and six inches high, with full black beard, and thick luxuriant hair. Rather solid and stout, having the appearance of a man of business." Moody questioned the interviewer in respect to American politics and social and religious conditions.

In an editorial of the same date, the *Herald* states: "The Americans are disposed to welcome kindly Messrs. Moody and Sankey. They wish to see what these famous apostles will do. They have certainly achieved a popular success abroad, and they will be severely, but fairly, judged."

A five-column article on August 16 reports interviews with prominent ministers which are for the most part warmly sympathetic. In the same article the writer continues:

> The arrival here on Saturday of Messrs. Moody and Sankey, the great evangelists, who like the apostles of old, have turned the world upside down, have created no little stir in the community. Not only are the religious of New York and other cities of the United States interested in them, but the general public is anxious to see and hear the two men, who

have aroused the stagnant and formal religion that was spreading itself not only over Europe but over America also. It is true that on both sides of the Atlantic the English speaking people have ever had a certain degree of reverence and respect for religion; but never during the century has there been such a religious awakening, and springing apparently from inadequate sources, as that under Messrs. Moody and Sankey. Comparatively insignificant in the United States and almost wholly unknown in Great Britain, they went forth to that land of steady habits, and there has not been seen such an awakening among the dry bones there since the days of Wesley and Whitefield. And yet these men went there unheralded. Very few, save their most intimate friends on this side, knew anything about their departure when they left these shores over two years ago. And when they landed on British soil they were unknown, unhonored, and unsung. But now every movement they make is a matter of interest to two continents, every word they utter, almost, will be read in the ends of the earth. What has produced this result? These men are just as modest and unselfish to-day as they have ever been, and they are probably no more pious to-day than they were two or more years ago.

The article continues to analyze the men to discover the source of their success. It is

not eloquence certainly, not high culture, not high-sounding titles, not the singing of Mr. Sankey, [not in] fine physical constitution only, [nor in their] eloquence, culture, titular theology, nor the ordinary respect of a preacher by hearers, [not their] crude methods of presenting the gospel merely—these have never opened pockets and hearts at the same time;

these have never served human souls by the thousand and gathered hearers of the gospel by the millions. . . . The secret of success and the source of power must be sought elsewhere. And we find it in the remarkable intimacy of the two evangelists with their Redeemer and God; in their firm faith in his personal presence at all times in their religious assemblies; in the simplicity of their message of salvation, and in the fact that they are laymen.

CHAPTER XXXVI

MOODY went immediately to Northfield and on August 17 a dispatch appears in the New York press describing his homecoming. The return was attended by no formal welcome. He is reported as "cordially welcomed by one of his brothers who quietly drives him to the old homestead in a rickety buggy, scarcely less honored by time and service than the careful and gentle steed which hauls them." Occasionally he is recognized by an old neighbor who casually bows as he passes.

At the farmhouse table of his venerated mother [writes Dr. Cuyler] he related some of his experiences. When I asked him who had helped him most, he replied, "Dr. Andrew A. Bonar and Lord Cairns. The first one helped me by inspiring hints of Bible truth for my sermons; the other one by coming often to hear me, for the people said that if the Lord Chancellor came to my meetings they had better come too." He might have added, if his characteristic modesty had allowed, that Cairns had said that Moody gave him a new conception of preaching.

Another visitor was Major Whittle, a former associate and lifelong fellow worker. Several years before, while walking home from a meeting in his tabernacle in Chicago, stopping near a lamp-post where their ways were to part, Moody opened his Bible to II Timothy iv and, in reply to something his friend had said as to what could be done to arouse the people, read, "Preach the Word; be instant in season, out of season; reprove, rebuke, exhort with all long suffering and doctrine," adding, "This is our commission, Whittle."

An entry in Major Whittle's diary on the occasion of the visit to Northfield is revealing:

> Moody told me much of his experience in Great Britain. I asked him if he was never overcome by nervousness and timidity because of the position in which he stood. He said no; that God carried him right along as the work grew. He had no doubt that, had he known when he reached England what was before him, he would have been frightened. But as he looked back all he could think of was Jeremiah's experience—that God gave him a forehead of brass to go before the people. He had such a consciousness of the presence of God in his meetings in London, that the people—lords, bishops, ministers, or whoever they were—were as grasshoppers.

Moody's popularity did not make him spurn less conspicuous service. He immediately undertook a campaign in his home community. Under date of September 5, 1875, the *New York Herald* reports on the work at Northfield and states: "Nearly the whole town turned out and many came from long distances in carriages and business vehicles to participate in the services. The crowd was so large in fact, that it was necessary to abandon the church and Mr. Moody was obliged to preach in the open air." This was a preliminary service and the report further states that "next week the work of evangelizing will be commenced in thorough earnest."

That an evangelistic mission in a remote New England village should command the attention of the New York press was significant of the public interest already awakened by Moody. Within a few days articles from two to three columns in length appeared reporting fully the Northfield services, which lasted two weeks.

To his friends he appeared unchanged. When they meet him he is the same ingenuous soul whom they knew two years before. One friend who records his impressions at this time writes:

> The only change I see in him now is a growth of conscious power, and an ability for speaking with added weight and conviction. Praying alone with him, I found him humble as a child before God. Out in the work I found him bold as a lion before men. No hesitation, no shrinking, no timidity; speaking with authority, speaking as an ambassador of the most high God. . . . It troubled him somewhat in going to London that his sermons and Bible talks would all be reported, and his entire stock, the same he had used in other places would thus be exhausted; but, as he expressed it, "There was no help for it, so I just shut my eyes and went ahead, leaving it with God." He told me he spent but comparatively little time in secret prayer, and had no experience in being weighed down and burdened before God. He did not try to get into this state. His work kept him in the spirit of prayer and dependence on God, and he just gave himself wholly to the work.

With this humility Moody combined common sense. By championing no theological vagaries, he won the confidence of ministers; his meticulous attention to the finances of his missions commended him to men of business. In beginning his evangelistic labors in his own country he was ready to accept invitations to large cities believing that by first reaching great centers he could more readily reach the nation. "Water runs down hill," Moody would say, "and the highest hills are the great cities. If we can stir them, we shall stir the whole country."

Therefore, when Moody concluded his mission in

Northfield, he accepted an invitation to Brooklyn, where in October, 1875, he conducted his first large campaign in America.

Preparations had been made for these meetings, not only by providing places of assembly, and arranging a program for the exercises, but by the union of various denominations in holding meetings for prayer and conference, and pledging one another to a cordial coöperation in the effort of the evangelists, upon whose work in Great Britain the divine blessing had so signally rested. A rink was engaged for a month, and chairs for five thousand persons were provided.

From the first the work was attended with greatest encouragement. Large throngs attended the meetings and the music which had proved so great a factor in London was no less effective in Brooklyn.

The *New York Herald* described the opening scene as one "never before witnessed in any city on this continent," and editorially expressed surprise at "the lack of novelty or genius," and wonderment at the crowds. Nevertheless it continues to accord space to reports of the services. As the meetings proceed, the paper states, "The more we see of Messrs. Moody and Sankey, the more are we puzzled on account of their success."

Nor was the *Herald* the only paper that noted the work. An editorial in the *New York Tribune,* October 25, 1875, in respect to the Brooklyn mission states:

> All calculations with regard to the evangelists, Moody and Sankey, have been at fault. The numbers interested, the assistants at hand, the religious feeling awakened, have all been underestimated. This was not a result of mismanagement—on the contrary the management has been singularly good—but a misconception of the depth and earnestness of the religious feeling which awaited the coming of

the evangelists and stood ready at once to aid and respond to their efforts. This religious spirit had been lately aroused by various causes, chief among which we reckon the general trade and business depression which, now as always in the past, while multiplying men's trouble, tends to quicken their sympathetic and religious feelings. The demonstration yesterday in Brooklyn was expected to be noticeable and earnest, but in its magnitude it has proved a surprise. The reputation won by Moody and Sankey abroad especially adapted them to lead in a general revival, and led all to anticipate a great following to hear them, but that three or four times the numbers in attendance would have to be turned away was wholly unexpected. And instead of an effort being required to awaken interest and arouse dormant feelings, it was soon discovered that the audience was as intensely earnest and sympathetic as the leaders themselves.

Some of the indications of this spirit, as portrayed at yesterday's meetings, are curious. The morning meetings were begun at half past eight o'clock. Before six o'clock in the morning the crowd began to gather at the doors; at eight o'clock over five thousand were seated in the building, and three thousand or more had been turned away. In the afternoon twelve—possibly twenty—thousand were unable to gain admittance. . . . Additional car tracks had been laid by the street car companies to the doors of the building, and though cars were run at intervals of only one minute many thousands had to wend their ways homewards on foot. . . . It is not unreasonable to anticipate from such indications that the field is ripe for the harvesters, a great and general religious awakening in this part of the country—possibly also in its remotest sections. Such demonstrations will be frequent in the large cities of the East and when the evangelists shall have visited Philadelphia and other points near by, their coming to the metropolis will be productive of scenes the like of which were never witnessed in this city in the past.

Again at the close of the mission the same journal thus reviews the work:

> From beginning to end these meetings have been crowned with unexpected success. The interest felt in the services had continually accumulated with their progress, and the size of the audiences has uniformly increased. Nothing in secular affairs is capable of drawing off the interest excited; not even an election which aroused the citizens of Brooklyn to throw off a political yoke that has oppressed them for years. . . . It is difficult to estimate the numbers that have been present at these exercises. Counting in the "overflow meetings" the audiences must have included, especially toward the last, from fifteen to twenty thousand per day; perhaps a higher estimate would be nearer the fact.

The influence of the mission extended beyond Brooklyn; the *Tribune* again commenting editorially says:

> There is a common sense view to be taken of this matter as of every other. In the first place, why should we sneer because a large part of the multitudes crowding into the Brooklyn Rink are drawn there only by curiosity? So they were when they followed Christ into the streets of Jerusalem or the wilderness, yet they went to the healing of their souls. Or that a still larger part already profess Christianity, and all that Moody and Sankey teach? There is not one of them who will not be the better for a little quickening of his faith, and, we may add,

of his movements too. In the second place, with regard to the men themselves, there can, we think, be but one opinion as to their sincerity. They are not money-makers; they are not charlatans. Decorous, conservative England, which reprobated both their work and the manner of it, held them in the full blaze of scrutiny for months, and could not detect in them a single motive which was not pure. Earnest and sincere men are rare in these days. Is it not worth our while to give to them a dispassionate, unprejudiced hearing? Thirdly, in regard to their message. They preach no new doctrine, no dogma of this or that sect; nothing but Christ and the necessity among us of increased zeal in His service; which of us will controvert that truth? If the Christian religion is not the one hope for our individual and social life, what is?

And lastly, with regard to the method of these men in presenting Christ and His teaching. Men of high culture or exceptional sensitiveness of taste shrink from the familiarity of words and ideas, in which a subject they hold as reverent and sublime beyond expression is set forth to the crowd. They call it vulgarizing and debasing the truth. Granting that their opinion is right, from their point of view what is to be done with the crowd? They cannot all be men of fine culture or exceptional sensitiveness; they are not moved to believe or trust in Jesus through philosophic arguments, or contemplation of nature, or logical conviction, or appeals to their æsthetic senses; by classical music, stained glass, or church architecture; they are plain, busy people, with ordinary minds and tastes; yet certainly, as Christ died to save them, it is necessary that they should be brought to Him by some means, and persuaded to live cleaner, higher, more truthful lives.

> Christianity is not a matter of grammar for libraries and drawing-rooms, refined taste, or delicate sensibility. It was not to the cultured classes that Christ Himself preached, but to the working people, the publicans, fishermen, tax-gatherers; and He used the words and illustrations which would appeal to them most forcibly. If Messrs. Moody and Sankey, or any other teachers, bring Him directly home to men's convictions, and lead them to amend their lives for His sake, let us thank God for the preacher and let his tastes and grammar take care of themselves.

An editorial appears in the *New York Herald* under date of September 11:

> Moody and Sankey have begun their great revival work in this country. . . . There never was a time when a higher sense of the value of moral and Christian obligations was so necessary as it is now. Our politics are sordid and corrupt, and even our business principles are wanting in business men. The teachings of religion and the chiding of conscience seem to have lost their hold upon the hearts of the people. This downward tendency of public and private morality is not only to be deprecated but, if possible, to be remedied. Only a great awakening can show the people the danger of their situation, or make them earnestly strive against the evils which surround and threaten to destroy them. A religious revival, come in whatever form it may, will prove a blessing; but from no other source is it so probable, at this time, except from the two distinguished evangelists whose efforts at quickening the conscience of men have had such remarkable results abroad.

CHAPTER XXXVII

FROM Brooklyn Moody went to Philadelphia, beginning his mission there on November 21. Two circumstances might well have given pause to the committee inviting Moody, as well as to Moody himself. The distractions of the holiday season would doubtless interfere with a lively interest; the weather would be inclement. Furthermore, the city was engrossed in the approaching Centennial Exposition, the greatest enterprise of its character which had been held in America, to celebrate the anniversary of the signing of the Declaration of Independence. In addition to these considerations the city was unusually conservative. In the face of these obstacles, the projection of a mission demanded faith and daring on the part of its leaders.

But the history of the Philadelphia mission was like that of its predecessors.

The place selected for the meetings was a disused freight depot of the Pennsylvania Railroad. The growth of the city had made it no longer suitable for its original purpose, but its central location and accessibility to all parts of the city made it ideal for a large mission. The property had lately been acquired by Mr. John Wanamaker for a large department store, but alterations had not yet started. The railroad tracks were removed; the large space covering an entire city block was floored; and a large choir gallery and platform transformed the structure into the "Depot Church." It could accommodate ten thousand people.

The Philadelphia press at once accorded space and

prominence to the mission. The *Ledger* describes the opening service which was announced for eight o'clock on a Sunday morning.

> Long before that hour the rain commenced to fall, and by seven o'clock was coming down in torrents. It was hardly to be expected that a large audience would be collected at this early hour under such circumstances, but he who walked to the place of meeting with the idea that there would be an abundance of room quickened his pace as soon as he reached Market Street, for both pavements were filled with the people for several blocks, all directing their steps to the old freight depot. . . . At half past seven o'clock the front half of the auditorium was completely filled, and by quarter before eight only a small portion of the rear end of the room remained empty.

One writer says of the mission:

> Forty thousand dollars was raised, and a generous part of it went into advertising. The evangelists took no money for their own services. This was their invariable rule, and they did not believe in the collection for expenses that marred the closing days of later revivals. Sankey was John F. Keene's guest, and Moody was entertained in the Wanamaker home. All the expenses of the evangelists were met by these two men. A piano dealer, William G. Fischer, who, like Sankey, was writing hymns that were to live, gathered and drilled a volunteer choir of three hundred members, many of whom came from Bethany and were in Wanamaker's employ.

One meeting was set apart especially for intemperate men and women. At Moody's request, a large number of people who had been regularly attending the meetings remained away, that their seats might be occupied by those for whom the meeting was especially designed. The audience has been described as follows by a witness:

> Here and there could be seen the bloated faces of blear-eyed drunkards, glancing wildly around as though the strangeness of the situation was so overpowering that it required a great effort of will to remain; not a few were accompanied by mothers, wives, sisters, or friends, who, having exhausted human means, had determined to cast their burden upon the Lord.
>
> The great majority of those gathered in the Depot Tabernacle yesterday afternoon were as sad-faced and tearful a collection of humanity as it would be possible to assemble in one place. Those who had not directly suffered by intemperance grew at once into sympathy with the hundreds about them whose heavy sighs told stories of unutterable anguish, and this influence increased until a cloud of terrible depression seemed to hang over the entire congregation. Every class of society was represented in this throng, united so closely by such painful bonds. Close to the half-starved, long-abused, yet faithful wife of some besotted brute was seated the child of fortune and culture—child no more, but an old, old woman whose only son, still in his youth, had fallen almost to the lowest depths of degradation.
>
> Next her was a man whose every feature showed nobility of soul and rare talents, but whose threadbare coat and sunken cheeks betrayed him to all observers as the lifelong victim of an unconquerable appetite. Just behind this group was a young girl whose face, sweet as an angel's, was already furrowed by grief. Beside her was her father, who, broken

down in health and almost ruined in mind by the
excessive use of liquor, seemed at last to have resigned himself to hopeless ruin. He gazed about in a
half-asleep, half-childish way, and several times
attempted to get up and leave his seat, but the hand
of the child-woman held his very tightly, and each
time he would conquer his restlessness, and sit down.
By far the larger proportion of the congregation
were women, almost all of whom had evidently
clutching at their hearts the agonizing image of some
past or present experience with woe in its most
terrible form.

It was interesting to see the change that gradually
came over the audience as Mr. Moody declared over
and over again that the God who had once cast out
devils could do it then, and would do it if only asked;
and as fervent prayers for immediate help were
offered, the cloud seemed to rise from their hearts,
while the noonday sun poured upon them its blessed
rays of hope, and eyes, long dimmed by tears,
beamed with a new light.

The meetings were described as "unique in the annals
of the city." Tickets of admission were widely distributed and for two months with continued interest throngs
crowded the building. On January 8 it is reported,
"The building was completely filled within seven minutes
after the doors were opened last evening and thousands
were unable to obtain entrance."

In Philadelphia, as elsewhere, futile attempts were
made to explain the phenomenon of interest in the meetings and to analyze Moody himself. It is again the old
story everywhere recurrent. The gifts which are associated with power to move an audience are felt to be
lacking. Descriptions of his personal appearance are
commonplace, but a writer in the *Philadelphia Inquirer*

admits the inadequacy of his attempt at description but adds, "It would give but a poor idea of Mr. Moody's appearance while preaching when he seems to become a wholly different person."

To hold the attention of so vast an audience was a great achievement. The physical effort to make himself heard was attended with no little strain. But when, day after day, week after week, beginning before Thanksgiving and continuing through the entire holiday season, to speak in a way that would maintain the interest of his hearers, drawing them by thousands to sit in an old freight depot which had been temporarily made over into an auditorium, was amazing. It is reported that his address "scarcely lasted thirty minutes" and was "listened to with rapt attention by the immense audience."

Moody thoroughly believed in the application of business methods to Christian work. In announcing forthcoming services advertisements appeared in the daily press. One of these shows the way in which publicity was given and also explains the method employed by the committee in managing the mission. A statement of the estimated cost of the mission appeared over the names of the chairman and treasurer, both well-known gentlemen in Philadelphia. The estimate is itemized and totals $29,538.

> Services at Depot, Thirteenth and Market Streets, Next Week. The Noonday Meeting will be conducted by Mr. Moody with singing by Mr. Sankey
> The subjects are as follows:
> Monday—Reports of the week
> Tuesday—The Shepherd
> Wednesday—The Water of Life
> Thursday—The "Comas" of the Scriptures
> Friday—Prayer for the Intemperate

There is no expense for rent of the building or for the services of the Evangelists.

On Monday and Tuesday—from the close of the noon meeting—there will be in the Depot a continuous Inquiry Meeting, conducted by Moody and Sankey.

At the close of the meetings—the flooring and other lumber fittings, and also the furniture, will be sold at public auction for the account of this fund. Thus far there has been contributed $20,764.20. The Committee believes that to settle all the bills and to pay the expenses of the coming convention there will be required further contributions to the amount of some $8,000 to $9,000. All who desire to share in this good work are invited to send contributions, either large or small. There may be some who may wish to make thank offerings for blessings received. Please send money promptly to Jno. R. Whitney, Treasurer, Callowhill and Sixteenth Streets, or may be left with B. B. Comegys, Cashier Philadelphia Bank, or with Thomas K. Cree, Secretary, Thirteenth and Market Streets, or may be handed to any member of the committee.

While in Philadelphia, President Grant with his Cabinet and members of the Supreme Court attended the mission. The *North American,* December 22, reports among the distinguished persons present the Hon. George Bancroft, the historian, and Judge Strong of the Supreme Court. At the evening service "President Grant with Mrs. Grant and Col. Fred Grant and his wife attended the meeting, also ex-Speaker Blaine, Postmaster-General Jewell, General Hartranft, General Garfield, and Col. Thomas A. Scott."

Here rumors which Moody had encountered elsewhere persisted to the effect that he had some mercenary objective. It seemed hard in spite of repeated refutation to disabuse the public mind of this, but in this effort the press denied the allegations again and again. It must have been gratifying at the close of the mission when an editorial in the *Philadelphia Inquirer,* January 21, referred to this rumor regarding Moody and said, "They make no money; do not seek to make money, but are doing their Master's bidding without fee or reward."

The mission which began in Philadelphia on November 21 closed January 20. According to R. L. Duffus who terms Moody "next to Jonathan Edwards, the most striking figure in American religious history," his work had extraordinary permanency of character. Fifty years after his mission in Philadelphia it was said: "His coming made a greater stir than that of any evangelist who has visited the city before or since. Policemen, firemen and even reporters were among those who succumbed to his eloquence. He would single out helpless individuals regardless of their pitiful embarrassment."

According to the same authority, "In Moody's crusade to the British Isles he began with meetings of fifty persons and in two years had addressed two and one half millions."

CHAPTER XXXVIII

FROM Philadelphia Moody went to Princeton, on the invitation of faculty and undergraduates, for a brief visit before going to New York. His visit is thus described by a contemporary:

> The revival influence at work among the students is one of notable power. The movement is of recent origin. While Messrs. Moody and Sankey were in Philadelphia the students indicated to President McCosh their very general desire that the evangelists should be invited to spend a day at the college. The Doctor gladly undertook to extend the invitation. Visiting the gentlemen at Philadelphia, he obtained from them a promise that they should spend the "Day of Prayer for Colleges" at Princeton.

Preparatory services were held in which Dr. W. M. Taylor and Dr. Theodore Cuyler participated. Before Moody arrived at the college there was an awakened interest among the undergraduates. In the few addresses Moody gave there was no effort to adapt his message. Wisely he addressed himself to them as to others. But the same directness of speech and simplicity of statement of the gospel appeal met with the same response as elsewhere. It is doubtful if in so brief a time Moody's labors were ever greater than in that one day at Princeton.

That Moody had a message which would be listened to in centers of academic training was a revelation to others as well as himself. The college boy, critically observant, was thought to be prejudiced readily by grammatical errors. But the average youth is quick to recognize sincerity. It was Moody's candor and fearlessness that immediately won the respect of his hearers and in coming years his work among college students both in America and Great Britain was to be increasingly sought. Strange as it may seem, Moody, an untutored layman, later found one of the most fruitful fields of labor in youthful academic circles.

Moody himself was greatly impressed by the brief visit to Princeton. At its close he said:

> I saw more zeal when I was in Princeton last Sunday than I have in many a year. I was talking to the students there about their souls, and after I had been talking for some time, quite a group of young men gathered around me, and the moment that one of them made a surrender and said, "Well, I will accept Christ," it seemed as if there were twenty-five hands pressed right down to shake hands with him. That is what we want—men that will rejoice to hear of the conversion of men.

CHAPTER XXXIX

In June, 1875, while Moody was still engaged in the London mission, a movement was set on foot to bring him to New York City. A preliminary organization extended the invitation, and upon its acceptance a general committee was formed of prominent ministers and laymen of which Mr. William E. Dodge was chairman. A New York minister writing to a friend in Philadelphia described the arrangements:

> As in Philadelphia, the location of our Tabernacle is in the very centre of the city, accessible from every direction by all classes. On one side of it lies the homes of wealth, the avenues of fashion, and the great hotels, on the other the masses of middle classes, and a little beyond, the crowded abodes of the poor and the dens of wretchedness and vice. It is the old depot of the Harlem Railroad, and occupies the block bounded by Madison and Fourth Avenues and Twenty-Sixth and Twenty-Seventh Streets. . . .
>
> The committee have rented this structure at one thousand five hundred dollars a week and spent ten thousand dollars in fitting it for the meetings. It has been divided into two great halls, one seating six thousand five hundred, the other four thousand, while between there is a wide space enclosed for enquiry rooms, and for the evangelists, with a passage from one to the other for their use. It is expected that after speaking in the large room Mr. Moody and Mr. Sankey will pass over to the other

or overflow meeting, where, meantime, addresses and prayers are to be made by clergymen and laymen, chosen for their adaptation to such work.

During the months Moody was in Brooklyn and Philadelphia preparatory arrangements were perfected, including the training of inquiry room workers and volunteer ushers.

The mission began on Monday evening, February 7, 1876, and continued to April 19. Apparently the preliminary work had been well done and the opening of the mission was all that could be wished. An observer remarks a spirit of earnestness on the part of the audience rather than of curiosity. One reporter is impressed with the phenomenon of thousands facing the inclemency of mid-winter weather to attend religious meetings in such a cheerless auditorium as the "Hippodrome." People thronged the services to listen to the "uncouth exhorter."

As elsewhere, every evangelical denomination was represented upon the committee of management and the audiences were constituted of all kinds and conditions of men. Rich and poor, learned and ignorant, cultured and destitute came day after day during those months to hear the simple gospel or be present in the inquiry rooms.

In an editorial of February 12 the *New York Times* says:

> Their motives are beyond all question—they are doing good; in an age when the teachers of infidelity are so numerous and so active the exertions of these two gentlemen to bring home to what is called the common mind the truths of Christianity deserve the warmest sympathy and encouragement. They do not even court publicity, and we can quite believe that it would be far more agreeable to their feelings to be left to do their work quietly, and not to have their sermons reported in the newspaper. Through

the columns of the press, however, their appeals may reach many thousands who are beyond the sound of their voices, and this is the only good reason that can be given for publishing reports of their daily proceedings.

Another editorial in the *Times* notes that

> certainly Moody possesses little rhetorical power, less culture and no learning; yet his unusual earnestness and simplicity keep all hearers enchained. The impression left is that there is some truth behind the man, greater than he. It is to be observed too, that he trusts little to appeals of fear and the pictures of future torment do not figure in the oratory of these revivalists as they did in the past generation. The simple Scriptures are the great armories of these preachers, and from that they draw their weapons. It cannot be said either, apart from the public features of the meetings, that there is much that is exciting or sensational in them. There is, indeed, preparation and organization. Mr. Sankey's use of recitative and lively airs he has introduced are very attractive and effective for his objects, and Mr. Moody has quite a large force of assistants at work in aiding him.
>
> The entire absence of the controversial and denominational elements in this meeting is a suggestion to our clergymen which will be heeded. The day has passed in which a great preacher will command influence principally from his devotion to a sect, or as a controversialist. He must speak to Humanity, and be filled with sympathy for man as man. We cannot but think that the Protestant churches of this city will derive much permanent good from this religious awakening. The great difficulty of the day in the way of religion is indifferent-

ism, and whatever breaks that up is useful. Many will have their attention turned to truths which were before dim to their minds. The great ideas of the reformed sects will work afresh on the popular mind. Perhaps a new barrier will be raised to the increasing tide of greed and dishonesty. Possibly a generation will arise with higher aims than the one whose views and corruptions have become rank before Heaven. For, after all, public morality is only private honor, and the best "defense of honor" is the fear of God. . . . Why will not some of our most public-spirited Christian men of business set forth about founding a public and enduring memorial of this "revival" in a large, free Protestant place of worship for both rich and poor?

In an editorial on March 25 entitled "Revivalists and Modern Skepticism" there is an answer to an attack on Moody and Sankey by an atheist who styled them adventurers and charged that through their meetings people have become unbalanced and even insane.

> In this city, they may be said to have checked insanity, in that they have broken up habits of drinking in numbers of persons and sent them back to their homes reformed men and women, though madness in its worst form, delirium tremens, was threatening them. Nor can the influence of the revivalists here be called exciting or sensational. There has not been the usual manifestations of feeling in these meetings which are common in revivals. No physical excitement has been apparent. The audiences have been singularly calm and still. . . . It is a single instance of the narrowness of modern "Liberalism" that such writers do not see that men like Moody and Sankey are above all preaching an "ideal out of one's self" and that they hold forth

incessantly the embodiment of the "principle of love," and that the drift and purpose of their teaching is for men to come out of themselves, to forget themselves, and to be filled with a belief and ideal which is far beyond and above feeble humanity. If Socrates taught the absolute devotion to truth, they teach it more fully. If Buddha was filled with compassion for suffering humanity, they present One who has carried the very name of "the man of sorrows." If Confucius inculcated the principle of humanity they preach Him who has embodied human brotherhood. Why cannot the skeptical school analyze modern Christianity as well as Buddhism? Surely the one is as worth study and fair treatment as the other. . . . The drunken have become sober, the vicious virtuous, the worldly and self-seeking unselfish, the ignoble noble, the impure pure, the youth have started with more generous aims, the old have been stirred from old ways of grossness, a new hope has lifted up hundreds of human beings, a new consolation has come to the sorrowful, and a better principle has entered the sordid life of the day, through the labors of these plain men.

Moody's prodigious physical vitality impressed many. After weeks in Philadelphia with their tax upon his strength he began the work in New York with unabated vigor. A contemporary writer says:

> Instead of lessening, his incessant toil in Philadelphia seemed to have redoubled both his physical and mental energy. In his style of delivery he had much improved, and never had he in any city before commenced his work with such a powerful sermon. God was evidently with him. All things were ready, and a great awakening was anticipated. Mr. Moody closed his sermon by saying, "The mighty spirit of

Elijah rests upon us to-night. Let us go to our homes, and cry to the God of Elijah, 'Here I am, God, use me,' that we may be ready for all his services." Here was the keynote of the awakening.

There were very apparent results of the mission. Large accessions on confession of faith were reported in churches in the city and suburbs, and many lives were salvaged from the ravages of alcoholism and degradation. But perhaps one of the greatest benefits to the community was in the unifying influence among the churches themselves. Denominationalism might still be recognized as meeting the needs of differing temperaments but was realized to be no barrier among Christians for united effort in service for Christ. The life of the churches was strengthened by the quickening of their members in service in inquiry rooms and religion was a topic of conversation easy of approach.

These months in New York gave to Moody a wide acquaintance and formed close friendships. In subsequent years he found many whom he first knew in those meetings in the seventies all over England, in Brooklyn, Philadelphia and New York who loyally assisted him in the various forms of educational work in which he later engaged. Among this number were such lifelong friends as William E. Dodge, Morris K. Jesup, D. W. McWilliams, R. R. McBurney and John Wanamaker. In fact, there were literally scores, if not hundreds, who might be included in the list, for Moody truly had a genius for friendship.

During the New York mission Moody was the guest of Morris K. Jesup whose home was on Madison Avenue. An incident occurred at this time which may appear trivial but at the same time reveals that sensitiveness of which few were cognizant and the spirit which prompted him to be considerate of the feelings and even prejudices of others. Often in preaching Moody would perspire so freely that it would necessitate an entire change of clothing on returning to the place where he was staying. He would frequently put on a velveteen lounging coat or smoking jacket, although he did not smoke and was strongly averse to the habit. On one such occasion he came to dinner in this coat when a young man, a student at Yale, was present who took a strong prejudice against Moody for what he felt to be a great breach of etiquette to the host and hostess, and in consequence would not attend the mission or listen to Moody preach. Years afterward a member of his family inquired why he did not use a lounging coat which elicited the relating of this incident and Moody said, "Of course, I did not know I had done anything to offend anyone but I would never again risk hurting anyone's feelings in such a way."

During the New York meetings he came into close relationship with Richard C. Morse. In the reminiscences of the latter he refers to another phase of the mission:

> In connection with the farewell meeting, Moody following his usual course was desirous of announcing and accomplishing some large undertaking, vitally related to all the churches, in which the awakened energies of Christian workers might give expression, both to gratitude and consecration. Some years later, when he was expressing to me his disappointment that his recent work in some city was not followed by such an expression on the part of the workers, he said: "It is not the failure to get the money that troubles me, it is the lack of that spiritual 'fruit of his labor' which Paul is ever vigilantly looking for." Upon careful deliberation it was agreed that Moody's worthy purpose could best be carried out by an effort, in which all would unite, to

raise a fund of $200,000 to increase the efficiency of the New York Young Men's Christian Association, as an agency of all the churches. Such a valuation of the Association by this group of churchmen of all denominations was a very gratifying acknowledgment of all the good work it was accomplishing in the city. It was agreed that the best use of such a fund would be to remove the mortgage of $150,000 upon the Twenty-Third Street Association building, then the only one in New York City, and also to secure a building for the vigorous Bowery branch, where daily evangelistic meetings were held as part of a practical work of rescue and reclamation for men who were "down and out."

During this mission Dom Pedro, Emperor of Brazil, attended a service when Moody spoke from the text, "What shall I do then with Jesus which is called Christ?" One who was present remarked that the distinguished visitor "paid the strictest attention, bowing his head in assent to the remark, 'Even a great emperor cannot save his soul, with all his wealth and power, unless he bows himself at Christ's feet, and accepts Him.'"

CHAPTER XL

At the conclusion of the meetings in New York Moody made a hurried trip south to join his family who, owing to illness of one of the children, had been obliged to avoid the rigor of the north. It was the first visit he had made to the South since the war excepting two brief missions, in New Orleans and Mobile, and the kindly reception accorded him was an evidence of genuine Christian brotherliness.

After three such missions as those in Brooklyn, Philadelphia and New York it would have seemed that rest was imperative for Moody; but such was his energy and endurance that after a brief visit in Augusta, Georgia, he returned north to Chicago. Since funds from the hymn book royalties had become available to complete the Chicago Avenue Church, which was the outgrowth of his early Sunday school work, the erection of the building had been completed. The entire cost of the church had been eighty-nine thousand dollars and toward this sum five hundred thousand children had given five cents apiece immediately after the fire. However, there still remained approximately thirteen thousand dollars to be raised.

A letter written from Philadelphia on November 26, 1875, reveals Moody's opinions on the appropriateness of dedicating a church while still encumbered with debt. Evidently he had been urged to be present at the dedication service and in reply he wrote:

> To the Officers of the Chicago Avenue Church,
> Dear Brethren: Though not permitted to work

with you at present my thoughts are often with you and my prayers go up continually that you may be blessed and led in all things. My heart has been cheered as I heard from time to time of the earnest workers among your number. . . . But one thing impresses itself strongly on my mind and that is, that we have no right to dedicate anything to God that does not belong to us; therefore, we cannot rightfully dedicate a building to God's service which we are not able to call ours until paid for. Anxious as I feel for the building to be ready for use, I could not give my consent to its dedication until paid for. I am thoroughly convinced that it is a great mistake dedicating any building for religious services with a heavy debt hanging over it. My experience has been that it has always been a drag and a hindrance to successful work. . . .

I would be glad to come to Chicago to assist in the dedication services when the building is completed and the money raised to pay for it, but not until the building is owned by us can we dedicate it to God's service. I would further advise that the work should go on slowly, as the funds on hand warrant; and, if a sufficient amount to finish cannot be got, then shut up the building until the sufficient amount is raised for its completion. May God guide you in this as in all other matters and bless you more. Your friend and brother, D. L. Moody.

Evidently this letter stimulated the church to renewed effort, and the necessary funds were raised, for Moody took part in the dedication of the Chicago Avenue Church July 16, 1876.

Within the next month he returned to his mother's home in Northfield to enjoy the first real holiday he had had for years or for that matter had ever known. But holidays are an acquired habit. Here in the little quiet village of his boyhood he soon engaged in work in behalf of associates of earlier days and neighbors from adjoining communities. Although looking forward to arduous work during the coming winter in Chicago and Boston, he readily responded to invitations to speak in towns in the vicinity of Northfield.

In September of this year he entertained his friend P. P. Bliss and enlisted his help. Under date of September 18, 1876, Bliss writes: "Just returned from a week with Brother Moody, in his home at Northfield, driving one hundred miles over Vermont, Massachusetts and New Hampshire hills, and holding eleven meetings." Moody's conception of rest was a source of amusement to friends who often regarded the spending of a holiday with him as somewhat taxing.

It was during these weeks in Northfield that he gave a series of Bible readings to which his neighbors were invited. Doubtless this was the embryo from which came the General Christian Workers' Conference. Moody believed that the Bible was a fascinating study and needed only to be taught to attract attention. This he fully demonstrated. The proverbial indifference toward a prophet in his own community seemed inapplicable, for once a week, after arduous toil on the farms, neighbors would drive in from miles around in all kinds of nondescript vehicles, overflowing the house and the porches of the old farmhouse. While seated at the table under an old-fashioned kerosene lamp Moody would put forth the same efforts in behalf of his neighbors that he had expended before the great audiences in metropolises.

Sundays all through the summer months found him preaching, if not in the pulpit of the Northfield Church, in some neighboring town. Often the smallest communities in remote mountain districts seemed to offer the greatest attractions to him. The genuine and unaffected

Cartoon in "Chicago Tribune" in 1898

evidence of welcome which with New England self-consciousness and diffidence is not readily expressed, he felt deeply. Not infrequently in some little church in a town far removed from the turmoil of the outside world with which it would not even have railroad communication, Moody was really heard at his best. His phaeton and old gray mare, Nellie Gray, were a familiar sight for twenty miles in the country round about.

CHAPTER XLI

CHICAGO which had been the scene of his first efforts in religious work was the next place in which Moody held a mission. In the earlier days his unconventional methods and great zeal had won for him the sobriquet of "Crazy Moody," partly in ridicule and partly in condescension. But his indefatigable labors, sympathy and self-denying devotion won the hearts of the uncouth children of his Sunday school and when they called him Deacon Moody it was a term of affection. Slowly the community began to appreciate the character and value of his work and he became Brother Moody. When in 1876 he returned to Chicago with the prestige of the recent experiences, he was thenceforth known as Mr. Moody, or simply Moody, and the former terms were never again used to any degree either by the press or in the street.

From October, 1876, to January 16, 1877, was the time determined for the Chicago mission. This was the occasion of the Hayes-Tilden presidential campaign, one of the bitterest contests ever waged in American political history; feeling ran high and acrimonious charges and recriminations in the public press further accentuated partisan antagonism. Politics occupied an unwonted attention and to plan for a mission at such a time was at once evidence of faith and courage. Added to all this was the season of the year, for the lake cities in the late autumn are subject to sudden changes of weather and many would naturally hesitate to attend services in a temporary structure. Another distraction was the Christmas holidays.

But in spite of all seemingly adverse conditions the meetings began with a large attendance. In the *Chicago Tribune* Moody is described as "in all respects a plain man, reaching plain people by his very plainness, and cultivated people by the power of his sincerity of belief and earnestness in stating that belief. . . . He has not the remotest suspicion of cant in his talk, and yet his talk abounds with quaint piquant originality."

Later there appears an editorial in the same journal reflecting the impression that he makes upon his hearers. "His idea of religion," says the writer, "is the true one; it cuts deep, like the gospel which he preaches, and it knows no distinction of sinners. Board bills must be paid by his converts, or he will not acknowledge them." The editorial then comments upon the ethical significance of Moody's preaching.

Five years had elapsed since the great fire in Chicago which had so greatly disorganized the work Moody had built up in his Sunday school and church, and three years had elapsed since he had left Chicago for the protracted evangelistic work abroad. Now returning to the familiar scenes it must have been deeply gratifying to have such a reception. But evidently he was not conscious that his personality was a factor. If in all his incessant labors he thought of himself at all it was with a sense of almost bewildered surprise that he, with all his limitations, was accorded such a privilege of service.

It may be fitting to quote from another editorial: "He seems further to be a shrewd, clear-headed man of the world, fitted by much mingling with men to address himself with force and effect to the most stimulating tendencies in the human heart. Every line of his unstudied—yet carefully prepared—address attests this."

Early in this mission Moody was called upon to pass through a great bereavement; his youngest brother Samuel, for whom he had so great affection, died suddenly. The news was conveyed in a laconic message "Samuel is dead"; there was no warning or preparation and it came just as Moody was about to confront an audience of eight thousand people. It was a severe shock and he hastened to his mother upon whom the blow fell with the greatest severity. But after the simple obsequies and such ministry of comfort as he could render Moody again resumed his work in Chicago.

The mission in Chicago continued through October, November and December with unabated interest. Here where Moody was known as in no other city, he seems to have had accorded him the same cordial hearing as elsewhere. Day after day throngs attended meetings and visitors from adjoining towns came to participate in the mission.

The services in Chicago which began under the cloud of personal bereavement closed with a tragic loss which cast a shadow not only over Moody himself but over his fellow associates and for that matter over the community. This was the death of P. P. Bliss and his wife in a railway accident at Ashtabula while on his way to join the work in Chicago.

For Bliss, Moody entertained a deep affection. He had turned to him first as his helper in Great Britain and it was a great disappointment when Bliss was unable to go. Bliss was a man of exceptional gifts, endowed with qualities both as solo singer, choral leader and composer. He was a thoroughly trained musician, sharing with Mr. George C. Stebbins the distinction of being easily the first in evangelistic work in this respect. In single-hearted devotion to the cause in which he was enlisted he combined a rare winsomeness of personality and a keen sense of humor. At the memorial service held on the Sunday following the accident, which occurred on Friday, December 29, 1876, Moody spoke with difficulty of his beloved friend and associate. "I have been looking over his hymns to see if I could find one appropriate to the occasion," he said in his brief address, "and I find they are all like himself, full of hope and cheer. In all the years I have known and worked with him I have never once seen him cast down."

A significant feature of the work in Chicago as elsewhere is awakened interest in the Bible. A reporter of the *Chicago Times* wrote under date of December 31, 1876:

> Among the results of the revival meetings of Messrs. Moody and Sankey the increased demand for Bibles is worthy of attention. This is not without interest from a commercial point of view, and it is quite significant as indicating the increased study of the book. To ascertain what the increase has been a *Times* reporter called during the week at the principal book stores.

Then follows the returns given by these stores indicating from two to four times the number sold during the corresponding season of the previous year.

CHAPTER XLII

In going to Boston after the Chicago missions, conditions confronted Moody that he had not encountered heretofore. Twenty years ago he had left the little shoe store on Court Street to try his fortune in Chicago and now he was returning to the Athens of America to proclaim his message. Boston was the citadel of liberal theology in America. Emerson, Theodore Parker and Channing were men who had made their impress upon the thought life of many. Cambridge is just across the river from Boston's Back Bay district and the influence of Harvard, which was distinctly Unitarian, was potent. And what a coterie of names there were at that time: Longfellow, Whittier, Elliot, Lowell, Holmes, Fisk. To many the character of Moody's message savored of medievalism and the preaching of the cross was an offense. The biographer of Theodore Roosevelt describes a class among the late President's hearers that would be applicable to some in Boston who came, from curiosity, to hear Moody.

> No doubt among those who listened to him in each place there were carping critics, scholars who did not find his words scholarly enough, dilettanti made tepid by over-culture, intellectual cormorants made heavy by too much information, who found no novelty in what he said, and were insensible to the rush and freshness of his style.

On the other hand there were a group of earnest evangelicals ready to accord Moody support. In Phillips

Brooks he found a sympathetic well-wisher, while A. J. Gordon and Albert Plumb were whole-hearted supporters of the work. Two laymen are outstanding for their coöperation, Henry F. Durant and Henry M. Moore.

At one time during the mission Moody was for some reason unable to preach and asked Phillips Brooks to take his place. According to Bishop Brooks' biographer:

> Many doubted whether Mr. Brooks could hold a congregation drawn together by Mr. Moody's peculiar gift of earnest and direct appeal. But he was invited in the confidence that the thousands who were flocking nightly to the tent, or "Tabernacle" as it was called, where the services were held would not be disappointed when they knew of the change. The confidence was not misplaced. It was an event in the history of the revival that Phillips Brooks had taken part in it. On that evening the "Tabernacle" is reported as filled to its utmost capacity. Mr. Sankey sang "The Ninety and Nine." Other hymns were "Just as I am without one plea," and "'Tis the promise of God full salvation to give." The text from which the sermon was preached was the words of St. Paul describing his conversion. "Whereupon, O King Agrippa, I was not disobedient unto the heavenly vision."

Of the mission Bishop Brooks speaks with evident sympathy. "There is a good healthy religious influence, I think, and underneath our little work the deep thunder of the Moody movement is rolling all the time."

It was probably in Boston more than elsewhere that Moody met with those in inquiry rooms who were genuinely troubled with intellectual difficulties. There were of course the counterfeits whose obvious mental deficiencies debarred the possibility of any difficulty being intellectual. These Moody could readily deal with, often revealing the secret of trouble to lie in moral turpitude. On the other hand there were also the genuine seekers after truth, many of whom Moody would refer to his host and coworker, Mr. Henry F. Durant, who had come to an evangelical position only after many struggles with the same problems which perplexed the educated youth of the day.

The noonday prayer meetings were held in Tremont Temple. A daily paper reports, "Long before the time announced for the meeting to begin every available seat was occupied . . . and a large crowd of disappointed applicants outside besieged the doors and appealed to the inexorable policemen in vain."

Here too the journalists are mystified at the apparent success; an editorial in the *Globe* reads:

> It is a marvel to many people how the preaching of Mr. Moody produces the effect which evidently comes from it. He is not a learned man in doctrines or profound in theological study. He is not even strikingly original in thought or forcible in style of expression. He has few of the arts or graces of oratory, and yet he brings people together in greater crowds and apparently produces more effect upon their thoughts and feelings and conduct than the most brilliant and cultured of popular divines. What is the secret of his success? . . . The whole explanation of the mystery is probably to be found in one word—earnestness. His views may not be philosophical or even logical. They may be far from correct, but he has a thorough belief in them himself. In what he has to say he has no misgivings and no qualifications. To him it is Divine Truth and vitally important to every living man. . . . We may question as we will the soundness of the views of life and of the destiny of man which he promul-

gates; we may have doubts of the salutary effects upon the mind and the nervous system of his impassioned appeals and his representations of the duties of life and consequences of death; we may hesitate about believing that permanent good results from such revivals attend his preaching; but there is one lesson that all can learn of him. Earnestness of purpose and whole-souled devotion to an object, be it what is called the saving of souls, or be it any worldly pursuit whatever, are the real elements of success.

According to the *Transcript:*

> Any analysis of the charm of Mr. Moody's speech arrives finally at his transparent singleness of purpose as the bottom fact. The most skeptical must respect such honesty pure and simple, such unadulterated zeal to do good. . . . There is a tenderness as true and gentle as that of a loving parent to his child. [And the same journal finds after a week] the whole character and effects of the movement not only unobjectionable, but indicative of good. [Moody] exhibits sagacity, shrewdness and a wonderful skill in the plan of his ministrations. . . .

Boston's reputation for "philosophic dilettantism, apathy, frigidity and conceit of intellectual superiority" has no terrors for him and he appears "neither appalled nor disheartened by any opposition or difficulty he was likely to encounter from that quarter."

> Individuals, groups and coteries whose repute is of that character are wholly out of reach of Mr. Moody. Doubtless some of them may make him the subject of psychological study or essay, and may explain any degree of success he may meet, wholly independently of the agencies and means he will

ascribe to it. But this class of the favored and petted illuminati of Boston conceive that their philosophy of nature, truth and life sinks below any depths to which Mr. Moody's plummet has ever sounded. Yet as they realize how utterly powerless their ideal fancies and speculative ingenuities are to meet the real cravings of the common run of human beings, and to grapple with crimes, follies, woes, and miseries of human life, they will doubtless welcome any good results wrought in the character, habits and principles of men and women even by methods which they discredit.

Moody's "broad catholicity and toleration" impresses some journalists; others find criticisms "ineffective and unprofitable when such crowds of the learned and unlearned, rich and poor, high and low, flock to him for religious teaching and consolation."

The first years of Moody's return to America had been divided between five great centers—Brooklyn, Philadelphia, New York, Chicago and Boston. The next year, 1877-78, he decided to devote to the smaller cities of New England—Burlington and Montpelier in Vermont; Concord and Manchester in New Hampshire; Providence in Rhode Island; Springfield in Massachusetts; Hartford and New Haven in Connecticut.

The traditional conservatism of New England made some question the results of evangelistic work in the unresponsive atmosphere of small cities. But an article in the *Religious Herald*, December 19, 1878, recounts the general sympathy which Moody's work had evoked:

> Ministers of churches not in sympathy with the revival methods, not believing in the great doctrines of Christ, have been enforced to speak words of kindness in respect to the evangelists. The wave of sympathy has been so strong, that it seems to have

flowed out and covered everything else. . . . We discover first of all, that religion to have a great hold on men, does not need the inspiration of architecture or an elaborated ceremonial. How austerely plain is the edifice without embellishment of any kind! No richly carven pulpit, canopied with its pendent sounding board above, as in an English cathedral, no massive organ, no oaken stalls and screens, and cherubs' heads, softly darkened by time, no polished marbles, no lofty arches and groined roof, no painted window, mellow and radiant and historic, no symbols, not even a cross, or the trefoil of the Trinity, but instead of these a great plain room, perhaps four hundred feet long, and one hundred fifty feet wide, full of clear daylight, its only music drawn from such an organ as many of us have in our houses, and its only pulpit a handrail. Not austerity, but simplicity, a sheltered spot, warm and lighted, where thousands may sit down together, and be at the command of a single presence and a single voice. . . .

Realness, this is what you think of from first to last; no airs, no fine sentiment, no vague thoughts beginning somewhere and leading out nowhere. . . .

We may perhaps learn from him that we have been having too much of what is called culture in our pulpits and in our sermons; perhaps the Bible has been crowded out that other books may take its place. Perhaps, to use the old expression, our sermons smell too much of the lamp; and are too little redolent of the fragrance of grace. Perhaps they are literature instead of speech. If it be so, we have greatly erred; and perhaps by reason of it, leanness has entered into our souls. . . .

But the fact that the dailies were filled with religious addresses to the exclusion of matters artistic, literary, and political, indicates, as did the thronged audiences, that religion really holds a very prominent place in men's regard, and that when it is addressed in a tone, not doubting, nor wavering, but in confidence and in earnestness, it will respond more heartily and contagiously than to any other subject. And in an age like ours when a scientific scepticism has already begun to boast of having carried the day, and left the church nothing but rotting traditions and dead customs, and empty ceremonies, all soon to vanish, what a joy it must give us to have the certification that the religious nature of man cannot be extinguished. . . .

CHAPTER XLIII

The winter of 1878-79 marked a distinct change in the character of Moody's work. He turned from the large and intense mission to a service more protracted and more closely identified with the church. The permanency of an evangelistic mission, he felt, was to be measured by the numbers of those who became identified with the churches in the communities, for Moody, though unsectarian, was essentially a churchman. "If I had one drop of sectarian blood in my veins," he said to a friend, "I would let it out." But he believed in all the evangelical denominations constituting the "Holy Catholic church."

It was because of this that Moody refused association with the Salvation Army. One of Moody's friends who had become interested in the work of the Army, arranged a breakfast that Moody might meet "General" Booth. Moody was glad to meet with a fellow worker, and though he did not feel the appeal of the Army's methods, he was not disposed to be indifferent. What he disapproved was the Jesuitical autocracy of the leader and the assumption of the direction of every individual. It seemed to him that the system precluded the immediate guidance of the Spirit of God and the dictates of conscience. Another point of divergence was the attitude of General Booth to church membership and activity within the church itself of those who had become Christians through the agency of his coworkers.

"What is to be your attitude to the churches?" Moody asked the "General."

"I am not going to be involved with them," was the reply.

"Are you going to start a new denomination?"

"No."

Moody then submitted a case, hypothetically stated, but based upon an actual experience. "Here is a case upon which I would like to know what advice you would give," he said, addressing the general. "A young lady, who has been the child of godly parents and the object of their prayers, but has been indifferent to all religious things, is converted in the army. The parents are rejoiced and urge her to accompany them to the services of their church and join their fellowship. She comes to you for advice. What will be your attitude?"

"I would ask her where she had found life."

"Her answer," replied Moody, "will be 'In the army.'"

"Then," said "General" Booth, "I will tell her to remain where she found life."

"Are you going to start a new denomination?"

Again the reply was "No."

"What then is to be your attitude to the administration of the sacraments?"

"What sacraments do you mean?"

"The communion, for instance."

"I shall leave it alone. It was a mistake to have ever instituted it. The quarrels of Christendom have arisen around the Lord's table."

"Do I understand you to say our Lord made a mistake?"

"Well, I won't say that," replied "General" Booth, "but I will say that it would have been better if it had never been instituted." This determined Moody's attitude toward the movement which he felt lacked an essential element of spiritual permanency by its aloofness from the organized churches.

In his work in the large centers visited he felt that

D. L. MOODY

too often the great value of the interest aroused had not been used to advantage because it was disassociated, in the minds of many, with the church. Therefore when in 1878 he received an invitation to Baltimore Moody was desirous of adopting a new plan of campaign. He determined to spend the entire winter in the city, giving several weeks in different churches. It did not matter what the denomination of the church might be, but he sought to associate more closely the meetings with the regular services of a place of worship.

He spent the early autumn of 1878 in the Chicago Avenue Church and on October 29 began the winter's work in Baltimore. Week after week he spoke in various parts of the city and carefully avoided holding meetings which might interfere with regular church services in the community.

One notable service he rendered at this time was in the penitentiary. Here Sunday after Sunday he preached to the prisoners and the lives of many men were transformed. It is alleged that one of the officials stated that it would have paid the state to have kept Moody connected with the penal institution permanently as so many who had been repeatedly committed never came back after that winter.

While primarily he had announced that the year in Baltimore was to be one of preparation and study and in an early interview he intimated that he hoped to spend six hours a day thus engaged, it was not long before he was as actively enlisted in evangelistic work as ever. On November 16 the *American* says:

> In the present week he has preached thirteen sermons, each full of thoughts that must have been the result of patient study and reflection. . . . On Sunday morning he made a stirring appeal to over six hundred convicts in the penitentiary. An hour

later he was speaking to colored Methodists. At three o'clock in the afternoon he addressed a large congregation of colored Baptists and at eight o'clock he addressed about a thousand colored Presbyterians.

After the close of the Baltimore mission an account of the work appeared in a small book edited by two observers.

Silent and unseen, a strange, mighty influence seemed to fill the very atmosphere, and men everywhere began to think and to pray. The poor drunkard found his way into church and came out with Christ in his heart. The merchant forgot his business and sought for the waters of life. Rich and poor, old men and little children—all classes were brought under this mighty influence. Amid all this great movement the central figure was that of a plain, unassuming layman, yet one who in the hand of God has become a flaming herald of the Cross— the evangelist, D. L. Moody.

Usually Mr. Moody held his services in a large, centrally located tabernacle, and there the Christians of various denominations attended and labored. Although this plan would naturally attract many non-church-going people, yet it must be allowed that Christian laborers working here would lose many of the happy associations and the inspiration which would come to them at their own churches. The Baltimore plan was a combination of these two. Mr. Moody preached extensively in the churches, where, as men were turned to Christ, he would give them to the care of pastors. Immense throngs gathered also at public buildings—witness the Maryland Institute, the Fifth Regiment Armory and the German Street Hall meetings. The pastors of all evangelical denominations rejoiced to have a common platform on which to unite for Christian work. The first work of the committee was to divide the city into four districts—north and south of Baltimore Street and east and west of Charles Street. Out of these four districts certain churches were selected. . . .

In every church he visited the membership was largely increased, a new life seemed to be infused into the old members, and the new, by their bright experiences and earnest zeal, lent freshness to subsequent meetings. In the Methodist churches those very important organizations, the classes, were in some cases completely transformed. . . .

A very great part of his influence depended no doubt upon the matter of his discourses. He avoided all abstract reflections, all trains of reasoning, everything that could fatigue the attention or rouse the intellect to question or oppose. His preaching was based upon the most confident assertions, and it dealt almost exclusively with topics, which if firmly believed, can hardly fail to have a deep influence upon men. The utter depravity of human nature—the free salvation by Christ—the imminence of death—the necessity to salvation of a complete supernatural change of character and emotions, were the subjects upon which he continually dilated. . . .

CHAPTER XLIV

THE succeeding season, 1879-80, Moody spent in St. Louis. The results at Baltimore convinced him that he could achieve more by continuous labor in one large city than by itinerant work. Accordingly he rented a house and settled for a winter's work in this new field.

The *Globe-Democrat,* a paper having a large circulation throughout that section of the country, printed a daily report of the services and a verbatim report of his addresses. An incident of the conversion of a man who was serving in jail and was reached by this newspaper is recorded. The story as related by Moody was as follows:

> When I was holding meetings in St. Louis, Missouri, in 1880, the *Globe-Democrat* announced that it was going to publish verbatim reports of my sermons, prayers and exhortations every day. I made up my mind that I would weave in plenty of Scripture for the newspaper to carry into places that I could never enter.
>
> One night I preached on the Philippian jailer, and next morning the paper came out with a sensational headline: "How the Jailer at Philippi Was Caught." A copy of the paper was carried into the city jail, and fell into the hands of a notorious prisoner named Valentine Burke.
>
> This man was one of the worst characters known to the St. Louis police. He was about forty years old at that time, had spent about twenty years in jail, and was then awaiting trial on a serious charge.

As Burke glanced over the morning paper, the headline caught his eye. Thinking that it was some jail news he began to read it. He was so anxious to see how the jailer was caught. He thought he had once passed through a town called Philippi in Illinois, and supposed this was the place referred to.

Every now and then he came across the words, "Believe on the Lord Jesus Christ, and thou shalt be saved." That text was quoted nine times in the sermon.

Burke wondered what had happened to the *Globe-Democrat,* and looked at the date. It was that morning's paper all right. He was disgusted, but he could not shake off that text, "Believe on the Lord Jesus Christ, and thou shalt be saved." God used it to convict him, and a sense of his responsibility before God rushed upon him. There in his cell at midnight he prayed for the first time in his life. On the following Sunday he talked with the Christian friends who held service in the jail, and was led into the light of the gospel.

From that night Burke was a changed man. The sheriff thought he was playing the "pious dodge," and had no confidence in his professed conversion. But when he came to trial the case against him was not pressed, and he escaped through some technicality.

For some months after his release Burke tried to find work, but no one would take him, knowing his past history. He thought perhaps it was because of his ugly face, and he prayed God to make him good-looking. He went to New York, and was taken in by a member of the police who knew him, and who told him that he would shoot him dead if he abused his confidence. Being unsuccessful in New York he returned to St. Louis.

One day Burke received a message from the sheriff that he was wanted at the courthouse. He obeyed with a heavy heart.

"Some old case they've got against me," he said; "but if I'm guilty I'll tell them so. I've done lying."

The sheriff greeted him kindly, "Where have you been, Burke?"

"In New York."

"What have you been doing there?"

"Trying to find an honest job."

"Have you kept a good grip on the religion you told me about?" inquired the sheriff.

"Yes," answered Burke. "I've had a hard time, sheriff, but I haven't lost my religion."

"Burke," said the sheriff, "I have had you shadowed ever since you left jail. I suspected your religion was a fraud. But I am convinced that you are sincere as you've lived an honest life, and I have sent for you to offer you a deputyship under me. You can begin at once."

This was in 1880. When I was preaching in Chicago in 1890, Burke, who had not been off duty for the ten years, came to see me. During all that time there had been many changes in the administration of the sheriff's office, and they had changed every deputy but him. Finally they appointed that ex-convict "treasurer" of the sheriff's office.

I preached in St. Louis again in 1895. A short time before my visit an evangelist was called away in the middle of revival meetings. The committee wanted Burke to come and preach in his absence, but the sheriff said he had just levied on a jeweler's store, and had not had time to take an inventory and Burke was the only man he could trust to put in charge of it.

He was held in such confidence by the police that

they did a most unusual thing; they gave him the photograph they had of him in the Rogues' Gallery. He had his photograph taken again in 1887, and in sending a copy of this, along with the original Rogues' Gallery photograph, to Mr. T. S. McPheeters of St. Louis, to show the change in his features, Burke wrote a note:

"Notice the difference in the inclosed pictures. See what our holy religion can do for the chief of sinners." On the back of the Rogues' Gallery photograph he wrote: "He raiseth up the poor out of the dust, and lifteth the needy out of the dunghill, that He may set him with the princes, even with the princes of His people."

This incident shows what the grace of God can do for a hardened sinner. Not only can it save him, but it can keep him. Valentine Burke lived an active, consistent Christian life in the position until God called him home in 1895.

In different sections of the city Moody labored for several weeks until he had visited all parts. At this time Dr. Constans L. Goodell was one of the leading pastors in St. Louis and whole-heartedly supported the mission. His testimony to Moody's work expressed what many other pastors felt. He wrote:

> God has visited His people in this city through the coming of our beloved brethren, Moody and Sankey. Forty ministers met them in conference the day after their arrival. The city was divided into five districts, grouping the churches thus for a month's work in each district. No tabernacle was desired, the object being to work in and with the churches, and to quicken the churches themselves into more active effort and higher spiritual life. The second service they held was blessed by the special

presence of the Holy Spirit, and from that hour to this there has been no service in which there have not been inquirers and conversions in constantly increasing numbers. A great many cold Christians have been quickened. Persons formerly Christians in other places, but hiding the fact on coming here, and living apart from the Church, have appeared in great numbers, making confession of neglect and handing in their letters. . . .

Mission work in the waste places and suburbs has been extended, and all kinds of Christian work in the city have been vitalized and multiplied many fold. The colored churches have received new life, and the great German population has become awakened and interested in personal religion as never before in the history of this city.

Early in the season the Germans got up a Moody and Sankey play. One, personating Mr. Sankey, sang; another, representing Mr. Moody, gave a side-splitting sermon. Then they had inquirers and a bevy of converts, and at that point Satan came in on the stage and carried them all off and put an end to the scene, to the vast delight of the audience. But now all this is changed. A revival German preacher, once a famous infidel, but marvellously converted, Von Schluembach, is preaching every day to thousands of Germans, in their own tongue, with most gratifying results. The work of Gospel temperance is also very effective, and meetings are crowded nightly with drinking men. A canvass has been begun of the whole city, every house being visited, and parents invited to attend church and children the Sunday school.

Mr. Moody is discreet, courageous, effective, powerful; working day and night, month after month, with an energy and perseverance and wisdom only less remarkable than his love of souls, and his constantly fresh anointing from God for service. His work is marked for its spirituality, humility, modesty, and self-forgetfulness. . . . I heard the evangelists five years ago, week after week, when the work was at its height in London, and I bear testimony that there has been a gain in them of breadth, condensed power of statement, exhaustiveness in presenting themes, and mellowness in Christian graces. There is the might of the tempest and the gentleness of the lamb; the awful power and earnestness of truth, as in Christ's discourse to the Pharisees, mingled with the moving tenderness of tears, as when Christ wept over Jerusalem.

In the winter of 1880-81 Moody went to San Francisco. The occasion of this visit was in part due to the earnest solicitation of his friend Mr. Morris K. Jesup, a prominent New York business man, whose interest in Y. M. C. A. work was not limited to his own city but embraced every sphere of association activity.

In 1876 Mr. Jesup had occasion to visit the Pacific coast and was greatly impressed with the need of aggressive Christian work of the kind which had already been successfully carried on in New York City [says his biographer]. The Association of San Francisco was at this time deeply in debt and in need of a thorough reorganization. It occurred to Mr. Jesup that if Mr. Moody, who was then in the height of his success as an evangelist, could be induced to go to San Francisco, an impulse might be given to the Christian life of that city which would not only arouse an immediate interest in religion, but would put the Association upon its feet and make it the efficient instrument for Christian service which in his conviction it ought to be. Mr. Moody and Mr. Jesup had been friends for some years. During the evangelistic campaign which Mr. Moody had just completed in New York City he had been Mr. Jesup's guest, and the latter had gained an insight into his methods and had formed a high opinion of his judgment. He accordingly proposed to Mr. Moody to inaugurate a campaign in San Francisco similar to that which he had already conducted in New York. Mr. Moody accepted the invitation and, in coöperation with the International Committee, of which Mr. Jesup was at that time a member, a very satisfactory work was carried on by the evangelist, in the fruits of which the people of San Francisco and the Association alike participated.

BOOK V

CHAPTER XLV

"I AM a man of impulse," Moody once said to a member of his family. "The best things I have ever done have been decided on the impulse. I suppose when I die I'll just be up and off." His final settling in Northfield and the subsequent work which grew up about his home was determined by an impulse.

On returning to America after his mission in Great Britain in 1875 he spent some weeks in Northfield with his mother. One day he learned that a neighbor had been annoyed by his mother's hens trespassing into his cornfield which closely abutted upon the back of the little homestead. To avoid the recurrence of such an aggravation he sought to purchase a strip of land which was of inconsiderable value and could be procured, he thought, at a small outlay. Meeting the owner one day while driving on a country road Moody stopped and explained his purpose and asked if he would sell the desired land.

"No," replied the farmer, "I don't care to sell, unless it is the whole place."

"How many acres?" asked Moody.

"Twelve," was the reply.

"How much?"

"Well," said the neighbor, "I'll take thirty-five hundred dollars for the whole place with house and barns."

"I'll take it," Moody responded without a moment's hesitation, and the transaction was closed.

Moody intended to sell the farm, reserving only such land as he had originally wanted to acquire. On further consideration, however, he realized that it would be prudent to keep it for a few years as a home for his family. Since the Chicago fire he had been homeless, and he felt he owed it to his wife and children to provide some fixed abode, if only for a brief period in the summer.

Northfield has been richly favored by nature. Situated on the Connecticut River where Massachusetts borders New Hampshire and Vermont, its location is at the very gateway to the scenic attractions of New England. Far away on the Canadian border the river takes its rise. Through the first hundred and fifty miles it winds its tortuous course among the foothills of the White Mountains on the New Hampshire side and the Green Mountains on the Vermont side, marking the common boundary of these states. Often the hills rise abruptly from the banks of the river and the gentle flow becomes a foaming rapid as it rushes through the narrow defiles. From time to time cataracts break the river's course, while in the placid reaches the unruffled surface mirrors the wooded hillsides covered with maple, birch and elms, with their dark background of spruce, hemlock and balsam. Here and there upland farms and pastures overlook the valley, and the wild woodland changes to peaceful pastoral scenes. As the river enters Massachusetts, its character changes. The valley broadens, meadow lands flank the river banks, and the mountains recede. No longer in holiday mood, capricious frolicking gives place to the spirit of industry, and the music of the wilds to the whirring of wheels.

The impulse that determined Moody's home was indeed a happy one for the prospect, unobstructed, included river, valley and succeeding mountain ranges.

Simplicity was still the distinguishing characteristic of New England village life at the time and this he coveted for his children. The proximity to his mother in her declining years was also a strong factor in his deciding to locate in Northfield. Furthermore, his work had been so constant in recent years that no time had been afforded for reading. More and more he realized his own needs in this direction. No one was more keenly alive to the fact that the constant use of old material becomes inimical to effectiveness. It was imperative, therefore, for him to have a place where he could assemble a modest library and apply himself to systematic study.

The place he had purchased was unpretentious. The old farmhouse boasted of no modern improvements, even in the circumscribed use of the term in those days, and even for his small family was inadequate, necessitating a few alterations and additions. The farm as such, was poor, the acreage being mostly moss covered sand dunes. While the price paid was not high, it was all the place was worth.

During the summer of 1876 Moody and his family spent a few weeks in the new home where to his great joy he observed his children acquiring a fondness akin to his own for the place of his boyhood associations. Mrs. Moody, whose life had always been spent in a city, did not find it so easy to adjust herself to the novel experiences of country life but with characteristic self-forgetfulness she applied herself to the readjustment.

During the mornings Moody would withdraw to his library and work; afternoons he would give to renewing earlier experiences on the farm often assisting his brothers.

On one occasion he drove with his brother Samuel to a distant pasture to see some cattle. Returning home they passed a humble cabin, far up in the mountains. Sitting in the doorway were the mother and three daughters who eked out a meager existence by plaiting straw hats. The father was a helpless paralytic. Stopping by the wayside the two brothers entered into conversation with the cripple and his family whose intelligence and simple Christian faith impressed Moody. As they drove away Moody and his brother began to speculate as to the prospects which the future might have in store for the young people. A little district school on the mountain summit was the only educational privilege available. At that time there was no public high school nearer than the county seat, fourteen miles away but, in their circumstances, they could never pay their board while attending school, even if tuition were free. Two probabilities were before them, either they might marry and settle down on a mountain farm to a life of drudgery or they might become operatives in some factory in a neighboring town. In either case they would lack such an education as would liberate them from the thralldom of the immediate environment.

Then Moody realized that these girls but typified a general need, and slowly there evolved an idea for a school to meet the needs of the community. But for a time the seed which found lodgment in the heart and brain did not germinate. The plans for the coming year's work in Chicago and Boston precluded further consideration of such an enterprise, and also it is not at all improbable that Moody was conscious of grave misgivings as to his own qualifications for such an undertaking.

But when, in the following October, Samuel died, the plan which they had discussed together again took vivid form in Moody's mind.

CHAPTER XLVI

WHILE conducting the mission in Boston that winter Moody was the guest of Mr. Henry F. Durant, the founder of Wellesley College, with whom he talked over the prospective scheme of a school for girls in Northfield. In his host he found a sympathetic listener whose conception of the character of true education closely coincided with Moody's own views. He felt that if a university graduate and successful man like Mr. Durant held essentially the same views, he could take courage and still further develop his plans.

Henry F. Durant had been transformed in character by the sudden death of an only child in whom his every purpose in life had been centered. With his conversion he not only abandoned his former ambitions but also retired from the bar. He applied himself to Bible study and for nine years had given himself to evangelistic work in New England churches. But during all this time the thought of devoting his Wellesley estate to some form of Christian service had been evolving in his mind. Ever a champion of the weak and underprivileged, convinced that education was the prerogative of women equally with men, and realizing the inadequate provisions of colleges for those of limited means, he finally determined on the disposition of the estate. This home wherein his son was to have been surrounded by everything which should provide a broad culture, Durant dedicated to the higher education of women and primarily to those of limited means. "He gave himself," writes his biographer, "to the work with a lavish generosity which I say, deliberately, cannot be matched in all the histories of all the institutions of learning on earth. He built both the visible and the invisible Wellesley, in the closing ten years of a life crowded with achievement."

There were distinctive characteristics in Mr. Durant's conception of the educational system in this new college to which he had given a million dollars, in those days a princely fortune. It was to offer "to young women opportunities for education equivalent to those provided at Harvard; paramount to every other qualification in a teacher is that of vital Christianity; the charges are placed at the moderate sum of two hundred and fifty dollars per annum for board and tuition"; every girl was to share in the domestic work of the college. It was intended, as Mr. Durant expressed it, for "the calico girl."

It will be readily appreciated how Moody would endorse this conception of an education and he was full of inquiry as to how each problem had been met. Wellesley had opened in September, 1875.

Mr. Durant, at this time, was fifty-four and Moody was fourteen years his junior. From these days an intimate friendship ensued and Moody accepted a trusteeship of Wellesley College, Mr. Durant acting in similar capacity for Northfield Seminary when it was subsequently founded; in both instances the fiduciary service continued throughout life.

The purchase of a school site was characteristic of Moody. One day in the fall of 1878 he stood discussing the project with Mr. H. N. F. Marshall of Boston, when the owner of sixteen acres of land adjoining his original purchase passed them. They asked the man if he would sell, and learning his price, invited him into the house, made out the papers, and before the owner had recovered from his surprise the land had passed out of his hands. Three or four other adjoining lots were bought until the estate increased to one hundred acres, suitably located and commanding a pleasing view of the Connecticut Valley.

Moody had no private fortune like his friend Durant with which to build and endow a school. But he had friends and he used to say, "They constitute the greatest riches." From such he now received help.

In the spring of 1879 the erection of a recitation hall intended for one hundred students was begun. However, Moody could not wait for a dormitory to be built and altered his own home to accommodate the students, its capacity having been increased by finishing off a number of small rooms over a shed. Instead of the eight pupils expected twenty-five appeared. With these, the Northfield Seminary was formally opened on November 3, 1879, classes being held in the dining room of Moody's home until the recitation hall was completed the following December.

Moody was essentially an empiricist. He observed certain defects in the education of youth which required the introduction of supplementary, if novel, features into academic life. That he contravened tradition signified little to him.

The memory of early years had made him realize the value of forming habits of industry and thrift. In his judgment any well-rounded training should be comprehensive and not limited to the conning of books and the enjoyment of social intercourse; there was need of inculcating early in life a sense of individual responsibility and a practical knowledge of the value of labor and consequently of money. This object, he believed, could be best obtained by division of the household duties and the assignment of some specific task to each scholar. Latent ability would be developed in the individual and, under careful supervision, proficiency would be rewarded by successive advancement. Newcomers naturally began with the more menial duties while those who had passed through the novitiate assumed such responsibilities as the preparation of the meals.

Among other advantages of such a plan would be its democratizing influence. Those whose racial or religious background differed would find that prejudices disappeared in the intimate association of a common task; mutual sympathy and understanding would be promoted. The girl of studious habits and intellectual gifts would learn to appreciate the fellow student less gifted but whose dependability and industry were displayed in the discharge of her daily tasks.

There was another lesson that Moody believed would be taught by the introduction of such a system—a genuine understanding sympathy with those whose lot in life would be to earn their living by the labor of their hands. Sympathy with others, a recognition of the dignity of all honest work, and ability to teach the unskilled, all were involved in the scheme.

In this one feature of his system of education there was the economic consideration, dispensing with a staff of employees, as well as the practical training of the individual. It was in fact a clinic in elementary economics, social philosophy and Christian ethics. Side by side the daughter of sturdy and thrifty Puritan parentage worked with those from distant lands, with unfamiliar customs and strangely different traditions. Mutually they might learn what the classroom never could impart.

As the school was for those of limited means it was necessary that charges should be placed within the reach of this class. Moody therefore fixed the fees at one hundred dollars a year, inclusive of board and tuition, one-half of the actual cost. When remonstrated with on the plea that some were unable to pay even this half Moody's reply was characteristic: "If a student can't do her share she isn't worth educating. I am ready to meet any ambitious student halfway. If she raises one hundred dollars

I will raise the other hundred. It's better to help a person to help himself. I find you can do a real injury by doing too much for the individual."

But if the uniform charge was to be low it was obviously necessary that the school should be exclusively for those for whom it was established. He insisted he had no right to raise funds for the education of those who could afford to attend more expensive schools.

At first Moody's plan did not intend receiving students beyond the immediate vicinity of Northfield. His sympathy was enlisted primarily in neighbors' children. Probably his vision was circumscribed by the horizon, for he sought to purchase an old frame building, known as the "Beehive," in the village a mile from his home. But the need which he sought to meet was greater than he realized. From the first, applications for admission far exceeded the limited accommodations provided.

In four years the original recitation hall was found entirely inadequate, for a new dormitory had been built the following year and a house acquired and adapted the next season. As soon as the character of the school and the privileges offered became generally known applications poured in not only from adjacent communities but from all over the country.

Teachers were chosen for their Christian character as well as proficiency in their subject and the Bible was assigned an important place in the curriculum of the school. This emphasis on the knowledge of the Scriptures was given not only for moral and spiritual values but also for its educational importance. "No one who is ignorant of the Bible can be said to be well educated," Moody maintained, "while one who is familiar with God's Word can never be said to be illiterate." Therefore he insisted on Bible instruction for all.

Moody's conception of education was clearly outlined in a letter to a New York newspaper in 1896:

There are two things necessary to the life of this nation; one is knowledge, the other righteousness.

The founders of the republic recognized the need of education, and framed their policy accordingly. Educational advantages were to be widely diffused, so that the curse of ignorance should not rest upon the people. The same truth has been realized by nearly all reformers. Examine the theories of government put forward by socialistic writers and societies, from Plato to the present day, and you will find that emphasis is nearly always laid upon the establishment of schools and the diffusion of knowledge. In this country a good education has been put within the reach of the poorest. Rich men have devoted their wealth to the founding of colleges and other institutions, so that a higher education is accessible to those who desire it. Knowledge is increasing and becoming more general.

But of what use is knowledge alone, mere knowledge? It has no spiritual or moral power. The Bible says: "Knowledge puffeth up." It has not saved any of the old civilizations from annihilation. Egypt and Athens and Rome had knowledge, and yet they died of corruption. Education is powerless to prevent crime. In the state of Massachusetts, where education of every kind, public and private, has been longer and better established than in any other state of the Union, we had in 1850 one prisoner to every 800 of population; in 1880, there was one in about 450, and a year ago a Boston paper stated that one in every 225 was in jail.

Without righteousness, knowledge may become a keener instrument for wickedness. What we want is not education of the head alone, but rather regeneration of the heart by the Holy Ghost. Until the heart is made right all else will be wrong; for out of it are the issues of life. From within, out of the heart of man, proceed evil thoughts and all uncleanness. No amount of secular education can change its character. What is needed is a new heart, a knowledge of the true and living God. I believe this country is not lacking in regard to education, but we need a revival of gospel preaching—the plain, old-fashioned, unadulterated gospel of the Lord Jesus Christ. It is righteousness that exalteth a nation.

Sectarianism was ignored in the trustees whom he asked to serve on the board and the selection of a preceptress and teachers was without prejudice on the ground of denominational affiliations. All he sought was unity of purpose. From the students no religious qualifications were asked. All might be admitted but always the evangelistic spirit dominated the school.

That which contributed so greatly to Northfield's influence was the real spirit of sacrifice on the part of those who labored faithfully and zealously with Moody. Under the circumstances salaries were of necessity small and in the earlier years the facilities were meager. Moody never failed to recognize the contribution made by these co-laborers to the success of the work.

Unlike some educators, he placed great importance upon handwriting. Frequently he would offer prizes for the greatest improvement in letter writing and he would take personal interest in assigning the reward. Under date of May 30, 1896, he writes to Miss Evelyn Hall, principal of the school:

> I am glad to hear what you told me about the students regarding their handwriting this year. Now when I go from Chicago to Iowa I will have time to read letters. Will you ask all the students to write

me one thought they have got this school year that has helped them and then I can see their handwriting.

In dedicating East Hall, the first dormitory erected for Northfield Seminary, Moody said:

> You know that the Lord laid it upon my heart some time ago to organize a school for young women in the humbler walks of life, who never would get a Christian education but for a school like this. I talked about this plan of mine to friends, until a number of them gave money to start the school.
>
> My lack of education has always been a great disadvantage to me; I shall suffer from it as long as I live.
>
> I hope after all of us who are here to-day are dead and gone, this school may live, and be a blessing to the world, and that missionaries may go out from here and preach the gospel to the heathen, and it may be recognized as a power in bringing souls to Christ. . . .
>
> And now as we dedicate this building to God, I want to read you the motto of this school. [Then turning to Isaiah xxvii. 3, he read:]
>
> "I the Lord do keep it; I will water it every moment: lest any hurt it, I will keep it night and day."

In the corner stone of each of the school buildings proper a copy of the Scriptures has been placed. This is symbolic of the place that God's Word has held in the life of the schools. It is indeed foundation, corner stone and capstone of Moody's whole system.

CHAPTER XLVII

But what Moody had achieved for poor girls immediately raised inquiries if he would not also accept boys. To this he demurred. He was prejudiced against coeducation. "Let someone else take on the boys," his answer would be to oft repeated requests in their behalf. "I can't assume the responsibility for coeducation and my hands are full with what I've already undertaken."

It was at this juncture that Mr. Hiram Camp of New Haven, Connecticut, who had become acquainted with Moody during his mission in that city two years before, came to visit him at Northfield to consult him about making his will. After explaining that he had been successful in business and had provided amply for his family Mr. Camp said that he wanted to make bequests that would be helpful to the Christian community.

"Why not be your own executor?" Moody asked. "You've had all the work of acquiring your means, why not have the fun of seeing it do good?"

"Well, to what should I give?"

"What is your denomination?"

"I am a Congregationalist," said Mr. Camp.

"Well then, give to some one of the many societies of your church. They are well manned and it will be wisely used."

"But I want to give to something specific; I want to see what I do."

"All right. Here is the very thing," said Moody. "People have been after me to take boys into Northfield. I'm not going to increase my troubles that way. Then they would want me to start a school for boys on the same lines as Northfield, but I want someone else to do it. Now, Mr. Camp, there is something for you to do." Mr. Camp was at this time over seventy years of age and felt that he had lost contact with youth and would not be qualified to launch such a project, but he was deeply interested as Moody defined his conception of such a school as he would like to see established. Then Mr. Camp challenged Moody to undertake it, offering to make the initial gift of twenty-five thousand dollars. This placed Moody in an awkward position. So well had he defined the need and so enthusiastically described the plans and methods he would advocate in the hopes of having Mr. Camp assume this service, that he had unwittingly committed himself.

Two adjoining farms, totaling about two hundred and seventy-five acres, were purchased in Gill, four miles away from Northfield. The old farmhouses were altered to suit the school needs; they stood on an elevation overlooking the Connecticut Valley.

The school was named by Mr. Camp "Mount Hermon" after the ancient school for the prophets, "for there the Lord commanded the blessing, even life forevermore" (Psalms cxxxiii. 3). It was opened May 1, 1881, with the enrollment of one student. At this time Moody's design was to take candidates under sixteen years of age who were from homes of limited means.

No one was more ready than Moody to acknowledge mistaken judgment. Determined, persevering and patient, his mind was not closed to evidence nor did he confuse stubbornness and pride for faith and courage. Nowhere is this better exemplified than in his readiness to radically change the character of the work at Mount Hermon in respect to the student enrollment. Three years later, believing that younger boys had more opportunities to secure schooling and that institutional life was ill adapted for the young, the age limit was raised and it was decided to make sixteen the *minimum* age.

An added reason for this change was that applications for admission began to pour in from young men whose earlier education had for various reasons been meager and who wished to resume their schooling. Considering themselves too old to return to public school and without sufficient funds to attend private schools, though here too their age would be a matter of embarrassment to them, they longed for a place adapted to their peculiar needs. To supply this need now became Moody's aim.

In Mount Hermon the same policies which characterized Northfield Seminary were adopted. The student paid one hundred dollars which was half the cost of maintenance; Bible study was included in the schedule of every one. Here too the dignity and democracy of work was prescribed, two hours daily being assigned to each student. The laundry, the dining hall and a large farm with its varied forms of industry were carried on by the students under the supervision of a competent director.

Memories of his own youth made Moody sympathetic with a young man who was handicapped in life for want of an education. Mount Hermon, therefore, is an expression of his own sense of loss and an evidence of his loving sympathy for others like himself.

The growth of Mount Hermon was rapid and only a few months before Moody laid down his work he adopted a plan whereby more students could enroll, introducing a system of three terms of fifteen weeks each. In this way one and a half academic years could be comprised within a calendar year.

Moody's ambition was that the students should ever be loyal to the evangelical faith. On May 17, 1898, at the exercises attending the laying of the corner stone of Overtoun Hall, he said:

The thought I want to present to you to-day is that soon these schools will be under your control. I charge you to make Christ preëminent in whatever you do. People keep asking me, "Have you sufficient for your schools?" My reply is that we have a rich endowment in friends. Let Christ be preëminent, and there will be no want of funds. Make Christ first. Make Christ the foundation and corner stone of your lives. These schools would never have existed had it not been for Christ and the Bible. Live in Christ, and the light on this hill will shine around the world.

Moody used to drive some people to a certain eminence. "This," he would say, "is Temptation Hill."

"It is a beautiful view across the valley and far away into the New Hampshire hills—inspirational, in fact—but why Temptation Hill?" was the substance of the usual reply.

"Because I hope that here someone will yield to the temptation to build a chapel." But as the hint had not been taken, Moody's sixtieth birthday was made the occasion of an effort to provide this much-needed building. Knowing no personal gift would be acceptable, a number of friends in Great Britain and America raised, by voluntary contributions, the funds necessary to build a chapel on the site he had so long designated.

Although built expressly as a memorial of Moody's birthday, he would not allow this fact to be mentioned on the bronze tablet in the vestibule which reads as follows:

"This chapel was erected by the united contributions of Christian friends in Great Britain and the United States, for the glory of God and to be a perpetual witness to their unity in the service of Christ."

Thus, without previous thought Moody buys a little

home in a quiet and remote New England village primarily to relieve his mother of a trivial annoyance—the trespassing of her hens on a neighbor's field—the result, Northfield Seminary. His advice is sought on the drawing of a will and when he gives his counsel—lo! Mount Hermon.

CHAPTER XLVIII

Moody in his own generation was preëminently known as an evangelist; in the future he will be known more and more as an educator. In the fifty years that his schools have served the youth of the country over twenty thousand boys and girls have been enrolled. These have gone forth to serve their day and generation cherishing memories of their life at Northfield or Mount Hermon. By such Moody is remembered as the Christian educator. Even those of Moody's friends who viewed the entire scheme as visionary have come to attribute the success of the work to that which was novel.

People might well look askance when Moody assumed the rôle of educator. His own lack of academic training would have seemed a sufficient barrier to entering that field. But it is significant how far his powers of observation, analysis and synthesis could carry him. Moody's success in his chosen field did not lead him to treat scholarship with contempt; rather the consciousness of his own limitations awakened his sympathy for those who wanted "such an education as would have done me good at their age." But he did not consider education the *summum bonum;* simply to train the mind might result in developing "a clever rascal," as he expressed it. Education, therefore, should be a Christian education to develop a well rounded character.

In self-education Moody had made extraordinary progress. To be sure he had not retrieved the early losses in elementary schooling, a handicap of which he was most sensitive as only those who were close to him knew. But his was essentially a scholar's attitude. His humility of spirit made him willing to assume the position of a learner everywhere and always.

Moody read as much as possible and it was to encourage his "boys and girls" to read with discrimination and care that he would admonish them to enrich their minds each day with some new thought. It was his custom to challenge them with the inquiry, "What is your best thought to-day?" and thus teach them to be ever alert to appropriate the treasures available in good reading.

In the years following their opening Moody gave himself increasingly to the work of the Northfield Schools. He said of them, "They are the best pieces of work I have ever done." It was not that he undervalued the direct preaching of the gospel message. That was the supreme object of his life. Rather it was the conviction that through the Northfield Schools where would be the preparation of thousands for Christian service at home and abroad, and the work to which he had given his life would be augmented by hundreds of educated men and women, imbued with the same ideals and earnest purpose which had actuated him. He wrote to friends, "I have been able to set in motion streams which will continue long after I have gone."

It was because he felt the need for educated and trained men and women in varied forms of Christian work that Moody labored incessantly for his schools. It was an evidence of his belief in the power of the gospel as the only panacea for the world's ills. He hoped that all his students would become evangelists—each in his or her own sphere. Not that he would seek to have everyone enter public evangelistic service like himself, but, whether in professional or business life or in the humble duties of home life, he believed the great objective of life itself was to make known the abounding grace and love of

God to mankind. He strove that his boys and girls should be loyal to this high calling.

At first Moody knew every individual student; with the growth of the schools and with their increasing enrollments, even to the end of his career he was acquainted with a surprisingly large number. He followed the subsequent careers of all with keenest interest and every achievement on their part rejoiced his heart and any failure was a bitter disappointment.

Returning home in the spring from his winter's work as an evangelist he would give the most assiduous care to the affairs of the schools. It was not enough to consult with those in immediate charge but he would familiarize himself, as far as he felt capable, with every detail. He was interested in every phase of the school life, social, athletic, as well as academic.

Unsparing in behalf of his students and ready to exercise himself to the utmost in their behalf in raising funds to maintain the work, he watched to see that such funds trusted to him by friends were carefully expended. When he was at home it was not an unusual sight to find him visiting the kitchens and even examining the garbage to see that food was not wastefully thrown away.

From the first the Northfield work was an enterprise of faith. Each year the budget was raised by appeals to the public. Never did Moody seek to build up an endowment. He argued that if the two schools he had established remained loyal to their original principles, funds would be provided and endowment would grow from bequests. A "living endowment" was what he sought in the sympathy of friends who would give to current expenses. This was in his judgment the safest provision for the permanency of his schools. Thus when he laid down his work the combined funds of Northfield Seminary and Mount Hermon, after twenty years, were only five hundred fifty thousand dollars; but the history of subsequent years fully confirmed his judgment in an ever increasing endowment in bequests from those who, during their lives, had supported the Northfield enterprise by annual contributions.

His special care in the early summer, before the schools closed for the holidays, was to have a personal interview with each member of the senior class. He would inquire what their future plans were; where they purposed pursuing their studies, if they were going to college; what prospects they had of financial help; and many other intimate questions. Then invariably would come tactful and kindly questions respecting their relationship to Christ. The sympathy of his great heart always responded to perplexing difficulties and many a youth could testify to wise counsel being supplemented in some tangible way. Often the conversation would take place in a "buggy" ride; as he passed through the school grounds a cheery invitation might greet the student returning from class, or possibly he would make an appointment to take a drive before breakfast.

If in later years the Northfield schools acquired more beautiful buildings and better equipment than during the first twenty years when Moody was still among his students, it is doubtful if any who cherished the memory of those days would exchange them, if they could, for later advantages.

It may be well to pause to inquire how far time has vindicated Moody's judgment in respect to his schools. During his lifetime he saw the total enrollment of the two schools reach six hundred sixty-seven. Since then it has increased to nearly double that number.

From these Northfield schools, as Moody foresaw, there have gone forth streams of Christian influence to all parts of the world. Statistics show hundreds in the Christian ministry and various Christian activities in the homeland, while more than two hundred have gone to foreign missionary fields. In every profession and business are to be found Northfield girls and Mount Hermon boys whose application of the lessons of industry and thrift has been richly rewarded by distinguished achievement in their chosen field. Many are rendering valued service in their home churches and local activities. But above all are the thousands who have discharged the sacred trust of maintaining a Christian home and rearing a family in the reverential love of God.

A Mount Hermon student, now holding a high and responsible position in the business world, relates an incident from his life in the school. "I was assigned as my 'work hour' duty a peculiarly disagreeable task. I grouched about it a good deal. An older student was my companion in the assignment. One day when I had been specially complaining he said, 'Look here! This work has to be done, hasn't it?' I assented. 'Well, then someone has to do it, hasn't he?' Again I assented. 'Then,' said he, 'you're no better than any one else, so get on with the work and stop grouching.' That one lesson has stood me in good stead and many a time when I have faced a disagreeable task I have recalled that incident."

There is another story which exemplifies the work done by the Northfield schools. The story begins in the city of London with a young artisan working in a cabinet shop. He is a thoughtless, irreligious youth who finds diversion in singing parodies on some of the Moody and Sankey hymns in public houses, to the boisterous delight of his companions. One night with his "girl" he attends a mission being conducted in a parish church and here the miracle of conversion takes place. The very next day he drops into the public house, as has long been his wont, for the customary hot whiskey to begin his work. As he lifts the glass to his lips something warns him that this is not the place for a Christian to be and not the thing for a Christian to do; no one has told him so but he

September 2, 1855

Hon. ? Burditt	Mary M. Burditt
Ellen A. Kirkpatrick	Hannah A. Matthews
Seth E. Chandler	Mary Jane Chandler
	Lydia A. Beck

November 4th, 1855

Benjamin Crosby	Alexander Moon Stewart
A. J. Weymouth	George A. Rollins
James Cutter Jr.	

January 6, 1856

James P. Ellis	Helen S. F. Fleming
Abigail S. Kimball	Henrietta Leath
Daniel H. Dunham	Mrs. A. C. Dunham
Abby P. ?	?

March 2, 1856

Eliza Ann Drake	Ann A. Shedd

May 3, 1856

Ernest ? ?	Ellen A. Ball
Mary S. Coolidge	Mary Ann (her mark) Cliff
Mary S. Curtis	Emily B. Richmond
John L. Rollins	Aaron N. Rollins
E. H. Barrett	Lucy P. Rollins
Hannah M. Osgood	Benjamin Cliff
Eliza B. Botsford	Dwight L. Moody
Marietta F. Brown	

July 5, 1856

Elizabeth J. Greeley	Martha E. Temple
Abigail Hutchins	Samuel O. Pearl
Sis. L. Brigg's Beaton	
Sarah Woodside	

From Records of Mt. Vernon Church

feels it. So resolutely he sets down the glass. At the shop he accosts the foreman with the fearless announcement that he has become a Christian and the news is passed on to the fellow workers. So accustomed are they to his parodies and burlesque that they proclaim this as his very best. But soon they are made to realize that the declaration is in all seriousness for the zealous convert seeks to share his new experience with his companions. Then he yearns to give himself wholly to Christian service but is confronted with a sense of inadequate educational equipment. At this juncture he reads in an English journal of a school for such young men as himself, too old to return to regular school, but eager to retrieve lost privileges. He comes to America where he works his way through school by his trade. In a few years Moody is asked to recommend a man to take charge of a small church in Denver, Colorado. Without hesitation he thinks of this boy of earnest purpose and courageous spirit. A generation later a member of Moody's family is visiting Colorado and finds the selfsame London lad, now pastor of one of the largest churches of his denomination in the state, in demand in evangelistic work and conferences throughout the Rocky Mountain region.

Surely Moody "sets streams in motion" from Northfield which are continuing long after he has entered upon his reward.

It is a temptation to record more of the incidents and results of this venture of Moody's in the field of education. That his objective was achieved could be demonstrated by the ever increasing statistical reports.

CHAPTER XLIX

THE General Conference for Christian Workers was a natural outgrowth of Moody's general conception of education and service. Both, according to him, should be Christian and at Northfield, to the utmost of his ability, he would make them so. A social gospel without Christ was futile; an evangelicalism that had no concern for a neighbor was "sounding brass and tinkling cymbal." Service was the outward expression of spiritual relationship to Christ, but a Christless social gospel was a contradiction.

In a sense the General Conference had its beginning when in 1876 Moody invited his neighbors to Bible readings in his own home. Subsequently when the first recitation hall was finished meetings were held there when Moody entertained some distinguished guest. This was notably the case when Professor W. G. Blaikie of Edinburgh was with him in the summer of 1880.

The late Dr. H. B. Hartzler writing of early experiences which led him to the first conference says:

> In November, 1879, your father conducted an evangelistic campaign in Cleveland, Ohio, where I first met him. One morning it fell to my lot to conduct a meeting for prayer in Dr. Hayden's church. The topic was "Prayer for the Church." I made a brief opening address. Your father sat immediately before me. He listened with bowed head. Suddenly he lifted his head, flashed one glance at me, as if struck with a thought, and then resumed his former position. As soon as the meeting was closed, I

stepped down from the platform, just as your father came rushing by, catching me by the arm, and taking me with him into the pastor's study, in the rear of the platform where we sat down, and he said, abruptly, "I want you to come to Northfield next summer. Will you? I want to have a meeting to wait on God, and want you." I did not make any promise.

On August the fourth, 1880, I received the first letter that ever came to me from your father as follows:

"Enclosed you will find a circular that will explain itself. I got a start toward it when in your city and you spoke at the convention held there about November 1st. Now will you come? I *want* you above any other man in this *nation*, and I will pay all *bills* if you will come. Do not say me *nay*, but come and let us wait on God together."

I went, and to my consternation your father urged me to conduct the conference, which I, of course, declined, saying that *he* was predestined leader. He insisted that I repeat the address I had given in Cleveland, which was upon the absolute necessity of the Holy Spirit in order to succeed in the church, etc. I spoke several times, and conducted one meeting, and your father finally consented to take charge. I conclude, then, that the *thought* was suggested and *developed* in that wonderful mind and heart during the brief moments of that morning in Cleveland. I know not what you may think of this, but to me it is immensely suggestive.

The call, entitled "A Convocation for Prayer," was as follows:

Feeling deeply this great need, and believing that its reward is in reserve for all who honestly seek it, a gathering is hereby called to meet in Northfield, Mass., from September 1 to 10 inclusive, the object of which is not so much to study the Bible (though the Scriptures will be searched daily for instruction and promises) as for solemn self-consecration, for pleading God's promises, and waiting upon Him for a fresh anointment of power from on high.

Not a few of God's chosen servants from our own land and from over the sea will be present to join with us in prayer and counsel.

All ministers and laymen, and those women who are helpers and labourers together with us in the Kingdom and patience of our Lord Jesus Christ—and, indeed, all Christians who are hungering for intimate fellowship with God and for power to do His work—are most cordially invited to assemble with us.

It is also hoped that those Christians whose hearts are united with us in desire for this new endowment of power, but who cannot be present, will send us salutation and greeting by letter, that there may be concert of prayer with them throughout the land during these days of waiting.

D. L. Moody.

Only three hundred visitors responded to the first call. Those who could not be accommodated in East Hall, the one dormitory of the Northfield Seminary at the time, filled the recitation building and crowded the astonished town, some camping out in tents wherever a sheltered corner was to be found. The village church was scarcely large enough for a meeting-place, and a large tent was pitched behind Moody's house.

The second convention was held the year following; then, owing to Moody's campaigns in Great Britain, there was an interval of three years; but since a third gathering, in 1885, a conference has been held every successive year in the early part of August.

In 1892, when Moody was engaged abroad his friend, Dr. A. J. Gordon of Boston, was induced to preside. With this one exception, however, Moody himself conducted all the various sessions. When he realized that the time of his departure drew near he entrusted to his elder son the maintenance of the Northfield schools, especially charging him with the responsibility of the General Conference.

The general trend of these gatherings is evidence of Moody's own development. At first devotional in character, they changed to an emphasis on Christian doctrines; the succeeding phase was one in which the Bible itself became the subject of study, and in later years the burden of Moody's heart seemed to be Christian fellowship and self-examination with prayer for "power for service." Thus in 1899 when he issued the call for the last conference he himself was to conduct at Northfield, August 1 to 20, he sought "all of God's people who are interested in the study of His Word, in the development of their own Christian lives, in a revival of the spiritual life of the Church, in the conversion of sinners, and in the evangelization of the world."

He continues:

> The history of revivals proves that such a work must begin at the house of God. Who can doubt that if somehow the Church could be thoroughly aroused—not a mere scratching of the surface of our emotions, but a deep heart-work that shall make us right with God, and clothe us with power in prayer and service—the last months of this century would witness the mightiest movements of the Holy Spirit since Pentecost? . . .
>
> We are to have with us some of the most widely

known teachers of this country and England—men on whose labours God has already set His seal. There will be the great help that comes from close contact with hundreds of earnest men and women, almost all of them engaged in some form of Christian work. . . .

In response to this invitation the largest gathering ever held at Northfield met during the first three weeks of August. The Presbytery of New York engaged Weston Hall and fifty of its pastors and members were entertained there.

Four salient features of this gathering stand out as worthy of special mention, according to Dr. William Adams Brown:

"1. 'The deepening of the personal, religious life.' This was the dominant note of the conference from beginning to end. It was the theme of song, address and prayer. There was a spiritual uplift in the atmosphere of which one could not but be conscious. It was breathed in with every passing wind. It showed itself in the cheerful faces, in the absence of selfishness and irritation, in the gracious courtesy and ready kindness met with on every side. . . .

"2. 'Closer personal fellowship with the brethren.' In all, fifty members of the New York Presbytery were present at Northfield for longer or shorter periods. . . . Social prayer and conference deepened the impressions of private intercourse, and sowed seeds of kindly feeling which may be expected to bear rich fruit in the future.

"3. 'A stronger sense of brotherhood in Christian service.' Amid all the joys of the conference, the thought was ever present of the coming winter with its heavy responsibilities and perplexing questions; and the burden upon the hearts of all was that the new spirit of fellowship born of the gathering might be used of God to lead

Presbytery through every difficulty, into a broad path of Christian service. . . .

"4. 'An increased emphasis upon the things which unite.' This is the last point which there is time to mention, and it is not the least important. There were present among Presbytery's delegation to the conference men of very different theological opinions. There were some who held critical views of the Bible, while others felt that such views were mistaken and dangerous. Yet it was possible for all to unite in Christian fellowship upon the basis of devotion to Christ and zeal for His service."

If, in later years, emphases have changed from time to time, the purpose has ever been kept in mind which the founder had so often expressed, "Christian fellowship, Bible exposition and prayer," not for personal enjoyment, but for greater efficiency and power in service. And service meant primarily bringing men, women, and youth into vital relationship with Jesus Christ.

BOOK VI

CHAPTER L

Moody used to receive a constant stream of invitations to conduct missions in all parts of the country. These were indicative of interdenominational coöperation; in evangelism is the truest bond of church unity. Not infrequently these invitations were signed by hundreds of laymen as well as ministers and on one occasion he was astonished when a distinguished minister from abroad brought to the platform at the General Conference of Christian Workers an invitation which, with the signatures affixed, extended fifty yards across the entire width of the platform. But to that which was sensational he was strangely indifferent. None of these invitations can now be found and it is probable that they were destroyed.

An invitation was extended to Moody to revisit Great Britain in the autumn of 1881. This fact is significant of the estimate of the permanency of the results from the previous mission. Numerous accessions to churches, memberships awakened, and various forms of Christian activity stimulated, had been the common experience in the cities visited. It was the memory of former days, the present testimony of strengthened forces and the eager longing for further spiritual experiences that led to the resolution to accept the invitation and accordingly Moody planned a three-year campaign to Ireland, Scotland and various centers in England, concluding with a year's mission in London.

Moody entered upon the second mission in Great Britain with a series of meetings in Ireland in 1881. After a month's work here he proceeded to Scotland. During the autumn and early winter he spent some time in Edinburgh followed by six months in Glasgow and neighboring cities. Moody followed his more recent system and stayed a longer time in each city, keeping his work more closely allied with the various churches. The time would come when he would again respond to invitations to conduct series of meetings for large assemblages over a brief period but not until he had begun to experience the embarrassment of reputation and to find that the audiences he was addressing were largely of Christian people. Moody felt that his new plan lent itself more readily to permanency of results. Throughout the remainder of his life Moody was continually meeting with those who had become Christians during this mission or had been spiritually helped into effective Christian service.

A friend who had been closely associated with the work eight years previous thus records in her diary the impressions received at the time of the second mission:

> Mr. Moody is among us again, and we are right glad to have him. He is the same simple, straightforward and affectionate man we knew him to be in former years; a right loving tender heart is his. In preaching he is also the same; he preaches the same old Gospel, and the same power accompanies the preaching in as great—we think even in a greater degree than formerly. His style also is the same, but quieter. We think he is quieter altogether, probably the difference that eight years naturally makes in a man, the difference between thirty-seven and forty-five. So it strikes one at first, but we are not long beside him till we find there has been a mellowing power at work, not all of nature. He is the same, but quieter—the same, but one feels that he has grown much heavenward. . . . I have missed much this time, those little peculiarities—partly American,

partly personal—which used to attract and amuse us so much. Speaking critically, I daresay it is all in the way of improvement, but like most improvements it has carried away something we would rather have kept, and in this case some of the uniqueness and piquancy that we loved so well. But all those little things are of no consequence; the Gospel preached is the same. The unction is there, and the same earnestness and devoted zeal; he seems to be always seeking after souls, nay, hungering for them —travailing, till those hearing the Word receive it into their hearts.

Again friends who had assisted Moody on the occasion of his previous mission in seventy-three rallied to his assistance, among whom was Henry Drummond, now a professor of Natural Science in New College, Glasgow, and in charge of a mission church at Possilpark which was connected with Renfield Free Church of which Dr. Marcus Dods was pastor. The old fellowship of earlier days was renewed. Drummond writes to a friend:

> Moody too has made me promise to "hitch on to him" as he calls it, for the summer. [Later he again writes:] I was with Moody all summer in Scotland, Wales and England. I have been very busy, and have not had a holiday for a year and a half. . . .
> I hope you will see something of Moody when he is in your neighborhood in the early year. My admiration of him has increased a hundredfold. I had no idea before of the moral size of the man, and I think very few know what he really is.
> [The following March in a letter to the same friend he writes:] I am going to Liverpool next week to work for a short time with Moody. . . . Moody has asked me to go to America with him, but I do not think I shall be tempted. From your letter

I see you are afraid my book will not be orthodox, but I hope you will not find this to be the case. I am getting sounder and sounder.

A young pastor, the son of one of Moody's friends, invited him to speak in his church in a small community. In writing of the brief visit the Rev. R. W. Barbour says:

> I had a hundred great bills printed the day before, and a lad and myself went over the whole place the afternoon of Wednesday posting them and personally inviting the people. . . . Yesterday forenoon I again spent in bill-posting and publishing. At three I heard Moody give his Bible Reading on "God's Love." . . .
>
> At 4:30, he, Stebbins, Gray Fraser, and the "Christian" reporter, drove out with a carriage and pair to the manse. Charlotte had tea in the drawing-room for them and for some of our people. Moody had his arms open at once for Freeland, and said as he took him, "This is the fourth generation." I marvel at his absolute disengagement from everything except the matter in hand. . . .
>
> Almost all Cults was there. I think every house had masters or servants, old or young, representing it. Perhaps this mixing of classes was the finest outward feature of the meetings. Town and country, rich and poor, saints and sinners, were all mingled together. By six o'clock the place was packed. . . .
>
> His wealth of Biblical reference was amazing, only more powerful than his anticipation of every possible objection or question of the human hearts before him, and then reading the Scriptures into the face he had read. The effect of each successive experience, caught and carried back to you with a text at its heels, was very impressive.
>
> Toward the end he began to plead with the people individually. I saw nothing, but I know now heads

were going down all over the church; and then, to my intense delight, he began to call upon those who wanted prayer to rise. The Spirit of God seemed moving on the face of the waters, and raising, literally raising one after another. It was unspeakable to hear how he pleaded and pleaded for another and another before he should pray. Twenty-three rose and sat down again.

He did not spare himself. He spoke on for more than an hour. You would never have imagined that he had an audience of between two and three thousand waiting him half-an-hour away. We seemed to be the only people he had ever preached to, or would ever preach to. He might have been living among us by the way he took hold of the entire wants and state of the congregation. Young men, women, children, parents, all got their own message. His closing prayer was most pathetic. His petitions for my people and me, and for the mother of our old minister, and for you next week, were just brimful of affection and understanding.

He told us he had come here in order to keep a promise to you; you were going to be among us next week (the words he used of you were very high but most discerning), and he had just come to make a beginning. The humbleness, as well as the gigantic strength of the man, shone out radiantly all through his address. What touched a High Church lady who is staying with us, and who only knew him from hearsay, was his exquisite tenderness.

Repeatedly one is impressed with the physical endurance of Moody. A reporter refers to his apparently inexhaustible energy:

How do Mr. Moody and Mr. Sankey stand it! Take a specimen of their program. Any day will almost do; but suppose we take Good Friday. At twelve both put in their usual appearance at the noon meeting. Mr. Moody presides and speaks. As a variation from the Bible reading a children's meeting has been announced for four o'clock in the St. Andrew's Hall. To hold six thousand children for an hour is a feat which few men would attempt. I fancy it has never been done in this country before. . . . At seven o'clock preacher and singer thread their way through a dense crowd choking the aisles of Dr. Andrew Bonar's Church. The audience is mixed. . . . They then attend a meeting at eight in a Circus at the very antipodes from Dr. Bonar's Church. The perpetual freshness of the work must be a hard thing to maintain . . . but it is one great secret of their power.

In the late summer Moody conducted missions in Cardiff and Swansea, Wales, and preached in Paris during the greater part of October. During the following winter he returned to many centers he had visited on the occasion of his former mission. From Hull to Torquay he conducted missions in all the largest cities and from the accounts in the religious press everywhere there were the same interests and results as before.

To this statement there would not be universal assent. Sir George Adam Smith writes of this second mission that it "was not so powerful as that of eight years before, but much real work was done." If *power* is to be measured by great aggregations of people or by spectacular evidences of interest, he is right. But these phenomena were the very things that caused Moody misgivings. Not only did he seek to bring the gospel message to the individual but he had learned by experience that if there was to be growth there must be service in behalf of others. In the briefer periods, there was not time to set the converts to work. In other words Moody believed it was God's purpose not only "to make men good, but to make them good for something."

Moody also met criticism for what was thought to be a change in the nature of his message at this time. Dr. R. W. Dale writes to a fellow minister in 1884:

> You remember the kind of criticism to which Mr. Moody was subjected nine years ago. It was said that he did not preach Repentance; taught men that they were saved by believing something, and so forth. During his present visit no such criticisms have been general. Mr. Gill, a clergyman at Lee, wrote to the *Guardian* in that strain, but his letter called out several strong protests. When Mr. Moody was in Birmingham early last year, I was struck by the change in the general tone of his preaching. He insisted very much on Repentance—and on Repentance in the sense in which the word is used by "Evangelical" as well as other divines, as though it were a doing of penance instead of a *metanoia*—a self-torture, a voluntary sorrow, a putting on of spiritual hair-shirts.
>
> Now observe the effect of this. He was just as earnest, as vigorous, as impressive as before. People were as deeply moved. Hundreds went into the inquiry room every night. But the results, as far as I can learn, have been inconsiderable. Evangelical clergymen, Methodist, my own friends, all tell the same story. I have seen none of the shining faces that used to come to me after his former visit. From first to last in 1875 I received about 200 Moody converts into communion, and I reckon that 75 per cent of them have stood well. As yet I have not received a dozen as the result of his last visit.
>
> In 1875 he preached in a manner which produced the sort of effect produced by Luther, and provoked similar criticism. He exulted in the free grace of

God. The grace was to lead men to repentance—to a complete change of life. His joy was contagious. Men leaped out of darkness into light, and lived a Christian life afterwards. The "do penance" preaching has had no such results.

If there was a new emphasis on repentance it was because his experience had demonstrated the necessity for this if conversion was to be genuine. Emotions and ecstasies in themselves were not safe criteria of spiritual power. Mass psychology he understood better than many realized and if he could sway the emotions of great assemblages by the sheer force of his personality he also knew the consequent dangers. He had come to know that unless there was a genuine turning from known evil in life and thought, there was little permanency of change. Those who ever heard Moody preach his well-known sermon entitled "Sowing and Reaping" from the text, "Be not deceived, God is not mocked, for whatsoever a man sows that shall he also reap," will recall with what depths of feeling he warned against the obvious penalties of sin.

Dr. Dale's own biographer gives the following discerning differentiation between popularity and power; the former of which Moody distrusted and the latter yearned for deeply:

> There is a wide distinction between popularity and power. Popularity may be, and often is, the result, not of a man's strength but of his weakness; it may be won by inflated rhetoric, by eccentricity, by the avoidance—whether unconscious or deliberate—of unpalatable truth, by stimulating and satisfying the craving for sensational excitement. But power—the power that builds up a church; that sustains its energies and vigour through many years; brings comfort in sorrow, strength in weakness, succor in

temptation; that transforms abstract truth into a living fact and a controlling law;—power of this kind is no common gift; where it is found, it cannot exist apart from some high and noble qualities; though the qualities vary in different men.

CHAPTER LI

MOODY went to Cambridge at the invitation of a group of undergraduates and the success of the meetings was largely due to the efforts of Mr. Studd's son who had been converted in London eight years before. With his brothers he had become renowned as a cricketer, all the brothers playing on the Eton eleven and in course of time, four playing on the Cambridge eleven. In fact three brothers in successive years had captained the university team and at this time "J. E. K." was holding that position. His prestige in undergraduate life was great and he gave his heartiest support to the movement.

The story of the Cambridge University Mission is best related in the words of another undergraduate, the late Rev. W. H. Stone, Vicar of St. Mary's, Kilburn:

> On returning to Cambridge after the long vacation, I was invited by J. E. K. Studd and the Cambridge Christian Union to join the sub-committee in carrying out the arrangements for a mission conducted by Mr. Moody at the invitation of the Union. The Corn Exchange was secured for the Sunday evening meetings, and the gymnasium in Market Passage, now the Conservative Club, for the week-day evenings. A large choir of University men met regularly to practice those hymns which were likely to be required. A committee, including members from nearly all the colleges, handed a personal invitation to every undergraduate member of the University. The daily prayer-meeting was well attended by the men; all was now ready, and on Sunday evening,

November 5, we proceeded to the first meeting in the Corn Exchange.

The great building and annex had been seated to hold some twenty-five hundred persons. On the platform, in front of the choir, were the Revs. H. C. G. Moule, John Barton, James Lang, Henry Trotter, and a few others. Seventeen hundred men in cap and gown were counted entering the building. Every one was provided with a hymn book. In they came, laughing and talking and rushing for seats near their friends. Little attention seemed to be paid to the preliminary hymn-singing of the choir. A firecracker thrown against the window caused some disturbance.

Then Mr. Moody asked a clergyman on the platform to pray, but men shouted "Hear, hear!" instead of Amen, and Mr. Sankey's first solo was received with jeers and loud demands for an encore. The reading of the Scripture was frequently interrupted, and Mr. Moody's address was almost unheard by reason of the chaffing questions and noises which came from all parts of the Exchange. Still the evangelist persevered with the most perfect good temper, until a lull in the storm enabled him for five minutes to plead with "those who honoured their mother's God" to remain for a short prayer-meeting. After the singing of another hymn, during which many left the building, some four hundred remained for a brief prayer-meeting, amongst whom many of the rowdiest men were seen to be quiet, impressed, and apparently ashamed of their recent behaviour. With heavy hearts we took our way to our respective colleges, but Mr. Moody seemed undaunted and full of hope for the ultimate success of the mission.

On Monday we assembled in the gymnasium, and the sight was enough to depress the spirits of the most sanguine, for only a hundred came to the meeting. After the address Mr. Moody spoke to every man in the building. When, on asking a man if he were a Christian, he received the answer, "No, but I wish to be one," we saw that the effort was not to be in vain, for on that night one who was afterwards to row in the "varsity" boat, and then to become a missionary in Japan, decided to serve the Lord Christ. A few more came on Tuesday night. On Wednesday a letter written by J. E. K. Studd appeared in "The University Review," reminding the members of the University that Messrs. Moody and Sankey had been invited by certain undergraduates to conduct the mission, and that they were entitled to the treatment usually extended to invited guests. This letter had an excellent effect throughout Cambridge and some two hundred came to the evening meetings.

On Thursday afternoon Mr. Moody gathered a meeting of some three hundred mothers of the town of Cambridge in the Alexandra Hall to pray for University men as "Some Mothers' Sons." Mr. Moody described this meeting as unique in his long experience. Mother after mother, amidst her tears, pleaded for the young men of the University.

That night the tide turned. Who that was privileged to witness it will ever forget the scene? I may remind old Cambridge men that there is a gallery in the gymnasium used as a fencing room, and approached by a long flight of steps from the gymnasium below. The preacher's subject was "The Marriage Supper of the Lamb." At the close of his address he asked any who intended to be present at that marriage supper to rise and go up into the gallery—a terrible test. Amidst an awful stillness a young Trinity man arose, faced the crowd of men, and deliberately ascended the stairs. In a moment scores of men were on their feet, following him to that upper room. Many that night made the great decision. Some of the men who then received the Lord Jesus Christ as their personal Saviour are known to me to-day as honoured servants of God in positions of great importance. On Friday night there was an increased audience, but no meeting on Saturday.

What would happen on the last Sunday night was the question in every one's mind. Eighteen hundred men assembled in the Corn Exchange for the final service. In perfect stillness the great gathering listened to a simple address on "The Gospel of Christ." The annex was arranged for the after-meeting, and one hundred and sixty-two men gave in their names at the close as desirous of receiving a little book which might prove useful to those who were seeking to know the power of the gospel of Christ.

Many men came to see Mr. Moody at his hotel, some to criticise, some to apologize for the unseemly behaviour of the first night, and some to receive that help he was so fitted by God to give to those who were seeking the way of peace.

The impress of this mission still rests upon the religious life of Cambridge. Its influence is felt in many parishes at home and in many of the dark places of heathendom.

The Rev. J. Stuart Holden of London thus refers to Moody's influence upon the religious life of undergraduates at Cambridge University:

> The formation of the Inter-Collegiate Christian Union at Cambridge actually preceded Mr. D. L. Moody's mission to the University by a year or two.

The influence, however, which that time of revival and blessing exerted upon the newly constituted Society, was so great and so deep that the two events are always thought of as having been interrelated. For the C. I. C. C. U. was then stamped with a definitely Evangelistic character and purpose which it has never lost. . . .

Much of all this, especially the firm retention of its unapologetic Evangelistic purpose, is rightly attributed to the influence which Mr. Moody exerted upon the first generation of Christian Union members. From his flaming torch their lamps were lighted, and, year by year, on going down, they have passed them on to their successors. As one whose membership of the C. I. C. C. U. extends well over thirty years, and who, as one of its permanent officers has had not a little to do with its activities over a long period, I am constrained to say that I am always conscious of the fact that the C. I. C. C. U.'s aggressive and God-blessed Evangelism in the University is an illustration of a man who, being dead, yet speaketh. And that man is D. L. Moody.

The late Professor James Hope Moulton of Manchester writes that he was a freshman in Cambridge at this time and throughout life "regarded that week as the most momentous week in the religious history of this country during my lifetime, for it is certain that it was then the Student Christian Movement was born."

CHAPTER LII

At Oxford Moody's experience was not dissimilar. In a large hall the crowd which assembled filled all the available space and a neighboring hall was secured to serve for an overflow. The opening of the service, however, soon demonstrated that it was not as a mark of sympathy that so many were in attendance. They received the reading of the Scripture with exclamations of "Hear, hear!" This was too much for Moody and he rebuked them and asked those gentlemen to rise who wished him to continue, and the whole assembly with the exception of a few young men, instantly did so. The result was striking and effective, and there were no more interruptions during the evening. The second and third nights there was still a manifest intention to make fun of the services. The second evening Moody preached on "Repentance," and the third night on "Sowing and Reaping." He had not proceeded far in his discourse on Wednesday evening before it was evident, from the audible adverse criticisms, that there were many present who were not inclined to give the speaker a fair hearing.

A large company returning from a champagne supper attended the meeting, and their boisterous conduct made it difficult for the speaker to be heard. Hymns were applauded, and derisive "amens" accompanied the prayers. This same company, intent on mischief, attended the second meeting and undertook to break it up. With his usual readiness of resource Moody proceeded in the plainest, though most courteous, terms to tell the young men what he thought of their reprehensible conduct. Addressing them simply as those who, like himself, would lay claim to the title of "gentleman," he said: "I have always heard of the proverbial love of the English gentleman for fair play. As an invited guest to Oxford I expected at least to receive a fair chance to be heard. I am here at the invitation of your fellow collegians, and your condition after a champagne supper is the only explanation I can give of your conduct."

One who was present with Moody at that time recalls the incident which occurred the following morning:

> We were in a little private sitting room having just finished breakfast when it was announced that a number of undergraduates wished to see Mr. Moody. He sent word to have them shown up and at the same time asked Mrs. Moody and myself to remain. They were a clean cut, well set up, manly group that came in. Without any hesitancy or delay they made a straightforward apology—such an apology as to have made a disturbance worth while. How Moody responded! It seemed as if there was almost immediately a mutual recognition of elemental virtues that distinguishes real men in all places and times. Mr. Moody's heart went out to these manly boys, mischief-loving, carefree, but ready to frankly acknowledge wrong and prompt to make amends. They on their part sensed a genuine soul to which youth ever is ready to respond. To Mr. Moody's prompt and ready response to their apology came the further inquiry what could be done to make amends. "Well," said Mr. Moody, "come to-night and take front seats and show your fellow students by your presence you want to make amends!" "We'll be there!" was the reply. That night the front seats were occupied by the selfsame

group, including among them several who were prominent in athletics.

From this time the strength of the opposition was broken, and on the following evening the Clarendon Assembly Room had become too small for the growing numbers of undergraduates that attended and they met in the Town Hall. Moody's subject was the value of moral courage in a bold confession of Christ before men, and many instances from the Scriptures illustrated this. Having dismissed the first meeting and gathered a large number of men near the platform, Moody mounted one of the seats and adopted a more colloquial form of address.

> It will be a cross to you [he said] to confess Christ to-night, but the best thing to do is to take it up. If you intend to see the Kingdom of God, you will have to take up the cross. It will never be easier than now. "Whosoever therefore shall confess Me before men, him will I confess before My Father which is in Heaven." Think of Jesus Christ confessing you and saying, "This is My disciple." Is there not someone here who is willing to take up the cross and say right out, "I will"?

One voice sounding forth the response gave courage to others, and a stream of "I wills" came thick and fast.

> Thank God [said Moody]. I like those "I wills." Young men, you don't know how cheering this is; it is worth a whole lifetime of toil. Thank God for giving you courage to speak out. Is there not another here who will take a bold stand for Christ? Perhaps some of you will say, "Why can't I do it at home?" So you can, but it is a good thing to do it here.
>
> I remember the first time I stood up to testify

for Christ. My knees smote together and I trembled from head to foot; my thoughts left me; I spoke a few words and then sat down; but I got such a blessing to my soul that it has followed me until now. It helps a man wonderfully to take a bold stand and let the world—both friends and enemies—know that you are on the Lord's side. It is so easy to serve Him after you have taken your stand. If a number of you were to come right out for God together, you would change the whole tone of this University. I could stand all night and hear those "I wills." They are about the sweetest thing one can hear outside of Heaven.

Moody had taken a strong stand from the outset, and he knew that he had won the day. It would have been easy to stop here, but those who knew him could not expect to have the matter end simply with a confession of Christ. He hazarded a further test; he suggested that those sitting in the first three rows in front should vacate them, and that those who had just spoken should come, and, kneeling there, dedicate themselves to the Lord. The request was scarcely uttered before some five or six rows of seats were filled with a solid phalanx of kneeling figures.

In the Oxford meetings it was surprising to note those who were impressed by Moody's message. One was Canon Liddon, acknowledged at once as a brilliant preacher and a high churchman. Speaking from the University pulpit at Oxford, he gave testimony to the character of the work in the following words:

> Last year two American preachers visited this country to whom God had given, together with earnest belief in some portions of the gospel, a corresponding spirit of fearless enterprise. Certainly they had no such credentials of an Apostolic minis-

try as a well instructed and believing churchman would require . . . and yet, acting according to the light which God had given them, they threw themselves on our great cities with the ardour of Apostles; spoke of a higher world to thousands who pass the greater part of life in dreaming only of this, and made many of us feel that we owe them at least the debt of an example which He who breatheth where He listeth must surely have inspired them to give us.

Dr. Robert F. Horton was present at these meetings and thus recalls the scenes he witnessed:

It was while I was working in the New College as a Fellow Lecturer. I went one evening to the Clarendon Rooms, and found a large congregation of undergraduates. In the after meeting three young men came in, who had obviously dined. They were prominent "blues," well-known to everyone. They sat down in front of me, were loud and hilarious; they were very resentful when I mildly asked them to be quiet. Mr. Moody saw the men and came down and talked to them, and presently took one of them, named Webb, a very noted cricketer, into the corner of the room. I saw the two, as I left, in close talk. Next evening I went to the meeting, and sat on the platform. The room was full, but for three vacant seats in the very front. Just before the opening the three "blues" came in and walked up the aisle and took those three seats. Mr. Moody gave an arresting address on Sin. And at the close he turned to the three in front, and said something of this sort: "You three men have behaved well; you have kept your word"—this to three "blues" in the presence of all their fellow undergraduates! I was near enough to see their faces; tears started to their eyes. I do not know what became of the other two, but Webb from that time forth was a brave and active Christian. If I remember aright (it is nearly half a century ago) he taught in a Sunday school after he went down from Oxford; one Sunday he entered his class and bowed his head in prayer, but did not raise it again; his heart had failed. But I never saw anything in Christian work more striking than this piece of fishing for men. I gathered then, and at the great meeting in the Agricultural Hall in 1875, that this personal dealing was Moody's distinctive charisma.

Moody thoroughly understood youth.

His understanding resourcefulness impressed me in his relations to students [says one already quoted]. He was invited to "take tea" with a group of students in their college room. It was an apparent gesture, and Mr. Moody cordially responded arranging that I should accompany him. On entering the rooms he suspected that the object of "the tea" was the staging of an argument. Immediately alert he took the lead in the conversation; for half an hour he asked questions about English undergraduate life, social, athletic and intellectual. Withal it was done in a courteous way but at no time did he lose the lead. I recall the glimpse I caught of the expressions of some of the men as we left. Appreciating the adroit way in which Mr. Moody had sized up the situation and avoided the pitfalls laid for him they enjoyed the discomfiture of the ringleaders and admired the tact and courtesy that had been displayed.

Both at Cambridge and Oxford one distinguishing feature marked the mission in the general interest awakened. The influence of the meetings was confined to no one class. The "blues" and "honor" men alike were arrested by the note of genuine sincerity and earnestness of the speaker and the simplicity and forcefulness of the message. After a generation the impressions received in those undergraduate days echo from many sources. Thus W. J. Locke describes the meetings at this mission in the old Corn Exchange in his *Septimus*. When an inquiry was addressed to the novelist respecting the passage he wrote to an English editor: "I did actually hear the 'With this rod, sir,' speech when I attended Moody's meetings in those far off Cambridge days."

A. C. Benson, brilliant, cultured in his expression of religious experience, with the reservation of one reared in the home of the Archbishop of Canterbury, also came under the influence of Moody at this time. It was while at Oxford that he attended a service which he thus describes:

> Our host carelessly said that a great Revivalist was to address a meeting that night. Someone suggested that we should go. I laughingly assented. The meeting was held in a hall in a side street; we went smiling and talking and took our places in a crowded room. . . .
> Then the preacher himself—a heavy-looking, commonplace man, with a sturdy figure and no grace of look or gesture—stepped forward. I have no recollection how he began, but he had not spoken half-a-dozen sentences before I felt as though he and I were alone in the world. The details of that speech have gone from me. After a scathing and indignant lecture on sin, he turned to drawing a picture of the hollow, drifting life, with feeble, mundane ambitions —utterly selfish, giving no service, making no sacrifice, tasting the moment, gliding feebly down the

stream of time to the roaring cataract of death. Every word he said burnt into my soul. He seemed to probe the secret of my innermost heart; to be analysing, as it were, before the Judge of the world, the arid and pitiful constituents of my most secret thought. I did not think I could have heard him out —his words fell on me like the stabs of a knife. Then he made a sudden pause, and in a pervasion of incredible dignity and pathos he drew us to the feet of the crucified Saviour, showed us the bleeding hand and dimmed eye, and the infinite heart behind. "Just *accept* Him," he cried, "in a moment, in the twinkling of an eye, you may be His—nestling in His arms—with the burden of sin and selfishness resting at His feet."

Even as he spoke, pierced as I was to the heart by contrition and anguish, I knew that this was not for me—He invited all who would be Christ's to wait and plead with him. Many men—even, I was surprised to see, a careless, cynical companion of my own—crowded to the platform, but I went out into the night, like one dizzied with a sudden blow. I was joined, I remember, by a tutor of my college, who praised the eloquence of the address, and was surprised to find me so little responsive; but my only idea was to escape and be alone. I felt like a wounded creature, who must crawl into solitude.

CHAPTER LIII

The growth of the schools which Moody had established demanded his presence in America for a brief sojourn during the summer of 1883, but before sailing he had definitely promised to return in the early autumn to conduct a mission for eight months in London. Upon his arrival Moody was again welcomed to the hospitality of the Richmond Terrace home.

A large committee of laymen had been formed of which Mr. Hugh Matheson, a prominent merchant devoted to every good cause and with special interest in evangelistic work, became chairman. Mr. Matheson briefly relates the nature of the plans of the committee for the mission.

> It took charge of arranging for the whole work in England, and very specially for the erection in London of large buildings of corrugated iron and wood. This work devolved chiefly upon Mr. Robert Paton and myself. We had to select the sites, arrange with Messrs. Croggan the plan of the buildings, and generally manage the whole business.
>
> To the amazement of the committee, who were discussing with Mr. Moody at a large meeting the method to be followed in London, a plan which I prepared on the spur of the moment while occupying the chair, and which defined the order to be followed in the missions of the various districts north and south of the Thames, and the dates of each, was absolutely accepted by Mr. Moody, and this plan or programme was followed in the minutest detail all through the London campaign, and with a success

that was quite remarkable. Two halls were built by Messrs. Croggan—one at Islington, in the grounds of the Priory, and the other at Wandsworth. When the Islington meetings were finished, and we went to Wandsworth, the Islington Hall was taken down and erected at St. Pancras, and while St. Pancras was being occupied, the Wandsworth Hall was removed to Clapham, and so on, north and south being alternately occupied for three weeks in each place, until practically the whole town had had the opportunity of being present at the services. It was a wonderful time, and made a very deep impression.

The whole mission cost over twenty thousand pounds, and this sum was raised by special contributions. A similar arrangement about the royalty on hymn books was made to that on the former occasion, only Messrs. Quintin Hogg and Robert Paton were associated with me this time, and shared the responsibility. We arranged in detail with Messrs. Morgan and Scott the royalties to be paid upon each edition of the book, and at the end I was able to remit to America, to trustees for the new Northfield Schools which Mr. Moody was desirous of founding, and which have since attracted so much attention, no less a sum than ten thousand pounds.

At this time the Bishop of Rochester addressed a letter to the vicar of St. John's, Blackheath, expressing his desire that the vicar

> should give counsel and sympathy to our kinsmen, the American evangelists, who propose to help us with our overwhelming work in South London this winter. [He said that these men were personally known to him.] More than once I have come across their track in their own country, and I have heard nothing but good of them. To call them schismatics

is to trifle with language; to suspect them of sectarian motives is to do them a great injustice. Their religious services are simple, reverent and deeply impressive. Their recent labours, not only in our largest towns, but also in our two great English universities, are standing the hardest test, that of time. Should anyone doubt if their doctrine is pure or their work solid, let him do what I myself have done, and hope to do again—hear and judge for himself. My own desire is that God will raise up ten thousand such men to proclaim His redeeming love.

In referring to the meeting the first week, the *Pall Mall Gazette* said:

> Cultured society will blush to know anything about Messrs. Moody and Sankey, and others of their crowd. Revivalism in religion, and American revivalism in particular, is desperately vulgar; but unfortunately the same might be said with equal truth of every popular movement, religious and irreligious, of all kinds. Almost every religion has its origin among men of low degree, and the sons of fishermen and carpenters who create or revive the faiths and superstitions of mankind are, as a rule, very objectionable persons in the estimation of the men of light and leading of their time. It is only when the first fervour of the new faith begins to cool, and its vitality to disappear, that polite society condescends to investigate its origin, and to study the phenomena, sociological or otherwise, which it presents. The enchantment of distance renders it possible for self-respecting sons of culture to study, after the lapse of a century, religious revivals which, to their contemporaries, were too vulgar to be noticed except with a passing sneer.
>
> It is somewhat irrational, however, to subject the

scoriæ and lava of extinct volcanoes to the most minute analysis while craters in full eruption are treated as non-existent; nor can a plain man see the sense of poring over dreary tomes, describing the enthusiasm of some preaching friars of the Middle Ages, often as dirty and bigoted as they were vulgar, while the labours of such latter-day friars as the American revivalists who have now pitched their tent—in this case a portable iron building capable of holding five thousand persons—in the north of London are disregarded.

Moody and Sankey are not, it is true, graduates of any university. They are men of the people, speaking the language and using the methods not of the refined, but of the generality. Yet they have probably left a deeper impress of their individuality upon one great section of English men and English women than any other persons who could be named. Whatever we may think of them, however much their methods may grate upon the susceptibilities of those who have at length succeeded in living up to their blue china, these men are factors of considerable potency in the complex sum of influences which make up contemporary English life. As such they merit more attention than they have hitherto received from the organs of public opinion, and for that reason a full account of the American revivalists and of their services last night, which we publish in another part of the paper, may be studied with interest by some of our readers, and passed over—let us hope without too great a shock to their feelings—by the rest.

The halls which were erected seated five thousand and had been specially designed for the purposes of the mission with adequate provision for an inquiry room. In

1875 the mission had been held in large buildings at four different centers; but in the second mission the halls were taken to the crowded districts, the object being to get nearer to the people who could not or would not go to the larger and more central halls. To this end the temporary buildings were admirably adapted. In the Nazareth synagogue the Savior quoted the prophecy from Isaiah that "the poor have the gospel preached unto them"; while no class was excluded during these series of meetings, the poor especially were reached. The Rev. J. Guinness Rogers wrote to the (London) *Congregationalist* at the time:

> Mr. Moody's conduct of the entire meeting was a remarkable manifestation of the way in which the fervour of his zeal is helped by his extraordinary sagacity, and by the tact of a shrewd man. Sanctified common sense is characteristic of the many everywhere, and quite as much depends on details, and great care is given to the veriest trifles. He remembers, too, what many of those who claim to be scientific forget that men have bodies as well as souls, and that these two act and react upon each other; and he does his utmost to guard against the discomfort and weariness which may so easily mar the effect of the best sermon. His one aim is to get that into the hearts of the people; and if he sees anything which seems to hinder him in this, he spares no effort to get it out of the way.

During the mission that winter, meetings were held in all parts of London, as may be judged by the fact that the temporary buildings were erected on eleven different sites, from Hampstead Heath in the north to Croydon in the south, and from Stepney in the east of Kensington in the west. During these months Moody spoke in crowded halls at least twice a day, and on several occasions four or even five times. It was estimated that during the London mission he spoke to over two million people. At many of the meetings entrance was by ticket only, of which over four million were issued during the eight months.

On May 27 a three weeks' mission was begun on the Thames Embankment, in the hall situated on the vacant ground near Temple Gardens. The opening service at Temple Gardens Hall was the beginning of the end. Since the work had included the outlying portions of the metropolis during the previous seven months, it was fitting that the great campaign should terminate in the very heart of the city. The attendance was very large, embracing all grades and sections of the community, from peers of the realm to the poorest of the poor.

The mission was closed by a conference for Christians, June 17-19. In the afternoon of the last day the Lord's Supper was observed, after an address on the Holy Spirit by Moody. In his invitation to the congregation to remain for the memorial feast, he emphasized the fact that only those who had received Christ and were in communion with the Lord could rightly observe the ordinance, so that all who should remain would do so as a confession of faith in Christ. The sight of the thousands who gathered around the sacred emblems was deeply touching when one remembered the divergence of thought on minor matters that was represented there.

At the close of the mission, Moody accepted an invitation to spend a few days for rest and recreation at the country house of T. A. Denny and later at the home of his brother, Edward Denny. With him were also invited a score or more of those who had assisted in the work in London, including, among others, Professor Drummond, who had returned from a tour into the interior of Africa in time to be present during the closing weeks of the meetings. Those were very delightful days for Moody who, free from the care and strain of work, gave himself up to the privilege of truest fellowship with his friends. During this period of rest Moody made frequent attempts to draw from Drummond a little of the wealth of information that he possessed. At that time Drummond was at the zenith of physical strength and was standing before the Christian world as the suddenly famous author of *Natural Law in the Spiritual World.*

On one beautiful Sunday afternoon an urgent request was made of Moody to give an informal address. "No," was the response, "you've been hearing me for eight months, and I'm quite exhausted. Here's Drummond; he will give us a Bible-reading."

Drummond reluctantly consented, and taking from his pocket a little Testament, he read the thirteenth chapter of First Corinthians. Then without a note and in the most informal way, he gave that exposition of the passage which has since become so widely known to scores of thousands under the title of "The Greatest Thing in the World." Three years later, when visiting Northfield, at Moody's special request the same exposition was repeated both at the Students' Conference and the General Conference, and it was in response to Moody's urgent plea that it was later published in its present booklet form. Moody often said that he wished this address to be read in the Northfield schools every year and that it would be a good thing to have it read once a month in every church until it was known by heart.

Incidents connected with Moody's missions would require too great space to relate, but one occurrence was of peculiar interest. While Moody was conducting the Stepney mission in the east of London he announced that on a given evening he would specially address himself to skeptics and atheists. It was at the time when Charles Bradlaugh's influence was being widely exercised, and it is alleged that he himself urged the members of various "free thinkers" clubs which he had organized to attend. It was indeed a unique audience for evangelistic meetings. Moody spoke on "Their rock is not as our rock, even our enemies themselves being judges." So earnest and urgent was his appeal that the attention of the great body of men was riveted on the speaker from first to last. It was less an appeal to reason than to the heart and will. Moody simply assumed the verities with which all who have been brought up in a Christian land are familiar. The fact of sin and the need of strength required no demonstration. At the close Moody gave out a hymn and announced, "While we sing the ushers will open all the doors. Any who must leave may do so. We will then have the usual inquiry meeting for those who desire to be led to the Savior."

One who was present writes:

> I thought all will stampede and we shall only have an empty hall. But instead, the great mass of a thousand men rose, sang, and sat down again. Moody then simply spoke on "receiving" Christ and challenged anyone who would respond to His call to speak out bravely. A number responded. Then someone shouted, "I won't." With evident emotion Moody exclaimed, "It is 'I will' or 'I won't' for every man in this hall to-night." Then suddenly he turned the whole attention of the meeting to the story of the Prodigal Son, saying, *"The battle is on the will, and only there.* When the young man said, 'I will arise,' the battle was won, for he had yielded his will; and on that point all hangs to-night. Men, you have your champion there in the middle of the hall, the man who said 'I won't.' I want every man here who believes that man is right to follow him, and to rise and say 'I won't.'" There was perfect silence and stillness; all held their breath, till as no man rose,

Moody burst out, "Thank God, no man says "I won't.' Now who'll say 'I will'?" In an instant the Spirit of God seemed to have broken loose upon that great crowd of enemies of Jesus Christ, and *five hundred men sprang to their feet* shouting, 'I will, I will,' till the whole atmosphere was changed and the battle won.

The meeting is recalled by Sir Kynaston Studd but not in such full detail as given above:

I well remember during the Stepney mission, Mr. Moody gave out that on a certain night he would speak specially to sceptics and atheists and that as a result quite a number of local atheists were present, and that an impressive service was held, but the details given in the article you speak of are entirely unknown to me, and I never heard of them. The text, the meeting, and the satisfactory result of the meeting still remain with me. The incident with regard to the "I won't" and "I will" is I believe true.

Another is impressed with Moody's tact and resourcefulness:

It was in London, at New Cross [she writes], that one of his marvelous halls with such excellent acoustic arrangements was erected and I conducted there a lady who was not converted and for whom I was specially anxious that she should hear Moody hoping his simple and bold language might strike fire. . . . We did not succeed in obtaining tickets and my companion was decided to return home but we were standing at the door of the Hall and I entreated her to wait there till it would be opened, when a nimble fat gentleman approached us asking whether he could be of any assistance to us. It was Moody and we did not know it. I said that we had been unable to get tickets but that I was anxious my friend should hear Moody; could he tell us whether she would be permitted to come in when the doors would be opened. . . . He asked us to come with him and past the ticket man who looked at us aghast, and through a place which looked like an empty stabling he conducted us into the hall and seated us on the platform. When the choir had collected and the ministers were standing in front, a man in the first row close to the platform shouted, "There you are, you Christians, as you call yourself; you must have a higher place to stand upon and we poor sinners can sit here below. I don't see that making such a difference is anything Christian." Murmurs were heard around him and a good deal of laughter. Mr. Moody spoke to him, "My dear friend, I am very sorry you should have taken offense by misunderstanding our purpose but please take my chair if you like to be on the platform. You are heartily welcome to it. My friends, the ministers who are standing here in the front are taking this place in order that their voice should reach the end of the hall and the others who are gathered at the back of the platform are friends who kindly formed a choir to make the meetings more pleasant for you by their beautiful singing." The man would not come up nor cause any further disturbance.

As we were leaving the hall we found it was impossible to cross, the road being closely blocked by a crowd increasing every minute. The police called Mr. Moody out asking him whether they had better send for the mounted police, the crowd having grown beyond any possibility of their power being sufficient to restore order as there were nearly two thousand clamoring to enter the hall. "Wait a minute," said

Mr. Moody. "May I jump over this hedge and cross the field?" "Yes," said the constable, and Moody jumped over the opposite hedge, climbed up a bus, whispered something into the driver's ear and went to the back of the bus which served him as a pulpit; he began to speak to the crowd assuring them how delighted he felt to see so many anxious to hear the word of salvation but that it was impossible for him to hold again a meeting without any rest as he had to speak at night (here I could not catch the name of the place) he would be glad to see any of those present who could manage to be there that day. While he was talking the bus moved on gently and the crowd following. Without any further effort the crossing was cleared and every danger of a crush averted. I may say I admired this latter act of presence of mind so much that it enhanced the value of the address.

As in 1873-75 cable dispatches appeared in the American press reporting from time to time the progress of the mission and Robert Laird Collier in the *Boston Herald* reports attending the meetings at Blackfriars Bridge on the Embankment where "the building is crowded as often as its doors are thrown open" even when the mission is drawing to a close in the month of June after continuous service throughout the city since November. Moody had assisting him Major Whittle, Messrs. George C. Stebbins and James McGranahan.

In the Camberwell mission a young doctor, keen and athletic, who is on district service, passes the hall one evening and notices the announcement of a young men's meeting to be addressed by C. T. Studd and Stanley Smith, whose athletic fame is widely known. The doctor drops in a little while, but becomes restive during a long tedious prayer by some clergyman who seized the occasion to eulogize the Almighty. The young doctor reaches for his hat but is arrested by hearing the stout gentleman who is presiding announce, "While our brother is finishing his prayer we will sing number 75." Years later in Labrador, Sir Wilfred Grenfell, the erstwhile medical student, has become the missionary physician, and attributes to Moody's closure of a lengthy prayer the change of his own life objective.

The widely experienced editor of the *Christian World* of London says:

> I'm always meeting men who, when the ice has been broken and a confidential mood has been established, confess that they are Moody converts. One of the finest men I know, a sanitary inspector who went through the retreat from Mons as a stretcher-bearer, surprised me one day by saying that D. L. Moody made a man of him. Mr. A. C. Benson has confessed in one of his books that Moody at Cambridge made religion a reality to him—son of an Archbishop as he is. Dr. Grenfell is a Moody man, too. It was Moody's adroit closuring of a man, who was offering an inordinately long prayer at his Whitechapel Mission, that captured Dr. Grenfell, who was groping for his hat to beat a retreat out of the tent. He stayed, heard Moody, and resolved that his Christianity must henceforth be of the mainspring of his being. Through Moody's influence he volunteered for medical missionary work among the deep-sea fishermen on the North Sea trawlers. With them he went to the Labrador Coast, and, finding both the white men and the Eskimos suffering from sickness and disease, and eternally harassed by debt, he started his Labrador mission. What he has done for Labrador is comparable with what Livingstone did

for Central Africa. He opened the country for commerce, and healed an open sore of servitude to exploiters which was akin to the slave trade that Livingstone's journeys brought to an end. In short, he has civilized Labrador. Another "Moody Man," the Rev. Charles W. Abel, my third missionary hero, is at once a wit, a sportsman, a statesman, a captain of industry, a splendid platform speaker and a missionary whose resourcefulness and enterprise have always made him a problem to the missionary committee in London which administers his field of operations.

Proportion is not easily maintained in recording the events of a life so full and active, but even at the risk of according undue space to this London mission one feature should be alluded to. This is the notable group of young people who so loyally assisted in the work. Among the number were several of social prominence. A group of young men from Cambridge included those who had achieved distinction in athletics. These young men and women, from eighteen to twenty-four, were cultured and educated and from homes where there was every privilege which wealth and prestige confers, yet, through eight months, they gave themselves to the work of the London mission.

On the close of the London mission Moody was interviewed by the representative of the *Pall Mall Gazette*.

> Compared to your last visit to England, how does this stand? [Moody was asked]. Better [was the reply], better in every respect. There has not been so much newspaper sensation. . . . We have had more meetings, better meetings, and the work has been of a more satisfactory character in every way. For the last eight months I have addressed on an

average ten thousand people every day. We always rested on Saturdays, but we had on an average twenty-five thousand at our Sunday services. . . .

The interviewer noted that during that time he must have addressed over two million, two hundred thousand people.

BOOK VII

CHAPTER LIV

Moody returned to America in August, 1884. Whatever organization or leadership might develop after Moody was gone, it was certain that during his life the varied lines of work he had undertaken needed his presence periodically. In the Northfield Seminary and Mount Hermon the crude equipment with which they had begun soon was found to be altogether inadequate to meet the rapidly growing needs of the work. The Chicago Avenue Church was ever turning to him for advice and at long range it was difficult to give wise counsel. Increased membership was continually resulting in situations where the presence of one whom all loved and whose judgment was esteemed was urgently needful. In an interview Moody intimated that for the present he purposed remaining in America.

The years immediately following his return from England were given to evangelistic work throughout the United States and Canada. It is probable that there was no city of any size in which he did not hold meetings. His sermon notes he kept in large linen envelopes, the theme written in his large bold handwriting on the outside and the occasions when the address had been given. This was the nearest approach to a record of his labors which he left and this was only intended for his own information to safeguard repeating addresses where he had already given them. But it is from this source that, in part, his rapid journeys throughout the country can be traced, for he was again returning to earlier methods and staying a shorter time in each center and thereby responding to more invitations to visit a larger number of places. Thus in 1885 he is largely in the Southern states. He was welcomed cordially and visited Selma, Alabama; Richmond, Virginia; Charleston, North Carolina. He then went to Kansas City, Pittsburgh and Chester, Pennsylvania. Notations on the envelopes indicate meetings the following year in New Orleans, Houston, Wheeling and western New York state.

Moody never kept a diary. Three reasons effectively prevented. First, he had no time to write in it; secondly, he would have no time to read it; and finally he was too humble to believe it would be profitable to anyone.

The first part of 1887 was devoted to launching still another movement, this time in Chicago. Experience had led him to believe that the Christian church had potential resources in its young laity. He recalled his own early zeal which might have been made more effective if only there had been Bible instruction available.

In Chicago there was a Miss Emma Dryer, a teacher in the public schools of the city, herself a normal school graduate, who was interested in the work of the Chicago Avenue Church, by which name the former mission was now known. Since Moody's return from England in 1875 they had been consulting on the best means of using the services of the young people. Something in the nature of experimentation was already undertaken. Several houses were rented adjacent to the church and a group of young women gave their time to church visitation in return for Bible instruction. This work had steadily grown and Miss Dryer was compelled to give herself exclusively to its development.

But this was only a work for young women and Moody wished to extend it to young men. Here there were complications. It was necessary to more thoroughly organize, with a head of a men's department and some thoroughly trained, spiritually discerning and tactful superintendent. Courses of study had to be arranged, with a staff of capable instructors. But there were no other institutions conceived on exactly the same plan and no one who from previous experience could greatly help him.

One of Moody's earliest and hardest experiences was in dealing with those whom he regarded with warm affection but whom he felt were unqualified to assume the administration of the work. It had been known heretofore as the Chicago Evangelization Society, but was now to become the Chicago Bible Institute.

Moody was at great pains to explain in the religious press and from the platform his purpose in founding this institution. It was not an implied affront to theological seminaries, for Moody again affirmed his belief in a trained ministry and was opposed to short cuts to the pulpit. This school was established for young men and young women of mature years and with the equivalent of a high school education, whose circumstances did not permit them to pursue a regular course of study in other institutions of learning to equip themselves for Christian service. Primarily he had in mind men and women, already experienced in life, feeling impelled to enter home or foreign missionary work as lay workers. For such he felt there was need of a thorough training in the Bible, accompanied by practical Christian service, the opportunities for which are amply afforded by a great city.

The burden was probably the greatest Moody ever undertook. Even when he was called to lay down his life work he did not feel that he had yet achieved the end for which he had labored. To be sure he lived to see success attained numerically, but this was not his measure in Christian service. Shortly before his going he referred to "his whistling through the woods" when asked about the work of the Chicago Bible Institute.

At this time Dr. Charles F. Goss was pastor of the

Chicago Avenue Church, or, as commonly called, the "Moody" Church. He thus recalls these dark days through which Moody was called to pass:

> For many different reasons he had been compelled to postpone the accomplishment of his plan for their education from year to year; but at last, in 1889, he came to Chicago determined to carry it out at all hazards, and I had the good fortune to be able to study the operations of his mind during the gestation of this great enterprise. It was to me the most impressive mental and spiritual exhibition I had ever witnessed. The fervor, the intensity of feeling, the prodigious energy of will, the confident faith, were like the mighty forces of nature. One day a few weeks previous, and while riding with him in his buggy in Northfield, he drove up a beautiful and quiet valley and began to talk about his plans. His eyes kindled, his face glowed. Suddenly he stopped the horse, took off his hat, and said, in tones that sent a positive physical thrill through me, "I am awfully concerned about this matter. Let us pray God to help us consecrate ourselves to it!" That prayer went to heaven if anything ever did! It was propelled by a spiritual force that would have carried it across infinity. It filled my mind with an indescribable awe.
>
> When we arrived upon the ground ready to begin, such was my curiosity about his mind that I studied its processes as a jeweler does the movements of a watch. He came to the scene of operation as a general would to a field of battle, seizing with lightning-like rapidity upon the strategic positions, utilizing every means toward his end; but utterly without previous definite preparation. Very little money (if any) had been promised, no pupils were actually in

sight, the location had not been selected when he swooped down upon the field.

There were no moments in his life more full of interest to the student of his strange nature than those in which he was incubating (if I may say so)— when his mind was hatching its thoughts. His manner was an "absent" one. His eyes seemed turned inward. He was not quite as talkative as usual, although he "came out of himself" suddenly and easily, but sank back again quickly. His brow was not often "knitted," and the mental effort was not a painful one, at least apparently. Instead of straining itself after a conclusion I should have said his mind sank into a quiescent state, as a bird sits on a nest, and that his "conclusions" came to him, rather than awaited his approach.

To his son Moody writes at this time of great stress:

It is Saturday night and I am thinking of you and wishing I could be with you. I will only have two more Saturdays away from you and then we will all be together if all is well. I am to leave here on Tuesday night and go toward home. It is comforting to think I will soon see dear old Northfield and all of my family. I got two thousand pounds to-day from Mrs. MacKinnon for the work. It did me good. It is grand to have such good friends. I think my dark days in Chicago are nearly over. I am getting out all right but it has been a hard pull. I am so thankful that it is behind me and not before me, for I would not like to see another three years like it.

CHAPTER LV

Moody was ever young in spirit; therefore he had an understanding of youth. Early in life he had been drawn to the Y. M. C. A. where, as he had written home, he could enjoy exceptional privileges. Later in Chicago he had worked for the upbuilding of the association, serving as both secretary and president; but more especially did the spiritual needs of the work appeal to him.

Early in the history of the Y. M. C. A. conferences were held for the mutual help from the interchange of experiences, the discussion of methods and for furthering in every way the interests of the movement. Richard C. Morse who later was to become the veteran secretary of the International Committee of the Y. M. C. A. was for some time associated with the *New York Observer*, a religious weekly journal, and he was assigned to report a convention called by the association in New York in October, 1867. He writes: "Among the speakers was Dwight L. Moody from Chicago." The speakers impress the young reporter "by their evangelistic enthusiasm. . . . Moody especially made this impression. He spoke often, but in each instance for not more than five minutes." From that time the two men met occasionally in association work and Mr. Morse is greatly impressed with Moody's accomplishments.

Shortly after the close of Moody's London mission, a group of young men, many recently graduated from Cambridge and others who were in the army and all of whom had assisted in the inquiry room and in work among young men, had decided to dedicate their lives to missionary work in China. As they were all men of social position and several had national renown as athletes, it aroused unusual interest. They were known as the "Cambridge Seven" and prior to their departure for China they did deputation work among the universities and churches throughout the land. The first to volunteer was C. T. Studd, a brother of J. E. K. Studd, through whose example and influence others made the decision.

In 1885, at Moody's invitation, J. E. K. Studd, later Sir Kynaston Studd, Lord Mayor of London, visited America. His coöperation had contributed greatly to the success of Moody's work in Cambridge three years before, and he had rendered yeoman's service in the London mission of 1883-84. Through the collegiate department of the association Moody found openings for him to visit the leading colleges and universities of the United States and Canada where he recounted the spiritual awakening in the British universities.

The story of this work among students awakened an interest in all the American colleges and among the number so aroused was a young freshman in Cornell, John R. Mott, whose name for a generation has been identified with international student life and missionary enterprise.

Later in his reminiscences Mr. Morse thus recalls the beginning of the Northfield College Students' Conferences:

> One afternoon, Moody invited Studd, Wishard, Ober and myself, with our wives, to visit Mt. Hermon with him to see the boys' school and the new building, the first Crossley Hall, which had just been completed. At first we declined, under pressure of our work, but he insisted that we should take a holiday, so we accepted the invitation, little thinking of the long chain of events of which it was the first link. We went in a large four-seated wagon. Moody him-

self handled the reins in his usual and original manner. Most interesting was the story he told of his plan for the Northfield and Mt. Hermon schools, and what he wished their names to stand for, disclosing a purpose and plan now known and valued round the world. . . .

Moody's errand at Mt. Hermon that day was to give a talk to the boys on "How to Be a Good Public Speaker," a theme of which certainly he was master. He desired us to visit the grounds and buildings while he was talking to the boys, but we insisted on hearing the talk! It was altogether the best treatment of the subject to which I had ever listened, and came from the brain of a master workman, who had been taught in the high school and university of life-long experience. As we talked I was reminded of what his aged mother had once said to me, in the house where he was born: "When Dwight was only a little boy, he was fond of going up into the garret and trying to make a speech all alone!" . . .

As we rode through the woods behind the Mt. Hermon buildings our driver pointed out among the trees a frame building and said, "There is a house which was used by the men who put up Crossley Hall. Why couldn't you bring a group of Association secretaries up here next summer to spend your vacation time in studying the Bible together as you have been doing this summer? I will give them the use of this and other buildings if they will come!" . . . We told him that our secretaries had a conference early every summer like the one he had addressed in Baltimore in 1879, and that it would be difficult to bring them here to a second meeting of the kind he had suggested. "But," said Wishard, "we might bring college students." "Well," said Moody, "bring them along. What I want is to have the buildings used to help in Christian work and Bible study."

The plan suggested was that Moody should gather a group of undergraduates about him in Northfield and lead them in a daily study of the Scriptures. Moody listened to the project and then definitely declined; he felt that he knew his own limitations. He made a counter proposition, however. If these gentlemen would relieve him of the necessary work in making known the plan and would enlist the students he, for his part, would make available the Mount Hermon dormitories and lecture halls and gather about him a group of Bible teachers who, he felt, were better qualified than himself to teach college students.

This was the plan adopted, resulting in the first College Students' Conference, held during the entire month of July, 1886, at Mount Hermon. The attendance exceeded the most sanguine expectations, delegates coming not only from all the leading Eastern institutions of learning but from the far south and numerous Western states.

The succeeding year the Northfield College Students' Conference was transferred to Northfield Seminary where greater facilities were available for the entertainment of guests and has continued, under Moody's direction during his life, and for twenty years after.

To this gathering of eager youth Moody invited the best men he could find. One year it was Henry Drummond, again it was Sir George Adam Smith. Moody invited prominent evangelical leaders from Great Britain and the United States, and American leaders in all religious thought were also given a cordial welcome, even if in many directions their views did not accord with Moody's. There was, however, a platform or common belief requisite to speaking at Northfield—the acknowledgment of the deity of Jesus Christ, the efficacy of His atoning work upon the cross and the final authority of Holy Scriptures in all questions of conduct and doctrine. No human theory of the atonement was insisted on; assent to the fact was required. Inspiration was left undefined. From this position Northfield has never departed.

Among the group of students attending that first conference were two young men who were planning to dedicate their lives as missionaries in India, Robert P. Wilder and John N. Foreman. The presence of several missionaries and the brilliant authority on missionary history, Dr. A. T. Pierson, naturally called the attention of many to the cause of foreign missions. The result was the formation of a group of young men who banded themselves together as prospective missionaries. They termed themselves Student Volunteers, an organization which in forty years has done so much to recruit the forces of missionary effort.

Enthusiasts, even in the best causes, incur the risk of a narrow outlook. Although the Student Volunteer Movement had its origin at Mount Hermon, Moody never sympathized with the form of the pledge adopted by the organization. He maintained that it was a dangerous thing, especially in so important a field as foreign missionary labors, to overurge any individual to pledge himself. It was Moody's conviction that since the kingdom of God is comprehensive of all peoples, everywhere, the scene of a man's life work matters little; what is essential is for a man to be in the will of God; the place and manner of service will then be made known through His guidance. But this was not enough for some who criticized Moody for want of missionary zeal. His attitude was rather an evidence of his wide experience and whole-hearted sympathy with the foreign missionary work and his great admiration for the missionary heroes of the church.

There was no other evidence needed to prove his interest in foreign missionary work than the fact that so many of those who came under his influence gave themselves to this service. In this number were included hundreds of students who attended the Northfield student conferences as well as the large number of students from Northfield Seminary and Mount Hermon.

It should also be added that his sympathy was enlisted in behalf of the regular denominational missionary boards. So-called faith missions he viewed with a certain degree of misgiving. He believed that all missions were essentially maintained by faith, and to publish and constantly reiterate that any particular mission was dependent upon prayer and the voluntary gifts of Christians constituted in itself an appeal. To stress the point that there was no appeal was but an astute method of soliciting.

"This telling a person to 'look to the Lord for support on the field and to us for directions' is not a sign of faith," Moody would say. On one occasion his friend Dr. A. T. Pierson wanted to inaugurate a Northfield Missionary Board, which should raise funds and commission missionary candidates. In a public meeting in which there had been unusual missionary interest and enthusiasm he had called for subscriptions for an independent missionary enterprise with the result that a considerable sum was at once pledged. But Moody's sound judgment immediately asserted itself. With a group of friends that night, he pointed out the wastefulness in duplicating existing agencies, the lack of experience of all present to constitute an efficient board and the implied lack of confidence in the long established boards and his unwillingness to have the name of Northfield associated with such an enterprise. "The boards of the different denominations are manned by the ablest men," he averred. "Just look at their secretaries. Where will you find abler men than Robert E. Speer, James Barton, Henry Mabie and a score of others I could mention? We want to uphold their hands and not embarrass them as such a course of action on our part must do."

Of Moody's zeal combined with sound judgment Bishop Thoburn, the great missionary apostle to India, bears testimony in an article written many years after Moody had laid down his work.

> Among the letters awaiting me on arrival was one from Mr. Moody inviting me to visit Northfield, where his annual summer assembly of young people was in session, and I lost no time in proceeding to that place. I found five hundred or more young people of both sexes gathered there, with nearly as many adults, and a deep religious feeling seemed to pervade not only the public meetings, but every group of friends and all the conversation heard on the ground. Mr. Moody wished me to speak on practical missionary work, but in doing so to utter a word of caution against some teachings which had been advanced on the subject of trusting God alone for support. Some youths were inclined to accept literally the command to take neither purse nor scrip, but to go out into the wilds of Africa trusting God for everything, and Mr. Moody wished me indirectly to correct the notion, and in doing so to put a more practical and healthy ideal before the young people. In the evening of my arrival I was asked to speak briefly at an outdoor meeting, and the next day I was asked to address the main audience in the auditorium. I saw at a glance as I rose to speak that I had a rare opportunity. Hundreds of students of both sexes, and many Christian workers of mature years, sat before me, and they were evidently "hearers" and not merely idle spectators. I gave them a plain,

practical account of our work, and incidentally remarked that thousands of poor misguided creatures were willing and ready to become Christians, but that we could not give them the most elementary teaching. I added that the small sum of thirty dollars would support a man who could teach a little while learning more himself, but gave no hint that I wished anyone present to give anything for the purpose. The audience gave the closest attention, and I felt at once that I was in touch with them. When I closed the young people began to applaud, but Mr. Moody sprang to his feet and stopped it peremptorily. "If you want to cheer this man," he said, "you can do it better by supporting a lot of those men on thirty dollars a year. I am going to support one. Mr. Sankey will take one. Messrs. A., B., and C. are going to take one each—here, come on. They are taking down names here," etc. In a very short time one hundred pledges were recorded. I sat in a state of half-bewildered amazement. If three thousand dollars had dropped out of heaven it could not have seemed to come more directly from God. My visit to America was indeed of His ordering, and I felt assured that He would be with me wherever I should go.

The evening papers all over the country told the story of my address and Mr. Moody's big collection, and now I needed no introduction East or West. Invitations came from many places and I knew beyond a doubt that God had put His seal upon my visit to America, and would be with me wherever I should go. Before leaving I promised to return and attend Mr. Moody's larger meeting of Christian workers, a month or six weeks later. I went from Northfield to Ocean Grove, a resort at that time retaining more of the features of an old-time camp meeting than have been apparent in recent times. Here I found an immense audience and was received most cordially, but an inflexible rule of the organization made it impossible for me to take a public collection, or even mention the object of my visit to America. In private, however, I found friends, and not only received some liberal contributions, but was invited to other important places which I could visit later.

Among college students Moody became increasingly a force. In the leading institutions, from time to time, he was invited to preach or hold brief missions. Of his visit to Harvard, Dr. Francis G. Peabody in his *Reminiscences of Present Day Saints*, says:

> Moody immediately impressed all hearers as completely single-handed and sincere, and his addresses, like those of Abraham Lincoln, were packed with anecdote, reminiscence, wit and genuine feeling. He was genuinely conscious of his own limitations; and while a guest in my home, with his wife, for a week of meetings with Harvard students, inquired one morning about the duties of a professor. Being told that one usually lectured four or five times a week during the whole winter, he said across the table to his wife, "Emma, this is no place for us; I only last three weeks." . . . His prodigious popularity had not cost him his simplicity or humility. He remained a plain man, who knew himself to be about his Father's business.
>
> Beyond the extraordinary powers of popular appeal which Mr. Moody possessed, he maintained two principles of his work which were conspicuous but fundamental. The first was derived from his observation that the emotional excitement of the crowd must be steadied and reënforced by the specialist's

care of the individual. His converts must be followed, sustained, confirmed. . . . The second principle he had reached was derived from his own sense of limitation. His hope for the future of religion was set on the discovery of young men who should be intellectually as well as piously fit to direct these clinics of the soul. The first principle, of individual conference, drew Drummond to Moody; the second principle, of selected diagnosticians, led Moody to see in Drummond a providential instrument.

As from year to year these gatherings grew in attendance and interest, the work in the colleges grew correspondingly. This entailed increased secretarial work resulting in a larger budget to be raised by the International Committee. Here again Moody proffered his services and for more than ten years assisted in raising funds by appealing through letters, over his autograph.

In 1893 a group of young women who were in Northfield at the time of the College Students' Conference came to Moody to ask if he would do for the women's colleges what he had done for men's. So for nine years college women to the number of four or five hundred convened each summer. Similar in character to the previous gatherings Moody not only presided at the sessions but sought to bring those to address the students whom he felt to be especially helpful by extended experience. The idea originated with Miss May Whittle who, in later years as Mrs. W. R. Moody, was to start a Northfield Young Women's Conference when the College Girls' Conference withdrew from Northfield in 1902.

Rev. Dr. John Timothy Stone of Chicago recalls his impressions of Moody from his childhood days and later as a student at Amherst.

"We lived in my boyhood in Springfield, Massachusetts, and when Moody was holding evangelistic meetings in the city in 1878 I first saw and heard him. At that time I had an alto voice which an intimate friend of the family, who was a good musician, had taken pains to train. I sat far to the front and in some way apparently attracted Mr. Moody's attention. To my bewilderment he pointed to me and said, 'Here, boy, come up and help us sing.' With great diffidence I found my way to the platform and he asked me what I could sing. I said I was fond of 'Dare to Be a Daniel.' 'Sing it,' he said, and there I stood before that large audience in the Rink, singing the verses while he enjoined the congregation to take up the chorus. Nine years later as a sophomore in Amherst I attended the college students' conference at Northfield in 1887. It was on the occasion that Professor Henry Drummond and Dr. H. Clay Trumbull were on the program. Early in the conference I met Mr. Moody and remarked that I had met him previously and alluded to singing for him as a boy. To my great amazement he vividly recalled the incident. With the thousands he had met in the intervening years it was an indication of his remarkable ability to recall faces. One day Dr. Trumbull was to address the conference and as he arose and stepped to the platform he drew from his pocket a manuscript. Immediately Mr. Moody spoke up, 'Doctor, do put that up. What these boys want is just a talk on how to bring young men to Christ.' Hesitantly, Dr. Trumbull, who felt that he was not a public speaker, laid aside the manuscript and there for over an hour talked to us out of his personal experience and gave what later appeared in book form as *Individual Work for Individuals*. At another service Professor Drummond gave that address on the thirteenth of Corinthians which appeared in book form as *The Greatest Thing in the World*. At the close of the address Mr. Moody arose and with evident feeling said, 'Young men, you have heard a great address. I prophesy that this will live and will be translated into twenty languages.' The truth of Mr. Moody's prophecy has been fully confirmed."

Dr. James Vance spoke at Northfield seventeen years after Moody had passed to his reward and recalled the far-reaching influence which Moody exerted among the students:

> There was one incident in that conference that was dramatic and that has been most significant in its effect upon the student life in the South since. A young Vanderbilt student from Nashville made an address on the need for Christian work among the students. He talked out of his heart. Mr. Moody listened to him, "Well, Brockman, you think there ought to be a secretary, a student secretary, for these Southern colleges, do you?"
>
> "Yes," said Brockman, "I do."
>
> "Well then," said Mr. Moody with that directness which was so characteristic of him, "what is the matter with your being that secretary? Suppose we call you to that this morning, will you accept it?"
>
> And Brockman had only one answer to the proposal under those circumstances, and he said, "Yes."
>
> Then Mr. Moody said, "How much money will it take to support you?"
>
> Well, the young man was a little bit modest about that and did not seem anxious to say.
>
> "Will fifteen hundred dollars support you?" asked Mr. Moody.
>
> "That would be perfectly satisfactory," replied Brockman.
>
> Then Mr. Moody turned to the audience and said, "We will raise that salary here and now."
>
> It was started with a gift of five hundred dollars, and the money came so rapidly that it was hard to stop it at fifteen hundred dollars. Within less than

five minutes the money was raised. And then, then —oh, I shall never forget how Mr. Moody called that young man to the platform and, laying his hands upon him, set him apart to his work with prayer. And Brockman went out. You know something of his work since, how only recently he has been recalled from the mission field to succeed Doctor Mott as student secretary of the Young Men's Christian Association.

I got a blessing at that Northfield Conference that has followed me through all the years. I think everybody that comes to Northfield with an open mind and a hungry heart goes away with a great blessing. I know nothing better for a young student, especially for young theological students, than to come to Northfield for a conference.

When I began to think of coming back, I was wondering whether it was changed. I was wondering whether the old spirit survived. Of course, I have been hearing of the Northfield Conferences through the years, and how they have grown in numbers, how the schools as well as the conferences have grown. And, oh, I have been so delighted to find that not only has Northfield grown in the development of its schools and in the widening of its conferences and in the number reached, but that the old spirit survives, unabated and unquenched.

CHAPTER LVI

MOODY's sympathy was not limited in later years to the privileged youth of the colleges. The general work of the Y. M. C. A. always appealed to him and when emergency arose ever found in him a loyal friend and supporter. Mr. Morse, probably as familiar with the associations throughout the country as any, thinks no list "can show a total amount which represents to any degree the financial help that came to the Association through his agency." In New York City, San Francisco, Chicago, Pittsburgh, Scranton and a score of other centers he gladly and freely undertook the raising of funds. Through his direct efforts large sums were raised not alone for buildings for the association but for aggressive Christian work both in the homeland and abroad. Through his influence the committee to which the royalties of the hymn book were made over for the benefit of various Christian organizations, contributed fifteen hundred dollars yearly and in one season twenty-five hundred dollars, the largest single contribution for running expenses received up to that time.

In 1875, at the close of the evangelistic campaign in Brooklyn, he turned to the Association as a valuable helper of the churches in caring for the converts [writes Thornton B. Penfield, secretary of the Brooklyn Young Men's Christian Association]. The Association was crippled for want of means, and its discontinuance was threatened. Although Mr. Moody was much wearied by his extensive labors, he did not leave Brooklyn until he had secured subscriptions of $8000 to relieve it of its indebtedness, and to enlarge its activities and usefulness. From that day the Association has never taken a backward step. In 1884 he became interested in raising the endowment fund of $150,000, coming to Brooklyn more than once to aid in that effort. The largest church collection ever taken in our city for the Association was at the close of a statement made by Mr. Moody which occupied about ten minutes, concerning the value and the necessity of Young Men's Christian Association work; and expressing his great indebtedness to the Association for what it had done for him. In 1885, Mr. Moody laid the corner-stone of the Central Building at 502 Fulton Street; and even on that occasion made so pointed an appeal that some of the workmen employed on the building were led to Christ. . . .

In the winter of 1879-80, when I was general secretary in St. Louis, the Young Men's Christian Association of that city was a young and comparatively weak organization occupying rooms. The Association was instrumental in getting Mr. Moody to come to St. Louis and spend the winter in a great evangelistic canvass. The organization was very active in the work, and it was my happiness to be closely associated with him for the whole of that winter. At the close of the campaign he voluntarily undertook to raise $37,500 in order to purchase, for cash, the property of the Union Methodist Church, at Eleventh and Locust Streets, and present it to the Young Men's Christian Association. Although a conservative community, and up to that time but little interested in Association work, Mr. Moody's great ability and influence carried the plan to success. The amount was raised; and the property was sold by the Association for $128,000, which sum was the foundation of its present splendid building and widely extended work.

In Philadelphia the central building of the Association was begun and finished during the financial panic of 1873 and the hard times that followed. As a result, the building, when completed, had a debt of $200,000 upon it. In 1882 this debt had increased to $400,000 of which sum $200,000 was in notes. The Association was in a critical condition, and seemed to be about to lose its property. This would have been disastrous to the work in Philadelphia, and the moral effect would have been felt throughout the entire country. The case being presented to Mr. Moody, he at once came to the rescue with all his unselfishness and great executive ability. He had a large appropriation made from the hymn book fund, in addition to which he secured contributions from prominent citizens of New York City. He came to Philadelphia with $60,000 obtained outside of the city, and then, by his own exertions, secured $140,000 in Philadelphia, making up the sum of $200,000 with which the floating debt of that amount was entirely paid, leaving only the mortgage debt of $200,000. Thus by his personal interest and individual effort this valuable property was saved, and a great shock to the credit of the Young Men's Christian Association in the United States was averted. The trustees recently refused an offer of $750,000 for the piece of property thus preserved by Mr. Moody's efforts.

He came to Philadelphia again several years afterwards, and started a canvass for $200,000 with which to pay off the mortgage remaining upon this property. This last effort was seconded by the Hon. John Wanamaker and others; and $150,000 was collected and paid upon the mortgage in this second canvass. In the first canvass Mr. Wanamaker was associated with Mr. Moody and contributed $50,000 himself. In the second canvass also, Mr. Wanamaker contributed largely both in time and money.

In briefly stating these two cases that come within my knowledge, I may add that Mr. Moody carried on this work of money-raising in the spirit of Christian service in such a way that it proved a great blessing to all with whom he came in contact.

Mr. S. W. Travers writes: "I am satisfied that we owe our Association in Richmond largely to Mr. Moody, for which the city owes him a lasting debt of gratitude; and I am positive that his memory is warmly cherished by all our people. . . ."

Frequently Moody's indirect influence in behalf of the associations was no less strikingly helpful. A former secretary of the Albany Association writes:

> In 1886 Mr. Moody held a series of services in Albany, N. Y., in the management of which the Young Men's Christian Association took a prominent part. Mr. Moody, as was his custom, at the closing service of the convention, made an earnest appeal to the people of Albany to provide better facilities for the work among young men, and earnestly advocated the need of a building for the Association, stating at this service that the organization had, under God, done more in developing him for service than any other agency. The suggestion bore fruit. Mr. Charles F. Waterman was led to make a generous subscription and to advocate earnestly the need of such a building. Through Mr. Waterman and the earnest advocacy of the movement by Mr. Moody, Mr. James B. Jermain became interested and made the Association a gift of its present building, and later largely increased this gift, so that his benefactions to the Association exceeded $100,000. I fully

believe that credit for the suggestion of the erection of this building belongs to Mr. Moody.

When in 1898 the United States became involved in war with Spain, the occasion was viewed as an opportunity for the Y. M. C. A. to render service for the recruits in camps and embarkation ports. A special Army Committee was formed to have oversight of this new phase of association work, of which Moody was made a member and he subsequently headed the sub-committee on evangelistic work. Into this work which so vividly recalled his war work a generation before he entered with characteristic zeal. He imposed the condition that he should be permitted to raise funds independently, to send experienced evangelists and Christian workers into camps to preach the gospel, feeling that when men were confronted with danger and freed in many cases from home prejudices and environment they would be specially accessible to Christian influences. "I am not interested in providing writing paper and current literature, as many will do this who have no concern for men's souls," he said. "What I want to do is to reach men with the gospel." In this one project he raised tens of thousands of dollars enabling him to send scores of men to work among the soldiers in the great training camps throughout the South during the summer of 1898.

Moody was ever solicitous that the association should be primarily a spiritual movement and that the evangelistic note should dominate. Educational privileges and opportunities for athletic prowess he recognized as secondary to the original plan and purpose. The association, to his mind, was a means to an end, and he had little sympathy with the spirit that willingly sacrificed the preaching of the gospel to what are called association methods. He was strongly opposed to the exclusion of women from the Sunday gospel meetings of the association, believing that in many instances mothers, sisters, or friends might be counted on as efficient helpers in bringing to the meetings the very men whom the association should reach. Instead of poorly attended gospel meetings supported by a few Christian men, he believed the association meetings would be well attended by the very class they should reach, if they were but thrown open to mixed audiences.

These views he often expressed, and in consequence some felt that Moody was disloyal to the organization. But if he was able to serve the association in earlier years, the last twenty-five years of his ministry showed still greater results of his service in their behalf. Early in his evangelistic work in America, Moody seized every opportunity to secure the coöperation of local associations, and on his part never lost an opportunity to work for their interests.

CHAPTER LVII

THE last invitation which Moody received to visit Scotland in the autumn of 1891 was, perhaps, the most impressive which was ever extended to him. It was presented to him at the Northfield General Conference of that summer. It was in the form of a scroll, containing twenty-five hundred signatures, representing fifty different cities and towns and all the churches of Scotland. He was unable to respond immediately to the invitation but later consented to undertake the proposed mission. In accepting, he offered to meet all appointments the committee might arrange for the fall and winter months in Scotland. The task he assumed was tremendous. Referring to this campaign he afterwards explained that in "ninety-nine days I visited ninety places, speaking three and four times daily."

The winter's work was preceded by a large meeting held in Edinburgh November 13, 1891. In various towns where missions were of brief duration the local ministers gave their whole-hearted support, union prayer meetings being held each night for a week previous to the mission, a good choir was organized and trained and the town thoroughly canvassed by volunteer workers to invite the public to attend the meetings.

The old Free Assembly Hall, rich with associations of former days, was the scene of three large meetings at the close of the mission in which Moody addressed himself to Christians on the need for personal work and the necessary qualifications for it.

Now was to be realized a long anticipated privilege of

visiting the Holy Land, the scenes of his Master's earthly career. At the close of the strenuous mission in Scotland Moody, his wife and their youngest son went to Palestine as the guests of Mr. and Mrs. Peter MacKinnon. The party visited Rome en route and of this city Moody spoke freely, but of Palestine he said little. Bethany, Gethsemane and (Gordon's) Calvary were peculiarly sacred associations. For nearly forty years Moody had served Jesus Christ with increasing devotion; now that he saw the scenes of His earthly life silence alone expressed the depth of his emotions. Mrs. MacKinnon relates:

> The missionaries, hearing that Mr. Moody was in Jerusalem, had come to him on Saturday to ask him to preach, and it had been arranged that he would have a service on the skull-shaped hill outside the city walls. We all proceeded there, and found a wonderfully mixed company of many nations and various costumes.
> It is not easy to write of this meeting; the occasion was so solemn; our feelings were at such a pitch of intensity that words are a very poor medium to convey an adequate impression of it. . . .
> The Hon. and Rev. E. Carr Glyn, later Bishop of Petersborough, offered the opening prayer on Mount Calvary, as it is commonly called here in Jerusalem, and the children of the English school sang very nicely. One of the hymns we sang was the appropriate "There Is a Green Hill Far Away," but we were standing on it. Mr. Moody began by saying he had been preaching for twenty years, but never had he felt so solemnized as at that moment, never had he felt so much that he must put the shoes from off his feet, for it was holy ground. He continued by tracing Abraham's trial of faith; and he himself was melted with tender feelings at the thought of what

the faithful and obedient patriarch must have suffered. From that he went on to speak of the love of the Father, who had not spared His only Son from Heaven. . . .

On Monday morning Mr. and Mrs. Moody went together to the Mount of Olives for the last time; they also visited the Tombs of the Kings, which I need not describe, except to mention that there is a stone there that formed the door to a chamber, and it gives a good illustration of how "the stone" could be "rolled away." . . .

We left Jerusalem at noon, escorted to our carriages outside the Jaffa Gate by a delightfully varied company. The beggars of Jerusalem, I am sure, never had such a good time as when Mr. Moody went about its streets. They soon learned to watch his coming out of the hotel, and followed him about, and now they were here to see him off. The lepers were at their accustomed place outside the gate; the blind and maimed followed him; the Americans who live in Jerusalem waiting the return of Israel to their own land, the missionary brethren, the Rev. Carr-Glyn, Lady Mary Carr-Glyn, accompanied by Miss Grenfell, all gathered to say farewell. And so the evangelist of the nineteenth century had seen for himself the scenes of the Great Transactions which he had spent his life in proclaiming.

I must not omit the story of the young Greek priest. We were attracted by his appearance on board the *Rahmanieh*. He had a most beautiful face. He spoke a little English, and Mr. Moody had some talk with him. He was a very earnest soul and was going to Jerusalem full of holy zeal and enthusiasm to see the Holy City and the Holy Places. When we were again at the Church of the Holy Sepulchre we met him, and Mr. Moody and he had a hearty greeting. He looked very sad and downcast and expressed himself as astonished and grieved at all the superstitions, I fear I must say deceptions, of his church. Mr. Moody most earnestly besought him to speak out, to go back to his country and protest, and then preach the gospel of Jesus Christ. "You may be another Luther." The young man had tears in his eyes, and dear Mr. Moody, his face beaming with love and sympathy, pled very earnestly. I do not know that we ever saw him again.

Returning from the Holy Land, Moody resumed his work in England and subsequently went to Ireland for the month of September. Apparently reinvigorated by the vacation he manifested such energy and endurance as few could equal. The program for one week will confirm this. Concluding a short mission in Southampton on Sunday night, Moody started for Dublin on a train leaving after midnight, which carried no sleeping-car. Arriving in London before daybreak, he caught the train for Holyhead, and had a four hours' passage across the Irish Channel which completely prostrated him with seasickness. Dublin was reached by six o'clock in the afternoon, where, after a hasty repast, Moody addressed a large meeting. The audience had been waiting for some time, and the atmosphere was heavy. At the close of the meetings numbers of old friends pressed forward for a handshake and words of welcome, and it was near midnight before Moody was able to retire. He was entertained by Mr. Peter Drummond, who lived some distance out of the city, and he had to take leave of his host early, drive to Dublin, and get the seven o'clock train for Belfast on Tuesday morning. It had been arranged that he should conduct a two weeks' mission in the large Convention Hall in Belfast a week later, and on his arrival the committee of ministers and laymen, at whose invitation he came, met him for conference regarding plans, and lunched with him at the house of the Rev. Dr. Williamson.

That evening in Londonderry he had time for only a hurried supper after his arrival, before going to a crowded meeting, and it was late that night before he had any opportunity to rest. Wednesday, Thursday and Friday he visited six other towns speaking in crowded halls and twice in the open air. The very hospitality added to the demands upon his strength for he was entertained at meals where others were invited to meet him. Saturday, however, brought a much-needed rest at the home of Mr. William Young, of Fenaghy, and on the following day he began his Belfast mission by addressing ten thousand people in the crowded Convention Hall. "And so day after day did panting time toil after him in vain."

Convention Hall in Belfast was a temporary structure which had been built for a political demonstration. The daily paper thus describes the service:

> It is not too much to say that no other man, whether minister or layman, could draw such audiences to hear the gospel preached as Mr Moody, the American evangelist, is at present drawing in the city of Belfast. There were those who prophesied that the cool, clear-headed people of Belfast had not enough of interest in Mr. Moody or his methods of conducting evangelistic services to fill such an immense hall as the Convention Building. It has now, however, been proved that they were false prophets. The attendance last evening was almost as large as those at the opening services on the Sabbath day previous. Doubtless many were in hopes yesterday evening that owing to the very inclement state of the weather it would be possible to find a front seat if one were there half an hour before the time ap-

pointed for opening the meetings. All such hopes, however, were doomed to disappointment, as the hall was comfortably filled at half past seven o'clock, while at eight the time advertised for beginning the services, the entire floor space and almost all the gallery was occupied. Some regard it as a hopeful sign of the times that while on the way to the regular services of the sanctuary on the Sabbath-day there is but here and there a traveller, multitudes flock together on Sabbath-day and week-day alike to attend services conducted altogether out of the ordinary line followed by any denomination of Christians. This in fact is one of the great magnetic powers which Mr. Moody possesses. He has the courage to do things out of the ordinary line, and the multitude admire him and his ways.

Returning to London in November Moody concluded his last visit to Great Britain by conducting a two weeks' mission in the Metropolitan Tabernacle where for so many years his old friend Charles Haddon Spurgeon had proclaimed the gospel. Twice daily throngs crowded the meetings; the eagerness of so many of his old friends to see and hear him filled the great auditorium in advance of the announced hour of the service. When he arose to speak and found that his audience was almost entirely made up of Christian people, he addressed them as such, with almost a twinge of disappointment at times, for much as he prized friendship the passion of his life was to proclaim the gospel to those outside the Christian faith.

During these meetings in London Moody suffered from huskiness. At the earnest solicitation of friends he consulted Dr. Habershon who, in making the general examination, discovered an irregularity in Moody's heart action. Dr. Habershon wished Moody to see Sir Andrew

Clark to have a confirming opinion. Sir Andrew was far too busy to waste time on unessentials and had acquired in consequence a certain reputation for brusqueness.

In reply to Moody's inquiry concerning what he had done to bring on the difficulty, and how he should avoid increased trouble in the future, the celebrated doctor asked how many times a day Moody was in the habit of speaking.

"Oh, I usually preach three times a day; but on Sunday four or even five."

"How many days in the week?"

"Six days in the week, but during the last winter seven."

"You're a fool, sir; you're a fool! You're killing yourself," declared Sir Andrew.

"Well, doctor," said Moody, "usually I take Saturday to rest; this year has been an exception. But may I ask how many hours a day you work?"

"Oh, I work sixteen or seventeen."

"How many days a week?"

"Every day, sir; every day."

"Then, doctor, I think you're a bigger fool than I am, and you'll kill yourself first."

And with these pleasantries the two men parted, the physician to continue his ministry of healing for little more than a year, while Moody was permitted to work on for seven years.

CHAPTER LVIII

A BRIEF visit to Oxford closed this mission to England. The contrast between this visit and the one ten years earlier was striking. There was no "rowdy reception," a correspondent notes, but rather, "there were five hundred undergraduates among the large audience and their reverent and respectful attention was notable."

After an absence of over twelve months, Moody secured homeward passage for himself and his son by the North German Lloyd line. A small company gathered at the station in London to see him off, and he started for Southampton. The journey found Moody in the best of spirits. To be again on his way home had been a long-anticipated pleasure, and it was expected that a week later would find him back in America. The last good-byes were said, and the party went on board the *Spree*, at this time one of the fastest vessels of the line.

> When about three days on our voyage, I remember [says Moody in describing this event] I was lying on my couch, as I generally do at sea, congratulating myself on my good fortune, and feeling very thankful to God. I considered myself a very fortunate man, for in all my travels by land and sea I had never been in any accident of a serious nature.
>
> While engaged with these grateful thoughts I was startled by a shock as if the vessel had been driven on a rock. I did not at first feel much anxiety—perhaps I was too ill to think about it. My son jumped from his berth and rushed on deck. He was back again in a few moments, exclaiming that the shaft

was broken and the vessel sinking. I did not at first believe that it could be so bad but concluded to dress and go on deck. The report was only too true. The ship's passengers were naturally roused, but in answer to frightened enquiries they were assured that it was only a broken shaft.

The serious nature of the accident soon became evident, however, as other passengers rushed on deck declaring that their cabins were rapidly filling with water. Later it was found that the two fractured ends of the shaft, in revolving, had broken the stern-tube, admitting water into the two aftermost compartments, which were immediately filled. The bulkheads between the compartments were closed at once and braced with beams to resist the pressure of the water. For two days the ship drifted in this helpless condition, in momentary peril from the tremendous force of water in the flooded compartments, which beat frightfully, as the ship rolled, against the next compartment. But for the skill of Captain Willigerod and his efficient engineers, the ship would soon have foundered.

The officers and crew did all that they could to save the vessel. But it was soon found that the pumps were useless, for the water poured into the ship too rapidly to be controlled. . . .

The lifeboats were all put in readiness, provisions were prepared, life preservers were brought out, the officers were armed with revolvers so as to be able to enforce their orders, and it was only a question of whether to launch the boats at once, or wait. The sea was so heavy that the boats could hardly live in it.

At noon the captain told the passengers that he had the water under control, and was in hopes of drifting in the way of some passing vessel. The ship's bow was now high in the air while the stern seemed to settle more and more. . . . The night closed in without the sight of a sail.

That was an awful night, the darkest in all our lives—several hundred men, women and children waiting for the doom that seemed to be settling upon us! No one dared to sleep. We were all together in the saloon of the first cabin—Jews, Protestants, Catholics and skeptics—although I doubt if at that time there were many skeptics among us. The agony and suspense were too great for words. With blanched faces and trembling hearts, the passengers looked at one another as if trying to read in the faces of those about them what no one dared to speak. Rockets flamed into the sky but there was no answer. We were drifting out of the track of the great steamers. Every hour increased the danger of the situation.

Sunday morning dawned without help or hope. Up to that time no suggestion for religious services had been made. To have done that would almost certainly have produced a panic. In the awful suspense and dread that prevailed, a word about religion would have suggested the most terrible things to the passengers. It was necessary to divert their minds, if possible, or they would break under the strain. But as that second night came on, I asked Gen. O. O. Howard, who was with us, to secure the captain's permission for a service in the saloon. The captain said, "Most certainly. I am that kind, too."

We gave notice of the meeting, and to our surprise nearly every passenger attended, and I think everybody prayed, skeptics and all.

With one arm clasping a pillar to steady myself on the reeling vessel, I tried to read Psalms xci, and we prayed that God would still the raging of the sea, and bring us to our desired haven. It was a new psalm to me from that hour. The eleventh verse touched me very deeply. It was like the voice of divine assurance, and it seemed a very real thing as I read: "He shall give His angels charge over thee, to keep thee in all thy ways." Surely He did it! I also read from Psalm cvii. 20-31. One lady thought those words must have been written for the occasion, and afterwards asked to see the Book for herself. A German translated verse by verse as I read, for the benefit of his countrymen.

I knew my sins had been put away, and that if I died there it would only be to wake up in heaven. That was all settled long ago. But as my thoughts went out to my beloved ones at home—my wife, my children, my friends on both sides of the sea, the schools and all the interests so dear to me—and as I realized that perhaps the next hour would separate me forever from all these, so far as this world was concerned, I confess it almost broke me down. It was the darkest hour of my life.

I could not endure it. I must have relief, and relief came in prayer. God heard my cry, and enabled me to say, from the depth of my soul, "Thy will be done!" Sweet peace came to my heart. I went to bed, fell asleep almost immediately, and never slept more soundly in my life. Out of the depths I cried unto my Lord and He heard me and delivered me from all my fears. I can no more doubt that God gave answer to my prayer for relief than I can doubt my own existence.

About three o'clock in the morning I was aroused from my sound sleep by my son's voice. "Come on deck, father," he said. I followed him, and he pointed to a far off light rising and sinking on the sea. It was a messenger of deliverance to us. It proved to be the light of the steamer *Lake Huron*, bound from Montreal to Liverpool, whose lookout had seen our signals of distress. . . . Oh, the joy of that moment when those seven hundred despairing passengers beheld the approaching ship! Who can ever forget it?

But now the question was, "Can this small steamer tow the helpless *Spree* a thousand miles to Queenstown?" Every moment was passed in the intensest anxiety and prayer. It was a brave and perilous undertaking. The vessels were at last connected by two great cables. If a storm arose these would snap like a thread. . . . But I had no fear. God would finish the work He had begun. The waves were calmed, the cables held, our steamer moved in the wake of the *Huron*. There were storms all about us but they came not nigh our broken ship. Seven days after the accident, by the good hand of our God upon us, we were able to hold a joyous thanksgiving service in the harbour of Queenstown. The rescuing ship that God sent to us in our distress had just sufficient power to tow our steamer, and just enough coal to take her into port. Her captain was a man of prayer; he besought God's help to enable them to accomplish their dangerous and difficult task; and God answered the united prayers of the distressed voyagers, and brought us to our desired haven.

The experience of those days upon the Atlantic left a lasting impression upon Moody; but through it all he was thinking of others. His tender heart torn by the scenes of anguish, as mothers wept over their children, and fathers pleaded with God to spare them the sight of their son's destruction.

His son reported that during the first few hours after the danger was known, he had little to say and that once he said of the probable outcome of the accident, "I had hoped to have a few more years to work. I had planned to preach the gospel in Chicago next summer; and I want to do some more work on the schools at Northfield and Chicago. But, if my work is ended, why, it's all right. It's hard for you, though, with your life-work just beginning. If it's God's will, however, it's all for the best." And there he left it.

CHAPTER LIX

In January of 1893 Moody resumed evangelistic missions in America. From notations on his sermon envelopes it is evident that he spent a greater part of the time in Southern states and revisiting Baltimore.

But the great work of the year was to be undertaken in the summer months. This was the mission in Chicago from May to November during the World's Fair. It had been determined to observe the four hundredth anniversary of Columbus' discovery of America by an exposition in which the progress in every phase of modern civilization should be suitably exhibited. All nations were invited to exhibit that which was peculiarly characteristic of their life, both in industry and culture. A world-wide publicity campaign had aroused the interest of people everywhere and it was anticipated that during the summer months of 1893 Chicago would be thronged with great crowds.

The most experienced pastors and laymen of the city looked forward to the Fair with misgivings and apprehensions altogether reasonable. "It was a question," said a leading pastor, "what was to become of us during the six months. We knew it would be a time of great excitement, and what should become of the spiritual life of the churches we knew not."

As far back as his Palestine trip, Moody had looked forward to this work. When seated on Mount Olivet, watching the city over which the Savior wept, he thought of the city where he had begun his early Christian efforts, the city with its noble churches and earnest preachers, its faithful Sunday school and Y. M. C. A. workers, devoted Christians and philanthropists. Side by side with the city of temples and saints he saw another one, inhabited by men who cared for none of these things; he saw the gilded gambling halls and the dingy barrooms, the parlors of shame and the miserable dives, the sacrilegious concert rooms and the vulgar variety shows. He saw, as few men see it, the chasm which divided the classes; and he knew that even with a church on every block in Chicago there would still be a vast unchurched population, a city in a city in which many were going down to death crying piteously, "No man careth for my soul!"

Into the city of wealth and culture and piety, and the city of poverty and ignorance and crime, he saw a multitude pouring from every state and territory in the country and from every nation under heaven. The White City, the goal of all, would be visited, but what then? Would there be closed church doors and open saloons, a darkened house of God and brilliantly lighted resorts? The contrast was an inspiration to Moody and he worked with one great object in view.

When the fair managers decided to keep open on Sundays, some said, "Let us boycott the fair"; others, "Let us appeal to the law and compel them to close on Sundays." But Moody said, "Let us open so many preaching places, and present the gospel so attractively that the people will want to come and hear it."

His plan of campaign was simple. Chicago, as has been stated, is naturally divided into three sections by the forking river. In each section a church center was selected; Chicago Avenue Church in the north, the First Congregational Church in the west, and the Immanuel Baptist Church in the south. Later many other churches were offered and occupied.

Chicago is a polyglot community. During the summer

of 1893 the confusion of tongues was even greater, and many strangers from distant lands could only be reached through their own language. Moody therefore enlisted the coöperation of well-known evangelists from other lands; Poles, Hebrews, French, Germans and Swedes, all heard the gospel "every one in his own tongue."

In all Moody's career there never was a time when his resourcefulness, tact, executive ability and power as a preacher were so evident. Every available opportunity was seized for gospel meetings and for services for Christian workers. Meetings were held in churches, halls, tents and in the open. In residential districts, in business centers, in proximity to the fair grounds and in the slums of the city, the work was extended.

When Moody announced a meeting in Tattersall's with its seating capacity of ten to fifteen thousand, he said: "We've got something better than the Military Tournament, and we must get a bigger audience than they." And the great throng that attended was all that could be desired.

Forepaugh's circus came to Chicago in June, and established itself on the lake front. The manager rented the tent to Moody for Sunday morning, but reserved it for his own shows in the afternoon and evening. When the circus advertisement appeared, the manager had included the morning meeting in his announcement as follows:

> Ha! Ha! Ha!
> Three Big Shows!
> Moody in the Morning!
> Forepaugh in the Afternoon and Evening!

An observer thus describes the scene:

> The surroundings were the usual circus furniture —ropes, trapezes, gaudy decorations, etc., while in an adjoining canvas building was a large menagerie,

including eleven elephants. Clowns, grooms, circus-riders, men, women, and children, eighteen thousand of them, and on a Sunday morning, too! Whether the gospel was ever before preached under such circumstances I know not but it was wonderful to ear and eye alike.

When that mighty throng took up the hymn, "Nearer, My God, to Thee," a visible sense of awe fell upon the multitude. After an hour of singing and prayer, Moody rose to preach, his text being, "The Son of Man is come to seek and to save that which was lost." The spirit of God was present; the hush of heaven was over the meeting. Towards the close of the address there was a slight disturbance, and a lost child was passed up to the platform. Moody held her up so that her parents might see her; and when her anxious father reached the platform, Moody placed the child in his arms and said, "That is what Jesus Christ came to do, to seek and to save lost sinners, and restore them to their Heavenly Father's embrace."

Moody rented this circus tent for two Sundays. It was a revelation to the circus manager that so many people would come to listen to songs and sermons. His afternoon and evening shows were so thinly attended that he abandoned Sunday exhibitions, and asked Moody to keep him supplied with an evangelist to hold gospel meetings in the tent on Sundays in other cities, promising to bear all the traveling and other expenses of such an arrangement. However, there were serious objections to complying with such a request.

Every variety of gospel meeting was held: men's, women's, children's meetings; temperance, soldiers', jail meetings; open-air and cottage meetings; meetings for Germans, Poles, Bohemians, French, Jews, and even for the Arabs in the fair grounds; meetings for praise and for prayer; all-day and all-night meetings.

As the closing weeks of the campaign came on the work was further extended.

> It seems as if we had only been playing during the past weeks [Moody said]. Now we are going to work. We have just been fishing along the shore; now we are going to launch out into the deep. Friends, help fill up the churches. Let us see whether we can't wake up this whole city. There is now before us the grandest opportunity for extending the kingdom of God that this country has ever seen. Hundreds of thousands of people will come in during these last weeks of the World's Fair. It is possible to reach them with the gospel message. We want to get still more buildings for meetings near the fair grounds. We'll hire all the theaters we can get. I'll use all the money you will give me to push the work. We are spending now about eight hundred dollars a day in this work, and could spend eight thousand dollars a day if we had it. We are getting new places for meetings as fast as we can. We want to press these closing days of the World's Fair as never before.

On certain Sundays not less than one hundred and twenty-five meetings were held under Moody's directions, the staff of speakers, singers and clerks all having to be provided by him. It was estimated that the aggregate attendance each Sunday at these services exceeded a hundred thousand.

It is of interest to learn Moody's estimate of this Chicago work as given in an interview at the close of the meetings:

> The principal result of our six months' work is that millions have heard the simple gospel preached

by some of the most gifted preachers all over this land and have been brought to a deeper spiritual life and aroused to more active Christian effort for the salvation of others.

"Have you learned any new lessons or suggestions about Christian work from your experience and observation during the six months' labor?" he was asked.

"I have learned that the summer, so far from being the worst, is the best time to carry on Christian work in our cities. I have learned to appreciate more than ever the power that there is in concentrated and united Christian action. I have been impressed with the fact that it is the Christian people of the land that take an interest in and patronize such expositions as the World's Fair."

"Would such an extensive, long-continued series of gospel meetings be practicable and advisable at other times and places?"

"Certainly. A gospel campaign such as that in Chicago this summer would be practicable, I believe, in any other large city, even where there was no fair."

"What do you consider to be the most effective agency, or agencies, in the prosecution of your campaign?"

"The preaching and singing of the old gospel and the power of the Holy Ghost."

"Will you gratify a curious public by stating what has been the aggregate expense of your entire six months' labor?"

"The entire expense, exclusive of the ordinary expenses of the Institute, was $60,000; an additional large expenditure had to be made to enlarge the buildings before the beginning of the campaign."

"Do you mind telling how these enormous expenses have been met?"

"By gifts of generous Christian individuals and societies all over the United States, Canada and Great Britain. Some of this money was given in answer to personal appeals, some without any suggestion from me."

"What assurance, if any, had you at the beginning that the means would be provided for the prosecution of the work?"

"Only that I knew the work ought to be done, and that I knew we have a God who will always sustain us in doing what we ought to do."

It should be remembered that this work was assumed upon Moody's sole responsibility, at the close of a hard winter's work, at the season which he usually reserved for rest and study in his home at Northfield, and after he had been warned not to overtax his strength because of the condition of his heart. No committee shared the responsibilities with him for the simple reason that he feared that such a committee would be reluctant to assume expenses which he felt must be incurred to successfully prosecute the work. His energy and genius in marshaling forces, his tact in overcoming petty differences among his staff; his readiness to reinforce by his own efforts any place where there was poor attendance, were all manifested in this campaign. Then there was the heavy financial responsibility to meet attendant expenses in hiring halls, entertaining speakers, and providing for their expenses, and maintaining the necessary staff of clerks and assistants. All this was in addition to the heavy burden he was carrying in connection with the other varied interests in which he was enlisted.

Great as some of his campaigns in evangelistic work had been in former years this six months in Chicago exceeded all experiences both in numbers reached and in the demands upon Moody's resources. But Moody courted a difficult task. Obstacles were a welcome challenge. If once he realized a cause was worthy he threw himself into it with enthusiasm and labored with genuine zest. Opposition called forth his resources to the utmost with a spirit at once genial and free from any personal pique.

CHAPTER LX

Moody was a man of "consecrated common sense." It was this combined with his energy and unselfish spirit that won the confidence and esteem of many who did not share his religious zeal and convictions. Men of affairs recognized in him qualities which could successfully administer large enterprises and they respected these abilities directed in non-material interests. From many such he received help for the work which he was conducting; the gift was often a personal tribute, though Moody would never recognize it as such.

It is related that on one occasion a business man in New York City was asked why Moody found such ready access to men of wide interests when others representing worthy philanthropic enterprises could not get a hearing. "He is one of us," was the reply.

The attitude of the press is largely to be attributed to this personal respect. Moody, on his part, was deeply sensible of the potential power of the press in Christian service. If his gospel message was carried farther by reports in the newspapers, he would do his utmost to coöperate with their representatives. To reporters he was always accessible and cordial. Even with the sensational papers he would coöperate saying, "They enter places into which I can never go and if I can get the message of the gospel where it is needed that is what I want."

It was often amusing to see him turn the tables on an interviewer if he did not wish to be drawn into a controversy. With the passing of the years a mutual spirit of regard led to mutual confidence. On one occasion during the Spanish War it was rumored that the Pope might offer to act as intermediary to effect peace between the United States and Spain. The city editor of one of the New York papers called on Moody, who happened to be in the city, to secure an interview. In answer to the first inquiry, "What would be your position if the Pope should offer his services to mediate peace?" Moody promptly and firmly declined to be drawn into any such controversy. The visitor then asked, "Mr. Moody, will you give me your opinion, not for publication?" "Certainly," was his reply, with an abandon of all reserve. "If the Pope is so concerned to bring about peace why didn't he offer long before when both parties were Catholic?" Some one who was present asked how the fact of both belligerents belonging to the Catholic faith would alter the situation. "Give me half an acre of purgatory," replied Moody, "and I will stop all the wars in the world."

On another occasion a New York daily asked him to discuss a certain type of pictures which were permissible under the guise of "art." To this he assented. Enlisting the help of one who knew, in his special sphere of criminal investigation in New York, of this phase of evil, Moody prepared an article which dealt, in general terms, with chastity and the necessity of safeguarding the appeal to sense through the eye as well as through the ear.

Moody was to be in New York on Sunday, preaching in Carnegie Hall. During the week street cars carried advertisements of the forthcoming Sunday issue and gave prominence to the announcement of Moody's article. This placed Moody in an embarrassing position. His strong aversion to the Sunday papers was well known both for the unnecessary labor they entailed on railroads and news venders and because he believed that they constituted a great factor in diminishing church attendance and Sunday observance. When the article eventually appeared, illustrated by pictures in the nude reproduced from paintings in the homes of people of social distinction, Moody was further embarrassed.

To the credit of the paper it should be said that a note the subsequent week declared that Moody's known disapproval of the Sunday press entitled him to a public apology for the appearance of the article in their Sunday edition, through an inadvertence on their part for which they would express their sincere regret, etc.

Moody seldom replied to misstatements in the newspapers; but when early in his evangelistic career, it was stated in the press that he was making a good thing financially out of his religious work, he referred to the criticism. There were tears in his eyes, and his voice quavered as he said:

> As I know my heart, before God, I have never let the desire for money determine my conduct in any way. I know I am weak and come short in many ways; but the devil has not that hold upon me. I have never profited personally by a single dollar that has been raised through my work, and it hurts me to be charged with it, above all things. May God forgive those who say this of me.

More than $1,125,000 was received from royalties on the hymn books, which was used for benevolences. Moody was a good financier; he appreciated the value of money, but he never used it to build a fortune; he simply wanted to use it in doing good.

On two other occasions Moody made a public denial of newspaper reports—not for the sake of personal gratification, but solely because of injury to his work. In 1877 the Boston papers accused him of having purchased a racing horse for which it was claimed that he had paid four thousand dollars. Finding that the statement was being credited by some, and that these were prejudiced by it, Moody made a plain statement of the facts of the case. He had bought a roadster whose special virtue was its gentleness as a family horse—not its speed as a racer. The price, he also stated, had been exaggerated, and there should be deducted from the amount claimed thirty-seven hundred and fifty dollars, as he had only given two hundred and fifty dollars.

The second statement that brought forth a public denial from Moody was a newspaper report circulated in Richmond, Virginia, while he was conducting a mission in that city. One of the local papers printed a letter in which the writer stated that on a certain occasion he had heard Moody make most disparaging references to Generals Robert E. Lee and "Stonewall" Jackson. The rumor was at first ignored. Later it was found that the meetings were being seriously affected and that a bitter opposition was rapidly growing. Fortunately Moody's addresses had all been printed at the time it was claimed he had made the offensive remarks. Absolutely denying the charge at one of his meetings, he brought out this fact, and challenged anyone to find any reference to the disparagement of either of the two brave generals, for whom he had the highest personal regard. What was apparently a serious obstacle to the work was then turned to the good of the meetings, and a most successful mission followed.

In 1897 he wired his son who was then engaged in the work of the Mount Hermon School to join him immediately in New York. On arrival Moody briefly instructed his son, "I've engaged Carnegie Hall for a week, mornings and afternoons, two weeks from now. I want you to fill it for Meyer." Further inquiries elicited the information that some time previous he had asked Rev. F. B. Meyer of London to visit America to address ministers and Christian workers and had promised to make suitable preparations. Mr. Meyer was well known to a large number of the readers of his books and to others who had heard him at the Northfield General Christian Workers' Conference and elsewhere. Moody had inquired if a certain prominent church would be available for the meetings and had been told that possibly the vestry might be put at his disposal. Immediately he was determined to demonstrate that there was as much interest in spiritual things as ever there was and to provide the widest opportunities to all to hear the eminent preacher. Then Moody gave instructions as to how to fill the hall. For a week in advance announcements were to be inserted in all the daily newspapers stating that tickets might be obtained by calling at the hall or sending a stamped return envelope. Such tickets were only good for seats up to five minutes of the advertised hour when the doors would be opened to the public. During a week of extremely inclement February weather the hall was filled, often to overflowing. When it was objected that the amusement column was hardly a proper place to announce meetings Moody's rejoinder was, "It's where people look; so put it where they'll read it." His judgment was vindicated by the results.

The advertising columns of the daily papers were used in accordance with the same principles that are recognized to be helpful in the business world. "Some ministers think it undignified to advertise their services," he once said. "It's a good deal more undignified to preach to empty pews, I think." He believed that the Christian minister should have an audience, and that services intended to reach those who were not under church influence should be brought to the attention of the public.

With such devotion to the Scriptures it is not surprising that plans for increasing its study should continually occupy his mind. In 1881 he urged Major D. W. Whittle to prepare a scheme of daily Bible readings, with notes,

D. L. MOODY

and publish them regularly. This was done as a supplement to a periodical just then about to make its appearance, the *Record of Christian Work*, itself the outgrowth of Moody's suggestion, having for its purpose the report of evangelistic missions, missionary efforts, and plans of Bible study. For nearly fifty years this monthly has appeared regularly, its daily Bible notes being read by thousands. During the last months of Moody's life he took a still deeper interest in this effort, and arranged to make this magazine a special organ of the various institutions he had founded, in which there should appears the reports of the leading addresses at the Northfield Conferences and other news not only of Northfield and Mount Hermon but of the progress of "the Kingdom" throughout the world.

Moody was always fearful lest his connection with some publication should be considered as a money-making scheme on his part. For this reason he was loath to consent to any authorized edition of his sermons. They were published, however, in the daily press and numerous publishers were very ready to adapt these to book form, so that *Moody's Sermons* appeared in every conceivable shape for a number of years before any authorized works were issued.

A volume of sermons resulted from each of his series of meetings in the states. The meetings in New York, Philadelphia, Boston, Chicago, and other leading cities were reported verbatim by one or more papers; and at the close of the meetings the reports were collected in book form. Moody had no part in their compilation and no profits accrued to him or his work from their sale, which was exceedingly large.

His reluctance to sanction any volume was first overcome in connection with the unpretentious work entitled *Twelve Select Sermons*. This was issued in both Great Britain and the United States; but for several years after its appearance he would not consent to give his approval to the publication of any additional compilation. Convinced at last of the numbers who might be reached by this means, and annoyed by the fragmentary character of many of the sermons printed, he supplied other small volumes, which appeared at irregular intervals.

One of his early publications was entitled *Heaven*. One day on the railroad train he heard a newsboy, with a bundle of books under his arm shouting, "Here you are, Ingersoll *On Hell*." Moody caught the boy, and placed a copy of his own book in his hand, saying, "Here, my lad, here is another book; give them that at the same time." The boy went on through the car shouting, "Ingersoll *On Hell;* Moody on *Heaven!*"

The high valuation Moody placed upon the influence of the press in the presentation of the gospel will readily explain his interest in bringing good reading within the reach of the largest number. In 1894 he was conducting meetings in a Western city when he wanted to purchase certain religious books suitable to give to some friends. He was greatly surprised and disturbed to find that in the local bookstore no religious books could be obtained, though the shelves were loaded with all kinds of cheap fiction. "Religious books don't sell," he was informed by the clerk.

This challenged Moody's interest. He made inquiries widely only to learn that in one of the great states of the Middle West there was not one bookstore that pretended to carry even a limited assortment of religious books. Determined to do something to fill the gap which he had discovered, he returned to Chicago and consulted prominent Christian workers, who said, "People won't buy religious books; they are too expensive."

"Then the price must come down," said Moody. The only way to reduce the price without working on a charity basis would be by printing larger editions, and Moody organized a colportage department in connection with the Chicago Bible Institute.

At first ordinary methods were adopted to bring about the sale of good books, the price being lowered. In the spring of 1895, however, the distinctive feature of the work was formulated and put into execution. It was difficult to get just the books that were wanted, and Moody was not yet satisfied as to the price. It was felt that, before the work could become in any way extensive, a class of books must be secured that it was at that time impossible to obtain. The Colportage Library was therefore planned to combine these salient features: (1) popular, readable style; (2) well-known authors, or books of existing reputation; (3) strictly undenominational; (4) first-class workmanship; (5) low price.

An order for one hundred thousand copies of one of Moody's own books, *The Way to God*, was given at once.

So rapid was the growth of this work that, in four years, Moody saw it spread over not only the whole continent but to foreign lands. In addition to the English editions there were, in the Colportage Library, books in German, Danish, Norwegian and Swedish; and there were requests on file for translations in Spanish, Polish, Bohemian, Dutch, French, and other languages.

In 1895, Moody heard to his amazement that no less than three quarters of a million men and women in America belonged to the distinctly criminal class; that is, the number passed continuously in and out of jails and prisons. He could scarcely believe it until he had investigated. He began to inspect the jails and prisons in every state that he visited, and found that the county jails in many places were entirely neglected as to religious work. Only here and there were Christian people who took any interest in these jails. Libraries and reading matter were found in the penitentiaries, but a great many jails that he visited—among others one containing three hundred prisoners—were destitute of all good reading.

When he asked the prisoners if there was anything he could do for them, they said that if they had something to read it would help to kill the time. In answer to his inquiry if they would read sermons or religious books, they replied that they would, and he sent some into that prison. There were among them those who could not read, and they insisted that those who could should read aloud to them. They read Spurgeon's and other sermons that Moody sent, and before long he began to hear of conversions. Then he sent Testaments, and became so interested that he began to write to the sheriffs of all the different counties (there is a jail in nearly every one of the twenty-seven hundred counties in the United States). Of all the letters written only one brought a disrespectful reply.

During the last four years of his ministry he scarcely ever left a town without making a special plea for the prisoners, with very gratifying results.

> It must not be supposed [he said] that all prisoners are hardened criminals. Many a young man has committed a crime in a moment of anger, or under the influence of liquor. The records show that nearly half the prisoners are under twenty-five years of age. At this time of life a young man is not supposed to have become settled in character. If he can be reached by the gospel message before he begins to sink lower and lower, there is every hope of his salvation for this life and the life to come.

The prisoners fear idleness more than anything else. With his knowledge of human nature, he believed that this was just the time to reach a man, and to make him think, when cut off from old associations, and away from whiskey and gambling.

That is what you want a man to do [he said]. What brought home the prodigal? He began thinking. These prisoners begin to realize what wretched lives they have been living, and this is the opportune moment to strike them. They are glad of a book or paper to occupy their minds, and Christian influences may be brought to bear on them by this channel and their whole destiny changed for good.

Moody's plan was to get people sufficiently interested to send one book, if they could not send more, and then follow it with their prayers.

The scope of the influence which Moody foresaw would continue long after he had passed away is noted in the last annual report of the society. Nearly nine million books, published in six languages and under one hundred and forty-seven titles have been disseminated, carrying the gospel to the uttermost parts of the world. Approximately half of these have been actually purchased, implying that they have been read by several in the family, often in some remote district. The report also indicates that four million, four hundred thousand have been distributed in prisons, hospitals, orphanages, mines and through numerous agencies to all kinds and conditions of men.

CHAPTER LXI

Zeal for Christian service had resulted in ever increasing burdens of responsibility. Rest and study, the object which Moody had in mind when he settled in Northfield, were less and less available. Summer evenings, which in former years were spent with his family, were now devoted to writing appeals or signing typewritten letters soliciting contributions. Of these he signed thousands, often affixing his signature to two or three hundred in an evening.

For some years the annual amount which Moody had to raise for the work at Northfield and Chicago exceeded $120,000, while he also collected additional sums for the Y. M. C. A.

Instead of seeking relief from burdens, as the years passed, Moody seemed to be ever assuming new ones. When at last he laid down his work it was found that this which might be termed his summer's pastime engrossed the time of two mature men, while in his life work, evangelism, there was no one to succeed him.

To what is to be attributed his success in raising funds? The answer that would be first elicited from him would be that funds came in answer to prayer. On one occasion some appeals were being prepared by his son and after they had been mailed Moody turned abruptly on him and said, "Did you pray over those letters?" "No, I didn't." "Well, how do you expect to get responses if you don't pray?" Moody asked.

But prayer was accompanied by work and a spirit of self-denial on his part. Though Moody's own testimony

D. L. MOODY

to the efficacy of prayer is taken, there were other factors that made prayer effective and won the confidence of the public. Moody was absolutely disinterested personally. He never received any emolument for such labor; he was in no sense a professional money raiser. All that he did was the spontaneous expression of confidence in what he was seeking to help and the conviction of the genuine service the effort would be to the cause of Christ. His own generosity in freely giving of time and labor was contagious. If he was so convinced of the value of an object to give, others were influenced thereby. Business sagacity, sound common sense and experience were recognized in methods adopted in the work as well as in the manner of approach. Moody knew men and was familiar with business-like directness. Unctuous phrases he hated.

Finally, Moody's own standard of living was simple. When he traveled he preferred the less ostentatious hotels, though he went where he could be protected from the importunity of cranks and where the acknowledged respectability of the place was a guarantee against being the victim of any effort to place him in a compromising position. No man was more careful of his manner of life to avoid not only the appearance of evil, but even the possibility of misconstruction.

His own home, an enlarged old farmhouse, was simple and unpretentious. The original outlay was thirty-five hundred dollars and it is doubtful if during the twenty-four years he lived in it there was further outlay of more than four thousand dollars. Only during the last six years was there steam heat in the house; prior to that an old-fashioned furnace, which heated only four rooms, had sufficed. Although gas was provided in the school buildings, kerosene was the only illuminant Moody had in his own home. Such conditions could hardly answer the description that "his house, if not luxurious, had certainly every accommodation that the most exacting could require." Moody could appeal to others because he was denying himself to serve.

Many interesting narratives Moody used to relate of experiences in raising funds. Often the unexpected sources whence help came in time of emergencies afforded evidence of his contention that help came primarily in answer to prayer. But these incidents he never spoke of publicly.

On the other hand, he had many humorous experiences. While engaged in a series of meetings in Scranton, Pennsylvania, he was impressed with the need of a well-equipped Y. M. C. A. building for the greater effectiveness of its service. At once he began to work for a fund of seventy-five thousand dollars and announced that a collection for this purpose would be taken at an evening service. Rev. S. A. Taggert, who was active in this endeavor, writes:

> In the meantime the alert board of managers of the Association had taken advantage of the occasion to invite a special company to dine with Mr. Moody at the hotel that evening. Around $25,000 was subscribed for the new building. One who had been especially invited to be present, and from whom, by reason of his wealth, they hoped for help, was not there. Mr. Moody proposed to go and see him at once before the meeting of the evening. Some shook their heads and said they feared it would be of no use. Mr. Moody said to Colonel Boies, "Get your sleigh and drive around with me to see this man before the meeting; I like to talk to rich men, particularly if they don't want to give. They are a neglected class and need a missionary. No one ever thinks of speaking to them about their souls or their stewardship." He called to see this man and said to him, "We need a Moses to lead the way for the young men of Scranton. The Association is out on

the street nearly all the time begging for its living, when it ought to be trying to save the ten thousand young men of the city. We want you to give $20,000 to lead the way for a building." This request staggered the old gentleman for a time, and he could make no reply, but finally said that he could not give. Mr. Moody then talked to him of $10,000, but with no satisfactory understanding. He said to him, "You will be at the meeting to-night?" "Yes," was the reply. "Well, I want you to take a seat on the platform." When the time for the meeting came we had worked our way with difficulty to the platform. Mr. Moody said to me, "Do you see Mr. X—— anywhere?" Before I could reply he caught sight of him on the edge of the platform and worked over as near as he could get, and in a shouting whisper said, "How much is it—ten, ten?" "Oh, no," was the reply, "just the half, just the half." When the name of this man, among others, was announced that night as giving $5,000 it produced a deep impression. He was known as slow in giving, and yet for that very reason it seemed to inspire the whole city with confidence that the project must go through to success. From that hour this man took the deepest interest in the building project, and was greatly blessed in his gift. The result of the subscriptions and collections that night was less than $35,000 but the sequel showed that Mr. Moody understood the situation. He had been informed that many who were interested in the business enterprises of Scranton lived in New York City and elsewhere, and he assured the people of Scranton that the building would soon be erected.

At the close of the meetings there still remained forty thousand dollars to be raised and Moody turned to men in New York whose large financial interests in the anthracite coal fields would in Moody's judgment lead them to help. Securing by telegraph an appointment with Mr. Samuel Sloan, president of the Delaware, Lackawanna and Western Railroad, a coal carrying road with large interests in the vicinity of Scranton, he enlisted his support with a contribution of five thousand dollars. At first Mr. Sloan had demurred, offering the objection that he was appealed to for every object and did not know why people always came to him when there were so many much better able to give. Moody replied: "There was a man once who went to solicit money and came to one who made your objection. 'Why don't you go to the people who never give, instead of us who do give?' to this the solicitor replied, 'If you wanted a good pail of milk, would you go to a cow that was milked regularly or to one that was only milked once in a long time?'"

Mr. Sloan found the argument unanswerable and after he had given evidence of his sympathy, Moody then asked if he could advise where he could turn next. "Yes," said Mr. Sloan, "there is Mr. B——. He has large interests in that region, is very wealthy and ought to give, although he is not noted for that." "How can I approach him?" asked Moody. "I'll send for him," was the reply and immediately a messenger was despatched to summon one of the leading magnates. Moody used to relate with genuine relish the encounter which ensued. "Old Mr. B—— came rushing in breathlessly fearing the bottom might have dropped out of the market. His silk hat was on the back of his head and his collar button had come undone and he was fastening it with a shaking hand. Mr. Sloan greeted him familiarly and told him to take a seat. Mr. B—— 'was in too great a hurry,' 'couldn't stay' and 'had to keep an appointment.' But all to no avail; he had to be seated. Mr. Sloan told of my being in Scranton, my feeling there was a need of a Y. M. C. A. and that he promised me to help in the work with five thousand and added that he was sure Mr. B—— would do the same. Yes, he had heard of Moody who had been turning things upside down in Scranton, but couldn't do anything for Scranton. Why did people always turn to him—— Mr. Sloan interrupted, 'That's what I said. Moody told me a story you want to hear.' 'No time.' 'Yes, you have; Mr. Moody, tell him that story.' And Mr. B—— had to listen while I told again the story of the milk pail. This time Mr. Sloan laughed heartily but no response came from the other. 'Mr. Moody,' said Mr. Sloan, 'he pretends he doesn't see the point but he will be telling the story all round the Street. You can count on another $5,000 from him. The story is worth it.'"

In a short time the added subscription was received and still another of equal amount was made through Mr. Sloan's help. Again quoting Mr. Taggert:

> The result of Mr. Moody's efforts on his rest day in New York for the Scranton Fund was an assured increase of nearly $30,000 more, making a total of over $60,000 in less than four days; the whole amount needed, $75,000 was secured in less than six weeks.
>
> I had tried for some time [continues Rev. Mr. Taggert] to think of someone with whom Mr. Moody was not acquainted, to assist him with more than an ordinary contribution in his educational work at Northfield. After considerable thought I said, "I have a friend in the oil regions whom I have known for a long time. I knew him when he was poor, and he is now prosperous, and his prosperity has not hurt his Christian character. I wish you would write to him explaining your work and its needs." A short time after this I received a letter from Mr. Moody in which he said, "The Lord answers prayers, and I

must testify to His goodness. I wrote to your friend, and, after finishing the letter, I prayed that God might incline him to give the sum I had named, if he was able to give it. He has sent me his cheque for $5000. Some days afterward I was in the place where this man resided, and called upon him. He said to me, "I think you must have set Mr. Moody after me, as I have never met him. I received a letter asking me for $5000 for his schools in Northfield. When I read the letter I thought I could not give anything; then I thought I would send $500 anyhow. In a little while I raised it to $1000. On my way home to luncheon I thought of the hundreds of poor young men and women getting an education for $100 a year, and the large extra expense resting upon Mr. Moody, for which he must make provision; and the thought came to me, 'Make it $2500.' Before I reached home I thought, if my wife agreed with me, I would make it $5000. When I showed her the letter she said, 'Give him the sum he asks for.' This all occurred within an hour, and that afternoon I sent him my cheque for the full amount."

In his approach to men of affairs he was considerate of their time. He wasted no time on futile apologies or circumlocutions. He assumed that they would be interested in a worthy object, stated his case, and often left almost as abruptly as he called. On one occasion he was interested in raising a sum to serve as a guarantee fund for some evangelistic services to be held in New York during the summer months. He made several calls, briefly stating the need, making request for a definite sum and excusing himself, hurried on. That one afternoon and evening he raised the requisite five thousand dollars in five different gifts.

In his *Character Sketch of Morris K. Jesup* Dr. William Adams Brown refers to the warm friendship between the two men. In Mr. Jesup Moody found

an intelligent and sympathetic supporter in the various enterprises in which he was engaged. He was a frequent visitor at Mr. Jesup's home and valued the advice which he received there as much as the money which he carried away. It was a rare January which did not find among Mr. Jesup's early letters one from Mr. Moody. The following, chosen from several which have chanced to survive, is so characteristic of both the writer and of the recipient of it, that I shall be pardoned for quoting it in full:

"Mount Hermon Boys' School,
"January 2, 1891.

"My dear Mr. Jesup

"Excuse me for my boldness, but I know you will give away about so much in 1891, and if I can get my call in early enough I think you will remember me some time in the year. Mount Hermon has added $180,000 to your $5000. The Sem. has about $100,000 and the school at Chicago has property worth about $150,000 and the $100,000 as endowment. Now, if my friends will help me a few years longer I think I will then have them all endowed and in good working order.

"The last time I saw you you said you wanted results. I think we can show them to you now and if you call on me up here in the Spring I think we can cheer your heart. Thanking you for your help in the past and wishing you a Happy New Year and a joyful eternity, I remain,

"Your true friend,
"D. L. Moody."

CHAPTER LXII

"If anything happens to me I want you to destroy all my sermon notes," Moody enjoined his son. In reply to a remonstrance that many would prize these notes he replied, "No one can make them out but myself. They are largely catch words which remind me of an illustration or something which has happened in my own life. If they should fall into some people's hands I would be made to say the very opposite of what I stood for all my life."

Dr. Goss graphically describes Moody's style of preaching:

> Mr. Moody seemed to seize the idea that his messages were to be delivered over wires kept hot, and that there was neither time nor money to be wasted in their delivery. Brevity, precision, perspicuity, were from the first their prevailing traits. Words and sentences fell from his lips with rapidity and clearness.
>
> In passages of the same length (about 530 words chosen at random from printed sermons) I have estimated that Mr. Moody uttered thirty-six sentences: Bushnell, twenty; Spurgeon, twenty-one; Lacordaire, fifteen; Chalmers, nine.
>
> It would seem as if such brevity would have rendered his speech unmusical; but this was far from being the case. There was a flow and smoothness to its movement which gave an actual pleasure to the ear. In passages of intense excitement the sentences possessed an explosive quality suggesting a

pack of fire crackers set off by accident; but after he had gained control of his vocal organs, and of his inflammable emotions, there was nothing of this character.

In preparation Moody used to note down the main subdivisions of his address, using ordinary note paper. Then he would use some one word of a brief sentence which would call to mind some apt illustration of incident in his experience. The notes he kept in a large envelope; each time the address was given he would write on the envelope, as already described, the date and place where the address was given.

He did not hesitate to use a sermon repeatedly. In this respect he resembled George Whitefield, of whom Benjamin Franklin said:

> By hearing him often, I came to distinguish easily between sermons newly composed and those he had often preached during the course of his travels. His delivery of the latter was so improved by frequent repetition that every accent, every emphasis, every modulation of the voice was so perfectly well turned and well placed, that without being interested in the subject one could not help being pleased with the description. . . . When he had nothing before him except the audience whom he was addressing the judgment and imagination as well as the memory were called forth.

From the notations it would seem that many of Moody's sermons were used repeatedly over a number of years. As illustrative of this, between 1875 and 1897 he preached on the "Son of Man" one hundred and forty-two times; "Faith, Courage and Enthusiasm," seventy-three times; "Holy Spirit," during the last seven years of his life ninety-five times; and the "New Birth" between

1883 and 1894 one hundred and eighty-six times. "Sowing and Reaping" he used one hundred and thirteen times and his address on "Daniel" he gave seventy times. There were over four hundred sermon envelopes at the time of his going. "If I find a sword effective, why shouldn't I use it often?" was his response when questioned if he used a sermon more than once.

But all the sermons were always in the process of revision. Each time he spoke he added new material and each envelope contained material for several addresses. Some sermons he used but seldom, others he discarded as the subject matter was better dealt with under different texts.

Illustration he used freely. "It has often happened," he would explain, "that an illustration fixes a truth in the memory. They are hooks in the mind on which truths may be hung. Many times people have told me they have heard me years before and when I ask what I spoke on they have told me that they did not remember the text but recalled a story I'd told."

One illustration he used greatly in later years was so unusual that it is recalled after a generation. To illustrate the expulsive power of a life filled with the spirit of God he would take a glass of water and filling it to the brim, continue to pour in more water till the overflowing contents would spill onto the platform. Objects floating on the surface would be carried off and the constant stream would keep the contents clear.

His experiences in the Civil War afforded him an almost exhaustless fund of anecdotes while the contacts with all classes gave varied stories of struggles and victories of people everywhere. He was always careful to guard sacredly a confidence and never allow an incident to become susceptible of identification. If illustrations were homely they were for that reason more effective with the average man. It has been said that Moody was not a wide reader. This was true in respect to literature in general. Illustrations were usually drawn from daily life with which he was familiar. But at the same time historical allusions were often used. In his library the frequent markings in books were evidence of a wider reading than many assumed.

In those early days in the Northfield home before conferences preëmpted so much of his time he did much reading. It was his custom at this time to preach a new sermon in a hay loft to familiarize himself with the subject matter.

Moody's printed sermons lack the personality of the speaker. The intonation of his voice and his facial expression gave much force to the subject matter. First reported stenographically and then edited for permanent record, they lost much of the vigor and passion of the short and almost jerky phrases. This is doubtless true of most speakers but especially so of one who never followed a manuscript. Beyond the flexible Bagster Bible in which he inserted an elastic band to hold the barest skeleton of an address, chiefly catchwords, Moody took nothing into the pulpit. His addresses were the impassioned appeal of his own heart and from the heart and will of his hearers he sought response. He always insisted that what the church is in need of is "men who can think on their heels."

His intense humanity was ever present. In him the "love of God was spread abroad in his heart." Because of his great capacity for loving men he could say severe things without incurring the charge of rancor and bitterness.

Moody's theology has been the subject of much discussion. It would be difficult to determine his position in academic terms. "I am an Arminian up to the Cross," he would say. "After the Cross, a Calvinist." This he would illustrate by an analogy from Masonry, although he himself was not a member of any secret organization. "Supposing I want to join the Masons and seek admittance to the order. That is my part. It is the *whosoever*. When I gain admittance I know I'm elected." It was the "whosoever will" he emphasized to the outsider, the "elect according to the foreknowledge of God" to the professing Christians.

He would be termed a literalist. He believed the Bible "from cover to cover." But this did not mean he was a bigot. To him many things it contained were inexplicable. These he left. There was so much he could grasp, at least in part, that he placed his emphasis on what was within his comprehension. Speculation had no attractions for him. He knew the power of sin in his own experience and in what he observed in others. He knew the redemptive power of the gospel in the same way. The abounding love of God was a present consciousness with him. The truth such as he knew it, he held in a spirit of love.

In the first place Moody's theology was conservatively evangelical. The evangelical doctrines were the subjects of his preaching. It is of interest in studying his career to note the varying emphasis which he gave to certain truths. Early in his public work his emphasis had been upon retribution, a relic of the early Calvinistic views, representing God as a vengeful deity. This was followed by the influence of Henry Moorehouse and from that time the emphasis was wholly upon the love of God. But it was the love of God which was shed abroad that again brought a new emphasis into his preaching, a warning note against sin. Though God forgave sin, Moody realized that there was another equal truth, that there were certain consequences of sin, which even divine forgiveness would not eradicate.

This latter emphasis was the underlying thought in the sermon on "Sowing and Reaping," which he illustrated by so many dramatic examples. It was a warning to youth of the inevitable consequences of sin when he cited the case of a man who in drunkenness met with an accident and lost an arm. His drunkenness might be forgiven and he might be restored to respected citizenship, but this would never again restore to him the arm which he had lost.

There was another thing which characterized Moody's preaching and that was his sound judgment. This doubtless may be challenged by some, but he never would have held the thought and attention of the class of people who attended his services on mere sensation or the recognition of his zeal. Moody would have heartily subscribed to the definition that

> religion is the response of the whole man to that which is external to and higher than himself, and in this response, feeling, thought and will are all alike concerned. . . . The question at issue is really one of balance and proportion. We are all aware of the evils which follow from an over-emphasis of the emotional elements in the religious consciousness. But over-emphasis on the intellectual is equally productive of mischief, though of mischief of a different kind. . . . It is at least a matter of regret and productive of much confusion that religion should so often be presented to men as a body of truth rather than a life. It can only be the one as and because it is the other, and one of the merits of a psychological treatment of religion is that it shows that in any acceptable presentment of it both elements must be preserved. . . . Apart from reason the will is blind.

Religion was indeed to Moody a widening of the whole horizon of life. The same writer already quoted states that in evangelical circles it is not infrequently the case that those who have given every evidence of conviction of sin and conversion, and who are regarded as shining examples of the faith, do at the same time altogether fail to give evidence of any real Christianizing of character. It is quite possible to be soundly converted according to all the accepted standards and yet to remain censorious, uncharitable, and mean to a degree that is quite incompatible with any really Christian interpretation of conduct.

From this Moody would have dissented. Any profession of religion which was not attended by fruits of the spirit was lacking, and the evidence of a sound conversion was not in ecstasies or outward expression of emotions but rather in the nature of the life of the individual.

On one occasion a former graduate of Mount Hermon who made a distinguished record at Princeton University and Seminary returned to Mount Hermon on a visit. He was invited to conduct the daily chapel and spoke on the atonement. The emphasis was all upon the justice of God demanding satisfaction in sacrifice, and omitted the love of God in His suffering for sinners. It was suggested that this was an inadequate view of God's redemptive work, but Moody's response revealed his own experience. "It's well to begin in a conservative way. As one grows older the tendency is ever to broaden one's views."

At one time his son, recently graduated from college, was disturbed in his views regarding the atonement. Henry Drummond with whom the son was visiting pointed out that the fact of the atonement, which was clearly taught by all the New Testament writers, was the essential thing and that no human theory was adequate. Later in conversation with his father the same view was emphasized though from a different angle. "In the atonement you never lose sight of the fact of the oneness of the Father and the suffering Christ. The mystery of the atonement is the mystery of the Trinity. You cannot understand the sacrifice of Christ and its relation to God until you can understand the Trinity itself."

Moody believed in future punishment but it is notable how his conception contrasted with the preaching of Jonathan Edwards. Take as illustration the following extract from the latter's sermon "Sinners in the Hands of an Angry God," which reflects the belief of early Puritan theology:

> The God that holds you over the pit of Hell, much in the same way as one holds a spider, or some loathesome insect, over the fire, abhors you, and is dreadfully provoked; His wrath toward you burns like fire; He looks upon you as worthy of nothing else but to be cast into fire; He is of purer eyes than to bear to have you in His sight; you are ten thousand times more abominable in His eyes than the most hateful venomous serpent is in ours. . . .
>
> When the great and angry God hath risen up and executed His awful vengeance on the poor sinner, and the wretch is actually suffering the infinite weight and power of His indignation, then will God call upon the whole universe to behold the awful majesty and mighty power that is to be seen in it. . . . "And the people shall be as the burnings of lime; as thorns cut up shall they be burned in the fire."

But Moody's view is thus expressed: "God will not punish us. We shall punish ourselves. When we come before God He will turn us over to ourselves. 'Go and read the book of your memory,' He will say."

Reporting an address in Edinburgh a friend records:

> Speaking of the probability that we forget none of the events of our lives, and that this is, perhaps,

to be a means of punishment in a future state, he pictured an unrepentant sinner awakening in the other world, and his misdeeds coming back upon him. "Tramp! tramp! tramp! tramp!" he said suiting the action to the word. "Do you think that Judas, after nearly 1900 years, has forgotten that he betrayed his Saviour for thirty pieces of silver? Do you think that Cain, after 5000 years, had forgotten the pleading look of his brother Abel when he slew him?" he continued.

Dr. R. W. Dale spoke freely of his recollections of the missions conducted by Moody in Birmingham in both 1875 and 1882. "I have always felt," he said, "that Moody was the only man that I knew that had a right to talk about Hell, and that because he always did it with tears in his voice."

If Moody ever had doubts he never spoke of them. His whole duty as he saw it was to make known the power of God to save men's lives here and hereafter.

In later years he seldom referred to future punishment. When a noted infidel lecturer died, the secular press sought a statement from Moody as to the probable condition of such an one in the great beyond. All he could be induced to say was kindly references to his home life and

> how dark must be the life of a man for whom, by his own confession, it was like "a narrow vale between the peaks of two eternities; we cry aloud, and the only answer is the echo of our calling"; and for whom death seemed like "a leap into the dark"! How different from that of a believer in Christ! For him not only is the present life filled with the peace of God, but the future is bright with hope. He knows that for him death is only the exchanging of a shifting tent for an enduring mansion.

Dr. Charles F. Goss in speaking of his message and the nature of its preparation says:

> His mind had never been trained to logical reasoning nor scholarly methods, and, in fact, was perhaps incapable of proceeding in that manner to the discovery of truth. It was so constituted that it gathered its conclusions from multiplied impressions of many sorts, as a bee gathers the sweets of flowers and turns them into honey. And so where other and eccentric minds used this method to find quotations which substantiated their vagaries, he used it to discover those which supported the few great central conceptions which were the entire stock with which he did his great business. The result, therefore, of his patient, ceaseless, heroic struggles to master the sacred Scriptures was that he accumulated a vast fund of texts and stories to illustrate the truths which he wished to hammer into the minds of men. His Bible got to be at last (that portion of it which he needed) at his very finger tips. He never fell down on his method. He gave it finally an enormous vogue, and while the crowds of his servile imitators made themselves and the Book ridiculous, he used it to delight and instruct millions. In addition to the newness of the method was the marvelous freshness which his own simple and childlike apprehension gave it. Owing to the natural constitution of his mind, the works of the Scriptures took possession of his faculties in the same vivid way that they do those of a child. No one familiar with his utterances can doubt that he had an imagination of a very high order. Had it been trained to poetical expression it could have produced forms of great literary beauty. Before this powerful faculty the heroes of Scripture really lived and its

truths absolutely glowed. Faith is only a spiritualized imagination, and his imagination was spiritualized as truly as that of a great inventor is materialized. Most ministers and students of the Bible confess that it requires their strongest efforts to give reality and vitality to the facts recounted in the sacred oracles. Their minds have become suspicious by investigating all the evidences for and against the supernatural elements of the Bible. Their hold upon them is the result of effort. With Mr. Moody it was different. No question of their reality ever for a moment troubled him. They were as real as if he had seen them with his own eyes. Everyone who heard him speak felt this, although perhaps they were not always conscious of it, and this vivid apprehension of the facts of Scripture was the greatest source of his pulpit power. . . .

I heard him preach his sermon on "Elijah," in the city of Detroit, when it appeared to me that supernatural things were actually occurring in the room. The line of demarcation between the real and the imaginary seemed broken down. That solemn hush had fallen upon the audience which rests upon the world before a thunder storm. You would have thought that every listener had been nailed to his seat. In the final outburst we actually beheld the chariot swoop down from heaven, the old man ascend, the blazing car borne through the still air; and when the impassioned orator uttered that piercing cry, "My father, my father, the chariot of Israel and the horsemen thereof!" the excitement was almost unendurable.

I also heard him preach his sermon on "Whatsoever a man soweth, that shall he also reap" to 2500 men one night in the Chicago Avenue Church, when I am sure that an actual doom could not have made all the dreadful phenomena of evil seem more real. That was the sublimest exhibition of the power of one life over many that has ever been granted to me.

No one who has not heard him can ever imagine what this power was. No quotation can give any impression of the effects produced; but here is a random specimen:

I can imagine when Christ said to the little band around Him, "Go ye into all the world and preach the Gospel," Peter said, "Lord, do you really mean that we are to go back to Jerusalem and preach the Gospel to those men that murdered you?" "Yes," said Christ. "Go hunt up that man that spat in my face; tell him he may have a seat in My Kingdom yet. Yes, Peter, go find that man that made that cruel crown of thorns and placed it on My brow, and tell him I will have a crown ready for him when he comes into My kingdom, and there will be no thorns in it. Hunt up that man that took a reed and brought it down over the cruel thorns, driving them into my brow, and tell him I will put a scepter in his hand, and he shall rule over the nations of the earth if he will accept salvation. Search for the man that drove the spear into my side, and tell him there is a nearer way to My heart than that. Tell him I forgive him freely, and that he can be saved if he will accept salvation as a gift."

The most wonderful thing about this preaching was that the people never seemed to tire of it. Through all those wonderful years from 1871 to 1899 the crowds that thronged about him were as great as ever, surging around the doors and cramming the hall almost as soon as the doors were open, and all this time he was preaching the same old sermons! Some of them had been delivered seventy-five or one hundred times, and he finally ceased to care whether he had spoken them in the first place or not, for the people liked them the second time as well as the first, and the fifth as well as the second. If this is not a prodigy, what is? Let those who are disposed to take this man lightly remember that they can move across the continent and no one observes their progress or cares a farthing what they have to say; but whether it was in Chicago or London, San Francisco or Paris, Mexico or Alexandria, Cairo or Jerusalem, thousands upon thousands pursued him, until a careful statistician has concluded that he addressed in all more than twenty million human beings! For myself I must regard it as I do any great natural phenomenon. He was an elemental force in human society. And he did not lose this power even to the last. The meetings which he held in Kansas City, where his public life closed, were in some respects the most enthusiastic in his whole career, and his last sermon was delivered to fifteen thousand people!

Moody believed in the second coming of Christ. In early years it occupied a prominent place in the themes of his Bible readings. Among the earliest recollections of his children were Moody's visits to Round Top; he loved the panorama unfolding distant scenes up the Connecticut Valley, into the remote hills of Vermont and New Hampshire. Here he would love to talk about the personal return of his Master and once he exclaimed, "I would like to be here when the Lord comes." The outdoor meetings held at twilight during the summer months added many sacred associations to the spot in later years.

It would be wrong to infer that the broadening influences of life tended to a so-called liberal theology. Moody remained essentially conservative through life.

His breadth was rather tolerance toward other interpretations of truth.

During the last year of his life he entertained Sir George Adam Smith, the distinguished scholar and higher critic. Strong opposition had been made to his coming to Northfield to speak at the College Students' Conference, but, convinced of Smith's evangelical position, Moody paid no heed to it. At the close of an evening meeting he invited the most outspoken opponent to come to the house for a late supper. After supper the other members of the family retired leaving a small group of men. Moody sat at the head of the table, Sir George on one side of him and the invited guest on the other, the only others present being Dr. S. Parkes Cadman, Moody's son-in-law and eldest son. Moody began the conversation by turning to Sir George Adam Smith and in a kindly but very outspoken way deplored the effect of higher criticism in undermining the faith of the people in the authority of Scripture. To this Sir George emphatically dissented. "Should you return to Scotland to-day, Mr. Moody," he said, "you would find no more loyal supporters than the men who have gone out from our seminaries. The authorship of books of the Bible does not invalidate their message. Higher criticism may teach that traditional views of dates and authors demand revision but does not effect the content of the Scripture."

Thereupon the other guest asked if he believed certain passages were Messianic or not. The Scotch scholar averred his belief that they were not primarily so intended. This elicited the ungracious response that having studied higher criticism many years before when little more than a youth, he had come to the conclusion that there was nothing in it, and had abandoned further study for want of confidence in its conclusions. To this rejoinder Sir George made no reply. Moody added that times demanded the united efforts of all evangelical forces and that he deplored the spirit of antagonism, and the group broke up. As the door closed upon the belligerent guest Moody exclaimed to his son that the critic had hardly shown an irenical spirit, and then added, "Awful! awful! They (of whom Sir George was representative) often put us (conservatives) to shame by their more Christian attitude." It was said with an inexpressible note of sadness.

In epigram Moody excelled. Some one writes of his public addresses during the Brooklyn meetings of 1875:

> He has in perfection that faculty of epigrammatic statement which one often finds among the farmers and laboring people of New England, and this has sometimes the effect of humor. Thus preaching at the Rink from the text, "Where the treasure is, there the heart will be also," he remarked, "If you find a man's household goods on a freight train, you may be pretty sure to find him on the next passenger train." On another occasion he told of a woman who came to him saying that she had sought Christ without avail. "I told her there must be some mistake about this, because an anxious sinner and an anxious Savior could not need three years to find each other." Speaking of persons who were ambitious to make themselves prominent he remarked: "It does not say, 'make your light shine,' but 'let your light shine.' You can't make a light shine. If it is really a light it will shine in spite of you—only don't hide it under a bushel. Let it shine. Confess Christ everywhere." "Satan got his match when he came across John Bunyan," Moody said another time. "He thought he had done a shrewd thing when he got the poor tinker stuck into Bedford jail, but that was one of his blunders. It was there that Bunyan wrote 'Pilgrim's Progress,' and

no doubt he was more thankful for the imprisonment than for anything else in his life."

This use of epigram characterized Moody's sermons and impressed his hearers everywhere. One who knew him thus records some which appealed to him:

> I like the gospel because it has been for me the very best news I have ever heard. It has taken out of my path four of the bitterest enemies I ever had.
>
> It has taken away the fear of death. The Conqueror bursts the bands of death and shouts: "Because I live ye shall live also."
>
> It has taken away the burden of sin. It tells me: "As far as the East is from the West so far has he removed our transgressions from us."
>
> It takes away the fear of judgment. Christ declares: "He that believeth on Him that sent me is passed from death unto life."
>
> It takes away bondage to sin and gives me the spirit of liberty. Do I speak to a man who is a slave to strong drink? Christ can give you strength to hurl the cup from you and make you a sober man, a loving husband, a kind father.
>
> It is a free gospel. This good news I am bid to proclaim to every creature.

In preaching on the prodigal son Moody's analysis was most interesting. He said:

> The best men are in the habit of striking a balance sheet. Now let us see what this man's are. On the debit side he lost his money. On the credit side what has he got? An uneasy conscience and the knowledge that he had made a fool of himself.
>
> There is one thing he never lost, and that is his father's love. All through the years the father loved him through his wanderings and ill-doings. To

everyone here, God is waiting to embrace you, to show you his love, and to take you home again if you will go. Each morning he takes down the parchment and reads out of the psalms of David. His servants are gathered in. He prays for them and for his elder son, and then adds, "Oh, God, bless my wandering boy to-night."

Ask the elder son about the prodigal and he will tell you he is good for nothing. Ask the father about him and he will tell you he is a noble boy led away by bad companions, but he would add, "I am praying every day that he may come home again."

At an after-meeting, one who listened to Moody's words made the following notes:

> After we had all gathered he gave a few very touching remarks as he has often before on the words "receive," "believe," "trust," "take." It was so simple that a child could understand it; one would think no one could escape; so tender, that every heart must be touched; so appealing that one would think no one could refuse to take the water of life freely; to trust so loving a Saviour and not be afraid; to believe God; to receive his loving Saviour. . . ."

The same friend records extracts from meetings. Moody said:

> It will be found that more has been done by people of one talent than by those who have many. If each one with one talent would wake up to realize his responsibility, what a mighty work would be done—to wake up and say "Here am I, use me to do the work Thou hast for me to do." If you couldn't lead someone into the Kingdom after trying hard, there must be something wrong with you; you must be out of communion with God. . . .

Ex. xxv. 1, 2, etc., "Willingly." Goats' hair—the least valuable yet if brought willingly, as acceptable and as useful as the fine linen, the purple and the scarlet. Bring everything—your weakness, and ask Him to use it for His service. Moses' weakness—he couldn't speak, he said, God told him to take a rod—a wand—and go with that to Pharaoh. God made it the means of opening the Red Sea and bringing water out of flinty rock. . . .

If we take what we have got, God will use it. Let us work from Love. Look at the widow's two mites—her all; look at Mary's precious box of ointment. Empires have come and gone since then and are no more heard of, but her name has come through the ages with the sweet savour of her loving service. . . .

Some good words on faith: "Courage follows faith, always follows faith." "God uses men of courage, but there must be love. Show the love. There is no use working without love. A doctor, a lawyer, may do good work without love, but God's work cannot be done without love. . . ."

Trust. First what we should not trust—not in ourselves. I Cor. i. Then whom should we trust? God.

Ps. cxxv. 1; xxviii. 1; lvi; cv; Is. xii. 1, 2.

How to trust—Prov. iii., v. With all our hearts. When to trust, at all times. Ps. ix, x.

Who will trust? They that know thy name. I used to think I should close my Bible and pray for faith; but I came to see that it was in studying the Word that I was to get faith. Faith cometh by hearing. and hearing by the Word of God. . . .

If you want rest and peace, just take God at His word. There is not a greater honor you can give Christ than just to trust Him. . . .

> How bold and fearless he is. It braves one to hear such plain speaking. Sin is going to bring me to judgment, or I am going to bring it. If we do not judge ourselves and confess our sins, God will judge and condemn us. It must be pardon or punishment —which will I take? In the book of Revelation we find that we are, great and small, to be judged out of a book; God is keeping a record. I was myself near drowning; had been down twice, and was sinking the third time; in what must have been some seconds only my whole life passed in array before me; everything I had said and everything I had done. I do not know how that could be, but I know that it was so. Have this matter of sin settled at once; God is waiting to forgive. I pray God that everyone within the sound of my voice to-night will confess his sins, and God will forgive him for Christ's sake.

Again and again Moody's emphasis was upon the comprehensive nature of religion. Dealing not with peripheral religious ideas, but with a central dynamic controlling the life and impelling the motives. His experience with children in early life had been invaluable; as he himself testified, "One who can interest children can always interest adults." And it was doubtless the influence of these early years that emphasized to Moody the importance of use of illustration and striking apothegm.

The following are extracts from his sermons or outlines of his Bible readings:

> God's love is shown towards us in the way He dealt with our sins. Our love is very, very faint, these minds of ours can't grasp much. God's love is great, it is unchangeable, and unfailing. . . .
> There are four expressions to show how God deals with our sins—Sin blotted out as a cloud; sin cast

into the sea; sin removed from us as far as east is from the west; sin put behind God's back. That's a safe place to have our sins. . . .

Talk about zeal and excitement, there is more excitement in a saloon right here in New York than there is in all the churches in the city in twelve years. They get so excited that they shoot each other.

A man lay sick with the palsy and four determined men, who couldn't get him in by the door, made a hole in the roof and got him to the feet of the Savior. It was very irregular but the man's sins were forgiven and his palsy healed. Things have got to be done irregularly in this world. I tell you there will be lots of disorder in your well-kept graveyards on the resurrection morn. I don't know of anything better to wake a man up than these four determined men who carried in the palsied man. . . .

A good many preachers say I am lowering the pulpit. I am glad I am. I am trying to get it down to the level of men's hearts. If I want to hit Chicago, I would not put the cannon on top of this building and fire into the air. . . .

There are too many religious meetings which are sadder than a funeral. They are a hindrance to the cause. They give people an impression as chilling as an east wind in Boston in March. . . .

John the Baptist was the greatest preacher the world has ever seen and yet we do not see that he was called the Reverend John, or Dr. John, or John, D.D., or LL.D. Thoughtless wives have sent many a husband to the groggery for the solace he does not get at home. A man who embalms his troubles and lugs them around for his friends to see, as he might carry a mummy, is not a witness for Christ. The world is desperate because it has not found the true way to rest. God never made a promise that was too good to be true to the last. There would be a grand rush for Heaven if there was a back door and a way to get there without public confession. It is a good time to work with prodigals when they get in jail. They have plenty of time then to think. Ministers will not fill their churches until they get back to preaching all the Bible. The Bible and music have moved the world more than any other two agencies. It is worth living a life to help one man to his feet.

Moody's influence was extended to foreign centers far beyond his own land through the nationals of European countries. The Rev. Frederick E. Pamp in an address in 1927 recounted how the influence of Moody's sermons and Sankey's songs, translated into Swedish, was felt not only among the Swedes in America, but through them found their way to Sweden and greatly stimulated a revival movement which was then under way in the decade between the years of 1865 and 1875. "Many little communities," according to Mr. Pamp, "were without a preacher and people would gather in homes while someone read the sermons and sang the gospel songs in Swedish. Moody's English, which was largely of plain Anglo-Saxon words easily interpreted to Swedish immigrants, more readily brought him into touch with Scandinavia."

In an appreciation of Moody at the time of his going Dr. Goss thus sums up his estimate of the one whom he had closely and admiringly observed for many years.

> It always seemed to me to be one of the most remarkable things about him that he could never be induced to turn aside from the regular institutions of the Christian church, into any side issue or narrow sect. Two influences would naturally impel him to do so. In the first place, his clear conceptions of the lack of fervor and consecration to be found in

the ordinary denominations; and, in the second place, a natural capacity for organization and opportunity to identify his name with a great and new movement. . . .

With such self-knowledge as he possessed he must have clearly seen that if he had struck out, like Wesley or Booth, to form a new society he could have given it colossal proportions and have secured for himself an undying fame through the society which should subsist to perpetuate his memory and his ideals. But he deliberately turned away from this great temptation. He scorned to further divide the already sundered body of the Christian church. He decided that instead of communicating the mighty impulses of his life to a separate organization he would instill them as best he could into the church universal and be forgotten if need be. This we regard as the very noblest decision of his mind and the noblest impulse of his heart.

BOOK VIII

CHAPTER LXIII

WHAT was Moody like? Biographers and those who have sought to analyze him have failed to portray him as a living personality. There was much that seems paradoxical in their delineations, often for the simple reason that they have sought to account for him in terms of natural genius *only*. If asked to what he owed his success, Moody himself would have declined in genuine humility to make reply, unless to deny that any success was to be attributed to himself at all. The message he had to deliver was the only secret, if secret there was.

"Every man has his own gifts. Some start things; others can organize and carry them on. My gift is to get things in motion." This is Moody's own estimate of himself.

To many men such success as Moody achieved would have contributed to an unbearable conceit and been disastrous to character. But in Moody's case he had rather been humbled by what he had done. Praise and flattery never touched him. The press acknowledged his genius, tact, generalship and command of terse Anglo-Saxon; they were conscious of power which they attributed to native genius and extraordinary knowledge of human nature. To deny that he possessed these gifts to a remarkable degree would be contrary to the truth; but though he could not be utterly blind to the fact of their possession, he never gave evidence of such consciousness.

The success of all these missions Moody attributed to

"power from on High." He believed that, though without education or training, God had chosen him "that no flesh should glory." Others possessed rich gifts qualifying them, in his opinion, for greater service, but in his complete abandonment to the will of God it had pleased Him to effect a work which was not of man. In subsequent years he said this time and again.

"I never understand why people come to hear me as they do," he once said in conversation with a member of his family. "There are men who are more gifted and have eloquence which I have not. But God has given me the ear of the public and I am bound to use this to His glory."

At another time, when urging upon one of America's most gifted and brilliant preachers the work of evangelism, Moody sought to persuade him to preach for results. "That is for you, Mr. Moody," was the reply. "I could never do it. You can, for you have the ear of the public." "In the Temple worship there were silver trumpets," Moody responded. "You have that, and I only have a ram's horn. You can reach those who would not listen to me. In the meantime I will go on with my horn, but you use your silver trumpet."

A friend who closely observed his work writes:

> In private intercourse I have always found Mr. Moody as full of gentle courtesy toward others as he was of tender love for his Saviour. I never knew a man so free from selfishness or self-seeking as he. His friendship is as pure as a crystal, and his generous love flows out toward all whom he can serve or benefit. A nobler soul was never formed by grace and spiritual culture. His very presence as a guest is a blessing in any home.

It is not easy to describe his personal appearance; neither photographs nor paintings have caught the expression which so truly reflected the soul. A man of average height, he appeared shorter on account of his heavy build. He was approximately five feet ten inches in height. He weighed 270-280 pounds. He did not have the appearance of corpulence, for his flesh was hard. On his return from his first misison to Great Britain a reporter described him as having a black beard with thick luxuriant hair. Later years found the black beard turned gray and the luxuriant hair becoming perceptibly thin, but otherwise he remained in outward appearance much the same. He always wore a black or dark blue cutaway coat, a large old-fashioned black cravat that completely covered the shirt front; he wore no jewelry, even cuff buttons he dispensed with in later years. His whole attire was designed to be unobstrusive. He had a meticulous fastidiousness in the fit of his clothes, as he felt that this made his size less noticeable and he wanted nothing about himself to distract in any way the attention of his hearers.

One who had opportunities to observe Moody in his later years remarked his reticence about himself; efforts to induce him to recount what he had achieved were futile. He had a strong aversion to publicity. For years he would not have his photograph taken. It was not until he visited Paris in 1882 that he would yield to the importunities of his wife and children to be photographed and then only on the condition that the negatives be destroyed. When grandchildren came into the family circle sixteen years later he again submitted for their sakes. When a popular publication required his photograph to illustrate an article on the schools at Northfield it was with difficulty that the use of his picture could be obtained. His sensitive nature shrank from what others may accustom themselves to and his great objective was ever to submerge self and exalt his Master. Even in these little things this was evident.

People who knew Moody only as the public speaker little realized how keenly sensitive he was, not to personal slights which he did not cherish though he felt them, but to the sympathy and responsiveness of an audience. He wanted the attention of all his hearers; careless inattention seemed to be a challenge to him to exert every effort. On one occasion he was disturbed by a boy who was turning the leaves of the hymn book and apparently reading all the verses. "I told one story after another to capture his attention," Moody said in relating the incident, "but still he kept turning leaf after leaf. I tried not to see him, but I couldn't keep my eyes from him. I thought 'Will he never stop!' At last I could stand it no longer, so I told a story of a boy 'about the age of this boy reading the hymn book.' The book slammed together and from that time his eyes were riveted on me."

That which doubtless first impressed a stranger was Moody's nimbleness and energy. His physical reserves seemed illimitable. After his New York mission in the Hippodrome with its great taxation, he joined his family in Augusta, Georgia, for a brief respite from his work. His conception of rest may be inferred from a letter written by Mrs. Moody to Mrs. MacKinnon in Scotland:

> My husband came direct from New York here after ten weeks of meetings in that busy city. He looks none the worse for his hard work and felt quite ready for one meeting a day while he was resting(?) in this town. I thought the heat here would be more than he could bear, *with the work*, after New York's cool climate, but I think it would be too much rest and would really tire him to have no meetings.
>
> Yesterday, Sunday, he preached five times! but seems quite fresh this morning.

An incident which occurred during meetings which he was holding in Dublin in the autumn of 1892 illustrated the readiness with which he could relax under unusual circumstances. With Moody was a group of friends and associates. They had the use of a small sitting room on the second floor, insuring a certain degree of privacy. Moody was speaking three times a day, and after he had returned to the hotel at the close of an afternoon service and was chatting with a few friends, a visitor was announced. Moody turned to one of the group and asked him to see what the visitor wanted. In a few minutes, to the surprise of everybody, the stranger was ushered into the sitting room. He began his interview by explaining that he wished to see Moody on an important matter. Thereupon he launched forth on some question regarding baptism, giving clear evidence that, if not mentally unbalanced, he was at least one of those men who can only see one small aspect of a truth and ever wish to hold forth at great length upon their peculiar views.

Moody pointed out that he was in Dublin at the invitation of all the evangelical bodies and it would be very unbecoming for him to seek to introduce an issue which was bound to bring about dissent. But no explanation was sufficient, and Moody realized that he had a crank to deal with. He explained that after preaching to a large audience he sometimes felt the need of rest and he was sure his guest would not mind if he reclined on the couch. To this suggestion the visitor gladly assented, probably assuming that with Moody flat on his back, he would be at a disadvantage and could not run away. Sending his son, who was acting as his secretary at the time, for a pillow, Moody lay on the couch and, closing his eyes, assumed the attitude of a meek and receptive listener, but in less than half a minute, his deep breathing revealed that he was beyond consciousness.

The crank took in the situation and paused, which

awoke Moody for he looked up inquiringly and said, "Well!" Again the visitor launched forth and this time there was a distinct snore. Somewhat crestfallen, the caller rose and expressed regret that Moody was so tired; and the man who was uninclined to take a hint or listen to reason was at last overcome by Moody's ability to sleep.

Moody used to relate with genuine appreciation one incident which fully accorded with his own views. At the invitation of a group of ministers, he addressed their weekly meeting. While speaking he noticed in the audience Sam Jones, a Southern evangelist who combined picturesque piquancy with a generous heart and an unusual fund of sound common sense. Curtailing his own address, Moody called upon Jones to speak. In the course of the Southerner's remarks, with his inimitable drawl and with a kindly smile which took all the sting from his homely advice, he said, "We preachers are fishermen. Now some of you have been fishing in the same hole for years and caught nothing. Do you know what I'd do in such a fix? I'd change my hole or I'd change my bait."

Having expended every effort to the achievement of his task Moody always left the issue with God. In other words he lived his life free from worry.

Moody's mind was agile. Often it seemed as if he had a certain intuition that led to decisions that others would arrive at after laborious reasoning. But rather he had the faculty of having formulated certain principles based upon analogous experiences and on these principles he acted quickly.

On one occasion an invitation was received to visit a certain city while he was in Scotland. In order to know exactly what expenses would be involved in a mission the committee insisted that he should state his terms. Drummond, who was with Moody at the time, answered in his behalf explaining that there were no financial prearrangements; whatever the committee deemed wise would be perfectly acceptable to Moody. The committee was importunate and said the invitation was dependent on knowing what was involved. Tossing the letter across the table at which Drummond was seated Moody said, "Tell them I won't come." The tact of his friend later induced Moody to reconsider his decision when the committee, through the assiduous efforts of Drummond, was made to realize the futility of endeavoring to induce Moody to deviate from his rule.

Arbitrary! Well, perhaps. When Moody was convinced that he was right he was immovable. The lessons which he had learned in the school of experience were not forgotten. To argue, to explain, to debate, and to wrangle only wasted time and energy better expended in the work itself. He recognized that this laid him open to misinterpretation, which he greatly regretted. However, there were circumstances in which he would be as docile as a child. This was when he was unfamiliar with conditions and willingly placed himself in the hands of those with whom they were familiar. At other times he was adamant and would not willingly sacrifice the good of the work to gratify the whims or fancies of others. Since there was a limit to a man's strength and time they would be expended better in achieving the one great purpose of his life rather than in futile debates and inexpedient methods.

Although never active in politics he was none the less deeply interested in current events and followed the careers of the leaders of national life not only in America but also in Great Britain. During his last illness the Boer War was at its height. One day he appeared to be sleeping when, suddenly, he startled his son who was with him, by saying, "Do you know what I would do if I was old Krüger? I would write to Queen Victoria and say I was an old man who must soon appear before God. I would not want to appear before Him with the consciousness of greater bloodshed and I would ask her to state her own terms of peace." It was stated that possibly favorable terms would not be granted. "Yes, they would," was his reply. "After the fight the Boers have made England, they would have to grant favorable terms. The best sentiment in Great Britain and the world would demand it. Such an attitude would appeal to everyone and the old man would win."

Naturally such a temperament as Moody's implied a hasty temper, but early in life he had learned that one who was to master others must first master himself. If on rare occasions he was apt to speak hastily he was prompt to acknowledge the fault and make ample apologies. A friend who was present at a Bible conference relates incidents illustrating this characteristic of Moody:

> We were perhaps a hundred men, seated on the clean straw under the tent at noon, on Round Top. Mr. Moody was leading the conversation hour. He sat sturdily against the tent-pole. Out came the plump question:
> "Brethren, how many of you have so grown in grace that you can bear to have your faults told?"
> Many hands went up. Quick as a flash, but not sharply or insultingly, Moody turned to a young Episcopal minister in front of him and said:
> "Brother, you have spoken thirteen times in three days here, and perhaps shut out twelve other good men from speaking."
> It was true. The young man had been presuming and officious. Mr. Moody fitted him fairly. He had held up his hand as one willing to be chided for fault, but he could not bear it. He owned no fault or sorrow, but stoutly defended himself—or tried to

—only making his case really the worse. Then a real old Yankee vinegar-face on the outer rim of the circle turned loose and sharply berated Moody for his bluntness. The good man blushed, but listened until the abuse was over; then, suggestively covering his face, he spoke through his fingers:

"Brethren, I admit all the fault my friend charges on me; but, brethren, *I did not hold up my hand!*" . . .

At one of these meetings for Christian workers Mr. Moody presented a very high ideal for the ministry, and spoke severely of those who had failed in their sacred calling. His words were very pointed, and a young theologue who was present winced, and spoke out ingenuously:

"Mr. Moody, I don't see any such ministers as you describe." It was a frank and outspoken remonstrance, but not rude. Quick as a flash came the retort:

"You are a young man yet; you will see many of them. Tarry in Jericho until your beard be grown."

The reply was unjust and it hurt, yet there was too much life in the meeting for stopping. It went on with a clear sense that the evangelist had dropped a little from his standard of loving courtesy to his guests. He could have ignored it; the tide of his eloquence was full. Yet the most eloquent was to come. In my heart has ever since been written a memory which brings moisture into my eyes yet, and ranks itself unquestionably as the greatest thing I ever saw Moody do.

"Friends," he said, "I answered my dear young friend over there very foolishly as I began this meeting. I ask God to forgive me, and I ask the forgiveness of my brother." And straightway he walked over to him and took him by the hand. That meeting need no after-meeting. It was dramatically and spiritually made perfect. The man of iron will proved that he had mastered the hardest words of all earth's languages, "I am sorry."

Ever considerate of others he was always rigid with himself. This implied frugality in his manner of life. He who might have had every luxury refused to expend upon himself what many younger men in the employ of business houses would have felt to be perfectly warrantable. On several occasions in later life when a local committee had provided for his entertainment at a hotel on what he felt to be a lavish scale, he insisted on less pretentious rooms. And frequently he refused to accept the honorarium proffered as being excessive, and insisted on returning a part to be given to some local charity. He laid up nothing for himself; on his death it was found that he left an estate of five hundred dollars in the form of a mortgage to cover a loan he had made to a neighbor although the mortgage had been made out without Moody's knowledge. He made a modest provision for his wife which was in her name. This included the home. Beyond that, Moody owned nothing. He did not even have a bank account; Mrs. Moody took sole care of the finances.

It has been intimated that Moody could not be unconscious of his own powers and that his humility must, of necessity, have been assumed. "The greatest egotisms of the world have loved to put others forward with the subtle sense underneath that the putter-forward could do the work and do it better, if he would, or at any rate that he was the master of his substitute," says a writer in referring to Moody's habit of using other men. Those who knew Moody and his genuine humility will challenge this construction upon his character. Such a spirit would have revealed itself in the generation in which he was before the public. No one who witnessed his appreciation of the achievements of others would entertain any such misgivings.

When Moody was in Chicago laying plans for the Chicago Bible Institute two evangelists were in the city conducting meetings. Sensational reports of their methods were given prominence in the press and some of their remarks were, to say the least, uncouth. These were offensive to Moody's sense of good taste. At this time two friends called on him and asked his opinion of the movement. He replied in a critical way, basing his judgment upon the reported utterances. As the two left, one remarked to the other it was easy to account for the attitude of Moody who could not view the ascendancy of others to a place he had occupied himself. Ultimately this came to Moody. In later years some expressed surprise that he could work with these selfsame evangelists whose utterances so often violated every sense of propriety. He then related the incident referred to and said: "When I learned what was said of our interview I went to my room, fell on my knees and asked God if there was lurking in me, unbeknown to myself, a vestige of a spirit of jealousy He would forgive me and take it out root and branch. Then I sent to the evangelists to come to the Chicago Avenue Church and conduct meetings. Since then I have never allowed myself to say anything in criticism of other workers. I do not know if there was any such feelings. If there was I determined to deal with it then and there." Moody's humility was thorough.

His love for home made the long absences from loved ones ever a real sacrifice. And when he was in Northfield the days were made memorable with both work and play. Major Whittle relates an experience there:

Two weeks we passed in this beautiful mountain home of our brother. We met his widowed mother, his three brothers, his wife and children. We were made a part of the family, and taken over all the haunts of Moody's boyhood; up the mountain where he used to pasture the cows and pick berries and gather chestnuts, and where he passed the last Sunday alone with God before he sailed for England upon his last memorable visit.

We went with him to take dinner with his Uncle Cyrus, over the Connecticut River, and as we were crossing the beautiful stream, the valley sloping down on either side and the blue hills and mountains beyond, Bliss and Sankey sang together, "Only Waiting for the Boatman," and "There Is a Land of Pure Delight." Moody was helping the ferryman. We all thought the crossing very slow. After the third or fourth song Sankey looked around and discovered Moody holding on to the wire and pulling back while the ferryman pulled forward; his object being to get in a good many songs, not only for his own enjoyment, but for the good of the ferryman, a boyhood friend for whose conversion he was interested. Moody greatly enjoyed Sankey's discomfiture, and after a hearty laugh from us all, we joined in the song, "Pull for the Shore," and by keeping a watch on Moody, reached the shore as we closed.

It has been said that laziness and conceit were two characteristics with which Moody had little patience. On one occasion he had arranged with a distinguished English Bible teacher to give a course of lectures for a week at the Chicago Bible Institute. Writing to the one in charge at the Institute, during the summer, he explained that he would like to have the guest from abroad given the first hour in the morning and to have the one who at that time was conducting lectures, placed at another hour. On arriving in Chicago it was found that the arrangement had not met with favor on the part of the lecturer at the first hour, who said he would give way for nobody as he was given that hour in the first place and not even temporarily would he have the hour changed. Other arrangements had to be made but Moody was disgusted. He could not hide his sense of humiliation that an English visitor should receive such scant courtesy in an institution with which he was connected, or that anyone working for the Institute should have such a small spirit.

There was something about Moody of implied authority which impressed even strangers. During the last year of his life he happened to be in the Pennsylvania station in Jersey City on Labor Day. There was a great throng of holiday makers and the usual settees had been removed from the waiting room to give greater space for the crowds. A nursing baby was peevishly crying in its mother's arms. The plaintive note of the child exhausted the mother's patience and she slapped it repeatedly. Moody realized that if only the mother could be seated she could give attention to the child. Accosting her he said, "Do not strike that child again. Come with me." Somewhat taken back the mother meekly followed him and he led them to the gateman on the platform. Without making any requests, but speaking with authority, he ordered the gateman to lead the mother and child onto the platform where the worn-out woman could find a seat. For an instant the man hesitated, but glancing at Moody and his set face he was apparently impressed that this was somebody whose word he must follow. Therefore, he promptly obeyed.

In a mid-Western city Moody had to take the train for some western point. On arriving at the station he found that inadvertently he had left something at the hotel which he must have. The train was ready to start, and the hotel was several blocks away. He was advertised to preach the next day and must catch that train to make his appointment. Approaching the conductor he said, "Hold this train until I return. I shall only be a few minutes but on no account go without me." The conductor remonstrated that it was already time to leave, only to have Moody repeat what he had already said, leaving the conductor somewhat at a loss to know who this was who presumed to hold a continental express. On his return from the precipitate trip to the hotel Moody found the train still waiting for him.

Moody hated introductions. Anything laudatory of himself he abhorred. To avoid subjecting himself to an introduction he adopted almost any means. A friend relates how once he adroitly escaped a formal presentation. A union meeting had been arranged in a certain city with some difficulty, as a prominent, and somewhat pompous pastor was unwilling to join in the movement. Apparently pressure was exerted and later he joined his fellow ministers in inviting Moody to the city. When the program for the meetings was arranged this pastor expressed the wish that he be assigned the task of introducing the evangelist. All this was unknown to Moody. At the opening service Moody came onto the platform and immediately gave out a hymn and conducted the service without any introduction and thus avoided the prearranged presentation to which he had such an aversion.

Once a man, whose prayer had been interrupted because of its interminable length, remonstrated with Moody. The reply was characteristic. "You say I hurt your feelings. I am sorry for that. But you were hurting hundreds of people's feelings and I'd rather hurt one person's feelings that let anyone hurt so many."

In the Northfield conference, and in fact in any conference Moody led, he would sometimes do very unconventional things. On one occasion when Henry Drummond was speaking before a gathering of college students at Northfield, he especially inveighed against cant. Moody interrupted him. "Drummond, what do you mean by cant?" The prompt reply was, "A young man with the religion of his grandmother." The text and the sermon probably were not remembered by many, but that concise definition remained. In the epigram was comprised all that might be said, that was essential, in regard to the evil of assuming the experience and phraseology of others to express that which should be original.

Dr. Lyman Abbott relates the tactful handling of a difficult situation which he witnessed:

> Mr. Moody was holding, with the coöperation of the churches, a series of meetings in Brooklyn. One day had been set apart to be observed as a day of fasting and prayer. Henry Ward Beecher spoke in a quiet conversational tone and followed his address with a prayer in the tenderest and most spiritual mood. It recalled Christ's prayer at the Last Supper. Then there arose just behind me a shouting revivalist. He was oratorical, waxed louder and louder, grasped the back of the pew in which I was sitting and shook it in the vehemence of his real or artificial emotion. It recalled to me Elijah's scornful address to the priests of Baal: "Cry aloud, for he is a god; either he is musing, or he is gone aside, or he is on a journey, or peradventure he sleepeth; and must be awakened." When at length the orator stopped, out of breath with his vociferous devotion, I thought the meeting was destroyed; that nothing could bring it back to its devotional atmosphere. Mr. Moody rose and said, with that strangely quiet and penetrating voice of his: "Now let us have three

minutes of silent prayer." And the silence which he summoned erased the disturbing oration and restored the spirit of devotion.

When at Northfield Moody no longer wore the conventional dark clothes to which he was accustomed in public work. He would be seen driving around the village or on the school grounds with a dark velveteen coat and waistcoat and trousers of tweed of a yellowish tint. His family would joke with him by saying that at a distance he resembled a large bumblebee. His straw hat was soon out of shape, the front brought down to shade his face, and often in rainy weather he would wear rubber boots slit at the top as he could not find a size large enough for his calf.

In the beginning of the autumn term of school he would not infrequently drive to the railway station to meet trains and bring some of the teachers to their dormitories. On one such occasion he drove a covered three-seated democrat. It happened to be a rainy day and a great number of vehicles were there to meet the returning students. When the train drew in a gentleman accompanied by two ladies came up and told him to drive them to the hotel. Moody started to explain that he was there to meet somebody but the gentleman was peremptory. "These girls are not the only people to be served. Now you just take us right up to the hotel." Moody meekly acquiesced, appreciating the joke upon himself in being taken for a hack driver. As they left the station the ladies inquired the meaning of the crowd, and the gentleman explained that it was this school Moody had started for poor girls which was drawing students from all parts. Turning to Moody he asked what hotel he would recommend. Moody replied that the hotel connected with the schools would probably afford the best accommodation and he was ordered to drive there.

When the occupants descended from the vehicle Moody drove off. The gentleman hailed him saying that he had not received his fare. But Moody paid no attention. Turning to the bellboy the gentleman inquired who the driver was. The reply was "Mr. D. L." "D. L. who?" asked the stranger. "D. L. Moody."

At once the gentleman was greatly perturbed, explaining that he had come expressly to have some girl in whom he was interested accepted as a student. The next day he was profuse in his apologies, only to be assured in the most good-natured way by Moody, who appreciated the joke on himself.

He was always an early riser. During the conferences at Northfield it not infrequently happened that he was importuned to speak. This always embarrassed Moody. Many will recall his way of surmounting the difficulty by appointing a meeting, sometimes on the mountain side or on Round Top at six o'clock in the morning, an hour he could not assign to any invited guest, and one at which he would be assured that only those who were earnestly desirous of hearing him would attend. It could be said of him, as of George Whitefield, that some of these early morning services were among the most memorable in the lives of the audiences that he addressed.

It was not for youth in the aggregate that Moody was interested solely. He was intensely interested in individual students. Hundreds cherish memories of his deep personal interest. At times it was pecuniary help afforded in a tight place—provided he was convinced the student had put forth every effort to meet his or her needs. Unbelief was the sin against which he might preach but his family entertained a secret suspicion that in his innermost soul he abhorred laziness even more. "If a man's lazy, what can you do for him?" he would exclaim. "Other faults a man may overcome but I almost despair if a man is lazy." But in behalf of one who was persevering, industrious and ambitious what efforts would he not make?

It was remarkable how one who had been endowed with robust health and experienced no serious or protracted illness should have had so great sympathy with suffering. Any case of illness at once aroused his anxiety whether among distant friends, neighbors, or his "boys and girls."

Just at the beginning of a mission in Baltimore in 1893 he heard that his aged mother was ill and threatened with pneumonia. Moody was perplexed as to his duty, to fulfill his engagement which had already involved the committee in expense or to hasten to his mother. He wrote his mother:

> I am wondering if you have got up yet. I do hope you do not suffer. It would look strange to see you on the bed. Only think, my memory goes back for fifty years and I cannot remember your being laid aside. The Lord has been good to you to give you eighty-eight years of good health. How many have come and gone in your day. Napoleon the 1st was living when you were at school on the other side of the river. Nearly all that bore the name have gone and you still live. It will be fifty-two years in May since father died, a good long journey you have had alone, or without a husband, but I am thankful you have had children to keep you company, and we will all miss you much if you should be taken from us. If you think there is danger, you must let my wife know it and I will come to you at once. I would go now but the committee have put up or fitted up a large hall at great expense, and they can only keep it for two weeks. I do not know of anyone I can get to take my place but I will come to you anyway if you say so, and

if you think the Master is going to call you to Himself you must let me know for I want to have your blessing. You have been a good mother to us all and I do not know what would have become of us fifty years ago if God had not given you strength and courage to have kept us all together, and you will find a rich reward waiting for you when you get home.

If a case of bereavement came to his knowledge he sought with real solicitude to minister comfort to the sorrowing.

> Once I accompanied Mr. Moody on an errand of consolation to Mount Hermon [recalls one who was in the home at the time]. A telegram had come that the mother of one of his "boys" had died after a long illness, in a far distant state. It seemed unreasonable that Moody should feel that he must personally see the boy and assume the difficult task of this sad duty. And anyway he was only one of many boys. If it was necessary why not wait till the morrow for it was then late in the evening and a ten mile drive on country roads to Mount Hermon and return would occupy the evening. Perhaps I gave some intimation of my thoughts for Mr. Moody said very simply, "Poor motherless boy! Just put yourself in his place." This was warrant for any effort on his part, and at once effectually silenced my complaining spirit. Like his Master he loved greatly.

His interest in his "boys and girls" did not cease with their life in the schools. He followed their careers with the same concern. He wrote from Princeton University to his son, "McGaffin and Tildsley stand at the head of their class. McGaffin number one and Tildsley number two. How is that for Mount Hermon?"

For his contemporaries he is equally solicitous. Two neighbors who were boyhood acquaintances were engaged in litigation which aroused much rancor. The quarrel was no concern of Moody's, yet he put forth every effort to effect an adjustment and bring about a reconciliation, though it brought some expense to himself.

After one of the dormitories at Mount Hermon had been completed a hodcarrier wished to obtain permanent employment there. He turned to Moody explaining that drink was his besetting weakness; while working at the school he had not been subject to temptation and wanted to break the evil. A little cottage was built and the man had work on the farm where he spent the remaining years of his life. Though he was a Catholic there was no discrimination on account of creed.

An old Frenchman was employed in road construction on the grounds of Northfield Seminary in 1884. He too was addicted to drink and when the work was completed he wanted to remain in Northfield to avoid temptation. He had had a checkered career. A veteran of the French army, having served in Rome in support of the Pope and later wounded in the Franco-Prussian War, he came to America to find employment in the building of the Hoosac Tunnel. Then for a few years he wandered from place to place wherever he could find work. Finally Moody employed him to work in his garden. The old Frenchman responded to Moody's kindly interest and, distrusting his own strength to resist his ancient foe, asked Mrs. Moody to take care of his wages; in the years that followed he was rewarded by a respectable savings bank account. His loving loyalty to Moody was pathetic. There was no attempt to proselyte him but he understood the practical Christianity and he never lost an opportunity to attend services when Moody spoke. Probably he understood little of what he heard, but love for his friend brought to his heart a welcome message of the love of God. When at last his mind weakened and he was a possible menace to society Moody himself took him to a retreat. When at last Paul Dumenal died the family arranged for his funeral according to the rites of the faith in which he was born and of which he was a worthy communicant.

A coworker said of Moody:

> It is no uncommon thing in life to see men of such extraordinary intellectual and moral endowments, cold, hard, just and unloving. But tears start to the eyes of those who knew Mr. Moody well, at the thought of the absolutely inexhaustible depths of his love for all living things. Horses, dogs, cows, animals and birds—all excited the emotions of his heart. In the realm of human life, love for all classes was a master passion. Misfortune, poverty, ignorance, crime even, could not throw anyone out of the pale of his universal sympathy. He had his antipathies, but they were not directed against any class. They were as likely to be aroused by the rich as by the poor, by the learned as the ignorant. These antipathies were never enmities. He had no hard feelings. He was simply repelled. He gave men a wide berth if he did not like them. But if he did he opened his heart to its utmost capacity. Little children, whether his own, his grandchildren, or the children of strangers, fled to his arms as to those of a mother. There never has been a home outside of Eden more filled with the divinity of love than his. To be in it, to see the play of affection, the absolute confidence and rest of love, was a beatitude.

A letter to one of the New York daily papers in 1890 relates the impressions made on a casual observer by Moody's love for animals. The writer says:

A fashionable turnout—coupe and team—was being driven rapidly along Twenty-ninth Street towards Fifth Avenue when the off horse, making a misstep on the slippery pavement plunged a moment as he strove to recover his balance, then, with a twist of his body in the stiff harness that must have been exceedingly painful, fell heavily on his right side. The headway of the carriage and the rapid pace of the team could not be instantly stopped, and as the splendid animal struck the pavement he was carried along over the stones, lunging and struggling, a distance of seventy-five feet. The near horse, frightened by the plunges of his fallen mate, began to rear. His eyes flashed, his nostrils distended, and in a moment he would have been beyond the control of the driver, who shouted to the passers-by to seize him by the head. The struggles of the fallen horse were threatening each moment to disable, if not to break the legs of his mate, which stood trembling and panting and jumping at his side. Everyone tried to do something; no one did anything. Excitement and confusion seemed to paralyze every effort at extrication. The driver held the standing horse by the head but was helpless at the heap of troubles that confronted him.

At this moment a stout gentleman with a book under his arm, who had been an earnest observer of the early scenes of the accident, seeming to realize the need of a controlling head, handed his book to a bystander, and rushed to the frightened team, and, with a word of authority that had power enough in it to move a regiment, caused everyone present to realize that a general had command who knew what to do, and had force enough to have it done. "Loose that pole strap," was the first order. Easier said than done. The harness was tight, but the pressure of the fallen beast had made every strap as tight as a fiddle string. A strong hand pulled on the strap ineffectually. "Can't be done," he said. "Can't be done!" said the stout man. "It must be done. Get hold here," he said. And seizing the strap himself, with two others, a tug or two of the mighty power loosened the buckle, and the pole was free. "Now the traces," the stout man cried. It was wonderful to see how everyone took fire and jumped at his word. After a few short, swift tugs at the various straps the standing horse was free, and the prostrate horse slowly induced to rise, and the accident was over. The team was safe, not a strap cut, not a bruise on either beast, and a heavy burden lifted from every heart. A sigh of relief escaped from more than one mouth, and the driver looked as if he had inherited a fortune. The stout man resumed his Bible, for that it was, and walked quietly away, evidently in deep satisfaction. Few persons recognized that it was Mr. Moody, the great evangelist, who was returning from his afternoon meeting at the church on the corner of Twenty-ninth Street and Fifth Avenue. His warm heart had led him to give his life to saving his fellow men from sin, but it is big enough to be deeply touched by dumb beasts in trouble, and the same sympathy and energy that gives impulse to thousands in his daily addresses is also at the service of the lowest creature that needs a helping hand.

If not a Roman Catholic Moody was in a true sense catholic in the broadest meaning of the word—recognizing the essential Christian fellowship of all believers in Christ in whatever forms of outward observances it was expressed. His fellow townsmen belonging to the Roman communion wished to build a church. It is significant of their feeling toward Moody that they sought his help, and he made a modest contribution. On the completion of the place of worship they needed a harmonium and this Moody supplied. He was invited to be present at the dedication of the church and though he was unable to be present, he was represented by his son. From the chancel the officiating priest expressed the gratitude of the congregation for the help received from those who did not belong to their communion, with special reference to Moody. An interesting sequel occurred the next year. The church in which Moody worshiped in Northfield and which was attended by the students of the Northfield schools was to build a new church. From the chancel of the Roman Catholic church the priest recalled to his hearers the help they had received and asked such as could to proffer their help, if not with money, by voluntary service. In coming days these humble neighbors contributed by giving of themselves and their teams in hauling materials for the new church. Thus friendly relationships were strengthened and a practical demonstration was given of church unity—if not uniformity.

Chivalry and courtesy are more nearly inherent qualities of character than merely exterior graces. But Moody was not indifferent to these. Drummond who was ever the accomplished and cultured gentleman was to Moody an object of genial envy. "I love to see Drummond rise and open the door for a lady. I wish I could do it with his grace." Observant of others and valuing the outward accomplishments of early training which he felt he could never acquire, he was ever sensitive to atmosphere, considerate of the feelings of others and self-forgetful in the interests of others, resenting injustice or ruthlessness toward the weak. Surely this is what constitutes true chivalry and courtesy.

In his relations with women he was ever the gentleman but guarded against any careless familiarity. "He never let gushing women make a fool of him," says one writer who is not sympathetic with Moody's ideals, but was compelled to recognize his common sense and obvious discretion.

His tact was in part due to his understanding of human nature and often stood him in good stead. Sometimes by some surprising action or some apt reply he could relieve an embarrassing situation or overcome some grave difficulty. On one occasion he was preaching in a community where there was bigoted opposition. A number of toughs had determined to give him a rough handling and rumors reached his friends that even his life might be threatened. In grave anxiety they urged him to cancel the meeting but to no avail. He had never "shown the white feather; and I won't begin now," he assured them. Then he was advised to request the police department to provide protection but this he decidedly refused to do. He would not even accede to the advice that he should quietly retire after the meeting by a back exit leading onto an alley where a carriage should be waiting. He would not deviate in any way from his usual custom. At the meeting he spoke as he had planned and at the close of the service, taking his overcoat over his arm, walked down the center of the hall and out onto the street. He saw a gang of young men who by their appearance were bent on mischief. Going up to the one whom he judged to be the ringleader Moody handed him his overcoat and said, "Just help me on with my coat, will you please?" and to another, "Would you hold my Bible?" After the coat was on he said, "Thank you, gentlemen. When you get as old and stiff as I am I hope someone will be as kind to you." The leader of the group, with a muttered oath to the effect that no one had better molest the old gentleman, then insisted on taking his arm and accompanying him across the street.

His sound common sense was evident in what others

would think to be trifling. Returning home from a mission to a certain city he brought with him a massive gold-headed cane.

> Here, take this and put it away [he said to a member of his family with evident embarrassment]. Inquiry elicited the story of its being the gift of the choir. If I had known in advance [he said], I would have headed them off. I would look nice going about with a gold-headed cane! Once when I was a young man in Chicago an old minister gave me a gold-headed cane saying that he was soon going to die and he wanted me to have it. I only carried it once. It was too expensive a luxury. Everybody seemed to charge me double. Even a boot-black charged me twice the usual price for blacking my shoes. When I remonstrated, he replied, "A gent who can carry a gold-headed cane ought not to complain when a poor boy charges that for blacking his boots." That explained it all. I took that cane home and I never carried it again. Here, take this away.

Nothing seemed to take him unaware. Once in a Western city he was walking with two English friends to a meeting which he was to address. On the way they met a young man who was under the influence of liquor although this was not at first noticed. Moody frequently invited people to his meetings when he felt that he was not recognized and on this occasion he asked the stranger to join their party and go hear Moody. The retort was as unexpected as uncomplimentary, for the young man said if he went he would not go in such a company of evident topers and specially called attention to the rather ruddy complexion of one of Moody's companions. In an effort to distract attention from his friend Moody asked if the stranger would not consent to accompany him, eliciting a no more flattering rejoinder that there was visible evidence from his size of undue indulgence in beer. Though this was the sense the phrases employed were extremely offensive. Instead of taking umbrage Moody asked if the personal appearance of the third in the party would be such as to be compatible with his dignity. Apparently he was assured and consented to go with this one. The brisk walk dissipated the influence of the liquor and when the service opened and the poor man realized whom he had addressed he was greatly perturbed. "I don't know what my mother would say if she knew I had insulted D. L. Moody," he said to the one who had accompanied him. "In England mother always hears him when he is there and sets great store by him." That this was the occasion of one being turned from the error of his way was a rich reward to Moody who slyly enjoyed the discomfiture of his ruddy faced companion and genuinely felt for the embarrassment of the stranger when he became conscious of his unwitting affront.

Even criticism he could turn to favorable account. When a rather officious person explained that his want of grammatical precision offended, Moody acknowledged his handicap in the matter of education, but he rejoined, "I'm trying to do the best I can with all my shortcomings. Now what are you doing with your greater advantages?"

An amusing story of Moody and his method in raising money was told by Major D. W. Whittle. Moody, it seems, had called upon a gentleman to enlist his help for the Northfield Schools. In anticipation of an appeal for a large sum, the gentleman proffered a donation of one thousand dollars. In relating the experience to his friend Moody said, "I thanked him in reply, but said that I should not have insulted *him* by asking for that amount. He asked me why. 'I should have asked you for fifty thousand dollars. When a man makes money by jumps, I go by jumps.'"

Dr. Lyman Abbott writes:

> Without office in Church or State; without theological, collegiate, or even high school education; without a church or society behind him to support him or a constituency, except such as he himself created, to afford him moral support; without any of the recognized graces of oratory; and without any ambition to form a new ecclesiastical organization or a new school of theological thought; and perhaps without the ability to do so; nevertheless, Dwight L. Moody probably spoke to a greater number of auditors than any man of his time in either Europe or America, unless possibly John B. Gough may be an exception, and he spoke on spiritual themes to audiences which were less prepared therefor by any previous spiritual culture than those addressed on such themes by any preacher since Wesley and Whitfield.

President McKinley paid a great tribute to Moody's memory. A member of his family called at the White House to renew an invitation previously given by Moody himself, to visit Northfield. "Your father," said the late President, "was a great man." To which the reply was, "He certainly was a good man." "Yes," said President McKinley reflectively, "he was a good man and he was also great; greatness and goodness is a rare combination."

CHAPTER LXIV

Moody has often been referred to as a genius. This explanation of his career depends largely upon the definition that is given the term. Genius, according to Webster, is "extraordinary mental superiority, uncommon native intellectual power." The Century Dictionary defines it as "exalted mental power and distinguished by instinctive aptitude."

If genius is thus to be defined in terms of the intellect, there may be difference of opinion about Moody as a genius. But Rev. Charles F. Goss says of him:

> It is not by logical reasoning merely that that grandeur of the human intellect is shown. The mind has another power not less wonderful. While some of the great geniuses of history have been compelled to arrive at conclusions through long and subtle processes of reasoning, others have reached them by a mental spring as swift as lightning. This is the power which we call "intuition," and it was this power which Mr. Moody possessed to a degree which filled the minds of those who knew him with wonder. I never knew him to pass through such processes of "reflection" as bring out the best results of most men's thinking. All he seemed to require was to have a given problem set before him in the clearest light possible, and he instantly saw the answer in all its bearings. It was like the mental operation of those mathematicians who astonish the world by their power to compute without addition, multiplication, subtraction, and division.

If genius is that quality which sees what to do and when and how to do it, certainly Moody was a genius. And if it is simply the capacity for hard work, his career from early manhood justified the application.

According to Theodore Roosevelt:

> The average man who is successful—the average statesman, the average public servant, the average soldier, who wins what we call great success—is not a genius. He is a man who has merely the ordinary qualities that he shares with his fellows, but who has developed those ordinary qualities to a more than ordinary degree.

In two other respects which may not be ordinarily viewed as genius Moody was notable; he recognized clearly his own limitations and he could determine the qualifications of others even when they themselves were apparently unconscious of their own powers. To recognize what one cannot do is almost as great a power as consciousness of inherent gifts; and to recognize latent powers in others and to have the ability to waken them and direct them into useful service would in itself seem to be nothing less than genius.

If the simplicity of his spirit is emphasized then immediately there is recalled his remoteness; if he had an unaffected candor he had also a diffidence. It may be said of him what was said of Roosevelt, "He flocked by himself on a peak."

In *Heroes and Hero Worship* Carlyle says,

> I should say sincerity, a deep, great, genuine sincerity, is the first characteristic of all men in any way heroic. . . . The Great Man does not boast himself sincere, far from that; perhaps does not ask himself if he is so; I would say rather, his sincerity does not depend on himself; he cannot help being sincere. The great Fact of Existence is great to

him. . . . God has made many revelations; but this man too, has not God made him, the latest and newest of all? The "inspiration of the Almighty giveth *him* understanding"; "we must listen before all to him."

Sincerity was one of Moody's outstanding traits. Contemporary newspaper editorials repeatedly refer to his obvious "earnestness," "singleness of purpose," and "genuine sincerity." That which all observed in common was the reality of his zeal.

"Why do you go to hear Moody?" said a scoffer contemptuously to a fellow club member. "You don't believe what he preaches." "No, but he believes it, with all his heart, and it is refreshing to meet such a man in these days of doubt and uncertainty."

> The things which to most of us are mere theories or hopes were to him burning realities [says a friend]. They glowed before his imagination like fire instead of gleaming with the faint radiance of phosphorus. We linger with an irresistible fascination over the problem of this power—a power which shook men to the center of their beings; suddenly disclosed another world; agitated dull consciences; aroused the slumbering emotions; brought to life dead memories, and filled men with a sense of the realities of things which they had thought to be only dreams. We regard it as a mystery demanding our best efforts at solution.

To an old-time Chicago friend, upon his return to America in 1875, Moody confided in great earnestness:

> I am the most overestimated man in this country. By some means the people look upon me as a great man, but I am only a lay preacher, and have little learning. I don't know what will become of me if

the newspapers continue to print all of my sermons. My stock will be exhausted by and by, and I must repeat the old ideas and teachings. Brooklyn every Sunday hears a score of better sermons than I can preach. I can't get up such sermons as Drs. Budington and Cuyler and Talmage, and many others who preach here week after week. I don't know what I shall do.

If it was hard for others to reconcile some of the seeming paradoxes of his nature it was no less difficult for Moody himself to do so. His zeal which his early associates in Chicago days noted, was unabated throughout life, but with experience came wisdom. A year before he laid down his work he was in Arizona, traveling from Phoenix to Tucson. On this journey his son was engaged in conversation with a young man, a contemporary collegian, who had been an athlete. The young man had come West hoping to arrest tuberculosis with which he was fighting, but with evident failure. Paroxysms of coughing seized him from time to time, but he expressed assurance of his improvement. In his conversation he carelessly swore, then turning to Moody apologized for the inadvertence. Moody quietly disowned any personal slight and said that there was no need for apology. Later Moody said to his son, "I don't know what I ought to have done. How my heart went out to that poor fellow so hopeful but so evidently near the end. There was a time when I would have spoken to him about his soul, but to do so under the conditions would have been to alarm him and possibly have done him real injury. Oh, how we need wisdom. All we can do for him is to pray for him."

Here was one of many instances of conflicting qualities. The inherent instincts of a gentleman and the zeal of a missioner. But experience had taught him that there is a time for everything; that to do the right thing at the wrong time may bring serious consequences.

The impression Moody made upon his contemporaries, even upon casual meetings, is significant. The late President Woodrow Wilson thus refers to an occasion when, for a brief moment, their paths crossed:

> I was in a barber's shop, sitting in a chair, when I became aware that a personality had entered the room. A man had come quietly in upon the same errand as myself, and sat in the next chair to me. Every word that he uttered, though it was not in the least didactic, showed a personal and vital interest in the man who was serving him; and before I got through with what was being done to me, I was aware that I had attended an evangelistic service, because Mr. Moody was in the next chair. I purposely lingered in the room after he left, and noted the singular effect his visit had upon the barbers in that shop. They talked in undertones. They did not know his name, but they knew that something had elevated their thought. And I felt that I left that place as I should have left a place of worship.

For what was only external symbolism, Moody had a strong aversion. The spirit of worship was everything, but when outward formalism tended to smother this spirit he had little patience with it. Better the simple outpouring of praise by devout souls, out of doors, than the most elaborate ritual, if only formal, in the most stately cathedral.

In a newspaper report of a catastrophe at Fort Worth, Texas, Moody appears in the rôle of an intrepid spirit. The following newspaper account describes the scene:

> There were not less than five thousand present, and these had determined to stay after Moody had requested those who wished to retire to do so. "I am

here to preach if you want to remain and listen!" he said.

Outside the elements were in magnificent warfare and the heavens presented scenes of terrific grandeur. The thunders rolled, and crashed and pealed, the lightning flashed and darted through the sombre clouds and burnished them with fiery tints of silver and gold, while the waters came down in almost solid sheets and pattered upon the earth. To add to the awful splendor which illumined the heavens the wind screamed and shrieked like a thousand engine whistles.

While thousands of voices were swelling with melody the roof gave way and the panic became awful. The music stopped and shrieks of frightened women and children and the hoarse yells of men rose above the din of the storm. Nearly everyone lost reason temporarily, and it is a wonder that a number of women and children were not trampled to death. . . .

Contrasted with the frantic people was Moody, without a quiver of limb, without a tremor in his voice. The grand old man stood upon his platform and gave directions to the few who were in their senses to get the people out at the various exits. His courage was supreme, and if the angry winds had seen fit to have clutched every timber in the structure and scattered them to the four winds, that old man would have stood his ground and met his fate with all the composure and calmness which he would have shown had the affair been nothing more than a gentle whispering of a southern breeze at sunset.

An old ex-Confederate general who was present is alleged to have said, "I've seen many brave men in my life put into positions of great personal danger, and I believe I know a brave man when I see him tested. I want to say to you I have never seen a braver man than D. L. Moody."

He was humble in spirit but, paradoxical as it may be, he could also be autocratic. This has been cited as a weakness; on the contrary it was strength. This was shown in his work at Northfield. Here he would delegate work to others and in purely academic questions he would never interfere. But sometimes when a principle or a policy was involved he would listen to all that might be said and then render a final decision. On one occasion his son pressed a certain matter after Moody had given an adverse decision. The response was characteristic, "While I am responsible it will have to be done in my way. When the time comes when you have the responsibility you will have to do it according to your best judgment."

His decision was the result of mature experience; the public held him responsible; and he had to determine policies according to his judgment in the realm where he was familiar. His position was accepted with no irritability. It was the quiet and final decree and all his subordinates recognized the wisdom of his course.

When faith healing in the sense of dispensing with medical advice was being adopted by some of the students at the Chicago Bible Institute, it was rumored that this had been the sequence of some of the teaching. Moody did not examine into the matter to determine the ground for the report, but summoned to the office the superintendent and department heads. He stated that such a report had reached him, that he believed in the use of such means as medical science prescribed, emphatically stated that the prayer of faith in his judgment did not preclude the use of means and that he would not be responsible for having students in the institution who, in case of illness refused medical advice. One who was present on the occasion says, "It was a straight from the shoulder talk. As he finished he brought his fist down on the table with no unmistakable emphasis and said, 'If any teach that in sickness doctors are not to be summoned, *out they go.* That's all.'" And the group disbanded. Autocratic? Certainly. But one who is responsible has of necessity to define the policy.

"There's no use asking God to do things you can do yourself. Many prayers you can answer yourself. If I can give sufficient help to do something I had better give and not pray God to send the money." This was his position. Those who recall the earnest, simple, direct nature of his public prayers will testify that they were never long. He was never tolerant of long prayers in others. But in a sense Moody prayed without ceasing. It would be difficult to imagine a situation in which he could not pray. It seemed such a spontaneous and natural experience. Often in the company of coworkers or the home circle, when a problem presented itself, he would say quite simply, "Well, let's pray about it." And then and there, in a brief sentence or two, he would seek divine guidance. Some times on some unfrequented road he would rein in his horse and utter a brief supplication for needed strength or wisdom. Nothing could have been freer from cant. He believed in the immanence of God; that He hears and answers prayers and Moody simply acted upon that belief in everyday life.

To Moody life was defined in terms of service. Well did he exemplify the delineation of true character as stated by Florence Nightingale in the following words:

> Live your life while you have it. Life is a splendid gift. There is nothing small in it. For the greatest things grow by God's law out of the smallest. But to live your life, you must discipline it. You must not fritter it away in "fair purpose, erring act, inconstant will"; but must make your thought, your words, your acts all work to the same end, and that end not self but God. This is what we call *character.*

CHAPTER LXV

FRIENDSHIP was to Moody a sacred privilege. He was ever seeking to impress upon his children this conception. "If a man is to have friends he must show himself friendly" was a common proverb with him. Personal inconvenience or even sacrifice one should ever be ready to make in behalf of a friend. His genius for friendship was an outstanding characteristic. In every class of society both poor and rich, cultured and uneducated, young and old alike, he enjoyed the friendship of those who differed widely in temperament and position.

Naturally there were degrees of intimacy. In the inner circle of those to whom he confided there were very few. With Mrs. Moody there were no reservations; her advice and fellowship was sought in every plan and to her he divulged every purpose. He owed her more than can ever be known both in the furtherance of his life work and in deterring him at times in unwise impulse. To his children, as they grew older, he would turn for advice and he was never too self-opinionated to refuse suggestions from any source. In all his projects it was ever his intent to carry his family with him, sharing with them his purpose and enlisting their sympathetic interest.

In establishing the Northfield Schools Mrs. Moody was his unfailing confidant and collaborator. To her quiet and unobtrusive fellowship Moody owed much in the educational work he achieved.

Next to his wife, the two who probably shared most in Moody's confidence were Mr. D. W. McWilliams of Brooklyn and Mr. H. M. Moore of Boston. To them he turned in every perplexity. Their mutual affection was of many years' duration and continued to the end of life.

Mr. McWilliams Moody had first known in early days in Illinois. At that time Mr. McWilliams was connected with certain railroad interests, but his responsibilities did not preclude his active participation in Sunday school work and it was their common interest in work for children that first brought them together. Whenever Moody was engaged in New York, Mr. McWilliams was at his side. Two letters to this lifelong friend are so characteristic and revealing of the nature of their friendship as to deserve a place:

BELFAST, OCT. 5, 1874

DEAR McWILLIAMS:

Your kind letter and book are at hand. I wish I could see you for five minutes to tell you how much I love you and to thank you for all your kindness to me, but if all goes well I shall hope to be back next season and see you all. I need not speak to you of the work. You will see by the paper what I am doing, but if you could arrange your business to come over to London, say in March, you could be of great help to me and you would see something of the stream of grace that is now flowing in this land. Could you not bring your wife and stay three months in London, and then I will go home with you? Pray over it and arrange your business to do so if possible. It is one of the best fields in the world to work for Christ. It is the center of the Christian world, and if God only would use us to move that place, Eternity alone could tell us the result. Come if you can. Tell Dr. Cuyler not to forget his promise to write for the Christian. We are now sending it to all the ministers in the United Kingdom, 30,000 of them, and I want him to help reach them. It is going to cost two thousand pounds and now that I have raised the money I do not want it lost by sending out a poor paper. If you see anything real good for the paper I wish you would send it to me and I will have it put in.

Yours in haste, with much love to all,

D. L. MOODY.

DUBLIN, OCTOBER 31, 1874

DEAR McWILLIAMS:

I long to see you, but that is out of the question unless you come to this country. I want to write you on business. You wrote me a long time ago that —— would give $300 towards —— in Chicago, and I counted on that, but I am afraid that he did not do it, or if he did they failed to tell me. I find it difficult to do what I am over here to do and to keep my work up in Chicago unless I get some help. I have given between six and seven thousand inside of twelve months to keep the work up in Chicago, and would be glad to give twice as much if I could, but I do not see how I can do it, but the letters that come from Chicago tell me of awful dark days in money matters, and the more I give the more I have to do. You know that I am responsible for —— and —— which cost me $500. . . . But that is hindering me from doing what I would like for our church and Sabbath school, besides clothing, etc. Now I do not want you to give any more, but thought if —— would speak to a few friends, or ——, they might get $2000 to keep the work up until I get back. Of course, I would not like to have you say anything about what I am doing. If the Lord blesses them as I am in hopes He will, they will have enough sent in by another year to pay them for their services. I do not know who to write to, for I do not know who is bankrupt since the failure of so many men. Do not let this trouble you. If —— or someone else will not take it up let it go. The work grows better as we go from place to place.

     Much love to all,
              MOODY.

Mr. H. M. Moore was a business man in Boston. Only those nearest to Moody knew how greatly he valued the unsparing labors of Henry M. Moore in behalf of the Northfield work. A New Year's letter to his esteemed friend, characteristically brief, thus expresses his affectionate gratitude.

       EAST NORTHFIELD, MASS.
          December 31

DEAR MOORE:
  I cannot let the old year pass without thanking you for all you have been to me in this old year. And my prayer is that 1898 may be your best year. I inclose you a letter I think will interest you. With much love to you and all the family I am,
     Yours as ever,
          D. L. MOODY.

Space would not suffice to give in detail all the services of Moody's fellow laborers and associates during the thirty-eight years of his active life, from the time he gave up business until he answered the summons to lay down his work. There were some on whose help he counted to follow him in evangelistic work or to undertake missions in places where he could not go. Such was Major D. W. Whittle whose acquaintance began in Chicago in the days of the Civil War. Invalided home by a wound received at the battle of Vicksburg Moody was at once attracted to this young officer whose popularity in the city called forth a great demonstration in Chicago on his return. The American Express Company, in whose service he had been engaged, sent their employees with a band of music and all their wagons to escort him from the station. A few days later Lieutenant Whittle was asked to make a speech at a patriotic rally, where a number of prominent men had been invited to speak. Referring to this occasion, Major Whittle says:

> I, a boy of twenty-one, was put forward to speak, with Bishop Simpson on the platform behind me waiting to give his address. I was weak from my wound, and felt foolish at being in such a position. Directly in front of me, in the centre of the hall, a sturdy young man jumped to his feet and cried: "Give him three cheers!" I recognized the face of Mr. Moody as he led the cheering with great earnestness. This manifestation of sympathy nerved me for the few words that followed, and I have often thought it was a specimen of what his courage, faith, and example have been to me all through his life. When I told him sometime afterward of how much good his sympathy had done me that night, and how vividly I remembered his earnest determined look as he led the crowd, I was rewarded by his reply: "I took you into my heart that night and you have been there ever since!"

For P. P. Bliss and James McGranahan Moody had a grateful sense of indebtedness for their contribution to the service of song not only in public services, but also in editing the hymn books used in England and America as well as for his personal regard for their sterling character. There was also Mr. George C. Stebbins who was associated with Moody for twenty-four years in evangelistic work and in the conferences at Northfield. He was an accomplished musician and also contributed to the hymn books.

Three other friends to whom Moody frequently turned

for counsel and help in his work were William E. Dodge, D. Willis James and Morris K. Jesup.

In Northfield Seminary the early years gave evidence that there was needed a preceptress who could carry out the founder's ideas without impairing scholastic standing. In 1883 Moody's attention was called to Miss Evelyn Hall. He readily perceived that the qualities for the position were to be found in her—a modest estimate of her own judgment implying an open mind, an earnest Christian spirit, and executive ability. Miss Hall rendered twenty-eight years of efficient service, during which period enrollment increased fivefold, the original purpose and principles were conserved, and a spirit of loyalty and friendship ensued. It is to the credit of both these fellow workers that through years of varied experiences these two, each of whom was imbued with New England resoluteness, could together effect that which neither could have done alone, and that they achieved this common task in mutual respect and truest esteem.

It is not implied that Moody's fellow workers were at once permeated with all his ideals and were fully sympathetic with all his methods. What is remarkable is that they embraced his views and later made them their own. It was their love and loyalty to Moody, no less than their devotion to the work itself which has accounted for the continued growth and development of the schools.

In every section of the country were friends for whom Moody entertained a real affection and it is evident the regard was mutual. Thus the testimony of one of the prominent Christian leaders of the South, writing to a friend, refers to Moody as "one of the most distinguished and justly honored Christian men of the age."

Some have said that Moody would abandon a fellow worker when he could no longer use him. The implication is that loyalty was lacking. This is utterly false. Such a criticism sometimes arose where the critics knew they could assuredly count on loyalty to past friendship not to disclose the cause of the discontinuance of former associations. But Moody labored often in behalf of former associates, sometimes seeking other employment for them when, for any reason, the services of the past could no longer be rendered.

It is true that he could not always associate with himself those who in former years had been fellow laborers. In fact, it often happened that some indiscretion or some unfortunate statement had impaired their influence in the Christian community; Moody would not undertake to thrust such workers upon others and impair the effectiveness of a union movement. But even in these cases Moody never was known to drop a friend even if circumstances prevented him from laboring with him.

Such was Moody's ideal of the nature of friendship that sometimes it imposed a very difficult task. If news came to him of a friend being overtaken in a fault, Moody did not make it the subject of conversation with others but went direct to the one involved. This faithfulness cost him much. Because he was capable of loving deeply he was capable of suffering keenly. To lose a friend was to him a real calamity.

It was on his last visit to London in 1892 that he learned that a friend had taken offense for supposed deviation from the Truth. This man was one for whom Moody entertained a great respect and warm affection. In former years their association had been close. His generous interest in his fellow men and his zeal in Christian service had found expression in a unique work in London hospitals, a work to which he gave much time and money. Since the last visit of Moody this friend had become a close communion Plymouth brother, rigid in his adherence to the letter of what he believed to be the law, both on his own part and in his requirements of others.

Word reached Moody of the disaffection of his friend and he went to call on him. He asked what he had done to forfeit the old relationship. The reply was that Moody had not been loyal to the Truth in asking certain prominent Christian leaders to speak at Northfield. Then followed the brief conversation, as Moody recalled it later.

Moody: "We are both getting on. I may never come over to England again and we may never meet. Now you think I've done wrong and you know St. Paul says 'if a man be overtaken in a fault, ye which are spiritual restore such a one in the spirit of meekness.' Have you made any effort to restore me or don't you think I'm worth saving?"

Friend: "It wouldn't have done any good."

Moody: "How do you know? Anyway that does not release you from the responsibility of trying."

Friend: "Well, you had no right to have —— speak at Northfield."

Moody: "Well, on that we don't agree, but should it make any difference in our relations to one another? At morning prayers I read from Peter's epistle, 'Above all things have fervent charity among yourselves,' and I determined to come around and see you for I can never forget the happy fellowship of former times. Now would I increase the scope of my ministry if I joined your body or what do you think I ought to do?"

Friend: "Stay, Moody, where you are. You can do more for the Kingdom."

Moody: "Then won't you pray with me?"

As they rose from their knees the two old friends clasped hands. Among the Bibles Moody prized was one on the flyleaf of which was inscribed "To D. L. Moody from his friend"—and in one corner "Above all things have fervent charity among yourselves (I Peter iv. 8)."

CHAPTER LXVI

"CHARACTER is what a man is in the dark" was a definition Moody used frequently to quote. It might be paraphrased with equal truth that "character is what a man is in his home." Many who become accustomed to public life find home commonplace or at least look upon it as a kind of vent by which they may release all kinds of dispositions they would not display in public. Moody was the very reverse for in public he was engrossed in the matter in hand and sometimes gave the impression of being brusque while at home he was always the tender, considerate, affectionate husband and parent. Moody was seen at his best in his family circle.

No impatient word escaped him with his wife. Always thoughtful and ready to express regret for any inadvertence; no matter was too trivial to be unobserved. Even in domestic arrangements he was concerned and ready to adjust his plans to the convenience of Mrs. Moody. She was ever his first consideration.

With his children he was a most sympathetic companion. He could enter into their interests and was always accessible to them. Their joys were his, and their disappointments were his alike. His daughter-in-law recalls his anxiety over his younger son's difficulty in mastering a certain piece of school work. Finding the boy applying himself to his work early one morning Moody walked the floor waiting to see the results of his work. Unable to assist him in the subject, he would from time to time ask how he was getting on, and when at last the task was finished Moody ejaculated, "Good!" and gave a sigh of relief as though he himself had achieved the success.

In his letters to his children his interest in every detail of their life was evident. While engaged in work he was observant of things that would interest them. From Spokane Falls, Washington, he writes his boy at college: "This is a growing place bubbled up inside of eighteen months. The saw mills are going day and night. They have electric lights and the night is as light as the day. I thing it is going to be one of the great cities of the territory."

Again from British Columbia he writes at the time of the excitement of a presidential election:

> I am thinking of you having a good time in New Haven these days. I have kept out of it entirely the last two days and to-night they had a grand rally here. The smoke is still in the street. I hope Paul saw something of it.
>
> I am having a good work this fall and I shall do as much good this year or fall as any for a long time. . . . I am in a house that is three hundred feet into the bay and it is set on piles and when a boat comes in it swings around. There is twelve feet of water under the house and all around us. . . . I have some fish stories to tell you that seem incredible. It is a wonderful country for all kinds of game. . . . I must close now and go to bed. I have six meetings on for to-morrow and so must get some rest.

When Moody was to be absent for Christmas he wrote from the Pacific coast:

> I have been all day thinking and working to get you and Paul something for the twenty-fifth, but I have had to give it up. I will try and find something when I get to California and bring it with me. You

do not know how much trouble it is to find anything in a city like this. But I am so happy at the thought that you can be in Northfield. I think I enjoy the thought as much as you will. It always makes me happy to see you and the rest of the family happy. I shall look in on you a good many times in my thought.

Once he signs himself, "Your father in a hurry to get home."

To a son at school at Mount Hermon and living at home he writes:

> I have not got a word from you since I left you in New York. I wish you would write me a good long letter and tell me all about the farm on both sides of the river. . . . I have bought you a book about the southern war from their standpoint. I think you will be interested in it. It is written by their ablest general, without it is Lee. I have got also the "Life of Lee." I think you will be interested in both of them. All the people are kind to me now and seem as if they could not do enough for me. Goodbye, Much love.

He wanted to be kept informed on everything happening at Northfield. Some buildings are in the course of construction and he writes:

> Will you go through the church and tell me all you find? Also, the store and the two houses that are going up near the hotel and the one near the Phillips house. Also, will you go through the barns at my house and the schoolhouse and tell me if you think the hay will hold out? . . . I hope you will not forget to write mother a letter next Tuesday, her eighty-fourth birthday.

In every way he would share with his family in all his

plans for the future of his work. Thus he writes in the autumn of 1888 from California to his boy in college to whom he has divulged his purpose of a trip around the world visiting missionary fields.

> I know you will be glad to know that I am not going to India. When I got near this city the leading men came out to meet me and say that they shall hold me to my word. I promised last year that I would come to them this year so I am in duty bound to stay.... May the God of the ninety-first Psalm watch over you day and night is my prayer.

The spiritual welfare of his own children was not lost sight of in his solicitude for others and when he is not assured of their allegiance to Christ he is deeply concerned.

> MY DEAR WILL:
> I do hope you are taking an interest in the Bible. I am so ashamed to have you grow up and go away from my home with so little knowledge of the word of God.... Will you not take an interest in the word of God and give fifteen minutes alone each day in February, putting your mind on the portion you read, and one hour on the Sabbath and read with me the Gospel of John? I wish you would commit at least one verse a day so you can repeat it at any time. I shall pray God to help you do it and I will give the same time each day to the same book.... I do not like to bully, but I feel as if something should be done this year and your growing dislike to it is the greatest sorrow I have on earth.... I shall pray God to help you, dear Will, to serve Him from the heart. Goodnight and may the blessings of God rest on you day and night is my prayer.

When his daughter takes a Sunday school class he writes her:

I have had the secret of a happy life and have found it was in making others happy. My earnest prayer has been for ten years that my children should enjoy it with me and year after year I have tried to get you interested in the poor of this town and in the Sabbath school. To come home last month and find you so heartily engaged in this work made me spend one of the best thanksgivings of my life.

Simplicity was the order of the home. Moody himself was an early riser. The first hour was given to study and devotion. If he followed any prescribed rule in his Bible reading and prayer life no one knew, for into the sacred precincts of his devotional life no one intruded. That it was simple may be inferred from every other phase of his life. Alone in the quiet of the early hours, his only companion the Bible, he emerged to meet the day and its duties after a spiritual preparation.

By six o'clock he was usually driving, if weather permitted, inspecting the farms at Northfield Seminary or Mount Hermon. By seven-thirty he met with the family for breakfast and then outlined the plans for the day. Family prayers immediately followed; a brief portion of Scripture and an earnest prayer in which the special interests of the members of his household were remembered and in which the sorrows or anxieties of his neighbors were not forgotten. The mornings were largely given to the varied interests of the work at Northfield, and opening his mail which was always large.

After the midday meal he rested. But even his rest hours were given in part to study, and by three or four o'clock he was again to be seen driving in his familiar buggy and not confining himself to roads but traversing fields, wherever a skillful driver could safely venture.

A simple evening meal and an hour or two watching the glories of a summer sunset were the prelude to an hour or two of work signing letters. And usually by nine-thirty or ten the family retired.

In later years when conferences were held during July and early August, Moody presided at all public gatherings and the day's routine was accordingly modified. Perhaps that which most speakers and privileged visitors best remember of these days of meetings was the late supper after the services of the day were ended. Here about the dining table they would gather, and ofttimes it brought real relaxation, for Moody made it a rule to always divert his thought from his work before going to rest. He was a good story teller and thoroughly appreciated the gift in others. Dr. G. Campbell Morgan, a gifted raconteur, would be called upon, whenever present, to relate stories of Peter Mackensie, a quaint Cornish lay preacher, in whose unique ways and original sayings Morgan delighted. Wholesome laughter usually characterized these evenings, though at times the conversation was in a more serious vein. But whatever the nature of the conversation, these social hours ended with a brief prayer, usually led by Moody, seeking God's blessing on the day's work and committing his friends to His care and keeping.

The healthful sport of the students ever enlisted his sympathy. He followed their athletics with deep interest. On one occasion the Mount Hermon students essayed to play the Williams College football team and found themselves no match for the more mature and better trained collegians. Moody, hearing of their defeat, wrote his son: "The Hermon boys were stupid to play Williams. They got a good thrashing and should have known better than to take a lot of fellows who have played together so long."

Moody's love of teasing found full scope with his children. An old broom shop on the place he had made over into a playhouse for his children. Here, when his little girl was giving a party, he found them seated on the floor beneath an open window and to liven up things he dropped a little squealing pig into their midst.

When some children dressed up as gypsies Moody induced his nephew to disguise himself as a tramp and turn the children's plan of discomfiting others against themselves.

But if he played pranks on them he could take a joke against himself. When asleep one day his little daughter quietly did his hair up in ribbons. Awaking from his nap he rushed to address a meeting and only just in time found out the prank that had been played on him.

On one occasion a son had, in the absence of the father, planted a small elm tree near the house. On Moody's return he looked askance at it. "I am afraid it will shade the house." "All right, then," was the reply. "Cut it down." A year later when the son returned from college he noted another tree had been planted ten yards away, and Moody informed him that the second tree would outstrip the one he had planted. During the next few years an amusing contest took place. In Moody's absence the son would enrich the soil and water his tree and carefully remove all traces of what he had done. When it began to show signs of unusual vigor, Moody would seize the first occasion in the absence of the son to give a similar treatment to his tree. Thus the contest continued through the son's college course.

As his children grew into maturer years he continued the selfsame companion. College life interested him intensely. He could not advise regarding the choice of subjects; he could only state principles which might help. Of sports he knew little, but he learned if asking questions would teach him. He wanted his son's companions to visit the Northfield home and enjoyed them far more than some of the eminent divines he knew.

When his daughter returned from a trip to Germany

she brought two little souvenir busts of the Kaiser and Bismarck. One day Moody's attention was attracted to them. He knew the Iron Chancellor only as a great patriot and regenerator of Germany, a loyal subject and faithful servitor of William I. For the young emperor he had only a deep contempt. "Bismarck is all right," he soliloquized, "but I don't want that in the house," pointing at the bust of the young Kaiser. "Why, father, what's the matter?" asked the daughter. "Any man who treats his mother as he has and then turns from one who has done for his grandfather and father what Bismarck has will come to a bad end. Mark my words. I may not live to see it but he will die in disgrace, an exile from his own land." This was in 1891.

Moody's older son planned to become a doctor but Moody sought to dissuade him. A year later the young man again talks of taking up a medical course and then Moody for the first time divulges his own cherished plan for the youth: "I need you to help me in my work. Take the Bible Institute and direct the work." The son demurs on the ground that he is not prepared to assume such a work. "Well, then, take Northfield Seminary." But the son felt that as he was unmarried it would be questionable if he was suited for this. "Then take Mount Hermon. That's my best work. If anything happens to me my friends would rally round you as they would about no one I know." And so he appointed his son as his lieutenant.

In Moody's thoughtful and delicate attention to his aged mother he was an example to many a less busy man. Seldom a day passed when absent from home that he did not send her some message, either a short note or a newspaper report of his work, and when at home he was never so busy but that he found time to visit her to whom he owed so much. Her birthday fell on the same day as his own and his letters to her on successive anniversaries were peculiarly tender. The last one he wrote her was in 1895.

At the funeral services he offered the most affectionate tribute to that mother's wisdom and loving devotion. Holding in his hands the old family Bible and the worn book of devotions, he stood by the form of the departed one and said:

> It is not the custom, perhaps, for a son to take part in such an occasion, but, if I can control myself I would like to say a few words. It is a great honor to be the son of such a mother. I do not know where to begin; I could not praise her enough. In the first place, my mother was a very wise woman. In one sense she was wiser than Solomon; she knew how to bring up her children. She had nine children, and they all loved their home. She won their hearts and their affections; she could do anything with them.
>
> Whenever I wanted real sound counsel, I used to go to my mother. I have traveled a good deal, and have seen a good many mothers, but I never saw one that had such tact as she had. She so bound her children to her that it was a great calamity for them to have to leave her home. I had two brothers that lived in Kansas and died there. Their great longing was to get back to their mother. My brother, who died in Kansas a short time ago, had been looking over the Greenfield papers for some time to see if he could not buy a farm in this locality. He had a good farm where he was, but he was never satisfied; he wanted to get back to mother. That is the way she won her family, she won them to herself.
>
> I have heard something within the last forty-eight hours that nearly broke my heart. My eldest sister has told me that the first year after my father died mother wept herself to sleep every night. Yet she

was always bright and cheerful in the presence of her children. Her sorrows drove her to the Lord. I would frequently wake up and hear her praying. She used to make sure her children were all asleep before she poured out her tears.

There was another remarkable thing about my mother. If she loved one child more than another, no one ever found it out. Isaiah, he was her first boy; she could not get along without Isaiah. And Cornelia, she was her first girl; she could not get along without Cornelia, for she had to take care of the twins. And George, she couldn't live without George. What could she ever have done without George? He stayed right by her through thick and thin. She couldn't live without George. And Edwin, he bore the name of her husband. And Dwight, I don't know what she thought of him. And Luther, he was the dearest because he had to go away to live. He was always homesick to get back to mother. And Warren, he was the youngest when father died; it seemed as if he was dearer than all the rest. And Sam and Lizzie, the twins, they were the light of her great sorrow.

She never complained of her children. It is a great thing to have such a mother, and I feel like standing up here to-day to praise her. And just here I want to say, before I forget it, you don't know how she appreciated the kindness which was shown her in those early days of struggle. Sometimes I would come home and say, "Such a man did so and so," and she would answer, "Don't say that, Dwight; he was kind to me."

Friends, it is not a time of mourning. I want you to understand we do not mourn. We are proud that we had such a mother. We have a wonderful legacy left us. What more can I say? You have lived with her, and you know about her. I want to give you one verse, her creed. It was very short. Do you know what it was? I will tell you. When everything went against her, this was her stay: "My trust is in God."

When grandchildren came, there was a rejuvenation. "Do you know I have a granddaughter? I am taking a present over to her," he shouted from his buggy to a friend on the natal day of his eldest grandchild. And he pointed to a basket of doughnuts. Later that day he made a second trip to Mount Hermon to see the baby, this time bringing over an immense cauliflower, the best his garden had produced.

This same playful nature was shown in his first letter to little Emma Fitt, the second grandchild, when she was three weeks old:

> This is my first letter to my dear little grandchild. I wanted to get a letter to you before you got your first tooth. Hurry up and get them all before the hot weather comes on, for I will get you some candy and you will want teeth to eat it. I want you to hurry up and grow so I can come early mornings and take you out riding when your mother and father are fast asleep. We will slip over the river to see Irene, and have some good times. Your mother is so proud of you and your nurse is so fussy. Only think, Emma, what your mother said the other day—I, your grandfather, could not kiss you on your lips! Did you ever hear anything like that? But I got a kiss on your lips all the same, and I will get a good many more when I get home.

When the children were old enough to sit up he took them riding with him on his rounds and scoffed at the idea that he needed anyone to hold them. He insisted that he was as good as any nurse.

A beautiful picture of him is cherished in the memory

of his family, seated by his little grandchild who had fallen asleep on one of the many drives. On returning home, he would not allow anyone to disturb her though it meant that he must sit quietly beside her in the carriage until she awoke.

Moody was away from home when his third grandchild, his namesake, died. He wrote to the bereaved parents:

> We got the letter this morning telling us of the translation of little Dwight. I am thankful he suffered so little and that he has gone to a brighter and better world. All I can remember of him is his sweet smile. All else has gone from my mind. What a joy it was for you to have him for one year! What days they have been to you and how you will live them over and over again!
>
> I wish I was near you now, but I will remember you all in prayer and our cry is that the good Lord will comfort you and help you day and night. What a glad thought to think when the short night is passed and the glad morning dawns we will all be together for ever to go no more out. Dwight has gone to help get things ready and to give us a warm welcome. I like to think of him with the Savior, free from all pain and trouble. Dear little fellow, how I long to see him. He will be a strong tie for us all and a lode stone to draw us to a land of Eternal day and he will never lose his smile when you see him again.
>
> My heart leaps within me as I think of the future. Let us work on a few days longer and then eternal glory shall drive away all sorrow.
>
> With a heart full of love and sympathy from
>
> Your loving father
>
> D. L. MOODY.

When one of these children was seriously ill while he was away from home he insisted that he be kept daily informed of her condition by telegram, and when she recovered he telegraphed his deep thanksgiving.

When, during his last year, his eldest grandchild died after a protracted illness his grief was poignant and he entered with understanding sympathy into the sorrow of the stricken parents. He arranged every detail of the funeral, choosing the hymns, and as it was summer when many friends were in town, he had the simple service held in the shade of the spreading trees at his own home. Suppressing his own grief before his family, the suffering was doubtless a factor in his own breakdown three months later.

Such was Moody in the circle of his own family. Always the same loving heart and noble character as when in work in the outside world.

CHAPTER LXVII

In 1892 Sir Andrew Clark had warned Moody that he was overworking; he should speak only once a day and twice on Sunday. But the succeeding years showed no diminution in his work. During the six months of the World's Fair his labors had been greater than in any period of his life. His responsibilities in maintaining the various projects he had instituted also increased. He revisited many centers. Invitations came from every part of the United States and Canada, and once he made a brief visit to Mexico.

From his sermon notes it is evident that during the winter of 1894 he preached in eleven cities, holding missions in Washington, Providence, Lowell, Toronto, Birmingham, Richmond, Scranton, and Wilkes-Barre; in 1895 he was in New York, Boston, Philadelphia, Worcester and Bangor; in 1897 in Cincinnati, Chicago, Winnipeg, and St. Louis; and in 1898 in Jersey City, Montreal, Denver and other cities in the west; 1899 he gave largely to the southwest and the Pacific coast.

Increasingly Moody was perplexed, in his effort for distinctly evangelistic work, by the presence of former associates and friends in his audiences. For a generation he had been preaching continuously throughout the United States and Great Britain. This naturally gave him a wide circle of acquaintances and in revisiting places his meetings were attended by the Christian public. From the subjects on which he spoke it is evident that his message was adapted to his audience, being directed toward rousing Christians to a sense of their individual responsibility in their communities. If he could not preach to the non-Christians, he sought to induce others to do so.

It has been intimated that the character of Moody's message was changed with the passing of the years. This is not substantiated by the meager notations on sermon envelopes. "People say the old gospel has lost its power," he confided to one of his family near the end of his career. "I have not found it so. This year I preached the same sermon I've used for years, first at Yale University, then in the slums of a great city, and in one of the leading churches of New York. It seemed to me to bring greater results than ever. No, the world still hungers for the same message."

Again it was said that in later years Moody's influence with his old-fashioned gospel was waning. A newspaper raised the inquiry whether Moody was not a preacher of yesterday rather than to-day. An article written by Professor Cleaver Wilkinson of the University of Chicago shortly after Moody's visit to Chicago in 1897 is pertinent:

> Where the doubt was first raised it seemed to be resolved in a sense unfavourable to Mr. Moody's continuing hold on public attention. But is it true that this great preacher, at sixty years of age and more, has already done his work and declined from the meridian of his power? An incident in my own recent personal experience settled that point for me, and settled it in a sense decisively opposed to those conclusions of the newspaper press to which allusion has been made.
>
> Mr. Moody is, I fully believe, still among us in a degree of ability to affect the public mind no whit diminished from what it was in the prime vigour of his manhood. Is there any other preacher living,

on either side of the Atlantic, who could, by the mere announcement that at a given mid-day hour of a given business day he was to speak on a given religious subject, call out a multitude of people numerous enough to fill—to overfill and overflow—the most spacious auditorium in the city of Chicago? But that not long ago happened under my own observation in the case of Mr. Moody.

Of course it was not mere curiosity to see and hear for once a celebrated man that drew those throngs of eager people together. Mr. Moody had been for many years a familiar figure in Chicago. Beyond doubt, the great majority of his immense congregation had seen and heard Mr. Moody before. It was because they had seen and heard him before that they wished now to see him and hear him again—this, far rather than because they were intent on gratifying an idle curiosity.

A public speaker of whom this can be said has assuredly not yet lost his command of the popular ear, has not yet lost his power over the popular heart. It is in the most real sense a topic of living interest to study and to try to understand the phenomenon presented to us in the character and career of this noble herald of the Gospel. In the case of Mr. Moody the keeping is perfect between the man as he appears in his printed books and the man as he appears in the pulpit. In whichever of these two aspects he presents himself to your notice, an ample, a sturdy, an unaffected, a sincere, an earnest, an aggressive, a quite indomitable, even a somewhat domineering, personality confronts you. Impression of personality is by no means wholly due to personal appearance, though in this matter personal appearance counts for much.

You read or you listen, and you unconsciously say

to yourself, "Here is a man that practices no arts. He only speaks right on." You are at once and completely thrown off guard if you had come to his audience, whether in the book or on the platform, bringing with you any disposition to subject him to criticism and to judge him by rules. He does not challenge admiration; and you are not drawn aside from his purpose to consider whether or not he may be worthy of admiration. He has grappled you unawares. I set it down, therefore, as the most characteristic and the most salient trait of Mr. Moody's preaching and the main merely natural secret of his power, that he puts no barrier of charm between himself and his audience.

Another report of these meetings conducted in the Chicago Auditorium from a Tuesday to Friday is thus given by the Chicago *Times-Herald:*

> The attendance averaged twelve thousand each day. He talked without a note—save the Bible. He did not repeat. There was never a minute when he was eloquent. He would not have been logical if he could be. Moody does not care a cent for grammar. He never saw the inside of a geology. Once he tried to tell the names of the men who ran for the presidency last fall and failed. He scolded Christians and cuffed the ministers as a father might his children. There was not a single, solitary reason which could be applied to any other man why women should leave the breakfast tables in order to get a chance at a seat. Men would not have endured so many faults in any man but Moody.
>
> Moody will not admit it, but there is no other man in this country who could have filled the Auditorium as he filled it eight times. He held 48,000 men and women in the hollow of his hand, and they wept or

smiled as he willed. It may have been magnetism or it may have been acting. It may have been that the plain talk from the plain man was just what the plain people wanted, and the people were plain—plain from the standpoint of fashion. He congratulated the audiences because they were plain. He does not think it is any particular honor for a man to be rich. Once he gladdened the thousands into cheering by telling them all the honor he had was the result of his faith in the goodness and fairness of the poor. Some one brought to him word that there would be no fear about the expense of the hall in case he would hold boxes for the rich. This proposition was set upon so hard that the board under his broad foot was split in his indignation. This stands for his popularity. He is Moody—only Moody, rough, honest, sincere, flat, without frills, old-fashioned, consistently simple and grandly in earnest.

Moodyism—if it is fair to call a sentiment which has lasted more than a third of a century as ism—was as rampant yesterday as it was thirty years ago. The police detail was at the vestibule as the whistles were blowing for the husbands of the women to go to work. There were two or three hundred of these wives standing in the street. The wives were so set on getting into the building that they threatened to stampede the doors. They abused the officers, and Moody passing by said he heard one of them express her pleasure in the prediction that there would be no policemen in heaven. Milward Adams, from the Auditorium, watched the religious riot. There had been times when the house was so full that the thousand on the stage were nervous. He opened the way two hours before the time for the first hymn, and an hour before it was time for the sermon to begin there was not an empty inch of seat under the roof. A preacher in front confessed he had never thought there were so many souls in all the city as were banked from pit to top. It seemed as impossible to count it as a field of wheat on a hillside.

One observer of Moody confesses to a sense of perplexing wonder at his incessant activity. That which impresses people is the unremitting and inexhaustible physical resources combined with zeal and sound judgment. Whitefield is said to have remarked at the very end, "Lord Jesus, I am weary in Thy work, not of Thy work." But even this was not true of Moody. He seemed in spirit to be as tireless as ever, though the strain of incessant labors for so many years had told upon his physical strength.

The inquiry room continued as an important factor in the work and the experiences of a lifetime in evangelism had confirmed his earlier judgment that it was not enough to make known the gospel but that there was needed the personal contact which could only be effected in what Drummond termed the spiritual clinic. Moody was too sound a psychologist to undervalue the importance of some method of registering a decision and would always urge the one who had decided for Christ to publicly make known the step. To him the will was the citadel to be captured. It was burning the bridges behind, and nothing so strengthened the spiritual life of the young convert as helping others find the source of newly discovered joy and power.

As invitations to conduct missions increased Moody made his choice of spheres of labor where he could count on the whole-hearted support of the local ministry. The permanency of a work, he realized, depended to a large extent upon the sympathetic work of the pastors in following up the missions, bringing the converts into church fellowship, and assigning them to work in Christian activity.

His warm personal friendship for many theological professors and the prominence given to them at Northfield conferences should be a sufficient answer to the charge that his attitude was critical, in general, of theological training. He was opposed to arid scholasticism or dead formalism; he was loyally sympathetic with thorough training and educational preparation for the ministry.

But he did criticize any preparation which undermined the confidence of the young minister in the *authority* of the Scriptures or was concerned so much with the presentation of the message as to lose sight of the message itself. He would cite the instance of a young student who said that in the study of one of the books of the Bible weeks had been spent on a consideration of its authorship and historical setting and half the term had passed before beginning on the book itself.

When he was invited to Australia in 1898 Moody wrote in reply:

> The work in my own country has never been so promising as it is now. Destructive theology on the one side, and the no less evil spirit of extreme intolerance on the other side, have wrought wide dissension in many communities in America. Instead of fighting error by the emphasis of truth, there has been too much "splitting of hairs" and only too often an unchristian spirit of bitterness. This has frequently resulted in depleted churches, and has opened the way for the entrance of still greater errors. Under these conditions the question of the authorship of the individual books of the Bible has become of less immediate importance than a knowledge of the teaching of the Bible itself; the question of the two Isaiahs less urgent than a familiarity with the prophecy itself.

BOOK IX

CHAPTER LXVIII

"This winter I prayed God to give me a hard field. He has answered my prayer. This is the most difficult field I've known." This remark Moody addressed to his son in a small mining camp and railroad center in the Southwest in his last year. Audiences were small and interest had to be worked up. The throngs which he had been accustomed to elsewhere did not exist. It was a challenge which appealed to him. He was not dependent upon the numbers that constituted his hearers. The same earnest effort that he made for large assemblages was put forth for the few. Those who heard him in those days felt that his power was undiminished and he had the gratifying experience of finding his audiences grow from small gatherings to fill the buildings or churches.

On reaching San Diego, Santa Barbara and San Francisco his meetings grew to their wonted size, and the year was one in which he rejoiced in having the privilege of sharing the labors with those in home missionary work in hard places.

But the year was a severe strain upon his physical strength. Those who were near him realized that he was carrying a heavy load. He did not so readily shake off a cold as in former years and twice he had to send a substitute to take his meetings. For six years he had persisted in spite of the warning he had received to abate his labors, and in his sixty-third year, after a hard and continuous public career of nearly forty years, his vital forces were impaired.

Returning to Northfield in the late spring of 1899,

after spending some time in Chicago supervising the work of the Chicago Bible Institute, he made arrangements for the forthcoming summer conferences and the closing of the school year in Northfield Seminary and Mount Hermon. The coming months were overshadowed by concern for his eldest grandchild who was stricken with tuberculosis, and the anxiety for the little four-year-old child hung over him as an ominous cloud.

The little girl passed away in the summer of this year. Keeping his personal grief to himself, Moody devoted himself to seeking to comfort the stricken parents and to keeping their thoughts engrossed in work for others.

Even in the first moments of anguished grief his character was revealed. As the little life flickered and then went out, kneeling by the bedside, he poured out his heart in prayer of thanksgiving for the sweet fellowship of the four brief years, of earnest supplication for the parents and of grateful acknowledgment of the confidence of reunion. Then in an abrupt way so characteristic of him always he turned to the parents and said, "And now we must get to work for there is much to do."

At the funeral service of little Irene, unannounced and unexpectedly, he arose and paid the following tribute to the little life he loved so dearly:

> I have been thinking this morning about the aged prophet waiting in the valley of the Jordan, so many years ago, for the chariot of God to take him home. Again the chariot of God came down to the Connecticut Valley yesterday morning about half-past six and took our little Irene home. The one was taken at the end of years of active service; the other at the early dawn of youth. But the service of the prophet was no more complete than that of the little handmaid of the Lord, for God called both, and He never interrupts the service of His own.

Irene has finished her course; her work was well wrought on earth. She had accomplished more than many in their threescore years and ten. We would not have her back, although her voice was the sweetest voice I ever heard on earth. She never met me once, since she was three months old, until the last few days of pain, without a smile. But Christ had some service for her above. My life has been made much better by her ministry here on earth. She has made us all better. She has been a blessing to all the conferences here this year. She has brought a wealth of sympathy into the meetings such as we have never had before. During the young men's conference I tried to keep it secret but while I was on the platform my heart was over at the home. On the day after the conference closed she left for the Adirondacks, and we feared we might never see her again. During the women's conference my heart was yonder in the mountains at Saranac. The last night of that conference, while I was trying to speak to the young women words of cheer and encouragement, I was constantly thinking of the little girl, and within twelve hours I was by her side.

The last few days have been blessed days to me. I have learned many new and precious lessons. She was very fond of riding with me, and on Monday morning, twenty-four hours before she fell asleep, she asked me to take her driving, and at six-thirty we were out together. She never looked more beautiful. She was just ripening for Heaven. She was too fair for this earth. I thank God this morning for the hope of immortality. I know I shall see her in the morning, more beautiful in her resurrection glory than she was here.

CHAPTER LXIX

EARLY in November of 1899 Moody accepted an invitation to conduct a mission in Kansas City. He was largely influenced in this by the fact that two of his Mount Hermon boys were active in Christian work there. Charles M. Vining was among the early students in Mount Hermon and Moody had advised him to settle in business in Kansas City. Mr. Vining, by his assiduous and faithful attention to business, had attained to a position of responsibility in one of the largest banks in the city. The other was Mr. Sydney Bishop, who had also gone to Kansas City at Moody's recommendation, as secretary of the city Y. M. C. A. For both these men he cherished real affection and looked forward to their companionship and coöperation.

Mrs. Moody remained, at his request, with the bereaved parents of the little grandchild at Northfield and he was unaccompanied by any member of his family. In passing through Philadelphia he met his old friend, Mr. John Wanamaker, who later recalled how unlike himself Moody seemed. He told of his recent bereavement which his friend noted had greatly told on him physically. Referring to this interview Mr. Wanamaker said:

> Reviewing his life from the time I knew him first, about 1859, I can call to mind many who, during these forty years, have been distinguished in the business world, in railroad enterprises, and in public life; but I do not know of one who has made so much of his life, or who would not say, if he were to speak, that he would be glad if he had chosen the

course that Mr. Moody took to make his life potential for good. He has done the best business of us all. God's work looms up larger than ever to us to-day.

It is like a vision to me recalling my last interview with Mr. Moody, about the 10th of November last, when, in answer to his telegram, I met him in the Philadelphia railroad station on his way to Kansas City. He could only stop over a train, and his purpose was to ascertain the exact situation of his prospective winter's work at Philadelphia. We talked for nearly an hour upon the outlook; and I went to my home to tell my family that Mr. Moody looked to me that night as the prophets Elijah and Hosea must have looked; and I told them, as I tell you now, that his eyes were full of tears, and that he sighed again and again, saying, "If only it would please God to let me get hold of this city by a winter of meetings! I should like to do it before I die, and possibly from Philadelphia the influence would go out to other large cities." Somehow my heart grew heavier as he talked. I witnessed what seemed to me like an agony of soul in his care for the church at large and his anxiety for a revival. It was with this burden that he undertook a railway journey for a thousand miles of fatiguing travel, and under this burden he has staggered to the grave.

In Kansas City the meetings were held in the large Convention Hall where the attendance taxed the capacity of the building to its utmost and he began, apparently, with all his wonted vigor. The *Kansas City Journal* reports:

> Never have there been such elaborate plans made for any religious event in Kansas City, and never has there been such an ideal place for holding revival

services as Convention Hall. Mr. Moody several times has said he intended to make this series of meetings the crowning effort of his life. Convention Hall will seat several thousand more people than any hall that Mr. Moody has spoken to in the United States.

The same journal records that the meetings continually grew. This last mission which he held, struggling against a sense of increasing physical weakness and loss of sleep, was a fitting close to his public ministry.

Notwithstanding the threatening weather the afternoon service, according to newspaper reports, was attended by three thousand and in his closing words there seemed a prophetic note. But at the evening service he spoke upon "Excuses." His message was one of earnest appeal based upon the parable of the marriage supper in the fourteenth chapter of Luke. According to the *Kansas City Journal*, Moody closed his public ministry as follows:

> Let me tell you some of the excuses you will make to your consciences to-night for not accepting Christianity. I hear excuses are the devil's cradles in which he rocks men's souls to sleep. Let me tell you some made here in Kansas City, Missouri. Yes, right in this hall to-night.
>
> The first excuse is the old Book. One fellow says this book contradicts itself. It isn't true. I challenge any man to show me a single promise God has made to His people He has not kept. The people who know the Bible are not the people who revile it, but those who never read it, who know nothing about it, are its denunciators. One man who claimed to know it, and that he had read it through, I found once, but I didn't believe he had ever read it through. He could quote but one passage in it, and that was

the shortest verse in the whole Bible—"Jesus wept." People are ready to give their opinion on a new book only after they have read it two or three times, but they give their opinion about the Bible before they have read it—on hearsay only.

Another excuse is "I am not foreordained to be saved. If I am, I shall be saved, no matter what I do, so I don't have to stand up here and profess before all these people. If God wants me saved He will save me." Now, you try that in temporal affairs. Just you sit in your seats and if God wants you to go home to your family He will get you there, even if He has to carry you through the window head first and put you to bed. If He wants you to succeed in business He will see that you do so. You needn't move a finger. That's fine philosophy, isn't it?

Others give as excuse there were too many hypocrites in the church; others, the life was too narrow, they wanted liberty; others they couldn't believe.

Suppose we should write out to-night this excuse, how would it sound? "To the King of Heaven: While sitting in Convention Hall, Kansas City, Mo., November 16, 1899, I received a very pressing invitation from one of Your servants to be present at the marriage supper of Your only begotten Son. I pray Thee have me excused."

Would you sign that, young man? Would you, mother? Would you come up to the reporters' table, take a pen, and put your name down to such an excuse? You would say, "Let my right hand forget its cunning and my tongue cleave to the roof of my mouth, before I sign that." I doubt if there is one here who would sign it. Will you then pay no attention to God's invitation? I beg of you, do not make light of it. It is a loving appeal, God inviting you to a feast, and God is not to be mocked. Go play with forked lightning, go trifle with pestilence and disease, but trifle not with God.

Just let me write out another answer: "To the King of Heaven: While sitting in Convention Hall, Kansas City, Mo., November 16, 1899, I received a pressing invitation from one of Your messengers to be present at the marriage supper of Your only begotten Son. I hasten to reply. By the grace of God I will be present."

Mr. C. C. Case who had been engaged to assist in the meetings by assuming charge of the music thus describes the days previous to Moody's complete breakdown:

Tuesday morning at breakfast I saw that he looked pale and ate little. I asked how he rested, and he said, "I slept in my chair all night." I knew if he could not lie down he was a sick man. I asked him what was the matter; he said he had had a pain in his chest for a couple of weeks, and added, "I did not let my family know it, for they would not have let me come on here." I had to urge him for an hour or two before he would consent to call a doctor but finally he gave in. The doctor put a mustard plaster on his chest, which at once relieved the pain. He preached six sermons after that, but I could see that he was all the time growing weaker, and the last two days he had to be taken to the hall in a carriage, although it was only two blocks away. When he began speaking he did not show his weakness, but preached with his old-time fire and spirit; but when he got back to his room I could see that he was very much exhausted. I tried to make him advise his family of his condition, but he would not until the day he started for home.

I think he enjoyed his work in Kansas City as

well as any he ever did, from what he said to me. The crowds were greater than any that I had ever experienced with him. The singing pleased him very much, for I had nearly a thousand voices in the choir. We had an "Old Men's Quartet" that he particularly enjoyed. Their ages varied from sixty-seven to eighty-two, and he would announce their selections by saying, "I want my boys to sing so and so."

Near the close of one service, Moody leaned on the organ and asked the ministers: "Will you allow me to say a word to you?"

"Yes, yes; say what you want," they answered.

"Well, I'm not a prophet, but I have a guess to make that I think will prove a true prophecy. You hear so much nowadays about the preacher of the twentieth century. Do you know what sort of a man he will be? He will be the sort of a preacher who opens his Bible and preaches out of that. Oh, I'm sick and tired of this essay preaching! I'm nauseated with this 'silver-tongued orator' preaching. I like to hear preachers, and not windmills."

In conversation with Mr. Vining he talked of the institutions he had founded and of the bereavements that had occurred in his family during the past year; picking up a copy of his book, *Thoughts from My Library*, he read a comment on the text (Psalms xxx. 5), "Weeping may endure for a night, but joy cometh in the morning." The extract ends with the words: "I have heard it in the Land of Light from which I come. There is a time approaching, steadily if not quickly, when 'the Lord will wipe away tears from all faces.' This weary world shall obtain joy and gladness at last, and sorrow and sighing shall flee away. 'Wherefore comfort one another with these words.'"

In view of the approaching end, the following paragraphs from one of the last sermons in Kansas City are significant:

> I have no sympathy with the idea that our best days are behind us [and he smiled as he related the impression that he had a year before when he saw in the papers that "Old Moody" is in town]. Why [he said], I am only sixty-two; I am only a baby in comparison with the great eternity which is to come. We say this is the land of the living! It is not. It is the land of the dying. What is our life here but a vapour? A hearse is the most common sight. Families broken into. Over there is one who has lost a father, there a mother, there is a place vacant, there a sister's name is no more heard, there a brother's love is missed. Death stalks triumphant through our midst, in this world. Only yesterday I met a mother who had lost her babe. Death in front of us, death behind us, death to the right of us, death to the left of us. See the hospitals in our land, and asylums for the insane, and the blind and the aged.
>
> See the great number of jails in our land. Seventy thousand criminals in our country. But look at the other world. No death, no pain, no sorrow, no old age, no sickness, no bending forms, no dimmed eyes, no tears. But joy, peace, love, happiness. No grey hair. People all young. River of life for the healing of the nations, and everlasting life. Think of it! Life! Life! Life without end! And yet so many men choose this life on earth, instead of the life in heaven. Don't close your heart against eternal life. Only take the gift, only take it. Will you do it?

Under the imperative order of his physician, Moody reluctantly consented to cease work, and, leaving Kansas

City by the evening train, he traveled directly home without breaking the journey, which required a day and two nights on the road. On the way an incident occurred that cheered and encouraged him greatly. From St. Louis to Detroit the train was delayed by the burning out of the locomotive fire grate, and it was feared that connections would be missed at a later point. The new engineer, who was to take the train from Detroit to St. Thomas, learning that Moody was on the train, returning to his home seriously ill, sent word that he would do his best to make up the lost time. "Tell him," he said, "that I was converted under him fifteen years ago, and I owe everything to him." The division from Detroit to St. Thomas was covered in the darkness of that night at a speed averaging a mile a minute, including stops, and the connection for the East was made.

The first intimation that Moody's family had of his illness was a telegram: "Doctor thinks I need rest. Am on my way home." This was followed at short intervals by other telegrams: "Improving rapidly. Have not felt so well for a week." "Have had a splendid day. No fever. Heart growing better all the time. No pain. Am taking good care of myself, not only for the loved ones, but for the work I think God still has for me to do on earth."

On his arrival at Northfield, he telegraphed Kansas City friends: "Have reached home safely. Have traveled backward and forward for forty years, and never stood trip better. Regret exceedingly being forced to leave. Had I been with you to-night I would have preached on 'Thou art not far from the Kingdom.' I want to thank the good people of Kansas City for their kindness and prayers."

It was hoped that a complete rest would restore the weakened heart; and specialists were consulted who gave encouragement for an ultimate restoration of health, even if the old-time vigor could never again return. But day by day his weakness increased. At first it was almost imperceptible; but it grew steadily more noticeable, until the least effort seemed to tax his strength.

The days of inactivity were hard for one so accustomed to a strenuous life. No word of complaint was uttered by him and he had evidently learned that the time of uncertainty and waiting which is always trying, was of God's ordaining. He could testify to the truth of Gladstone's statement when forced from active work for a time: "Our duties can take care of themselves when God calls us away from any of them. To be able to relinquish a duty upon command shows a higher grace than to be able to give up a mere pleasure for duty."

God had tried His servant in many ways, but it is doubtful if he ever experienced a severer trial than that of the last few weeks. After sixty-two years of an unusually active life, with the remembrance of not more than one or two days of slight illness, to be suddenly laid aside to wait patiently and in extreme weakness for God's will was indeed a stern test.

As time wore slowly away—slowly to a man of such tremendous activity—he would say that every night he longed for the morning. As he grew weaker, he said he knew now what that verse meant, "The grasshopper shall be a burden." On Thursday, December 21, he had seemed rather more nervous than usual, but nevertheless spoke cheerfully about himself. Asked if he was comfortable, he said, "Oh yes! God is very good to me—and so is my family."

Springtime was a season toward which Moody looked with eager anticipation. He loved to see nature reawakening from the long winter months and assuming the evidences of life and growth. It was the symbol of resurrection. As the days grew shorter, even in the early autumn, he would begin to anticipate the next change in the season. When the winter solstice was passed he would exultingly exclaim, "The backbone of the winter is gone." When his family would imply that the severity of the season had only begun, Moody's reply would be, "Yes, but the days from now on will be longer and spring will soon be here." It was a strange coincidence that with the turn of the year, on December 22, 1899, Moody entered upon day eternal.

In the early hours of his last December morning Moody woke after a brief sleep. The watcher by the bedside was startled to hear Moody speaking slowly and clearly, "Earth recedes; Heaven opens before me." Thinking the patient was dreaming the attendant sought to arouse him, only to be reassured by Moody, "No, this is not a dream, Will. It is beautiful. It is like a trance. If it is death, it is sweet. There is no valley there. God is calling me and I must go."

When the family were summoned to the bedside Moody marshaled his strength and talked quietly, giving parting messages to each. "I have always been an ambitious man," he said, "ambitious to leave no wealth or possessions, but to leave lots of work for you to do."

Then it seemed as though he saw beyond the veil, for he exclaimed, "This is my triumph; this is my Coronation Day. I have been looking forward to it for years." Then his face lit up and he said in a voice of joyful rapture, "Dwight! Irene! I see the children's faces!" Then, before he lost consciousness, he said, "Give my love to them all." Turning to his wife he exclaimed, "Mamma, you have been a good wife to me!" and with that he became unconscious.

For a time it seemed that he had passed on, but he revived slowly under the effect of heart stimulants, and suddenly raising himself on his elbow, exclaimed, "What does all this mean? What are you all doing here?" He was told that he had not been well, and immediately it all seemed to be clear to him, and he said, "This is a strange thing. I have been beyond the gates of death and to the very portals of heaven, and here I am back again. It is very strange."

To the plea of his daughter that he should not leave the family he said, "I'm not going to throw my life away. I'll stay as long as I can, but if my time is come, I'm ready."

Then a new thought seemed to possess him: "I'm not at all sure but that God may perform a miracle and raise me up. I'm going to get up. If God wants to heal me by a miracle that way, all right; and if not, I can meet death in my chair as well as here." Turning to one of the attendants who was applying warm cloths, he said, "Here, take those away. If God is going to perform a miracle we don't want them, and the first thing I suppose we should do would be to discharge the doctor." He did not insist on this, however, but was determined to get up, and could not be dissuaded. He then walked across the room to an easy chair where he sat down for a few minutes. A second sinking turn left him exhausted and he was willing to return to bed, where he remained, quietly waiting the end, for an hour. To the very last he was thinking of those about him and considering them. Only a little while before he passed away, he said to his wife, "This is hard on you, mother, and I'm sorry to distress you this way. It is hard to be kept in such anxiety." The last time the doctor approached to administer the hypodermic injection of nitroglycerine, Moody looked at him in a questioning and undecided way, and said in a perfectly natural voice, "Doctor, I don't know about this. Do you think it best? It is only keeping the family in anxiety."

In a few moments another sinking turn came; and from it he awoke in the presence of Him whom he loved and served so long and devotedly. It was not like death, for he fell on sleep quietly and peacefully.

CHAPTER LXX

An elevation back of the old farmhouse which Moody occupied surmounts the adjacent grounds of Northfield Seminary and the modest home of his childhood. It had ever been a spot which he loved for the beauty of the view it commands in all directions. He had named it Round Top and during the summer months thousands had come to share Moody's love for the place, not alone for its natural attractiveness but for sacred associations which had gathered about it with the passing of the years. Here at the twilight hour many an impressive, though informal, service had been convened. Wide spreading pines afforded nature's cathedral and the variegated tints of the setting sun behind the distant hills diffused a light more glorious than that provided by any stained glass window. To many the place had already become sacred from the realization that it marked the spot where high resolve for Christian service had been determined, and thousands during the previous generation had gone from its slopes to render valiant service for Christ both in the homeland and upon the foreign field. Though Moody himself had never expressed any thought or wish regarding his own final resting place, here he was laid to rest among scenes so dear to him in life and in the midst of the work which his love for others and zeal for his Master had built up.

A cherished memory of Moody's family was the summer evenings when he gathered them about him and watched the sunsets from the western veranda of his home. "Delight in nature is a gift of the gods, some-

thing which one cannot get if one has not got it. . . .
I am inclined to distrust anyone who does not love
nature," was the judgment of Bismarck. Moody shared
this sentiment with the rugged pagan. But even more
beautiful than the setting sun in all its glory behind the
western hills, are the lingering lights of the afterglow.
The distant hilltops are touched with every changing
tint and in the diminishing light outlines soften in summer mists. New beauties are seen in the growing dusk
and far away, as the shades of night increase, the hills
slowly turn from the rosy tints to ever darkening degrees
of purple, and one by one, the stars appear in the canopy
of heaven.

So after Moody's passing the afterglow has lingered
in the generation of those who labored with him in the
projects he instituted and the lives he touched. And
when the last of those who knew him have passed on
there will be a permanent place for him in the religious
history of the nineteenth century for "they that turn
many to righteousness [shall shine] as the stars for ever
and ever."

In 1927 *New Age* said of him:

> Some day Moody will be viewed and valued properly by someone who understands the play and progress of American character, and will grasp the really important part he played in it—to say nothing of the extreme picturesqueness and personal flavor of the man. He was precisely suited to the need of the times and he did a marvelous job. You Americans are so struck with inventive and money success that you habitually under-rate those who have contributed to the development of character.

There was perhaps nothing more significant or touching in its simplicity than a letter received from a sailor, three years after Moody's going. From a port on the

Round Top

Pacific coast, the letter was addressed to "Mr. Moody, son of late evangelist Moody, in Massachusetts somewhere. All postmasters knows him." The contents read:

> I am an old man, seventy years old, I want to live a better life. I wish to get a good prayer book. One that's full of sledgehammer words for to wake up an old dead sinner. If you know of anyone or got one to sell, please let me know and the price. P.S. If anyone is in heaven your father is there.

Subsequent letters from the same man lead to the assurance that even when no longer present in body Moody's work of evangelism still continues.

According to P. W. Wilson in an article in the *New York Times*, it is not too much to say: "Fifty years ago he gripped decadence by the throat and, for the time being, at any rate, strangled it. Thousands of men and women decided once more to be their best selves and the public opinion of the nation was purified."

Moody's dictum with which this record of his life began, "What is important is how a man ends, not how he begins," was truly demonstrated in his own career. Fearless and resolute Moody began his life work and fearless and confident he laid it down. If the secret of his life would be known it is to be found inscribed upon the stone that marks the final resting place on Round Top:

> HE THAT DOETH THE WILL OF GOD ABIDETH
> FOREVER

Three years later Emma Revell Moody, that "good Christian girl" who had so unobtrusively and faithfully labored with him, was laid by his side. On the stone which marks the spot is inscribed: "His servants shall serve him; and they shall see his face and they shall reign forever and ever."

BIBLIOGRAPHY

BOOKS, PAMPHLETS AND NEWSPAPERS CONSULTED

ABBOTT, LYMAN. Silhouettes of Contemporaries.
ABBOTT, LYMAN (with Charles F. Goss), Pulpit Echoes—D. L. Moody.
Abraham Lincoln, by Lord Charnwood.
Adoniram Judson Gordon—A Biography, by Ernest B. Gordon.
Alexander Balfour—A Memoir, by R. H. Lundie.
ALLEN, ALEXANDER V. G. Phillips Brooks.
American Evangelists, The, Dwight L. Moody and Ira B. Sankey.
American Nation, The, A History Edited by E. E. Sparks, by A. B. Hart.
ANDREWS, E. BENJAMIN. The United States in Our Own Times.
BANCROFT, GEORGE. History of the United States.
BARBOUR, G. F. The Life of Alexander Whyte.
BARBOUR, ROBERT W. Letters, Poems and Pensées.
BEARD, CHARLES, The Rise of American Civilization.
Best I Remember, The, by Arthur Porritt.
BOARDMAN, GEORGE NYE. New England Theology.
BRADFORD, GAMALIEL. D. L. Moody—A Worker in Souls.
Brother Scots, by Donald Carswell.
BROWN, WILLIAM ADAMS. Morris Ketcham Jesup, A Character Sketch.
BUCKLE, HENRY THOMAS. History of Civilization in England.
CABOT, JAMES ELLIOT. A Memoir of Ralph Waldo Emerson.
CARSWELL, DONALD. Brother Scots.
CHADWICK, JOHN WHITE. Theodore Parker, Preacher and Reformer.
CHANNING, WILLIAM HENRY. Life of William Ellery Channing.
CHARNWOOD, LORD. Abraham Lincoln.
Chicago Yesterday, by Kirkland.
Christianity in America, by Dorchester.

CLARK, JOHN SPENCER. Life and Letters of John Fiske.
CLARK, RUFUS W. The Work of God in Great Britain under Messrs. Moody and Sankey.
COOK, E. T. Life of Florence Nightingale.
COOKE, GEORGE WILLIS. Unitarianism in America.
Critical and Historical Essays, by Lord Macaulay.
CURRIER, A. H. Life of Constans L. Goodell.
Customs and Fashions in Old New England, by Alice Morse Earle.
DALE, A. W. W. Life of R. W. Dale of Birmingham (Eng.).
DANIELS, REV. W. H. D. L. Moody and His Work.
DARLOW, T. H. Life and Letters of William Robertson Nicoll.
Disraeli: Alien Patriot, by E. T. Raymond.
D. L. Moody and His Work, by Rev. W. H. Daniels.
D. L. Moody—A Worker in Souls by Gamaliel Bradford.
D. L. Moody, His Message for Today, by Rev. Charles R. Erdman.
DODGE, D. STUART. Memorials of William E. Dodge.
DORCHESTER. Christianity in America.
DRAKE, FRANCIS S. The Town of Roxbury: Its Memorable Persons and Places.
DRUMMOND, HENRY. Impressions and Facts in the Life of D. L. Moody.
DUFFUS, ROBERT L. The Hound of Heaven, in *American Mercury*, April, 1925.
EARLE, ALICE MORSE. Customs and Fashions in Old New England.
EDWARDS, JONATHAN. Sinners in the Hands of an Angry God.
EGAN, MAURICE FRANCIS. Recollections of a Happy Life.
ELLIOT, SAMUEL A. Heralds of a Liberal Faith.
ERDMAN, REV. CHARLES R. D. L. Moody, His Message for Today.
FOSTER, F. H. History of New England Theology.
GEORGE, JR., HENRY. Life of Henry George.
GIBBONS, HERBERT ADAMS. John Wanamaker.
GILLIES, JOHN. Memoirs of Rev. George Whitefield.
GOODSPEED, REV. E. J. Moody and Sankey in Great Britain and America.
GORDON, ERNEST B. Adoniram Judson Gordon—A Biography.
GORDON, REV. ARTHUR. Life of Archibald Hamilton Charters.
GOSS, CHARLES F. (with Lyman Abbott). Pulpit Echoes—D. L. Moody.
HALL, EDWARD EVERETT. Memories of a Hundred Years.

BIBLIOGRAPHY 545

HART, A. B. The American Nation, a History edited by E. E Sparks.
Heralds of a Liberal Faith, by Samuel A. Elliot.
History of Civilization in England, by Henry Thomas Buckle.
History of Hadley, by Sylvester Judd.
History of New England from 1630 to 1649, by John Winthrop.
History of New England Theology, by F. H. Foster.
History of the Town of Northfield, by J. H. Temple and George Sheldon.
History of the United States, by George Bancroft.
History of the United States, 1850-1877, John Ford Rhodes.
HOGG, ETHEL M. Quintin Hogg, a Biography.
Hound of Heaven, The, by Robert L. Duffus.
HOWARD, PHILIP E. Life Story of Henry Clay Trumbull.
HUGHES, DOROTHY P. Life of Hugh Price Hughes.
IDE, JACOB. Works of Dr. Emmons.
Impressions and Facts in the Life of D. L. Moody, by Henry Drummond.
JAMES, WILLIAM. Varieties of Religious Experience.
John Wanamaker, by Herbert Adams Gibbons.
JUDD, SYLVESTER. History of Hadley.
KINGSLEY, FLORENCE MORSE. Life of Henry Fowle Durant.
KIRKLAND. Chicago Yesterday.
LAWRENCE, BISHOP. Reminiscences.
LEATHAM, W. H. Life of St. Francis Assisi.
Letters of Charles Eliot Norton.
Letters, Poems and Pensées of Robert W. Barbour.
Life and Labors of Dwight L. Moody, by Henry Davenport Northrop.
Life and Letters of John Albert Broadus, by Rev. A. T. Robertson.
Life and Letters of John Fiske, by John Spencer Clark.
Life and Letters of William Robertson Nicoll, by T. H. Darlow.
Life of John Bright, by George Macaulay Trevelyan.
Life of William Ellery Channing, by William Henry Channing.
Life of Archibald Hamilton Charters, by Rev. Arthur Gordon.
Life of R. W. Dale of Birmingham (Eng.), by A. W. W. Dale.
Life of Henry Fowle Durant, by Florence Morse Kingsley.
Life of Henry Drummond, by Sir George Adam Smith.
Life of St. Francis of Assisi, by W. H. Leatham.

Life of Henry George, by Henry George, Jr.
Life of Gladstone, by Viscount Morley.
Life of Constans L. Goodell, by A. H. Currier.
Life of Julia Ward Howe.
Life of Hugh Price Hughes, by Dorothy P. Hughes.
Life of Florence Nightingale, by E. T. Cook.
Life of Principal Rainy, by P. Carnegie Simpson.
Life of Alfred, Lord Tennyson, by Tennyson.
Life of Henry David Thoreau, by H. S. Salt.
Life of Alexander Whyte, by G. F. Barbour.
Life Story of Evelyn S. Hall, by Mary E. Silverthorne and Paul Dwight Moody.
Life Story of Henry Clay Trumbull, by Philip E. Howard.
Lincoln, by Nicolay—Hay.
LUNDIE, R. H. Alexander Balfour—A Memoir.
MACAULAY, LORD. Critical and Historical Essays.
MACKINNON, MRS. PETER. Recollections of Mr. D. L. Moody. (Printed for private circulation.)
MATHESON, MRS. HUGH M. Memorials of Hugh M. Matheson.
Memoir of Ralph Waldo Emerson, by James Elliot Cabot.
Memoirs of P. P. Bliss, by D. W. Whittle.
Memoirs of Rev. George Whitefield, by John Gillies.
Memorial History of Hartford County, Conn., by J. Hammond Trumbull.
Memorials of Hugh M. Matheson, by Mrs. Hugh M. Matheson.
Memorials of William E. Dodge, by D. Stuart Dodge.
Memories of a Hundred Years, by Edward Everett Hale.
Month with Moody in Chicago, A, by Rev. H. M. Wharton.
MOODY, MRS. D. L. Private Diary. (MS.)
Moody and Sankey in Great Britain and America, by Rev. E. J. Goodspeed.
MOODY, PAUL DWIGHT (with Mary E. Silverthorne). Life Story of Evelyn S. Hall.
MORLEY, VISCOUNT. Life of Gladstone.
MORLEY, VISCOUNT. Recollections.
Morris Ketcham Jesup, A Character Sketch, by William Adams Brown.
MORSE, RICHARD C. My Life with Young Men.
My Life with Young Men, by Richard C. Morse.
NASON, REV. ELIAS. The American Evangelists, Dwight L. Moody and Ira D. Sankey.
New England Theology, by George Nye Boardman.

BIBLIOGRAPHY

NICOLAY-HAY. Lincoln.
NORTHROP, HENRY DAVENPORT. Life and Labors of Dwight L. Moody.
NORTON, CHARLES ELIOT. Letters of Charles Eliot Norton.
Our Times, by Max Sullivan.
Our Unitarian Heritage, by Earl Morse Wilbur.
PEABODY, FRANCIS. Present Day Saints.
Phillips Brooks, by Alexander V. G. Allen.
PORRITT, ARTHUR. The Best I Remember.
Present Day Saints, by Francis Peabody.
Private Diary (MS.), Mrs. D. L. Moody.
Pulpit Echoes—D. L. Moody, by Charles F. Goss and Lyman Abbott.
Quintin Hogg, a Biography, by Ethel M. Hogg.
RAYMOND, E. T. Disraeli: Alien Patriot.
Recollections, by Viscount Morley.
Recollections of a Happy Life, by Maurice Francis Egan.
Recollections of Mr. D. L. Moody (printed for private circulation), by Mrs. Peter MacKinnon.
Reminiscences and Gospel Hymn Stories, by George C. Stebbins.
Reminiscences, by Bishop Lawrence.
RHODES, JAMES FORD. History of the United States, 1850-1877.
Rise of American Civilization, The, by Beard.
Robert Louis Stevenson, Man and Writer, by J. A. Stewart.
ROBERTSON, REV. A. T. Life and Letters of John Albert Broadus.
SALT, H. S. Life of Henry David Thoreau.
SHELDON, GEORGE (with J. H. Temple). History of the Town of Northfield.
Silhouettes of Contemporaries, by Lyman Abbott.
SILVERTHORNE, MARY E. (with Paul Dwight Moody). Life Story of Evelyn S. Hall.
SIMPSON, P. CARNEGIE. Life of Principal Rainy.
Sinners in the Hands of an Angry God, by Jonathan Edwards.
SMITH, SIR GEORGE ADAM. Life of Henry Drummond.
STEBBINS, GEORGE C. Reminiscences and Gospel Hymn Stories.
STEWART, J. A. Robert Louis Stevenson, Man and Writer.
SULLIVAN, MAX. Our Times.
TEMPLE, J. H. (with George Sheldon). History of the Town of Northfield.
TENNYSON. Life of Alfred Lord Tennyson.

Thayer, William Roscoe. Theodore Roosevelt.
Theodore Parker, Preacher and Reformer, by John White Chadwick.
Theodore Roosevelt, by William Roscoe Thayer.
Town of Roxbury, The: Its Memorable Persons and Places, by Francis S. Drake.
Trevelyan, George Macaulay. Life of John Bright.
Trumbull, J. Hammond. Memorial History of Hartford County, Conn.
Unitarianism in America, by George Willis Cooke.
United States in Our Own Times, The, by E. Benjamin Andrews.
Varieties of Religious Experience, by William James.
Wharton, Rev. H. M. A Month with Moody in Chicago.
Whittle, D. W. Memoirs of P. P. Bliss.
Wilbur, Earl Morse. Our Unitarian Heritage.
Winthrop, John. History of New England from 1630 to 1649.
Work of God in Great Britain under Messrs. Moody and Sankey, The, by Rufus W. Clark.
Works of Dr. Emmons, by Jacob Ide.

Newspaper files examined:
  New York:
    New York Herald.
    New York Sun.
    New York Tribune.

  Boston:
    Boston Globe.
    Boston Herald.
    Boston Transcript.

  Chicago:
    Chicago Democratic Press (later *Press and Tribune* and then *Tribune*).
    Inter-Ocean.
    Tribune.

  London:
    Revival.
    Christian.

INDEX

Abbott, Dr. Lyman, quoted, 243, 473, 486
Address to skeptics and atheists in London, 361
Anecdotes of the many-sided Moody, 20, 53, 54, 59, 65, 102, 108, 126, 182, 225, 364, 400, 416, 422, 428ff., 447, 462, 463f., 471f., 474, 480f., 483f., 485, 501f., 508f., 509f.
Archbishop of Canterbury, quoted, 221
Army and Navy Committee of the Y.M.C.A., 85
Attempted assassination in Liverpool, Eng., 196
Attitude toward slavery, 28, 68

Bagster, Robert, quoted, 220
Bainbridge, Cuthbert, 141
Baltimore American, quoted, 289
Barbour, Rev. R. W., quoted, 336
Barton, James, 382
Belfast paper, quoted, 399
Belfast Post, quoted, 187
Benson, A. C., quoted, 353
Bewley, Henry, 141
Bishop of Rochester, quoted, 356
Bishop, Sydney, 528
Bismarck, 510, quoted, 539
Blaikie, Dr. W. G., 161, 324
Blaikie, Mrs. W. G., quoted, 161
Bliss, P. P., 141, 200, 206; quoted, 274; tragic death, 278, 499
Boer war, 465
Bonar, Dr. Horatius, 165; quoted, 167
Booth, General, interview with, 287f.
Boston Globe, quoted, 282
Boston Herald, quoted, 365
Boston Transcript, quoted, 283
British Weekly, 155; quoted, 188, 232

Brockman, Fletcher S. (quotation from Dr. James Vance), 387
Brooks, Phillips, quoted, 281; biography quoted, 281
Brother Scots, cited, 168
Brown, Dr. William Adams, quoted, 328, 433
Burch, Isaac H., 57
Burke, Valentine, converted prisoner, 292ff.
Burns, Anthony, fugitive slave, 28
Burrell, Dr. David J., 94

Cadman, S. Parkes, 447
Cairns, Dr. John, quoted, 183
"Cambridge Seven," missionary group, 377
Cambridge University mission, 377
Camp, Hiram, finances beginning of Mount Hermon school, 313f.
Carlyle, 138; biography quoted, 138; quoted, 488
Carswell, Donald, quoted, 168
Case, C. C., quoted, 532
Catholic Christians, 17
Chadwick, Rev. James S., quoted, 75
Chalmers, 154
Change in character of Moody's work, 1878-79, 288
Changing conditions in Great Britain, 136ff.
Channing, William Ellery, 16, 17, 280
Character Sketch of Morris K. Jesup, quoted, 433
Charteris, Archibald, 165; biography quoted, 165
Chicago Avenue Church, site secured for new church, 130; debt defeats dedication in 1875, 272; dedicated July 16, 1876, 273
Chicago Bible Institute founded, 373

INDEX

Chicago Evangelization Society, see Chicago Bible Institute.
Chicago Times, quoted, 279
Chicago Times-Herald, quoted, 519
Chicago Tribune, 70; quoted, 94, 277
Christian, The, quoted, 143
Christian World, quoted, 217, 366
Civil War years, 84-91; on the battlefields, 86ff.; problems of decade following, 239ff.
Clark, Dr. Rufus, quoted, 115
Clark, James Freeman, 16
Coeducation not approved by Moody, 313
Coffin, Edmund, quoted, 203f.
College Girls' Conference, started 1893, 385
Collier, Robert Laird, quoted, 365
Colportage Library, 422; events leading to its establishment, 421
Congregationalism in the early years, 15
Congregationalist, The (London), quoted, 359
Connecticut Valley, migrations to in 1635, 4
"Consecrated common sense," a Moody characteristic, 416
Cuyler, Dr. Theodore, quoted, 247, 262

Daily News, The, quoted, 190
Dale, Dr. R. W., quoted, 194, 339, 442; biography quoted, 195
Darby, J. N., 101
Darwin, 138
Denny, Edward, 360
Denny, T. A., 360
Descent of Man, 138
Disruption, The, in Scotland, 153
Dodge, William E., 200; quoted, 201ff., 264, 269, 500
Dods, Dr. Marcus, 335
Dom Pedro, Emperor of Brazil, 271
Drummond, Henry, 164, 168, 176, 186; quoted, 233, 335, 361, 386, 464, 473
Drummond, Peter, 398
Dryer, Emma, 372
Duffus, R. C., quoted, 261
Duggan, Bishop, appeal to, 71f.

Durant, Henry F., founder of Wellesley College, 281, 305f.

East Hall dedication, East Northfield, Moody quoted, 312
Educational ideals, 310-312, 318
Elliott, Rev. Samuel A., 16
Emerson, Ralph Waldo, 16, 18, 280
English provinces visited, 192ff.
Enmity to the saloon, 173f.
Erdman, Dr. Charles R., quoted, 96
Erdman, Rev. William J., first pastor Illinois Street Church, 99
Events leading to the choice between business and Christian service, 65-68
Everett, Rev. Oliver Capen, early Northfield pastor, 14

Faith tried, 142
Fancuil Hall, 28
Farwell Hall, Chicago Y.M.C.A. building, made possible by Moody's work, 93; destroyed by fire in 1868, 94; second building, erected in 1869, burned in 1871, and third building, erected 1872-1875, both built with Mr. Moody's aid, 95
Farwell, John V., helper in new Sunday school, 48, 53, 57; gives site for Chicago Y.M.C.A. building, 93; vindicates Moody in Edinburgh, 160f.; suggests song book royalties to rebuild Chicago church, 200; trustee of royalties, 201
Financial burdens increase, 426
First purchase of land in Northfield in 1875, 301
Foreman, John N., 380
Franklin, Benjamin, quoted, 435
"Free Breakfasts," Glasgow, 176, 181
Friendships, 495-502

Gaiety Club, Edinburgh, 176
Garrett, Rev. Charles, 172
General Conference for Christian Workers, small beginning in 1876, 274; development of work, 324-329; purpose defined in call

INDEX   551

of 1880, 325; change of emphasis, 327; call of 1899, Moody's last conference, quoted, 327
Gladstone, 228; quoted, 536
Glover, T. R., quoted, 204
Goodell, Dr. Constans L., quoted, 295-297
Goodspeed, Rev. E. J., quoted, 186
Gordon, Dr. A. J., 281; presides at General Conference, 327
Gospel Hymns, Nos. 1-6, 200ff.
Gordon, Rev. Arthur, quoted, 165
Goss, Rev. Charles F., pastor Illinois Street Church, 100; quoted, 374f., 434, 443-446, 454f., 487
Great Britain, visited, in 1867, 103-111; in 1870, 120-122; missions, in 1873-74, 141-197; in 1875, 210-235; in 1881, 333-354; in 1883, 355-368; in 1891, 395-401
Greatest Thing in the World, 93, 386
Great Fire in Chicago, 123-127; Moody's reference to his sermon on that night, 124; his home destroyed, 126; relief and reconstruction work, 128-131
Grenfell, Sir Wilfred, 366

Hall, Dr. Newman, quoted, 110
Hall, Evelyn, principal of Northfield Seminary, 311, 500
Hardy, Keir, 168
Hartford, home of pioneer John Moody, 4
Hartzler, Dr. H. B., quoted, 324
Hayes-Tilden presidential campaign, 276
Heroes and Hero Worship, quoted, 488
Hogg, Quintin, biography quoted, 230-231
Holden, Rev. J. Stuart, quoted, 345
"Hold the fort," story of its origin, 205-206
Holton, Betsey, mother of Dwight L. Moody, 6; marriage to Edwin Moody, 6; care of family after husband's death, 8; Moody's devotion to, 476; tribute to, 511-513
Holton, William, pioneer ancestor, to Hartford in 1634, 5

Holy Land visited in 1892, 396
Home relationships, 503-515; companion of children and grandchildren, 508-515; devotion to his mother, 510; grief over loss of grandchildren, 514, 526
Horton, Dr. Robert F., quoted, 351
Howard, Gen. O. O., 91
Hyde, Rev. Thomas B., pastor Illinois Street Church, 100

Ideal Life, The, 165
Illinois Street Church, formed, 98; formation of creed, 98; pastors, 100
Indian hostility in Northfield, 5
Individual Work for Individuals, 386
Inglis, Charles, quoted, 121
Interest aroused in Scotland, 152, 156
International Committee of the Y.M.C.A., Moody aids in raising funds, 385
Ireland, missions in, in 1874, 187ff.; in 1881, 333ff.; in 1891, 398ff.

James, D. Willis, 500
James, William, discussed by Royce, 241
Jesup, Morris K., 269, 297, 500
Jones, Sam, quoted, 464

Kaiser, The, 510
Kansas City Journal, quoted, 529
Kansas City mission, Moody's last, 528; closing address, 530
Kelman, Rev. John, 152
Kimball, Edward, 32
Kinnaird, Lord Arthur, 230
Kirk, Dr. Edwin N., 32
Kruger, President, 465

Lake Huron, rescues the *Spree*, 406
Last days, 528-538
Lawrence, Bishop, quoted, 243
Letters quoted, 7, 8, 30, 36, 37, 38, 39, 41, 42, 44, 45, 47, 49, 52, 71, 72, 76, 78, 80, 81, 82, 86, 90, 105, 110, 112, 143, 147, 161, 163, 213, 220, 221, 233, 234, 242, 247, 249, 272,

INDEX

311, 335, 339, 356, 375, 433, 476, 496, 497, 498, 504-507, 513, 514, 522, 541

Liddon, Canon, quoted, 350

Lincoln, Abraham, 68, 75

Locke, W. J., quoted, 353; describes Moody meetings at Cambridge University in *Septimus*, 353

London Daily News, The, quoted, 204

London Times, The, quoted, 189, 216

London, visited in 1867, 105; in 1872, 121; missions in 1875, 210ff.; in 1883, 355ff.; in 1891, 400

Lowrie, Rev. R., 206

Mabie, Henry, 382

Manchester (Eng.) *Guardian*, quoted, 193

Marriage to Emma C. Revell, 86

Marshall, H. N. F., 306

Matheson, Hugh, quoted, 355

Meyer, Rev. F. B., quoted, 144; visits America, 419

Miller, Hugh, 154

Ministry of earlier and later years compared, 517-521

Missionary zeal evidenced by influence on students in schools and conferences, 381; sane attitude shown, 382

Missions in America—Brooklyn, 1875, 250ff.; Philadelphia, 1875-76, 255ff.; New York, 1876, 268ff.; Chicago, 1876-77, 276ff.; Boston, 1877, 280ff.; New England cities, 284-286; Baltimore, 1878, 289ff.; St. Louis, 1879, 292ff.; San Francisco, 1880-81, 297-298; cities in United States and Canada, 1884, 371ff.; at World's Fair, Chicago, 1893, 408ff.; various cities in 1894-99, 516; last mission, Kansas City, 1899, 528ff.

Mission in Northfield in 1875, 248

Mission work in Chicago begun, 46ff.

Moody as educator, 318ff.

Moody, Dwight Lyman, birth, 3; ancestry, 3ff.; early life, 10-12; religious background, 13ff.; education, 19-23; experiences in Boston, 24-35; interest in anti-slavery, 28; joins Y.M.C.A., 30; conversion, 33; joins Mount Vernon Church, 34; goes to Chicago, 36; interest in public affairs, 38; joins Plymouth Church, 46; opens mission Sunday school in 1858, 48; evangelistic work, 51; evening meetings started, 56; choice of life work, 65ff.; engagement to Emma C. Revell, 67; marriage August 28, 1862, 86; work with Christian Commission, 85ff.; at the front, 85-89; home is burned, 89; birth of first child, 90; president of Chicago Y.M.C.A., 92; first visit to Great Britain, 103ff.; Great Fire, 123ff.; loss of church and home, 126; resigns presidency of Y.M.C.A., 135; beginning of General Workers' Conference, 274; inception of Northfield Schools, 306; ideas as educator, 318ff.; Chicago Bible Institute, 373; Northfield Students' Conference, 377; Student Volunteer Movement, 380; visits Holy Land, 396-398; shipwreck on *Spree*, 402-407; mother's death, 511; waning strength, 525; last mission, Kansas City, Mo., 528; last address, 530; journey home, 534-535; Coronation Day, December 22, 1899, 538; at rest on Round Top, 541

Moody, Edwin, father of Dwight L., 6; marriage to Betsey Holton, 6; death in 1841, 8

Moody, George, 24

Moody, Isaiah, grandfather of Dwight L., to Northfield in 1796, 6

Moody, John, pioneer ancestor, 3; Governor Winthrop's allusion to, 3, 4; monument and home lot in Hartford, Conn., 4

Moody Memorial Church, outgrowth of North Market Hall mission school, 100

Moody quoted, 32, 35, 55, 56, 108, 114f., 117ff., 124, 129, 130, 174, 211f., 272f., 292, 310, 312, 316, 325,

INDEX 553

327, 349, 402ff., 412f., 418, 424, 425, 441, 442, 445, 449-454, 465f., 469, 484, 511ff., 517, 526f., 530ff., 533, 534f., 537

Moody's elusive personality, 459-494; humility, 459-460; secret of his success, 459; reticence regarding himself and his achievements, 461; sensitiveness, 461; energy, 462; agility of mind, 464; arbitrariness, 465; interest in public affairs, 465; readiness to admit faults, 466-468; simplicity of living, 468; love of home, 469; unconventionality, 474; sympathy, 476-479; tact, 483; sincerity, 489; bravery, 491-493

Moody's theology, 437-455

Moody's tribute to his mother, 511; to his little granddaughter Irene, 526-527

Moody, Samuel, son of John, settler in Hadley in 1660, 4

Moody, Samuel, brother of D. L., 87, 90; death, 277

Moody, Mrs. W. R., starts Northfield Young Women's Conference in 1902, 385

Moody's evangelism, 170

Moore, Henry M., 281; Moody's friendship with, 498

Moorehouse, Harry, 116, 120; influence on Moody, 120, 438

Morgan, Dr. G. Campbell, 508

Morley, quoted, 177

Morse, Richard C., secretary International Committee of the Y.M.C.A., quoted, 95, 270, 376, 377, 389-392

Morton, Rev. Charles, pastor Illinois Street Church, 100

Mott, John R., 377

Moulton, Prof. James Hope, quoted, 346

Mount Hermon School, events leading to the founding of, 313; opened in 1881, 313; original plan, 314; change of policy, 81; growth, 371

Mount Vernon Church, 32, 46

Müller, George, 103

McBurney, R. R., 269

McCormick, Cyrus, makes first cash gift to Chicago Y.M.C.A. building, 93

McGranahan, James, 200, 365, 499

McKinley, President, quoted, 486

MacKinnon, Mrs. Peter, quoted, 82, 163, 396

MacKinnon, Peter, 163

MacIntosh, C. H., 101

Maclaren, Ian, quoted, 165

McWilliams, D. W., quoted, 73; Moody's friendship with, 269, 496-498

National Christian Commission, 85

Natural Law in the Spiritual World, 361

Needham, Rev. George C., pastor Illinois Street Church, 100

New Age, quoted, 540

New spiritual power received, 129-130

New York Herald, quoted, 244, 246, 247, 254

New York Independent, quoted, 106

New York Observer, quoted, 376

New York Times, quoted, 215, 265-268, 541

New York Tribune, quoted, 250-254

Nicoll, Sir William Robertson, quoted, 155-157, 168

Nightingale, Florence, quoted, 494

Noonday prayer meetings in Chicago, 92; in London, 107; in Paris, 109

North American, quoted, 260

North British Daily, quoted, 174

Northern Whig, quoted, 187

Northfield, town grant obtained in 1673, 5; northerly outpost of civilization in New England, 5; Indian hostility, 5; second settlement in 1685, 5; description of, 302

Northfield College Students' Conferences started, 1886, 377

Northfield Schools, see Northfield Seminary, Mount Hermon School

Northfield Seminary, inception of idea of, 303; purchase of land for, 306; erection of first building in 1879, 307; principles on

which the school was founded, 307-312; requirements in teachers and trustees, 309-311; growth, 371
Northfield Young Women's Conference, 385
North Market Hall Sunday school opened, 48; plan for financing, 52; novel methods employed, 52; phenomenal growth, 75; Lincoln's visit, 75; response to President's call for troops, 76
North Side Tabernacle, 128
North-Western Hymn Book, published 1868, 205
Norton, Charles Eliot, quoted, 242

Oats, William M., quoted, 180
"One Hundred and One Night," Glasgow, 179
Origin of Species, 138
Overtoun Hall begun, Moody, quoted, 316
Overtoun, Lord, 168
Oxford University, mission at, 347-352; visited, 402

Palestine visited, 396
Pall Mall Gazette, quoted, 357, 367
Palmer, Mr., of Boston, quoted, 110
Pamp, Rev. Frederick E., quoted, 454
Paris Exposition visited, 111
Parker, Theodore, 16, 18, 280
Peabody, Dr. Francis G., quoted, 384
Penfield, Thornton B., quoted, 389-392
Pennefather, Rev. William, 141
Philadelphia Inquirer, quoted, 259, 261
Philadelphia Ledger, quoted, 256
Philips, Philip, 141
Phillips, Wendell, 16
Philpott, Rev. W. P., pastor Moody Memorial Church, 100
Pierson, Dr. A. T., 380, 381
Plumb, Albert, 281
Plymouth Brethren, 101-103
President Grant attends mission in Philadelphia, 260

Princeton visited, 262
Prison work inaugurated, 289; books and Testaments distributed, 423-425
Publication of works begun, 421
Punshun, William Morcley, 149

Quarrier, William, quoted, 174, 175
Queen Victoria, quoted, 213

Rainsford, Dr. Marcus, 230
Rainy, 154
Record of Christian Work, 421
Reform Bill of 1867, England, 136
Relief work for poor, 75, 171
Religion defined (quotation), 439
Religion in early New England days, 13-19
Religious Herald, quoted, 284-286
Religious situation in Scotland in 1873, 152-156
Remington, R. K., 128
Reminiscences of Present Day Saints, quoted, 384
Revell, Emma C., 67; engagement to Mr. Moody, 67; character and influence, 79-83
Revell, Fleming H., to Chicago in 1849, 78
Revell, Fleming H., Jr., 78
Revival, The, quoted, 107
"Revivalists and Modern Skepticism," 267
Revival music and hymn books, 198-209; publication of suitable books, 199; royalties to Christian work, 199-203, 211, 234, 389, 418; trustees of fund, 200
Rogers, Rev. J. Guinness, quoted, 359
Rome visited, 396
Roosevelt, Theodore, quoted, 488
Round Top, 446, 539
Royalties from hymn book publication, 199-203, 234, 389, 418; trustees of fund, 200
Royce, Professor, quoted, 241

Sacred Songs and Solos, 199, 200, 208, 209
Salvation Army, 287

INDEX

555

Sanford, George A., quoted, 190-191
Sankey, Ira D., 141, 199, 200, 215, 216
Saturday Review, quoted, 215
Scotland, missions, in 1874, 158-169; in 1881, 333-340; in 1891, 395
Sermon notes, disposition of, 434; making, 435; plan of keeping, 435
Sermons—preparation and delivery of described by Dr. Goss, 443-446; others, 448-454
Shaff, Dr. Philip, quoted, 193
Shaftesbury, Earl of, 230
Sloan, Samuel, 430
Smith, Sir George Adam, 176, 447; quoted, 164, 179-180, 338
Smith, Stanley, 365
Social gospel, The, 107-177
Speer, Robert E., 382
Spender, J. A., quoted, 136
Sphere of service widening, 141
"Spiritual Diagnosis," Drummond, 164
Spurgeon, Rev. Charles Haddon, 138, 230
Spree, North German Lloyd liner, 402
Stalker, Professor James, 176
Standards of living, 427, 468
Stand as to faith healing, 493-494
Stanley, Dean, 226
Stebbins, George C., quoted, 141, 200, 278, 365, 499
Stewart, J. A., on "Victorian Religiosity," 137
St. Louis Globe-Democrat, quoted, 292
Stone, Dr. John Timothy, quoted, 385-387
Stone, Rev. W. H., quoted, 342-345
Stuart, George H., 128, 200
Studd, C. T., 365, 377
Studd, Edward, 226
Studd, J. E. K. (later Sir Kynaston), 342; quoted, 363; visits American colleges and universities, 377
Student Volunteer Movement started at Mount Hermon, 1886, 380

Swan, Provost, 176
Taggert, Rev. S. A., quoted, 428, 431-432
Tait, Dr. (Archbishop of Canterbury), quoted, 221
"Temptation Hill," 316; memorial chapel given, 316
Thoburn, Bishop, quoted, 382-385
Torrey, Rev. R. A., pastor Illinois Street Church, 100
Tractarian Movement at Oxford, 138
Transcendentalists, 19
Travers, S. W., quoted, 392
Trustees of fund from royalties on hymn books, 200

Unitarianism, rise and growth, 15-19

Vance, Dr. James, quoted, 387
Vanity Fair, 215; quoted, 216
Vining, Charles M., 528, 533

Wanamaker, John, 128, 255, 269; quoted, 528-529
Watson, Rev. John (Ian Maclaren), quoted, 165, 177
Welfare work after the Great Fire, 128; new tabernacle built, 128
Whittle, Major D. W., 91, 365, 420; quoted, 205-206, 248-249, 470, 485, 499; Moody's friendship with, 498
Whittle, May (Mrs. W. R. Moody), 385
Whyte, Alexander, 165, 167
Wilder, Robert P., 380
Wilkinson, Professor Cleaver, quoted, 517-519
Williams, George, founder of Y.M.C.A., 103
Wilson, President, quoted, 491
Wilson, P. W., quoted, 541
Wilson, Rev. J. H., 152
Winthrop, Governor, quoted, 3, 4
World's Fair mission in Chicago, Moody's estimate of, 412-414
Wrecked at sea, description by Mr. Moody, 402-406

Y.M.C.A., outgrowths of interest, in—"Cambridge Seven," 377; Northfield Students' Conference,

377; Student Volunteer Movement, 380; funds raised and giving stimulated, 389ff., 426ff.
Young Men's Christian Association, Moody a member in Boston, 30; active in Chicago, 84, 90, 92ff.; elected president, 92;

York, Eng., association backs mission there, 142
Young, William, 399

Zeal in seeking truth from all sources, 101ff.
Zouave Gazette, quoted, 85

www.ingramcontent.com/pod-product-compliance
Lightning Source LLC
Chambersburg PA
CBHW021713300426
44114CB00009B/129